2 3 4 5

The Theoretical Evolution
of International Political Economy

S 67 F.

The Theoretical Evolution of International Political Economy

A Reader

Second Edition

Edited by

GEORGE T. CRANE

ABLA AMAWI

New York   Oxford
Oxford University Press
1997

Oxford University Press

Oxford   New York
Athens   Auckland   Bangkok   Bogotá   Bombay   Buenos Aires
Calcutta   Cape Town   Dar es Salaam   Delhi   Florence   Hong Kong
Istanbul   Karachi   Kuala Lumpur   Madras   Madrid   Melbourne
Mexico City   Nairobi   Paris   Singapore   Taipei   Tokyo   Toronto

and associated companies in
Berlin   Ibadan

Published by Oxford University Press, Inc.
198 Madison Avenue, New York, New York 10016

Oxford is a registered trademark of Oxford University Press

Library of Congress Cataloging-in-Publication Data
The Theoretical evolution of international political economy: a
reader / edited by George T. Crane, Abla Amawi.—2nd ed.
p.   cm.
Includes index.
ISBN 0–19–509443–3
1. International economic relations.
I. Crane, George T., 1957–.   II. Amawi, Abla.
HF1359.T44   1996   337—dc20   96–8401

Printing (last digit):   5 7 9 8 6

Printed in the United States of America
on acid-free paper

Contents

Preface

When the first edition of this volume was conceived, a decade ago, international political economy (IPE) was struggling for scholarly recognition within the fields of political science and economics. As the second edition goes to press, the interaction of international politics and economics has grown into a vast area of inquiry, with numerous theoretical twists and turns. Ten years ago, the three major schools of thought—mercantilism, liberalism, and Marxism—seemed to capture a good portion of theoretical work in IPE, but differences within and between these perspectives have proliferated to such an extent that a single volume cannot fully represent all of the relevant controversies. But teachers must start somewhere, students must be brought into the multifaceted conversations of IPE theory, and in that spirit we offer this second edition.

We have left the classical readings alone, not because they are the "best of all possible" but because readers have reported that these work well in the classroom. Four of the six chapters from the first edition have been revised; in each case a reading has been replaced with a new selection that either surveys more recent debates or makes a novel conceptual contribution in its own right. We have also added a new chapter on postmodern IPE. Inclusiveness is impossible but we hope that the new readings provide the widest possible introduction to the expanding field of IPE.

We would like to thank our colleagues and students at Georgetown University and Williams College. Comments and criticisms from Mary Geske, Kate Manzo, David Campbell, Mark Reinhardt, and James Mahon helped to improve the introduction and the selection of readings. For supporting each of us in our academic pursuits, our families are also due our thanks, especially our children, who were not here for the first edition but have enlivened the second in myriad ways. It is to them—Tara Fischbach, Aidan Crane, and Margaret Crane—that we would like to dedicate this volume.

Williamstown, Mass.
August 1995

The Theoretical Evolution
of International Political Economy

Theories of International Political Economy

Theories do not move in straight lines. Some circle around certain questions for long periods before jumping to new concerns; others fan out in many directions at once, erasing the boundaries between one theory and another. Describing how theories change over time is, therefore, a tricky business. A term like _theoretical evolution_ conjures in many minds images of linear progress driven by virtually mechanical responses to conceptual and historical stimuli, moving toward ever better explanations of the object of study. This scheme of theoretical change is rejected, in whole or in part, by writers as disparate as Thomas Kuhn, Imre Lakatos, and Michel Foucault. Even the father of modern evolutionary theory, Charles Darwin, distanced himself from overly formal and deterministic understandings of evolution: "After long reflection I cannot avoid the conclusion that no inherent tendency to progressive development exists."[1]

We must, then, keep squarely in mind that evolution of any sort is a highly contingent process and that theoretical change is especially so.[2] To suggest that classical liberalism has given rise to a notion of international regimes does not mean that it had to happen that way. Nor does it mean that contemporary explanations are necessarily superior to those of the past. Theoretical revision is not simply a universal scientific process that extends across the ages; it is a product of historical context. Today's arguments succeed because they have found niches in their political–economic environments, habitats that could be destroyed by political movements (think of the decline of "socialism"), economic dislocations, or intellectual ferment. Old arguments fade away because they have grown anachronistic; their moment is past.

In any event, whatever the change, some lines of thought persist. Questions of international political economy (IPE) have long been debated within and among at least three theoretical families: mercantilism, liberalism, and Marxism. The present volume collects representative samples of these traditions, together with modern examples that demonstrate the complex evolution of each. More recent arguments have moved beyond established theoretical boundaries and the book therefore includes contemporary approaches that cut across the major schools of thought or turn in very different directions. Before we can proceed to a discussion of these transformations, however, we must consider the field in which they all occur: international political economy.

What is International Political Economy?

The most direct answer to this question is found in the name itself. *Political economy* suggests a focus on phenomena that lie at the crossroads of the fields of politics and economics. It seeks to explain how political power shapes economic outcomes and how economic forces influence political action.[3] Although divergent beliefs are held as to the direction and strength of the relationship of politics and economics, exploring their interconnection is the stuff of political economy. But political economy is not simply an amalgam of the two traditional fields; rather, it attempts a new synthesis. Implicit in the endeavor of political economy is a critique of the scope and methods of both economics and political science.[4] To the political economist, *ceterus paribus* assumptions and numerous "exogenous" variables rob neoclassical economics of its explanatory power. Likewise, much of political science pays insufficient attention to how economic processes and structures might influence the play of power. By contrast, a theory of political economy should be judged precisely by how well it captures the interaction of politics and economics.

International political economy primarily, though by no means exclusively, concentrates upon activities taking place *among* international actors: states, global corporations, international organizations, social movements, and the like. Such a focus naturally impinges upon the customary domain of international relations. Indeed, IPE is in part a response to perceived shortcomings in the dominant realist paradigm of international relations. Realism tends to separate politics from economics and define power largely in military-political terms.[5] As Susan Strange argues, this limits understanding of "structural power," in which international structures of production play an important part.[6]

Moreover, unlike Kenneth Waltz's neorealism, IPE is not confined to an international level of analysis.[7] Although much IPE work is taken up by a few internationally oriented empirical topics (trade, finance, investment, development), a significant portion of the field looks *within* particular countries to understand how domestic forces influence international action. The boundary between the international and the intranational is not rigidly fixed in the IPE literature.

The task of defining IPE, therefore, is not an easy one. The lines between political and economic, as well as those between international and domestic, are blurred and the interrelationships inform myriad phenomena, from foreign policy to popular culture. Moreover, the variety of theoretical frameworks in IPE creates even greater difficulty in delineating the field of study, for each defines the field differently. A number of categorizations for the various theories have been put forth, but perhaps the most widely cited is Robert Gilpin's.[8] He points to three major schools of thought: "nationalist" (also referred to as mercantilist, realist, or statist), "liberal," and "Marxist." Each possesses a distinct universe of discourse with a long intellectual tradition as well as a variety of contemporary manifestations. Gilpin's typology is not perfect—it does not capture some rather important theoretical variations—but it can serve as a starting point in discerning the evolution of IPE theories.

The Rise and Fall of Mercantilism

The earliest systematic theorizing on IPE is the classical mercantilist thought of the sixteenth to nineteenth centuries. In the words of Jacob Viner, mercantilism is: ". . . a doctrine of extensive state regulation of economic activity in the interest of the national economy."[9] Eli Heckscher makes a similar point: "Mercantilism would . . . have had all economic activity subservient to the state's interest in power."[10] Drawing on the political realism of Thucydides, Machiavelli, and Hobbes, mercantilists argue that if formal authority does not constrain the pursuit of self-interest, the result is likely to be a brutal "state of nature." Mercantilist thinkers thus believe in the necessity of public authority to translate individual interests into universal good.[11] Their analysis tends to focus on collectivities instead of individuals; maximizing *state* power and wealth is the best means of ensuring *public* welfare. *Raison d'etat* is a central economic principle, and state interest does, and should, determine economics in mercantilist theory.

For early mercantilists, wealth inheres in the absolute amount of gold or silver held in the public treasury. Since these are tangible assets of state power, the government intervenes in the economy both domestically and internationally to maximize holdings of specie. Domestically, extensive intervention takes the form of consolidating the national economy and more effective collection of revenues. Internationally, intervention takes the form of protectionism, the lasting contribution of mercantilism to the lexicon of IPE. A state's balance of trade is considered a central element of the international balance of power. The country must run a balance of trade surplus, maintaining an inflow of specie, to support its position in the international system of self-interested states. Insofar as mercantilists see this world political–economic struggle as a zero-sum game, no effort should be spared in protecting the national economy.

Mercantilism served for decades as a way of looking at the world and as a guide for policy. Its acceptance made sense sociologically in that it evolved simultaneously with the rise of the modern state. State-building absolutist princes encouraged and embraced mercantilist thought. By the late eighteenth century, however, it began to run into vexing anomalies. Adam Smith posited a withering critique of mercantilism, arguing that state interests would not be maximized if prescriptions of intervention and protectionism were followed. Smith's theorizing eventually informed Britain's ideology of free trade, which, coupled with the U.K.'s economic hegemony, seemed to invalidate mercantilist claims.

Mercantilism does not die, however. Friedrich List recasts it in somewhat diluted form. Although it is a very pointed critique of liberalism, his revision of mercantilism ultimately accepts the logic of free trade. List's infant industry argument is basically ad hoc, arguing why certain states, Germany in particular, should be given a chance, through protectionism, to ascend the ranks to industrialized status. While his fervent nationalism maintains the spirit of mercantilism, he is unable to defeat the powerful logic of comparative advantage and free trade. The German Historical School also attempts to save mercantilist assumptions in the aftermath of List's compromise. Gustav Schmoller reasserts the nationalist premise that economic processes are fundamentally shaped by political forces.[12] He rejects the liberal focus on the individual, as does List, in favor of a focus on the state and other key sociopolitical institutions. Yet while Schmoller's work suggests an interactive relationship of politics and economics, some of his colleagues proposed unabashedly politicist arguments.[13]

The influence of the Historical School is rather modest. Its inability to develop a more widely accepted approach to IPE is rooted in its methodology. Schmoller has an aversion to abstract grand theory, which separates him from both liberals and Marxists. Instead, he emphasizes historical monograph, a method that limits the explanatory range of the argument. For the most part, the Historical School does not produce generalizations; it is more the shared intellectual penchant of a number of careful scholars. Thus, while economic nationalism lived on in the policies of countries such as Germany and the United States, and flourished during the political–economic crisis of the 1930s, the theoretical ground of mercantilism was fundamentally undermined by liberalism. It would take many decades until it was refurbished into a major school of IPE thought.

Smith, Ricardo, and the Origins of Liberal IPE

Adam Smith does much more than criticize mercantilism; he founds a new line of IPE theory.[14] At the core of his system is an assumption, made by mercantilists as well, of rational egoism. But for Smith this does not imply a Hobbesian "state of nature." Instead, the "invisible hand" of the market naturally ensures that the pursuit of self-interest, in and of itself, will lead to the public good. Freedom is a crucial element in this process. Freely functioning markets, based upon a division of labor, will ultimately maximize efficiency and prosperity. Smith recognizes that "irrational" political intervention or economic collusion, can, and in his time did, undermine the felicitious consequences of free markets. His arguments for freer trade and limited government intervention are therefore tempered by an understanding of political realities. Nonetheless, Smith clearly believes that economics has a logic distinct from politics and should not be unduly hampered by political machinations. He turns mercantilism on its head.

David Ricardo adds to both the content and the methodology of Smith's liberalism. In Smith's argument, gains from foreign trade are largely based on absolute advantage. Free trade is universally beneficial when each nation can produce some particular commodity more efficiently than any other. Ricardo takes the defense of free trade a step further. Even if a country has no absolute advantage, it can still derive gains from trade. His famous example of England and Portugal demonstrates how trade based on comparative costs necessarily leads to mutual economic advantages. Ricardo thus develops a point which Smith raises but does not fully explicate: specialization and free trade based on comparative advantage will increase efficiency and prosperity.

Ricardo also revises the methodological ground of Smith's liberalism. Smith is philosophical and holistic, placing political economy within a moral and historical context. Ricardo, on the other hand, is narrower in his focus but more rigorous.[15] He separates economic questions from political and sociological issues and generates more parsimonious explanations. Although Smith's insights into the functioning of free markets place individual economic actors at the center of political economy, it is Ricardo who builds the foundation of methodological individualism that becomes a hallmark of liberal IPE. By the end of the nineteenth century, liberalism conceptualizes political economy almost wholly in terms of interrelationships among rational individuals. This approach is applied in all contexts: individual consumers in a national economy; individual groups; individual national economies interacting with one another. Ricardo's analytic style, while not as formal and abstract as that of later economists, foreshadows a distinctly liberal methodology.[16]

Smith and Ricardo also draw out the implications of comparative advantage and free trade. As market mechanisms are carried from the national economy to the world economy, a certain equilibrium will be established in international economic relations. The quantity theory of money (originally mercantilist but refined by liberals), directly ties changes in reserves to changes in domestic prices. This ensures that, if markets are unobstructed, trade and payments imbalances should balance automatically. Additionally, if all countries specialize and trade, then economic prosperity is diffused throughout the world. Every country will find its niche and benefit if liberal principles are conscientiously followed. International equilibrium and growth should arise from comparative advantage and free trade.

The economic focus of classical liberalism raises a question of whether this is truly a theory of IPE (i.e., of both politics and economics) or whether it subordinates politics to the point of nonexistence. Closer inspection suggests that liberalism does embrace a theory of politics. It views politics as the rational management of a naturally harmonious community. This shapes the liberal notion of war and international relations. Nineteenth-century liberals argue that war is: "the natural state of men ignorant of the laws of political economy."[17] In other words, reasonable people should agree that, since the use of force undermines productive capacity and saps national wealth and power, peace is logically in the interest of every state. War is not an outgrowth of conflicting national interests but arises from "national interests ill understood." Political economy is "the science *par excellence* of peace." For early liberals, free trade is so powerful a mutual interest that international political institutions are not necessary to ensure world peace. Liberal IPE thus contemplates the relationship of economics and politics, albeit in a laissez-faire fashion.

Liberal arguments changed IPE as a field of study. Modern economics was professionalized on the basis of liberal tenets and texts. In academia and government alike, liberalism had many faithful defenders by the turn of the twentieth century. What explains the vitality of this approach? Quite simply, it appeared to be empirically progressive. Liberal free trade and comparative advantage arguments not only explained new "facts" of international economic life, but they also seemed to corroborate the economic success of Great Britain. Although most countries clung to protectionism, liberalism predicted ultimate failure of this course and those forecasts enjoyed credence insofar as the "beggar-thy-neighbor" trade conflicts of the 1920s and 1930s were seen as contributing factors to the Great Depression. Liberalism offered persuasive answers to central questions of IPE.

Additionally, prior to World War I, liberal notions of politics were very alluring, more for their logical coherence and rationalist optimism than their correspondence with realities. In this period liberalism influenced the rise of idealism in international relations as seen in Norman Angell's popular argument on the futility and economic waste of war.[18] After World War I, Wilsonian idealism departed from the liberal disdain of international organizations but continued to accept the key principle of fundamentally harmonious interests among states.[19] Thus, it would not be until after the Great Depression and World War II that liberal IPE would be faced with the need of revision in light of Keynesian theory. This is not to say that the early liberals went completely unchallenged. Besides the continuing practical application of protectionism (it speaks to the politician), Marxism presented a direct assault on liberalism.

Marx and the Early Marxists

One of the most problematic aspects of Marxist IPE is the dearth of Karl Marx's own writings on the international realm. His thoughts on IPE, found mostly in newspaper articles from the 1850s, are scattered and not systematically developed.[20] The evolution of this perspective relies heavily on those who have come after Marx. The heart of the argument is, nonetheless, of Marx's own making. Unlike mercantilism and liberalism, Marxism does not assume that people are immutable, rational egoists. Human motivations and orientations are largely shaped by the material environment of a particular time. This is the foundation of one of Marx's most basic premises: historical materialism. Marxists hold that the way society is organized to produce its economic necessities conditions political activity as well as individual consciousness. The relationship of economics and politics is interpreted, then, as being generally dominated by economic forces expressed in a historically specific mode of production.

For Marx, history is marked by epochal changes in modes of production (e.g., feudalism to capitalism); that is, historical materialism is a theory of history. Although he contemplates a vast sweep of historical change, Marx focuses on defining the "laws of motion" of the capitalist mode of production. Capitalism is marked by a distinct social organization: a class structure of owners of the means of production pitted against workers possessing only the capacity to work—labor power. This distinction is based on both alienation (of workers from the products of their labor) and exploitation (of workers by capitalists). Class structure thus provides the necessary social prerequisites for the accumulation of capital.

To simplify a complex argument, Marx contends that the surplus value capitalists reap by selling the commodities produced by workers must be productively reinvested. If a capitalist fails to accumulate, other direct competitors will drive him from the market. Accumulation is the driving force of capitalism; it is the primary source of unprecedented material wealth and technological innovation under conditions of capitalism.[21] But accumulation is not sufficient to guarantee the permanence of capitalism. Rather, crisis, breakdown, and revolution are an inherent part of this mode of production. Generally, Marx sees an intrinsic contradiction, the growing inequality of the two classes, that will eventually goad the working class to foment revolution and usher in a new mode of production.

Marx himself derives very few empirically testable IPE arguments from these central assertions. Indeed, the concept of "testing" itself has no place in Marxian epistemology. The methodology involves discovering historically specific manifestations of core truths, not the linear causation of antecedent to consequent. For example, he believes the economic power (i.e., the ability to accumulate) of the capitalist mode of production will change the world. Other modes of production are thus eventually subsumed by the social and productive relations of capital.[22] No specific theoretical explanation explains why capital must expand globally (this is developed by later Marxists). But the logic of historical materialism suggests that all countries must experience a stage of capitalist development: "The country that is more developed industrially only shows, to the less developed, the image of its own future."[23] In the later years of his life, there is some evidence that Marx began to revise his ideas. The "late Marx" suggests that the transition from one mode of production to another is more complex than suggested in his earlier writing.[24] The hints of revision, however, did not significantly influence those after Marx who constructed more thoroughgoing IPE arguments.

This enterprise is taken up by, among others, Rosa Luxemburg, Rudolf Hilferding, Nikolai Bukharin, and V. I. Lenin.[25] Each makes a specific contribution to subsequent Marxist IPE and, although often at odds with one another, they share a certain theoretical family resemblance. For Lenin, the central issue is imperialism, a stage of capitalism involving, among other things, the expansion of capital internationally. He explains both the causes and the consequences of imperialism, albeit in dialectical fashion. Borrowing heavily from Hilferding, Lenin argues that the internal dynamics of capital result in global expansion. He contends that competitive accumulation, and the resultant concentration of capital, lead to larger and larger national monopolies. As opportunities for continued growth and accumulation shrink domestically, these monopolies cast an eye to foreign lands. This process takes a number of different forms: the search for new investment opportunities, the need for new markets, or the demand for raw materials.

The existence of territorial states, however, complicates the internationalization of capital. The power of monopoly capitalists allows them to control their respective state apparati; state power is an instrument of class domination. As competitive accumulation is carried to the international arena, military force thus becomes a means of securing economic gain. At first, military power is used against the targets of imperialism in the "pacification" of colonies. Eventually, the logic of accumulation leads national monopolies to compete directly against one another, resulting in Great Power war, the ultimate political outcome of imperialism. Short of Armageddon, Lenin also suggests other effects of imperialism. He argues that as capital seeks new foreign outlets in the periphery of the world economy, these areas will experience accelerated capitalist development.[26] He reinforces Marx's expectation that capitalism will spread to all corners of the world. Moreover, Lenin states that as the centers of industrial vitality shift toward the periphery, the traditional metropoles of capitalism will suffer economic decay. Lenin therefore suggests that Europe must ultimately face a dilemma: world war or economic decline.

Marx and the early Marxists add a new dimension to IPE. At a moment when liberalism, in the thrall of Ricardo, is increasingly focused on economics alone, Marx broadens the scope of analysis in an epic theory of *political* economy. Although economic forces are given pride of place, political implications are very much a part of Marxist analysis. Furthermore, historical materialism is a theory of economic, political, and social change, promising an explanatory dynamism that liberalism lacks. It is also a rationale for revolution which draws the attention of political activists. Thus, while Marxism had a miminal impact on turn-of-the-century economists, it shifts the problematique and creates a new audience, a new political economy.[27]

In sum, by the early twentieth century, three major schools dominate the IPE landscape. The mercantilist tradition is, perhaps, in the weakest position. List's post-Smithian revisions are largely ad hoc, limiting their explanatory power. Protectionist practice may be widespread, but its theoretical underpinnings are rather suspect. Liberals and Marxists alike interpret the state, the crux of mercantilist thought, as an epiphenomenon. The grand theory of Marxism and the parsimonious rigor of liberalism attract wider audiences and more committed proponents. Changes in international circumstances in the post–World War II period would, however, profoundly influence all three theories.

Modern Revisions of Liberal IPE

A number of notable additions have been made to liberalism since the turn of the century. Some—Marginalist neoclassicism and the Heckscher-Ohlin factor-proportions theorem—are refinements of Ricardian method and theory. The greatest modern challenge to liberal notions of IPE before World War II, from within its own ranks, is that raised by John Maynard Keynes.

The Impact of Keynes on IPE

Quite simply, Keynes changed the language of liberal economic thought. The thrust of his complex and controversial argument is aimed at the liberal belief that markets inherently tend toward a socially beneficial equilibrium.[28] Instead, he contends that production and consumption more often than not balance where unemployment remains at a relatively high level. Keynes's response to this problem breaks with liberal precedent. He advocates state intervention in the economy to stimulate both employment and investment. Although such action, in Keynes's mind, should be countercyclical and complementary to market forces, it challenges the basic liberal argument that economic prosperity can best be gained without state management. Additionally, the Keynesian focus on aggregates, in place of methodological individualism, questions the traditional unit of liberal anlysis.[29]

In judging Keynes's contribution, it must be kept in mind that his work is a product of its theoretical environment. Keynes was writing when the analytic separation of politics and economics was the norm of his profession. He speaks directly to economists in the professional sense; his aim is to contribute to economic science, not political economy. Whether intentionally or not, however, Keynes does add to IPE theory.

Generally, Keynes argues that a country must have full employment as its primary economic goal to avoid debilitating and unnecessary recessions. This priority both influences and is influenced by international economic policies. To secure full employment, for example, a country will want to run a balance of trade surplus, since exports contribute to effective demand. By the same reasoning, every country will want a trade surplus, implying that protectionism may follow from domestic Keynesian policies. Although Keynes exhibits a nationalist streak, he is not a protectionist.[30] He understands that devastating beggar-thy-neighbor policies in the interwar years must be avoided. This is best accomplished through international economic cooperation; an end he ardently worked toward throughout his life. He actively lobbied against the Gold Standard, which forced domestic deflation and raised unemployment. And he supported efforts to create international institutions to provide national leaders with some flexibility in balancing domestic priorities with international obligations.

Keynes shifts the debate in liberal IPE away from the issue of whether international intervention should occur, to what sort of institutions should be created. The key is his basic acceptance of economic management, and consequently a role for the state at the international level. As with his domestic interventionist ideas, such management should complement, not contradict, underlying world market forces. Keynes thus stays within the purview of liberal thought.

By bringing the state into his analysis, however, Keynes poses new problems for liberalism. The issue of *how* states should intervene internationally eventually leads to the question of *why* states actually intervene as they do. A series of events in the late 1960s and early 1970s raised this issue. The Bretton Woods system disintegrated, calling into question liberal arguments regarding international cooperation. The Organization of Petroleum Exporting Countries' (OPEC) successful manipulation of international oil markets could not be adequately explained by liberal assumptions alone; the market was not free, and competition was far from perfect. In addition, many less developed countries were not gaining the benefits of comparative advantage, challenging liberalism's predicted international diffusion of economic development. These events suggest that markets simply behave differently than liberal theory holds; in a word, they appear to be politicized. The key anomaly facing liberal IPE today is explaining how politics shapes economic forces—the converse of the traditional expectation that economics should determine politics.

The Tenacity of Economic Orthodoxy

A second strand of modern liberalism ignores the anomalies at hand and retreats to neoclassical orthodoxy. Although these arguments address relevant subject matter, they are not really theories of IPE as such; they do not explore the relationship between politics and economics. The neoclassical approach, true to its Ricardian roots, maintains the analytic separation of the two. Persistent and economically inefficient political intervention in the market is not explained; rather, it is dismissed as "irrational." This economistic impulse is hardly new; it has been extant since at least the Marginalist "revolution" and was buttressed against the onslaught of Keynesianism. One of the most pointed orthodox critiques of Keynesian IPE was Milton Friedman's argument against the fixed exchange rate system of Bretton Woods.[31] He argued that the self-regulating, self-correcting market dynamic would yield superior economic outcomes compared to interventionist policies. His position was based on a theory of economics alone; there was little consideration of why markets might in fact be politicized.

Neoclassical economic orthodoxy is a powerful theoretical tool, used by institutions such as the World Bank and the International Monetary Fund to justify market-conforming policies, but it is not very helpful in advancing liberal understandings of IPE. Instead of providing new facts, it merely repackages the old. By placing greater value on internal logical coherence than on interpretation of complex global realities, it is simply unable to meet the theoretical challenges of linking politics and economics.[32]

Interdependence

Analyzing economics and politics is very much the theoretical project of the interdependence approach. The term *interdependence* was coined in the late 1960s to describe the growing interconnectedness of national economies. Deepening trade, investment, and monetary ties among advanced industrial countries draw national economies closer together and create a truly global economy. The overall effect is debilitating to national autonomy. Each country is faced with a wider array of disrupting economic forces, but each has less capacity to control such disturbances. Interdependence thus creates a paradox; it produces incentives for both cooperation and competition. Successful management of transnational economic relations may best be achieved through policy coordination, but frustrated state leaders could also attempt to regain national economic control by means of damaging beggar-thy-neighbor policies. Interdependence analysis focuses on this tension of state and world market.

Some liberal analysts see the contradiction of interdependence ultimately resolving itself in favor of economic forces. States, they hold, must give way to markets. Perhaps the most daring propositions come from those liberals who analyze the rise of transnational corporations. State sovereignty is held "at bay" by the power of these gigantic companies.[33] National political structures, rendered increasingly obsolete by global economic forces, will have to surrender a measure of their authority to transnational organizations better suited to respond to the new international environment. These are eminently liberal expectations, consistent with the belief that economic logic should not be thwarted by "irrational" politics. Indeed, such optimistic interdependence liberals go further than their classical brethren, arguing that technological and market changes have now made it all but inevitable that economics will subsume politics.

Other interdependence analysts propose a different mix of politics and economics. In their landmark work on interdependence theory, Robert Keohane and Joseph Nye argue that economic changes do not negate politics but create a new type of politics.[34] Their alternative conception of interdependence is a combination of international relations realism and liberal IPE. While accepting the realist idea that military force can dominate economic relations, Keohane and Nye add the qualification that military power may be irrelevant to issues other than direct threats to vital national interests. American nuclear power is virtually meaningless in regard to international monetary policy. Moreover, power, especially in an economically interdependent world, is complex. The ability to affect certain outcomes at acceptable cost will vary from issue-area to issue-area. A country can dominate monetary affairs but may be more sensitive to harmful retaliation in trade matters.

States are also limited in their use of power by "international regimes"— tacit or explicit agreements on acceptable behavior within a given issue-area. The World Trade Organization (WTO) constrains the use of economic power in international trade with threats of costly counteraction against undue protectionism. What interdependence does, for Keohane and Nye, is to create new sources of power; it produces networks of "mutual asymmetric dependence" which leaders must consider when defining and defending state interests. Interdependence redefines politics.

Although Keohane and Nye stop well short of pronouncing the state irrelevant, their synthesis has a distinctively liberal hue.[35] In a sense, they save Keynesianism from itself by offering a justification for international economic management based upon a more sophisticated theory of politics. Furthermore, while the idea of "regime" raises some question as to liberalism's traditional unit of analysis, it is consistent with methodological individualism. As Keohane demonstrates elsewhere, regime creation and maintenance are in accord with the assumption of rational egoism.[36] The regime concept also returns to the question of how principles and norms can limit power, a primary concern of earlier liberal theorists. Keohane and Nye's approach to interdependence has its flaws; it is notably less successful in explaining North–South relations.[37] Their work, nonetheless, is an important revision of IPE liberalism.

Variants of Neo-Marxism

Liberalism is not the only IPE theory to undergo significant revision. Marxism is rife with internal disgreements on a number of key issues. The causes and mechanisms of imperialism have been reconsidered. The nature of state and class power have been the subject of pointed contention. To cover adequately all of these controversies is beyond the introductory scope of this chapter; competent surveys of much of this literature are already available.[38] The best way to proceed, then, may be to pick up where Lenin left off, with the expectation that capitalism will expand across the globe, shifting the locus of accumulation from Europe and America, ideas addressed by dependency and world-systems theories.

Dependency and World-Systems

After World War II, the notion that imperialism will bring capitalist growth to less developed countries (LDCs) is called into question. As the twentieth century unfolds, capital does expand out of the advanced industrial countries, but this does not necessarily lead to industrialization in less developed regions. Paul Baran is among the first to point out this problem.[39] He argues that the dialectical interaction of foreign capital and indigenous social forces does not always result in the creation of a typical capitalist mode of production in LDCs. Rather, surplus is expropriated from these areas and exported back to the advanced capitalist countries, yielding "underdevelopment" in Africa, Asia, and Latin America. Baran's insight paves the way for dependency theory.

Some dependency theorists assume a world-systemic perspective, analytically extending the internal dynamics of the capitalist mode of production, as originally outlined by Marx, to the world as a whole.[40] Their description and explanation of the position of underdeveloped countries within the capitalist world-system is analogous to the proletariat's situation vis-à-vis the capitalist. Underdevelopment becomes a *necessary* condition for the maintenance of the capitalist world system *as a whole*. Economic development in underdeveloped countries is as impossible as eliminating the "immiseration" of the working class.

One line of dependency thinking argues that underdevelopment is largely the result of forces external to countries on the periphery of the global economy. This point follows the assertion that a single mode of production, capitalism, dominates the world. From this vantage point, LDC class structures are an extension of the world-system of capital. The only chance of breaking out of the plight of underdevelopment, therefore, lies in cutting ties with the advanced industrial countries, ties that hold the periphery in debilitating dependency. The possibility of creating an alternative mode of production by "delinking" from the centers of capitalism is another revision of earlier theories of imperialism and contrasts with Marx's expectation that capital would transform the world.

A somewhat different theoretical strand returns to Baran and examines the interactions of foreign capital and domestic social forces. Fernando Cardoso (who has since moved away from his Marxist roots and assumed the Presidency of Brazil) suggests that the particular "historical-structural" conditions that exist in a given LDC may give rise to capitalist development when foreign capital is introduced.[41] But this sort of development is not equated with the process that earlier occurred in advanced industrial countries. Instead, the genesis of capitalist production in the periphery is "associated dependent development." By this argument, industrialization in LDCs occurs only in historically specific instances of a mutually advantageous interrelationship among foreign capital, domestic capital, and the indigenous state. Other theorists move in a direction similar to Cardoso, arguing that a number of modes of production may exist simultaneously in the world system.[42] This turn has spawned a "modes of production" literature that emphasizes domestic determinants of development and underdevelopment in the Third World. These studies focus less on the international context and engage in more detailed comparative political economy research.

The world-systems perspective returns to the transnational level, reasserting the impossibility of numerous coincident modes of production.[43] World-systems analysis, however, modifies the dependency argument by confirming the existence of a "middle class" of states as expressed in the concept of "semiperiphery." The economic growth and political stability of the system *as a whole* require a "middle sector" of countries. Thus, "limited opportunities for ascent" exist within the capitalist world-system. From this point of view, industrialization in LDCs is to be expected, but only for the limited few to which systemic opportunities are made available.

World-systems and dependency theories have faced a variety of criticisms from both Marxist and non-Marxist writers.[44] A fairly common complaint is the overemphasis on global forces in determining domestic political and economic conditions, which applies more to world-systems arguments than the historical-structuralism of Cardoso. Yet even with Cardoso's greater attention to domestic political forces, the question of the potential autonomy of the state vexes much Marxist theorizing. Arguing that the state is a crucial element in the industrialization efforts of Latin American countries, Cardoso is very hesitant to recognize the possiblity of a state interest distinct from the interests of the ruling class. Instead, the state must reflect the class structure of society.[45] Yet he also suggests class analysis does not allow for a complete explanation of particular cases of development or underdevelopment.[46] Thus, he recognizes the analytic constraints of Marxist IPE but does not move outside of them.[47]

Prominent class analysts are aware of the problems inherent in a neo-Marxist conception of the state. Fred Block argues that state power ought to be considered sui generis, not necessarily reducible to class interests. He flatly asserts that structuralist neo-Marxism is reductionist.[48] Ralph Miliband reaches a similar conclusion and suggests that the class/state relationship is best considered a "partnership" in which the state is not necessarily "junior partner."[49] These conclusions point to a problem for Marxist IPE: If historical materialism, a distinguishing feature of all the various strands of Marxism, is to be maintained theoretically, the possibilities of autonomous political action and the role of the state require reconsideration. This is happening in continuing debates on globalization and the condition of postmodernity.

Globalization and Postmodernity

Robert Cox, building upon the work of Italian Marxist Antonio Gramsci, acknowledges the possibility of autonomous political practice.[50] State managers make their own history, though they are constrained by the exigencies of production and the nexus of social forces surrounding them. Relationships among state, social class, and production are, in Cox's rendering, complex and malleable. The expansion of capitalism globally has been facilitated by specific political interests, even traditional balance of power intrigues. On the other hand, economic globalization has brought with it the "internationalizing of the state," the gradual redefinition of national interests to coincide with the requirements of global production and the empowerment of those bureaucratic elements (finance ministries, central banks, etc.) that serve these ends. These processes are never complete and, given the historical contingency of particular imbrications of politics and economics, "there is nothing inevitable about the continuation of either the internationalizing of the state or the internationalizing of production."[51]

Cox, among others, also emphasizes important transformations in the way globalized production is organized. Highly centralized, large-scale, integrated, mass production factories were the building blocks of "Fordism," the form of industrial capitalism that the United States rode to economic hegemony in the first three-quarters of the twentieth century. Fordist industrial structures have been giving way in the past several decades to more decentralized, globally dispersed, flexible forms of accumulation that raise yet newer possibilities for how states relate to the world economy and the political implications of production.[52]

Some Marxist theorists are exploring the cultural ramifications of post-Fordist production. David Harvey suggests that the cultural currents of postmodernism—the fragmentation of subjective identities, the loss of universalizing narratives, the ambiguity of meaning—are bound up with contemporary reorganizations of capitalism.[53] This notion is examined further below, but suffice it here to note that Marxist IPE is moving in many directions, some of which return to critiques of dependency and world-systems theory and others that take strikingly new tacks.

Neomercantilist IPE

Mercantilist theory has not had as robust an evolution as Marxism and liberalism; its family line thinned in the early twentieth century. Adam Smith's thought is carried on, with certain variations, by neoclassical Marginalists and Keynes; Marx has Lenin, Gramsci, and others. Few sons and daughters sit at the feet of Friedrich List, though a nephew or two may be found in Max Weber and the international relations realists.

Family Resemblances

Max Weber posits an interactive relationship between politics and economics. He neither denies the efficiency of the market nor rejects the power of social classes. The state, though, is at the center of Weber's political economy.[54] A monopoly of the legitimate means of coercion within a given territory, if effectively realized, gives those who control the state an obvious political advantage over rival social forces. The state can, therefore, under certain historical conditions, dominate both economic markets and social classes. The development of the modern state is dependent on the existence of a relatively advanced capitalist economy, but not merely in the Marxian sense of superstructure. The market cannot exist without the state; states grow out of markets. The two are intertwined in a complex and historically specific manner.[55] Weber argues that economic processes are not distinct from social and political processes. On the contrary, as the title of his magnum opus, *Economy and Society*, implies, these factors are interactive and interdependent.

Weber is similar to mercantilists and the German Historical School in two respects. First, he recognizes the potency of nationalism as a driving force of economic activity. Unlike some liberal interdependence theorists, he sees economic internationalization as heightening nationalist sentiments.[56] Second, he analytically places economic phenomena into a social and political context. Weber is, however, uncomfortable with historicism's lack of abstract theory. His ideal types are epistemological compromises of theory and history; heuristic and predictive devices, they suggest general trends that may be redirected by particular historical conditions. Although he concentrates on domestic political and economic forces, his conceptualizations are relevant to international relations as well.[57] For theoretical and sociological reasons, though, Weber's work did not immediately give rise to a further development and refinement of mercantilist IPE.

The contending liberal and Marxist variants of IPE were deeply entrenched at the turn of the century. Their wide acceptance obstructed the insinuation of a new theoretical approach. Market and class defined central intellectual debates; the state was by and large an afterthought. Additionally, a growing division of labor both between and within social science disciplines robbed mercantilism of friendly institutional confines. Weber's analysis was not only ignored but, ironically, also came to be associated with a perspective quite unlike his own.[58]

International relations realism also maintains mercantilist assumptions. Drawing on the same classical political philosophers who inspired the mercantilists, realism views international affairs as a struggle for power among individually sovereign states in an anarchic world environment. Their analytic focus is the distribution of "power" around the globe. Although power is seen as a complex phemonenon (including, inter alia, economic resources), its ultimate expression is a state's military capability. This suggests that realists tend to a narrowly politicist vision of the relationship between politics and economics. They ignore Weber's more complex ideas of political–economic interaction. Unlike the earlier mercantilists, realists do not give due consideration to the economic role of the state; they downplay the "low" politics of economic affairs while emphasizing the "high" politics of diplomacy and the use of force.[59] Many IPE topics are thus peripheral concerns of international relations realism. Moreover, when realists discuss economic issues they are vulnerable to criticism similar to that which undermined early mercantilists. Simply put, their theory of economics is inadequate.

The Critiques of Liberalism and Marxism

Although efforts were made to "bring the state back in" to IPE by a number of creative scholars, a neomercantilist approach did not arise until the 1970s.[60] At that time, certain writers were growing dissatisfied with liberal and Marxist interpretations of changing international events. The undoing of the liberal world economy (the fall of Bretton Woods, the OPEC oil shocks) and the apparent disutility of U.S. military force in Vietnam pushed liberal IPE toward interdependence. Some analysts, however, were less tolerant of core liberal assumptions and began to develop a unique line of inquiry. Robert Gilpin argues against what he calls the "transnational ideologists" and expands the political focus of international relations realism to include economic issues.[61]

Contrary to the then popular liberal belief that the state was declining in significance as an international economic actor, Gilpin contends that the political and strategic interests of states lie at the heart of much of the world's economic activity. He reasserts the state as the key unit of analysis and suggests that earlier realism is untenable because economic forces may constrain political action, just as political power shapes economic outcomes. Gilpin suggests that in the interrelationship of politics and economics, the former is especially important. In a manner reminiscent of Schmoller, he states: "politics determines the framework of economic activity and channels it in directions which tend to serve the political objectives of dominant political groups and organizations."[62] Other scholars have followed Gilpin's lead and contributed to the development of a state-oriented analytic framework as an alternative to interdependence theory.[63]

In a somewhat different vein, Theda Skocpol produces a state-centered critique of neo-Marxist political economy.[64] Arguing that Marxist insights are hampered by assumptions of the "relative autonomy" of the state, she is, at once, sympathetic and devastating to Marxism. Her thesis returns to Weber and is aimed directly at core neo-Marxist assumptions, suggesting that state actions do not always reflect the interests of dominant social classes nor the long-term interests of capital. The later works of Block and Miliband are, consciously or not, rejoinders to her analysis. Skocpol's work has its roots in class analysis but moves away from the premises of neo-Marxism toward a comparative historical alternative.

Neomercantilist IPE in the late 1970s is thus transformed in reaction to perceived shortcomings of both liberal and Marxist arguments. A theoretical school is rebuilt upon the revision of international relations realism and a rereading of Weber. It should be noted that neorealist IPE theorists are heirs to the *empirical* tradition of mercantilism, historicism, and realism, which emphasizes the importance of state power in economic affairs. They do not necessarily advocate protectionism or other normative prescriptions offered by earlier nationalists.

Two Contemporary State-oriented Approaches

At the core of neomercantilist IPE lies the premise that the state's semipermanent bureaucratic apparatus critically shapes economic processes on both the national and international level.[65] The state obtains this importance by its very nature. In its ideal typical form, the state is the only political–economic institution that claims external sovereignty and internal political predominance. In reality the state's sovereignty and authority are limited; it is precisely the gap between ideal and actual that forms the research agenda of state power theories. This approach does not assume that the political interests of the state will always dominate economic forces. Rather, it suggests a complex and interactive relationship between politics and economics. Through the analytic lens of the state, it seeks to specify conditions under which one may determine the other.

Nor does the neomercantilist perspective assume all states are alike. It conceives of the state as a pattern of institutional power relationships which result from historically specific political struggles. Particular organizational structures and capacities vary from one state to another; concrete definitions of state interests are diverse. All states, however, whatever their form, have as their primary purpose control of a certain territory. They are created to dominate domestic social forces and resist external threats. This similarity provides common ground for various arguments which fall under the rubric of neomercantilism.

The focus on the state has given rise to both international and intranational research. This is to be expected insofar as the state mediates global and domestic political–economic forces. From the international-systemic point of view, the analysis concentrates on the state's external relations with other states and revises the "structural realism" of Kenneth Waltz.[66] Gilpin's conception of the international system, for example, incorporates both political and economic forces.[67] Statist analyses further consider how the international political–economic system influences the behavior of individual states. Gilpin holds that structural change, an economic as well as political process, may spark large-scale international war. Somewhat less drastically, Stephen Krasner suggests that a state facing hegemonic decline may pursue more nationally oriented policies.[68] Elsewhere, Krasner contends that less developed countries are motivated—in part by their subordinate international structural position—to agitate for changes in international regimes.[69]

Neorealism also includes studies that focus on the character of domestic political structures and how they influence international economic policy. Early work along these lines suggests that the degree of centralization of state power and social forces significantly shapes the type of policy pursued.[70] More recent arguments concentrate on two characteristics of state–society relations: state autonomy and capacity.[71] Autonomy implies the state elite has a distinct power base which allows it to formulate policy independent of particularistic interests of powerful social forces. Capacity suggests that even if the state enjoys autonomy, it may not be effective in action. It must have the administrative apparatus required to implement its preferred programs. Using these concepts, neomercantilist writers attempt to show how the specific character of state autonomy and capacity explains economic performance in both advanced industrial countries and less developed countries.

This raises the question of whether a strict distinction should be made between the study of comparative and international political economy. Any attempt to rigidly enforce such separation would, however, weaken neomercantilist IPE. The two lines of thought address many of the same topics and complement one another.

Contemporary state-oriented approaches succeed in rehabilitating core nationalist assumptions and overcoming problems that have plagued mercantilism. They also contribute novel interpretations, ranging from the conditions for world war to the patterns of development in LDCs.[72] Neomercantilist theory is not without its problems, however. Perhaps most perplexing is the question of just how distinct state interests are, or can be, from the interests of capital. Yes, developmental states like that in Taiwan have been able to stand apart from particular social forces and enforce policies, such as land reforms, that serve state interests, but in many of these instances what benefits the state also promotes the process of accumulation, even if it works against specific capitalists. Neomercantilist interpretations of such issues cannot help but intersect some lines of neo-Marxist thought.

Crossovers and Combinations

The three major families of IPE theory have all experienced significant revision and development. Each has inspired lively debate on basic premises and specific applications. Much of this theoretical evolution is the result of arguments internal to each paradigm. The different approaches have, however, also influenced one another. Contemporary state-oriented theories are founded upon critiques of liberalism and Marxism. Interdependence theory is engaged in a dialogue with neorealism. Marxist ideas are integrated into non-Marxist analysis. Cross-fertilization is so pervasive now that it has bred IPE approaches that are not easily placed within any of the three major theories. Rational choice analysis, hegemonic stability theory, and regime analysis are examples of such theoretical crossovers.

Rational Choice Analysis

Sometimes called the *new political economy*, rational choice analysis is grounded in liberalism, constructing abstract models from the premise of rational egoism.[73] From this assumption, arguments are developed to explain why individuals make choices that lead to suboptimal economic outcomes. It employs the logic of economic analysis to explain why Adam Smith's vision is not realized. The parsimony of this approach allows it to be used across levels of analysis.[74] For instance, the persistence of protectionism, a continuing weakness of liberal theory in general, has been the focus of at least three different rational choice arguments. Building upon the early work of Mancur Olson, some rational choice analysts view the maintenance of free trade as an international public good.[75] It involves a "free-rider" problem in which each state tries to avoid the costs of maintaining free trade in the knowledge that it cannot be excluded from its benefits. This argument rests on the assumption that states are unitary rational actors which carefully calculate the costs and the benefits of international cooperation.

A second rational choice explanation of protectionism holds that protectionism is best understood as a result of bargaining among domestic interest groups.[76] From this perspective, rationality operates at the group or organizational level. Quite simply, there is a domestic "political market" for tariffs with a demand side (industry interest groups) and a supply side (government and civil service). Tariffs and nontariff barriers are a function of the balance of these two forces. Third, some rational choice theorists invoke game theory.[77] This perspective returns to an international level of analysis, where states are taken as unitary rational actors. From this point of view protectionism is seen as the outcome of a Prisoner's Dilemma game.[78] In an effort to avoid the "suckers payoff" of eschewing protectionism while others practice it, and in the hope of gaining the highest possible individual payoff by maintaining protectionism while others reject it, states are slow to reduce tariff and nontariff barriers.

Although there are notable differences among these three arguments, they all rest on a similar theoretical base. Each is a logical extension of the assumption of rational egoism under a specific set of circumstances. In each case, the political sphere is seen to bear distinct similarities to the working of a competitive market. All share the assumption that exogenous forces do not constrain rational actors from pursuing their own self-interests.

The theoretical strength of rational choice analysis is limited, though, by its abstractness. It extends the *ceteris paribus* assumption to such extremes that its predictions can be falsified by a host of "exogenous" variables. Thus, while some consider rational choice analysis a theory in and of itself, others view it as an analytic technique within a larger theoretical system. In the liberal sphere, Keohane uses a rational choice approach as one element of his further development of interdependence theory.[79] Indeed, rational choice analysis contributes directly to liberal IPE theory by explaining why political intervention thwarts the realization of liberal expectations. Other analysts, working outside of liberalism, have also invoked it. Gilpin employs rational choice analysis to explicate why states define their interests internationally.[80] The stated purpose of this work is to extend international relations realism to IPE theory.[81] Rational choice has also found its way into some Marxist analyses.[82] In this manner, what is essentially a liberal analytic tool is used to bolster contending theories. Rational choice has clearly been appropriated by nonliberal theories.

Hegemonic Stability Theory

While rational choice analysis grows out of a single theory and is extended to others, hegemonic stability theory arises almost simultaneously from all three major schools of thought. The common theme is the correlation of a relatively open international economic system and a concentration of global political–economic power in a single "hegemonic" state. The hegemon creates and defends a particular international economic order by absorbing costs of system maintenance and by compelling other states to accept certain practices. Under such circumstances, the worst excesses of debilitating economic nationalism are restrained by the hegemonic state. The United States and Great Britain have, at different historical moments, provided such leadership. Each has also faced gradual and relative economic decline, which theorists believe increases the likelihood of international economic conflict. Hegemonic stability theory explains structural political requirements for orderly international economic relations.

Differences exist, however, regarding the meaning and significance of hegemonic power. Charles Kindleberger's liberal interpretation suggests that the free-rider problem in global economic management requires a hegemonic power to provide public goods.[83] Without a hegemonic leader, economic nationalism could degenerate into international economic crisis, as happened in the 1930s. This implies the hegemonic power must rise above the fray and serve the interest of the system as a whole. Other liberals, such as Robert Keohane, take another tack, arguing that hegemons act out of self-interest. The most powerful state creates specific international regimes to defend its interests systemwide. But he holds that regimes, and therefore a certain economic order, will persist after a hegemonic power has declined, because rationally egoistic states will perceive the maintenance of regimes to be in their interest.[84]

Immanuel Wallerstein offers a different view of hegemonic rise and decline. His historical analysis examines the origins of hegemonic power. Uneven development and long-term cycles of world growth cause the locus of accumulation to shift periodically from one region to another. A conjunction of such historical forces produces a hegemon at certain times. Once established, a hegemonic state's interests are intricately bound up with the preservation of the global system and it will act accordingly to protect these systemic interests. The hegemon thus enforces a particular division of labor among advanced industrial countries as well as between core and periphery. Moreover, since it must defend the capitalist system as a whole, it works to liberalize and open international economic relations generally. For Wallerstein, hegemonic power is less a matter of overcoming a "free-rider" problem, or of providing specific regimes; it is an integral part of capitalism as a world-system.[85]

Neorealists also add to hegemonic stability theory. Krasner develops a "state-power" theory of hegemony in contradistinction to liberal interdependence IPE of the early 1970s.[86] He illustrates how states act upon interests defined in terms of economic power. Unlike Wallerstein's emphasis on the logic of capitalism, Krasner suggests the rise of a hegemonic power is the result of political struggles among competing states. On the other hand, Krasner agrees with Wallerstein that the leading state perceives its interests in systemic terms and therefore enforces a relatively liberal international economic order. When the hegemon's power fades, protectionism and economic nationalism revive. From another angle, where liberals emphasize the economic logic of hegemony, Krasner focuses on specific political interests. In an alternative neorealist approach, Gilpin employs rational choice analysis, grounded in liberalism, to explain a classically realist topic: the causes of war.[87] What unites Krasner and Gilpin, though, is the understanding that hegemonic power is a function of the competitive nature of interstate politics.

Thus, while the varieties of hegemonic stability theory are similar in their empirical observations, they differ in their interpretations and methodologies. Even among analysts working within one paradigm, neorealism for instance, there is disagreement on key questions. This diversity, moreover, has engendered criticism of hegemonic stability theory. Timothy McKeown notes that in the nineteenth century the U.K. did not act as the theory predicts.[88] A lively debate has developed on whether or not the United States has declined as a hegemonic power, a controversy popularized by Paul Kennedy's book *The Rise and Fall of Great Powers* and the various responses to it.[89] Keohane, who accepts the point of U.S. decline, shows how international regimes are un-evenly affected by a hegemon's demise. He concludes that hegemonic stability theory alone does not explain regime change and turns scholarly attention toward a more detailed analysis of international regimes.

Regimes and Epistemic Communities

The study of international regimes is another offshoot of liberal IPE. It is a central feature of Keohane and Nye's interdependence theory. But much like rational choice, regime analysis has also been integrated into contemporary state-oriented IPE. The regime concept thus draws together contending IPE paradigms. While such convergence opens new avenues of research, it also creates definitional problems. In a survey of the literature, Stephan Haggard and Beth Simmons uncover three meanings of the term *regime*, ranging from a very broad notion of patterned international behavior to a more restrictive idea of multilateral agreements.[90] Perhaps the most widely recognized defini-tion is that formulated in a volume edited by Krasner. Here, international regimes are viewed as networks of "principles, norms, rules and decision-making procedures around which actor expectations converge in a given issue-area."[91] Yet even if many liberals and neorealists accept this definition, other controversies remain.

Debate rages over the significance of international regimes. How do such networks of principles and norms influence the behavior of states and other transnational actors? Some IPE theorists dismiss the concept out of hand, arguing that principles and norms are tenuous reflections of more basic power relationships.[92] A number of liberals take the opposite position and see re-gimes as basic elements in the world political economy; regimes are found virtually everywhere and they can influence state action.[93] Between these two extremes, other political economists accept that regimes have only a limited impact on world political–economic relations. Some, though not all, of the work in this latter category falls within the liberal versus neorealist dichotomy.

On the liberal side, Keohane develops a "functionalist" theory of regimes based upon a notion of "political market failure" derived from neoclassical economics.[94] Although he accepts the proposition that regimes are usually created by self-interested hegemonic powers, Keohane's functionalism sug-gests regimes may come to possess a certain degree of autonomy vis-à-vis the interests of individual states. States abide by established regimes because violation in the context of interdependence entails national economic costs. Moreover, states seek to build regimes in the absence of a hegemonic power because their interests are best served by this form of international coopera-tion. Political interest is the initial impetus of economic cooperation, but the exigencies of interdependence ultimately constrain political interests. Alterna-tively, Stephen Krasner incorporates the regime concept into his neorealist theory of "structural conflict."[95] While recognizing a modicum of regime au-tonomy, his "modified realist" approach views regimes as reflections of the international distribution of power. Less developed countries try to change regimes because this is the most effective way for them to protect their national interests. For Krasner, regimes do not negate power politics, they redefine political strategies.

Krasner and Keohane, while they agree that regimes exist and can influence international relations, use contending theories to reach disparate conclusions on the significance of regimes. The broader debate on regimes, however, cannot be confined to differences between liberals and neorealists. Other neorealists, for example, either do not use the concept or reject it outright. In addition, liberals do not have a uniform approach to regime issues. Haggard and Simmons explicate four theories of international regimes, each with a distinct methodology. Some of these flow from liberal analysis (functionalism); others (game theory and structuralism) are consistent with liberalism but are employed by neorealists as well.

A recent variation in the regime literature is the emergence of the concept "epistemic community." Peter M. Haas argues that groups of technical experts, who share basic worldviews and cause-and-effect beliefs, may play a significant role in certain issue areas.[96] Epistemic communities are transnational, specialists are dispersed around the globe but can exercise influence on national policy; networks of expertise bring worlds of specific knowledge into domestic policy processes. Haas suggests that the nature of an epistemic community, its coherence as a transnational presence, and its existence in particular countries, help to explain the strength or weakness of certain regimes. The notion of epistemic community opens regime analysis to a consideration of knowledge as power in IPE. It also extends political economy arguments into many different realms, wherever influential groups of experts may have a role in policy-making, such as environmental studies.

The Postmodern Turn

Pushing beyond conventional IPE issues is very much the project of postmodern theorizing. It should be noted at the outset, however, that "postmodern" is a contentious title. It does not refer to a unified theoretical "paradigm" or "research program" but suggests a certain skepticism toward basic assumptions of positivist social science.[97] The social world, to many postmodern writers, is not driven by universal laws and unitary actors; it is a jumble of contradictory forces and conflicted identities that resists simple categorization and control. Theories that purport to explain politics and economics are likewise confused by the indeterminateness of meaning: How can we say that protectionism serves the national interest if we are uncertain what precisely the "nation" is? In denying the possibility of grand theoretical understandings or solutions, postmodernism often produces ironic critiques, stories of how the world has fallen apart without any attempt to put it back together again.

It is only in the past decade or so that postmodern thinking has been imported into international relations and IPE theory per se.[98] At least two sorts of contributions are evident.

First, postmodernism, in contesting foundational assumptions, raises many new questions for theoretical reconsideration. State sovereignty, for example, is most often either taken for granted as a hard reality or presented as declining in the face of the equally hard reality of world markets. Postmodern writers take a different tack, contending that sovereignty has never been a settled fact but is more of an attempt to overcome the ambiguities of national identity.[99] If the claim of sovereignty has no independent existence beyond the political practices that enforce it, then it is much more fragile and fluid than realists or liberals realize. The problem is not merely the market; it is the contingency and fluidity of existence.

Second, postmodernism can be seen as the cultural expression of global capital and, as such, adds a new dimension to IPE theory. Fredric Jameson offers one of the first, and perhaps most influential, arguments that "late capitalism"—with its accelerating pace of production and rapidly changing patterns of consumption—has transformed society and its artistic and literary creations.[100] Building on Marx's insight that, under capitalism, social and political conventions are constantly uprooted by capital's frantic search for profits ("all that is solid melts into air"), Jameson suggests that the global reach of capital now invades cultural productions everywhere. And if our understandings of personal identity and differences between one social group and another are derived from cultural practices and artistic imagery, then what we take as the most fundamental elements of social theory—who "we" are, who "they" are, and how we tell the difference—are subject to abrupt, even capricious, change, something akin to the volatility of futures markets. The commodification of virtually everything disrupts our sense of self and confounds the search for universal theories.

This has important implications for IPE. It suggests that the field is much broader than it might seem. Trade, investment, finance, and development take up a large portion of work in IPE, but given the postmodern turn, political economy now extends into literature, art, and popular culture insofar as they are expressions of late capitalism and reveal the full social and political consequences of globalization. Postmodern thought further informs IPE theory by challenging the very possibility of theory itself. As commodification intensifies, even the solidity of capital "melts into the air"—perhaps best seen now in derivatives markets—robbing theory of every possible foundation upon which to build grand explanations. This encourages a certain reflexivity, a heightened sense of the historical conditioning of theory, that reminds all IPE theorists of the difficulties, if not impossibility, of separating themselves and their ideas from their particular historical circumstances.

Conclusion

To summarize, IPE theory has moved in many directions. Within the three major theoretical traditions, significant transformations have occurred. Liberalism has fragmented along several lines, some of which are more successful than others as explanations of interrelationships of politics and economics; neoclassical economics fails as an IPE theory because it ignores questions of power, while interdependence theory explicitly focuses on the intersection of economics and politics. Contemporary Marxism is characterized by lively debate and frequent revision, even a stimulating engagement with postmodernism.[101] State-oriented theory has been remade from the remainders of mercantilist forebears and has enjoyed a renaissance of sorts. IPE theorizing has also moved beyond the three central schools of thought. Recent work in rational choice analysis, hegemonic stability theory, and regime analysis offers new avenues of inquiry. And the postmodern turn takes IPE in directions not contemplated before.

As can be seen, the theoretical evolution of IPE theory has not been linear and cumulative. Certain arguments have been discarded (e.g., the mercantilist definition of wealth as specie), with change driven more by historical circumstance than theoretical falsification. One strand of the multifaceted debate among Marxists has been inspired by the complex patterns of post–World War II development in the Third World. Revisions of liberalism and neomercantilism have been sparked by upheaval in the global political economy in the 1970s. Theoretical change has thus come in discontinuous fits and starts. For decades, mercantilist IPE stagnated, until it was revived in the 1970s. Similarly, Marxism and liberalism have experienced periods of uninspired rehearsals of well-worn generalities, punctuated by controversial and original revisions. Evolution is neither smooth nor predestined; it is abrupt and contingent.

In looking ahead, it seems unlikely that any grand synthesis of the three major schools of thought is, or indeed can be, imminent. Ontological and epistemological differences continue to pose obstacles to more thoroughgoing theoretical melding. Moreover, the crossovers that have been attempted thus far are more syncretic than synthetic, involving uneasy combinations of potentially contradictory elements. Does the methodological individualism of rational choice analysis undermine the theoretical bases of Marxism and neomercantilism? Analysts have handled such questions in a pragmatic manner, implying that if greater explanatory precision and more interesting arguments emerge from their eclecticism, then theoretical consistency may well be the hobgoblin of little minds. Although serious epistemological issues remain, theoretical *bricolage* will likely endure.[102]

Notes

1. Quoted in: Stephen Jay Gould, *The Individual in Darwin's World* (Edinburgh: Edinburgh University Press, 1990), p. 3.

2. Our use of the term *evolution* is not meant to imply continuous, linear progress. Rather, we subcribe to Gould's more sophisticated and nuanced understanding of the contingencies of evolution (see note 1). Thus we did not mean to imply that evolution is necessarily progressive, as suggested in Richard Leaver's stimulating critique of the first edition of this book: "International Political Economy and the Chang-

ing World Order: Evolution or Involution?" in Stubbs and Underhill, eds., *Political Economy and the Changing Global Order* (New York: St. Martin's Press, 1994), pp. 130–41.

3. "We can view international political economy as the intersection of the substantive area studied by economics—production and exchange of marketable means of want satisfaction—with the process by which power is exercised that is central to politics." Robert Keohane, *After Hegemony* (Princeton: Princeton University Press, 1984), p. 21. Robert Gilpin goes further when he states that IPE questions: "how the state and its associated political processes affect the production and distribution of wealth and, in particular, how political decisions and interests influence the location of economic activities and the distribution of the costs and benefits of these activities. Conversely, these questions also inquire about the effect of markets and economic forces on the distribution of power and welfare among states and other political actors, and particularly about how these economic forces alter the international distribution of political and military power." Robert Gilpin, *The Political Economy of International Relations* (Princeton: Princeton University Press, 1987), pp. 10–11.

4. Roger Tooze, "Perspectives and Theory: A Consumer's Guide," in Susan Strange, ed., *Paths to International Political Economy* (London: Allen and Unwin, 1984), p. 2.

5. Hans Morgenthau, a leading realist theoretician, was quite straightforward regarding the necessity of analytically separating politics and economics: "Intellectually, the political realist maintains the autonomy of the political sphere, as the economist, the lawyer, the moralist maintain theirs. . . . It is exactly through such a process of emancipation from other standards of thought, and the development of one appropriate to its subject matter, that economics has developed as an autonomous theory of the economic activity of man. To contribute to a similar development in the field of politics is indeed the purpose of political realism." Hans Morgenthau, *Politics Among Nations* (New York: Knopf, 1985) pp. 13–16.

6. Susan Strange, "International Political Economy: The Story So Far and the Way Ahead." in W. Ladd Hollist and F. Lamond Tullis, eds., *An International Political Economy* (Boulder, Col.: Westview, 1985).

7. Kenneth N. Waltz, *Theory of International Politics* (Reading Mass.: Addison-Wesley, 1979).

8. Robert Gilpin, *The Political Economy of International Relations* (Princeton: Princeton University Press, 1987), chap. 2. An interesting counterpart to this view of the literature is Alfred Stepan's three categories of theory in: *The State and Society: Peru in Comparative Perspective* (Princeton: Princeton University Press, 1978), chap. 1. The influence of Gilpin's analysis can be seen in Jeffery Frieden and David Lake, eds., *International Political Economy* (New York: St. Martin's, 1987). Stephen Gill and David Law also explicate the three major theories in *The Global Political Economy* (Baltimore: Johns Hopkins University Press, 1988). For other categorizations see: David H. Blake and Robert S. Walters, *The Politics of Global Economic Relations* (Englewood Cliffs, N.J.: Prentice-Hall,1987); Roger Tooze, "Perspectives and Theory: A Consumer's Guide." in Susan Strange, ed., *Paths to International Political Economy* (London: Allen and Unwin,1984); and R.J. Barry Jones, "Perspectives on International Political Economy," in R.J. Barry Jones, ed., *Perspectives on Political Economy* (New York: St. Martin's Press, 1983).

9. Jacob Viner, "Power versus Plenty as Objectives of Foreign Policy in the Seventeenth and Eighteenth Centuries," *World Politics* 1,1 (October, 1948).

10. Eli Heckscher, *Mercantilism* (New York: Macmillan, 1955), p. 15.

11. N. Keohane, *Philosophy and the State in France* (Princeton: Princeton University Press, 1980). Karl Pribram offers an analysis of different forms of mercantilism throughout Europe in his *A History of Economic Reasoning* (Baltimore: Johns Hopkins University Press, 1983), pp. 31–89.

12. "In every phase of economic development, a guiding and controlling part belongs to some one or another political organ. . . . It rules economic life as well as political, determines its structure and institutions, and furnishes, as it were, the centre of gravity of the whole mass of socio-economic arrangements." Gustav Schmoller, *The Mercantile System and Its Historical Significance* (New York: Peter Smith, 1931 [1895]), p. 2.

13. Schumpeter's discussion of Schmoller is informative, and Staniland points to the politicist followers of the Historical School: Joseph Schumpeter, *History of Economic Analysis* (New York: Oxford University Press, 1954), pp. 809–15. Also see: Martin Staniland, *What Is Political Economy?* (New Haven: Yale University Press, 1985), pp. 83–86.

14. For the paradigmatic importance of Smith see: Phyllis Deane, *The Evolution of Economic Ideas* (Cambridge: Cambridge University Press, 1978), pp. 6–7.

15. Schumpeter captures this nicely: "The comprehensive vision of the universal interdependence of all the elements of the economic system . . . probably never cost Ricardo as much as an hour's sleep. His interest was in the clear-cut result of direct, practical significance. In order to get this he cut that general system to pieces, bundled up as large parts of it as possible, and put them in cold storage—so that as many things as possible should be frozen and "given." He then piled one simplifying assumption upon another until, having really settled everything by these assumptions, he was left with only a few aggregate variables between which, given these assumptions, he set up simple one-way relations so that, in the end, the desired results emerged almost as tautologies." Schumpeter, op. cit., pp. 472–73. Ricardo's methodological break with Smith is also discussed in: Deane, op. cit., pp. 74–80.

16. "But if economics is essentially an engine of analysis, a method of thinking rather than a body of substantive results, Ricardo literally invented the technique of economics." Mark Blaug, *Economic Theory in Retrospect* (Cambridge: Cambridge University Press, 1985), pp. 135–36.

17. Edmund Silberner, *The Problem of War in Nineteenth Century Economic Thought* (Princeton: Princeton University Press, 1946), p. 280; other quotations in this paragraph come from the same source, pp. 280–82.

18. Norman Angell, *The Great Illusion* (New York: G.P. Putnam: 1913).

19. Edward H. Carr, *The Twenty Years Crisis, 1919–1939* (London: Macmillan, 1951), pp. 43–46.

20. Many of these can be found in: Shlomo Avineri, ed., *Karl Marx on Colonialism and Modernization* (Garden City, N.Y.: Doubleday, 1969).

21. Karl Marx, *Capital*, vol. I (New York: Vantage, 1976 [1867]), chap. 24.

22. "The bourgeoisie, by rapid improvement of all instruments of production, by the immensely facilitated means of communication, draws all, even the most barbarian, nations into civilisation. The cheap prices of its commodities are the heavy artillery with which it batters down all Chinese walls, with which it forces the barbarians' intensely obstinate hatred of foreigners to capitulate. It compels all nations, on pain of extinction, to adopt the bourgeois mode of production; it compels them to introduce what it calls civilisation into their midst, i.e., to become bourgeois themselves. In one word, it creates a world after its own image." From the *Communist Manifesto*, as quoted in Avineri, op. cit. pp. 36–37.

23. Marx, op. cit., 1976, preface.

24. Theodor Shanin, ed., *Late Marx and the Russian Road* (New York: Monthly Review Press, 1983).

25. An excellent review of all of these theorists can be found in: Anthony Brewer, *Marxist Theories of Imperialism* (London: Routledge & Kegan Paul, 1980).

26. V.I. Lenin, *Imperialism: The Highest Stage of Capitalism* (Beijing: Foreign Languages Press, 1975), p. 76.

27. Deane, op. cit., pp. 140–41, argues that Marx had little impact on mainstream economists.

28. Keynes states his position at the very beginning of the *General Theory*: "I shall argue that the postulates of the classical theory are applicable to a special case only and not to the general case, the situation which it assumes being a limiting point of the possible positions of equilibrium. Moreover, the characteristics of the special case assumed by the classical theory happen not to be those of the economic society in which we actually live, with the result that its teaching is misleading and disastrous if we attempt to apply it to the facts of experience." John M. Keynes, *The General Theory of Employment Interest and Money* (New York: Harcourt, Brace and Company, 1936), p. 3.

29. Mark Blaug, "Kuhn versus Lakatos, or Paradigms versus Research Programs in the History of Economics," *History of Political Economy* 7:4 (1975), p. 412.

30. This tendency can be seen in: John M. Keynes, "National Self-Sufficiency," *The Yale Review* 12:4 (1933), p. 755.

31. Milton Friedman, "The Case for Flexible Exchange Rates," in Milton Friedman, *Essays in Positive Economics* (Chicago: University of Chicago Press, 1953).

32. Susan Strange, op. cit., 1985.

33. This is, of course, a reference to Raymond Vernon's seminal work, *Sovereignty at Bay* (New York: Basic Books, 1971). Charles Kindleberger anticipated this analysis when he wrote: "the nation state is just about through as an economic unit." Charles Kindleberger, *American Business Abroad: Six Lectures on Direct Investment* (New Haven: Yale University Press, 1969), p. 209.

34. Robert Keohane and Joseph Nye, *Power and Interdependence: World Politics in Transition* (Boston: Little, Brown, 1977).

35. "although our analysis was clearly rooted in interdependence theory, which shared key assumptions of liberalism, we made no efforts to locate ourselves with respect to the liberal tradition. As we now see the matter, we were seeking in part to broaden the neofunctional strand of liberalism that had been developed by Ernst B. Haas and others in the 1950s and 1960s but that had been limited largely to the analysis of regional integration." Robert Keohane and Joseph Nye, "Power and Interdependence Revisited," *International Organization* 41,4 (Autumn 1987), p. 729.

36. R. Keohane, op.cit.

37. Michael Doyle, "Stalemate in the North–South Debate: Strategies and the New International Economic Order," *World Politics* 35,3 (April 1983); Vincent Mahler, "The Political Economy of North–South Commodity Bargaining: The Case of the International Sugar Agreement," *International Organization* 38,4 (Autumn 1984); John Ravenhill, "What Is to Be Done for Third World Commodity Exporters? An Evaluation of the STABEX Scheme," *International Organization* 38,3 (Summer 1984).

38. Brewer, op. cit.; Martin Carnoy, *The State and Political Theory* (Princeton, Princeton University Press, 1984); David A. Gold, Clarence Y.H. Lo and Erik Olin Wright, "Recent Developments in Marxist Theories of the Capitalist State," *Monthly Review* 27 (1975), no. 5:29–43; no. 6:36–51.

39. Paul Baran, *The Political Economy of Growth* (New York: Monthly Review Press, 1957).

40. Andre Gunder Frank, *Capitalism and Underdevelopment in Latin America* (New York: Monthly Review Press, 1967); Theotonio Dos Santos, "The Structure of Dependence," *The American Economic Review* 60,2 (May 1970).

41. Fernando H. Cardoso, "Associated-Dependent Development: Theoretical and Political Implications," in Alfred Stepan, ed., *Authoritarian Brazil* (New Haven: Yale University Press, 1973), pp. 142–78; Fernando H. Cardoso and Enzo Faletto, *Dependency and Development in Latin America* (Berkeley: University of California Press, 1979). It is important to note that Cardoso's work develops simultaneously with early dependency theory. Thus, he "solves" the anomaly of LDC industrialization even as the question is taking shape; see: Kate Manzo, "Modernist Discourse and the Crisis of Development Theory," unpublished manuscript, 1989.

42. Ronald H. Chilcote and Dale L. Johnson, eds., *Theories of Development: Mode of Production or Dependency?* (Beverly Hills: Sage Publications, 1983).

43. Immanuel Wallerstein, *The Capitalist World-Economy* (New York: Cambridge University Press, 1979); Christopher Chase-Dunn, *Global Formation: Structures of the World-Economy* (Cambridge: Blackwell, 1990).

44. Bill Warren, "Imperialism and Capitalist Industrialization" *New Left Review*, 81 (September-October, 1973); Theda Skocpol, "Wallerstein's World Capitalist System: A Theoretical and Historical Critique," *American Journal of Sociology* 82,5 (March 1977), pp. 1075–90; Tony Smith, "The Underdevelopment of Development Literature: The Case of Dependency Theory," *World Politics* 31,2 (January 1979), pp. 247–88.

45. "If the state has expanded and fortified itself, it has done so as the expression of a class situation which has incorporated capitalist development, as we have said, and policies of the dominant classes favorable to the rapid growth of the corporate system, to alliances between the state and business enterprises, and to the establishment of interconnections, at the level of the state productive system, between 'public' and multinational enterprises." Cardoso and Faletto, op. cit., p. 201.

46. "A simple 'structural' analysis, demonstrating the contradictions between social forces and the drawbacks of the process of accumulation with its cycles and crises, is insufficient to explain the concrete course of political events." Ibid., p. 207.

47. The early work of Peter Evans is a broader synthesis of Cardoso's perspective and world-systems analysis in an effort to rejuvenate Marxist IPE. Peter Evans, *Dependent Development: The Alliance of Multinational, State, and Local Capital in Brazil* (Princeton: Princeton University Press, 1979).

48. In a provocative riposte to the structuralist definition of the state as the "condensation of class interests," Block argues that: "A condensation cannot exercise power." Fred Block, "Beyond Relative Autonomy: State Managers as Historical Subjects," *The Socialist Register, 1980* (London: Merlin Press, 1980), pp. 227–42.

49. Ralph Miliband, "State Power and Class Interests," *New Left Review*, (March-April 1983).

50. "States undoubtedly act with a certain autonomy. Each state has evolved, through its own institutions and practices, certain consistent notions of interest and modes of conduct that can be termed its particular *raison d'etat*. This autonomy is, however, conditioned by both internal and external constraints. State autonomy, in other words, is exercised within a structure created by the state's own history." Robert W. Cox, *Production, Power, and World Order: Social Forces in the Making of History* (New York: Columbia University Press, 1987), p. 399.

51. Ibid., p. 254.

52. A good introduction to the debate on post-Fordism is: Stuart Hall and Martin Jacques, eds., *New Times: The Changing Face of Politics in the 1990s* (New York: Verso, 1990).

53. David Harvey, *The Condition of Postmodernity: An Enquiry into the Origins of Cultural Change* (Cambridge: Blackwell, 1990).

54. Bertrand Badie and Pierre Birnbaum, *The Sociology of the State* (Chicago: University of Chicago Press,1983), p. 17.

55. "On the one hand, capitalism in its modern stages of development requires the bureaucracy, though both have arisen from different historical sources. Conversely, capitalism is the most rational economic basis for bureaucratic administration and enables it to develop in the most rational form, especially because, from a fiscal point of view, it supplies the necessary money resources." Max Weber, *Economy and Society*, Guernther Roth and Claus Wittich, eds., (Berkeley: University of California Press, 1978), p. 224.

56. David Betham, *Max Weber and the Theory of Modern Politics* (Cambridge: Polity Press, 1985), p. 131.

57. Randall Collins offers a careful explication of Weber's significance for international relations; see: Randall Collins, *Weberian Sociological Theory* (Cambridge: Cambridge University Press, 1986), pp. 145–66.

58. Weber's work was appropriated by functionalist sociologists to bolster a decidedly society-centered theoretical perspective, a use since criticized as untrue to Weber's own inclinations; see: Badie and Birnbaum, op. cit., chap. 2.

59. Gilpin argues that only after World War II did realism lose sight of economic factors. Classical precursors of realist thought had a highly developed notion of political economy. Gilpin, 1984, op. cit., pp. 293–97.

60. Four authors stand out in this regard: Karl Polanyi, *The Great Transformation* (Boston: Beacon Press, 1944); Alexander Gershenkron, *Economic Backwardness in Historical Perspective* (Cambridge: Belknap Press, 1966); Gunnar Myrdal, *Asian Drama* (New York: Vintage Books, 1970); J.P. Nettl, "The State as a Conceptual Variable," *World Politics* 20,4 (July 1968), pp. 559–92.

61. Robert Gilpin, "The Politics of Transnational Economic Relations," in Robert Keohane and Joseph Nye, eds., *Transnational Relations and World Politics* (Cambridge: Harvard University Press, 1972).

62. Ibid., p. 403.

63. Perhaps the most significant work along these lines is that of Stephen Krasner: Stephen D. Krasner, *Defending the National Interest* (Princeton: Princeton University Press, 1978); and "State Power and the Structure of International Trade," *World Politics* 28 (April, 1976), 317–47.

64. Theda Skocpol, *States and Social Revolutions* (New York: Cambridge University Press, 1979).

65. Theda Skocpol, "Bringing the State Back In: Strategies of Analysis in Current Research," in Evans et al., *Bringing the State Back In* (New York: Cambridge University Press, 1985).

66. Kenneth Waltz, op. cit.

67. Robert Gilpin, *War and Change in World Politics* (Princeton: Princeton University Press, 1981).

68. Stephen Krasner, "American Policy and Global Economic Stability," in William P. Avery and David P. Rapkin, eds., *America in a Changing World Political Economy* (New York: Longman, 1982).

69. Stephen Krasner, *Structural Conflict* (Berkeley: University of California Press, 1985).

70. Peter Katzenstein, ed., *Between Power and Plenty* (Madison: University of Wisconsin Press, 1978).

71. Peter Evans et al., op. cit.

72. Gilpin discusses conditions leading to war in: *War and Change in World Politics*, op. cit. Atul Kohli presents a number of analyses of Third World development in: *The State and Development in the Third World* (Princeton: Princeton University Press, 1986).

73. For a general discussion of *new political economy* see: Martin Staniland, *What Is Political Economy*, op. cit., chap. 3. Although there are differences in their analytic focus and policy prescriptions, both game theory and public goods theory are here considered two variants of rational choice theory in that they operate on a similar level of abstraction and share many of the same assumptions. For distinctions between game theory and public goods theory see: John A.C. Conybeare, "Public Goods, Prisoner's Dilemmas and the International Political Economy," *International Studies Quarterly* 28,1 (March 1984), pp. 5–22.

74. Bruno Frey offers an explication and defense of rational choice approaches to international political economy in: *International Political Economics* (New York: Basil Blackwell, 1984); and "The Public Choice View of International Political Economy," *International Organization*, 38,1 (Winter 1984). The inspiration for much of the rational choice theory in IPE is Mancur Olson. His most recent work is possibly the most far-reaching application of this approach to IPE topics; see: Mancur Olson, *The Rise and Decline of Nations* (New Haven: Yale University Press, 1982).

75. Charles Kindleberger, *The World in Depression* (Berkeley: University of California Press, 1973).

76. Bruno Frey, *International Political Economics*. op. cit.

77. John A.C Conybeare, "Public Goods, Prisoner's Dilemmas and the International Political Economy," op. cit.

78. Game theory has also been applied to topics of international political economy in: Kenneth Oye, ed., *Cooperation Under Anarchy* (Princeton: Princeton University Press, 1986).

79. Keohane, *After Hegemony*, op. cit.

80. Robert Gilpin, *War and Change in World Politics*, op. cit.

81. Robert Gilpin, *The Political Economy of International Relations*, op. cit., p. xiii.

82. Good introductions to this literature are: John Roemer, "'Rational Choice' Marxism: Some Issues of Method and Substance," and Jon Elster, "Further Thoughts on Marxism, Functionalism, and Game Theory," both in John Roemer, ed., *Analytical Marxism* (Cambridge: Cambridge University Press, 1986). For a critique of "analytical Marxism" from a dialectical-Marxist perspective see: Andrew Levine, et al., "Marxism and Methodological Individualism," *New Left Review*, 162 (March/April 1987).

83. Charles Kindleberger, one of the earliest contributors to hegemonic stability theory, argues that: "for the world economy to be stabilized, there has to be a stabilizer, one stabilizer." Kindleberger, 1973, op. cit., p. 305.

84. Robert Keohane, "The Theory of Hegemonic Stability and Changes in International Regimes, 1967–1977," in O. Holsti, et al., eds., *Change in the International System* (Boulder, Colo.: Westview, 1980).

85. A Gramscian perspective on "hegemony" can be found in: Robert Cox, "Social Forces, States, and World Orders," *Millennium*, 10 (1981), pp. 126–55; and Gill and Law, op. cit., pp. 76–80.

86. Krasner, "State Power and the Structure of International Trade," op. cit.

87. Gilpin, *War and Change in World Politics*, op. cit.

88. Timothy J. McKeown, "Hegemonic Stability Theory and 19th Century Tariff Levels in Europe," *International Organization* 37,1 (1983), pp. 73–91.

89. Before Kennedy's book, skeptics of hegemonic decline included: Bruce Russett, "The Mysterious Case of Vanishing Hegemony: Or, Is Mark Twain Really Dead?" *International Organization* 39,2 (1985), pp. 207–32; Susan Strange, "The Persistant Myth of Lost Hegemony," *International Organization* 41,4 (1987), pp. 551–74. Then, Kennedy weighed in with *The Rise and Decline of Great Powers* (New York: Random House, 1987), stimulating counterarguments that the United States has not lost its global preeminence; Henry R. Nau, *The Myth of America's Decline* (New York: Oxford University Press, 1990); Joseph S. Nye, Jr., *Bound to Lead: The Changing Nature of American Power* (New York: Basic Books, 1990).

90. Stephan Haggard and Beth A. Simmons, "Theories of International Regimes," *International Organization* 41,3 (Summer, 1987), pp. 491–517.

91. Stephen Krasner, ed., *International Regimes* (Ithaca: Cornell University Press, 1983).

92. Susan Strange's article in Krasner, 1983, op. cit., is the most pointed of these critiques.

93. Donald J. Puchala and Raymond F. Hopkins, "International Regimes: Lessons from Inductive Analysis," in Krasner, 1983, op. cit.

94. Keohane, *After Hegemony*, op. cit.

95. Krasner, *Structural Conflict*, op. cit.

96. Peter M. Haas, "Do Regimes Matter? Epistemic Communities and Mediterranean Pollution Control," *International Organization* 43,3 (Summer 1989), pp. 377–403; see also the special edition of *International Organization* 46,1 (Winter 1992), on epistemic communities.

97. Jim George and David Campbell, "Patterns of Dissent and the Celebration of Difference: Critical Social Theory and International Relations," *International Studies Quarterly* 34, 3 (Fall 1990), pp. 269–300. For a discussion of the varieties of postmodern thought see: Margaret A. Rose, *The Post-Modern and the Post-Industrial* (New York: Cambridge University Press, 1991).

98. A notable landmark here is: James Der Derian and Michael J. Shapiro, *International/Intertextual Relations: Postmodern Readings of World Politics* (Lexington, Mass.: Lexington Books, 1988).

99. R.B.J. Walker, *Inside/Outside: International Relations as Political Theory* (New York: Cambridge University Press, 1993), chap. 8.

100. Fredric Jameson, *Postmodernism, or, The Cultural Logic of Late Capitalism* (Durham, N.C.: Duke University Press, 1991), chap. 1.

101. Jameson comments wryly on the combination of Marxist and postmodern theories: "the two terms (in full postmodernism) carry with them a whole freight of pop nostalgia images, 'Marxism' perhaps distilling itself into yellowing period photographs of Lenin and the Soviet revolution, and 'postmodernism' quickly yielding a vista of the gaudiest new hotels. The overhasty unconscious then rapidly assembles the image of a small, painstakingly reproduced nostalgia restaurant—decorated with old photographs, with Soviet waiters sluggishly serving bad Russian food—hidden away within some gleaming new pink-and-blue architectural extravaganza." *Postmodernism*, op cit, p. 297.

102. Claude Levi-Strauss uses the term *bricolage* to describe the cobbling together of diverse ideas in the process of mythmaking. Recent crossovers in IPE theory are similarly composed of a hodgepodge of concepts and methods. See: Claude Levi-Strauss, *The Savage Mind* (Chicago: University of Chicago Press, 1962), pp. 16–33.

Classical Mercantilism

1

Early Mercantilist political economy boldly asserts the centrality of politics. Economics is not separated from its political context, but instead is considered an important means of enhancing state power. Although the various strands of classical mercantilism do not form a unified theory, a general sense of the primacy of politics was the dominant view of political economy before Adam Smith, especially in the sixteenth and seventeenth centuries. The selections here, from Alexander Hamilton and Fredrich List, are not representative of the golden age of mercantilism; however, they both defend core mercantilist principles against the emerging liberal critique.

Alexander Hamilton (1755–1804) is most concerned with national economic development. His "Report on Manufactures," submitted to Congress in 1791, and his other analyses of public credit and a central bank are aimed at strengthening the flegdling economy of the United States. More of a practical statesman than social theorist, Hamilton invokes a number of classical mercantilist arguments in advocating the growth of manufacturing. Although he recognizes the importance of agriculture, he sees industry as providing additional dynamism to the American economy. Such diversification, in turn, will lessen the nation's vulnerability to external economic forces. The domestic market is a more reliable foundation upon which to build. Moreover, national security is best served by a self-reliant and complex national economy: "The extreme embarrassments of the United States in the late War, from an incapacity of supplying themselves, are still a matter of keen recollection . . ." Thus, avoiding economic dependence is an underlying theme, an idea consistent with earlier mercantilist thought.

The state, Hamilton argues, must take an active role in developing a manufacturing economy. Domestic obstacles to industrialization, such as inexperience and capital shortages, can only be overcome by government intervention: ". . . the public purse must supply the deficiency of private resource." Additionally, the state must promote and protect emerging U.S. industries, because this is common practice in the competitive international system. Adam Smith's notion of free trade is simply an inaccurate description of world political–economic realities. Hamilton, therefore, offers a series of protectionist measures that further American manufacturing interests. Yet his desire for protectionism differs from earlier mercantilist thought in that a positive balance of trade and an inflow of specie are not ends in themselves; they are the outcome of a strong manufacturing economy.

Hamilton thus draws on key mercantilist concepts (i.e., national security and self-reliance) but modifies others (the significance of a trade surplus). Interestingly, his rationale for U.S. economic policy is strikingly similar to the nationalist-oriented concerns of less developed countries in the twentieth century.

Fredrich List (1789–1846) operates more on the theoretical level. He directly assaults the liberal arguments of Smith and others of the "popular school." His critique centers on the invalidity of key liberal assumptions. The "cosmopolitical" world view assumes political stability and peace, even unity. This, List argues, misses the key point that the world is riven by pointed nationalist rivalries. Political economy must begin with a recognition of the inherently conflictual nature of international relations. The nation is, as early mercantilists held, the key unit of political–economic analysis. List's nationalist perspective reveals the politics behind international economic processes. "True political science," he contends, recognizes that the interests of the industrially developed economies are best served by a free trade regime; nations that have yet to industrialize are developmentally constrained in an open, competitive world economy. He concludes that protectionism is the necessary course for those countries interested in economic development.

Although List seems to offer a general theory of political economy, taking on Malthus as well as Smith, his argument is ultimately ad hoc. He suggests that "every separate nation" will discover its peculiar national means to economic development, but he is particularly concerned with Germany's economic future. Elsewhere in his book, *The National System of Political Economy*, he argues that the world can be divided into two regions, the "hot zone" and the "temperate zone." Only the latter is suitable for industrial development similar to that of Britain; the former should remain primarily agricultural. Thus, infant industry protection is not appropriate for every state, but only those deserving nations in the "temperate zone," such as Germany and the United States. Once these sorts of countries develop to a sufficient degree, then the mutual benefits of free trade can be realized. In sum, List recognizes the power of liberal arguments on comparative advantage and free trade. But he wants to make sure that, as these dynamics grow, Germany and others share in the wealth.

Report on Manufactures

ALEXANDER HAMILTON

The expediency of encouraging manufactures in the United States, which was not long since deemed very questionable, appears at this time to be pretty generally admitted. The embarrassments, which have obstructed the progress of our external trade, have led to serious reflections on the necessity of enlarging the sphere of our domestic commerce: the restrictive regulations, which in foreign markets abridge the vent of the increasing surplus of our Agricultural produce, serve to beget an earnest desire, that a more extensive demand for that surplus may be created at home: And the complete success, which has rewarded manufacturing enterprise, in some valuable branches, conspiring with the promising symptoms, which attend some less mature essays, in others, justify a hope, that the obstacles to the growth of this species of industry are less formidable than they were apprehended to be, and that it is not difficult to find, in its further extension, a full indemnification for any external disadvantages, which are or may be experienced, as well as an accession of resources, favorable to national independence and safety.

There still are, nevertheless, respectable patrons of opinions, unfriendly to the encouragement of manufactures. The following are, substantially, the arguments by which these opinions are defended.

"In every country (say those who entertain them) Agriculture is the most beneficial and *productive* object of human industry. This position, generally, if not universally true, applies with peculiar emphasis to the United

This is the text that has been printed in Jacob E. Cooke (ed.) *The Reports of Alexander Hamilton* (N.Y.: Harper & Row, 1964).

States, on account of their immense tracts of fertile territory, uninhabited and unimproved. . . .

"To endeavor, by the extraordinary patronage of Government, to accelerate the growth of manufactures, is, in fact, to endeavor, by force and art, to transfer the natural current of industry from a more, to a less beneficial channel. Whatever has such a tendency must necessarily be unwise. Indeed it can hardly ever be wise in a government, to attempt to give a direction to the industry of its citizens. This, under the quick-sighted guidance of private interest, will, if left to itself, infallibly find its own way to the most profitable employment: and it is by such employment, that the public prosperity will be most effectually promoted. To leave industry to itself, therefore, is, in almost every case, the soundest as well as the simplest policy.

"If contrary to the natural course of things, an unseasonable and premature spring can be given to certain fabrics, by heavy duties, prohibitions, bounties, or by other forced expedients; this will only be to sacrifice the interests of the community to those of particular classes. Besides the misdirection of labor, a virtual monopoly will be given to the persons employed on such fabrics; and an enhancement of price, the inevitable consequence of every monopoly, must be defrayed at the expense of the other parts of the society. It is far preferable, that these persons should be engaged in the cultivation of the earth, and that we should procure, in exchange for its productions, the commodities, with which foreigners are able to supply us in greater perfection, and upon better terms."

It ought readily to be conceded that the cultivation of the earth—as the primary and most certain source of national supply . . .—*has intrinsically a strong claim to pre-eminence over every other kind of industry.*

But, that it has a title to any thing like an exclusive predilection, in any country, ought to be admitted with great caution. That it is even more productive than every other branch of industry requires more evidence than has yet been given in support of the position. That its real interests, precious and important as, without the help of exaggeration, they truly are, will be advanced, rather than injured by the due encouragement of manufactures, may, it is believed, be satisfactorily demonstrated. And it is also believed that the expediency of such encouragement in a general view may be shown to be recommended by the most cogent and persuasive motives of national policy.

The foregoing suggestions are *not designed to inculcate an opinion that manufacturing industry is more productive than that of Agriculture.* They are intended rather to show that the reverse of this proposition is not ascertained; that the general arguments which are brought to establish it are not satisfactory; and, consequently that a supposition of the superior productiveness of Tillage ought to be no obstacle to listening to any substantial inducements to the encouragement of manufactures, which may be otherwise perceived to exist, through an apprehension; that they may have a tendency to divert labour from a more to a less profitable employment.

. . . . But without contending for the superior productiveness of Manufacturing Industry, it may conduce to a better judgment of the policy, which ought to be pursued respecting its encouragement, to contemplate the subject, under some additional aspects, tending not only to confirm the idea, that this kind of industry has been improperly represented as unproductive in itself; but to evince in addition that the establishment and diffusion of manufactures have the effect of rendering the total mass of useful and productive labor, in a community, *greater than it would otherwise be. . . .*

. . . . [M]anufacturing establishments not only occasion a positive augmentation of the Produce and Revenue of the Society, but . . . they contribute essentially to rendering them greater than they could possibly be, without such establishments. These circumstances are. . . .

1). . . . The Division Of Labour

It has justly been observed, that there is scarcely any thing of greater moment in the economy of a nation than the proper division of labour. The separation of occupations causes each to be carried to a much greater perfection, than it could possibly acquire, if they were blended. . . .

. . . . [T]he mere separation of the occupation of the cultivator, from that of the Artificer, has the effect of augmenting the *productive powers* of labour, and with them, the total mass of the produce or revenue of a Country. In this single view of the subject, therefore, the utility of Artificers of Manufacturers, towards promoting an increase of productive industry, is apparent.

2). . . . An Extension Of The Use Of Machinery, A Point Which, Though Partly Anticipated Requires To Be Placed In One Or Two Additional Lights

The employment of Machinery forms an item of great importance in the general mass of national industry. . . . It shall be taken for granted, and the truth of the position referred to observation, that manufacturing pursuits are susceptible in a greater degree of the application of machinery, than those of Agriculture. If so all the difference is lost to a community, which, instead of manufacturing for itself, procures the fabrics requisite to its supply from other Countries. The substitution of foreign for domestic manufactures is a transfer to foreign nations of the advantages accruing from the employment of Machinery, in the modes in which it is capable of being employed, with most utility and to the greatest extent.

3). . . . The Additional Employment Of Classes Of The Community, Not Originally Engaged In The Particular Business

This is not among the least valuable of the means, by which manufacturing institutions contribute to augment the general stock of industry and production. In places where those institutions prevail, besides the persons regularly engaged in them, they afford occasional and extra employment to industrious individuals and families, who are willing to devote the leisure resulting from the intermissions of their ordinary pursuits to collateral labours, as a resource for multiplying their acquisitions or their enjoyments. . . .

. . . . It is worthy of particular remark, that, in general, women and children are rendered more useful, and the latter more early useful by manufacturing establishments than they would otherwise be. . . .

4). . . . Promoting Of Emigration From Foreign Countries

If it be true then, that it is the interest of the United States to open every possible avenue to emigration from abroad, it affords a weighty argument for the encouragement of manufactures; which, . . . will have the strongest tendency to multiply the inducements to it.

Here is perceived an important resource, not only for extending the population, and with it the useful and productive labour of the country, but likewise for the prosecution of manufactures, without deducting from the number of hands, which might otherwise be drawn to Tillage and even for the indemnification of Agriculture for such as might happen to be diverted from it. . . .

5). . . . Furnishing Greater Scope For The Diversity Of Talents And Dispositions, Which Discriminate Men From Each Other

This is a much more powerful means of augmenting the fund of national Industry than may at first sight appear. It is a just observation, that minds of the strongest and most active powers for their proper objects fall below mediocrity and labour without effect, if confined to uncongenial pursuits. And it is thence to be inferred, that the results of human exertion may be immensely increased by diversifying its objects. When all the different kinds of industry obtain in a community, each individual can find his proper element, and can call into activity the whole vigour of his nature. And the community is benefitted by the services of its respective members, in the manner, in which each can serve it with most effect.

6). . . . Affording A More Ample And Various Field For Enterprise

 . . . . To cherish and stimulate the activity of the human mind, by multiplying the objects of enterprise, is not among the least considerable of the expedients, by which the wealth of a nation may be promoted. . . . The spirit of enterprise, useful and prolific as it is, must necessarily be contracted or expanded in proportion to the simplicity or variety of the occupations and productions, which are to be found in a Society. It must be less in a nation of mere cultivators, than in a nation of cultivators and merchants; less in a nation of cultivators and merchants, than in a nation of cultivators, artificers and merchants.

7). . . . Creating, In Some Instances, A New, And Securing In All A More Certain And Steady Demand, For Surplus Produce Of This Soil

It is evident, that the exertions of the husbandman will be steady or fluctuating, vigorous or feeble, in proportion to the steadiness or fluctuation, adequateness or inadequateness, of the markets on which he must depend, for the vent of the surplus, which may be produced by his labor; and that such surplus in the ordinary course of things will be greater or less in the same proportion.

For the purpose of this vent, a domestic market is greatly to be preferred to a foreign one; because it is in the nature of things, far more to be relied upon.

To secure such a market, there is no other expedient, than to promote manufacturing establishments. Manufacturers who constitute the most numerous class, after the Cultivators of land, are for that reason the principal consumers of the surplus of their labour.

The foregoing considerations seem sufficient to establish, as general propositions, that it is the interest of nations to diversify the industrious pursuits of

[handwritten: agr. is good for industry]

the individuals who compose them—that the establishment of manufactures is calculated not only to increase the general stock of useful and productive labour; but even to improve the state of Agriculture in particular, certainly to advance the interest of those who are engaged in it. . . .

If the system of perfect liberty to industry and commerce were the prevailing system of nations, the arguments which dissuade a country, in the predicament of the United States, from the zealous pursuit of manufactures, would doubtless have great force. It will not be affirmed, that they might not be permitted, with few exceptions, to serve as a rule of national conduct. In such a state of things, each country would have the full benefit of its peculiar advantages to compensate for its deficiencies or disadvantages. If one nation were in a condition to supply manufactured articles on better terms than another, that other might find an abundant indemnification in a superior capacity to furnish the produce of the soil. And a free exchange, mutually beneficial, of the commodities, which each was able to supply, on the best terms, might be carried on between them, supporting in full vigour the industry of each. . . .

But the system which has been mentioned, is far from characterising the general policy of Nations. The prevalent one has been regulated by an opposite spirit. The consequence of it is, that the United States are to a certain extent in the situation of a country precluded from foreign Commerce. They can indeed, without difficulty obtain from abroad the manufactured supplies, of which they are in want; but they experience numerous and very injurious impediments to the emission and vent of their own commodities. Nor is this the case in reference to a single foreign nation only. The regulations of several countries, with which we have the most extensive intercourse, throw serious obstructions in the way of the principal staples of the United States.

In such a position of things, the United States cannot exchange with Europe on equal terms; and the want of reciprocity would render them the victim of a system which should induce them to confine their views to Agriculture, and refrain from Manufactures. A constant and increasing necessity, on their part, for the commodities of Europe, and only a partial and occasional demand for their own, in return, could not but expose them to a state of impoverishment, compared with the opulence to which their political and natural advantages authorize them to aspire.

 . . . . It is for the United States to consider by what means they can render themselves least dependent on the combinations, right or wrong, of foreign policy.

The remaining objections to a particular encouragement of manufacturers in the United States now require to be examined.

One of these turns on the proposition, that Industry, if left to itself, will naturally find its way to the most useful and profitable employment: whence it is inferred that manufactures without the aid of government will grow up as soon and as fast, as the natural state of things and the interest of the community may require.

[handwritten: Invisible hand]

Against the solidity of this hypothesis, in the full latitude of the terms, very cogent reasons may be offered. These have relations to—the strong influence of habit and the spirit of imitation—the fear of want of success in untried enterprises—the intrinsic difficulties incident to first essays towards a competition with those who have previously attained to perfection in the business to be attempted—the bounties premiums and other artificial encouragements, with which foreign nations second the exertions of their own Citizens in the branches, in which they are to be rivalled.

Experience teaches, that men are often so much governed by what they are accustomed to see and practice, that the simplest and most obvious improvements, in the most ordinary occupations, are adopted with hesitation, reluctance, and by slow gradations. The spontaneous transition to new pursuits, in a community long habituated to different ones, may be expected to be attended with proportionably greater difficulty. When former occupations ceased to yield a profit adequate to the subsistence of their followers, or when there was an absolute deficiency of employment in them, owing to the superabundance of hands, changes would ensue; but these changes would be likely to be more tardy than might consist with the interest either of individuals or of the Society. In many cases they would not happen, while a bare support could be insured by an adherence to ancient courses; though a resort to a more profitable employment might be practicable. To produce the desireable changes as early as may be expedient, may therefore require the incitement and patronage of government.

The superiority antecedently enjoyed by nations, who have preoccupied and perfected a branch of industry, constitutes a more formidable obstacle, than either of those, which have been mentioned, to the introduction of the same branch into a country in which it did not before exist. To maintain between the recent establishments of one country and the long matured establishments of another country, a competition upon equal terms, both as to quality and price, is in most cases impracticable. The disparity, in the one or in the other, or in both, must necessarily be so considerable as to forbid a successful rivalship, without the extraordinary aid and protection of government.

But the greatest obstacle of all to the successful prosecution of a new branch of industry in a country, in which it was before unknown, consists, as far as the instances apply, in the bounties premiums and other aids which are granted, in a variety of cases, by the nations, in which the establishments to be imitated are previously introduced. It is well known (and particular examples in the course of this report will be cited) that certain nations grant bounties on the exportation of particular commodities, to enable their own workmen to undersell and supplant all competitors in the countries to which those commodities are sent. Hence the undertakers of a new manufacture have to contend not only with the natural disadvantages of a new undertaking, but with the gratuities and remunerations which other governments bestow. To be enabled to contend with success, it is evident that the interference and aid of their own government are indispensable.

There remains to be noticed an objection to the encouragement of manufactures, of a nature different from those which question the probability of success. This is derived from its supposed tendency to give a monopoly of advantages to particular classes, at the expense of the rest of the community, who, it is affirmed, would be able to procure the requisite supplies of manufactured articles on better terms from foreigners, than from our own Citizens, and who, it is alleged, are reduced to the necessity of paying an enhanced price for whatever they want, by every measure, which obstructs the free competition of foreign commodities.

But though it were true, that the immediate and certain effect of regulations controlling the competition of foreign with domestic fabrics was an increase of Price, it is universally true, that the contrary is the ultimate effect with every successful manufacture. When a domestic manufacture has attained to perfection, and has engaged in the prosecution of it a competent number of Persons, it invariably becomes cheaper. Being free from the heavy charges which attend the importation of foreign commodities, it can be afforded, and accordingly seldom or never fails to be sold Cheaper, in process of time, than was the foreign Article for which it is a substitute. The internal competition which takes place, soon does away [with] every thing like Monopoly, and by degrees reduces the price of the Article to the *minimum* of a reasonable profit on the Capital employed. This accords with the reason of the thing, and with experience.

Whence it follows, that it is the interest of a community, with a view to eventual and permanent economy, to encourage the growth of manufactures. In a national view, a temporary enhancement of price must always be well compensated by permanent reduction of it.

There seems to be a moral certainty, that the trade of a country which is both manufacturing and Agricultural will be more lucrative and prosperous than that of a Country, which is merely Agricultural.

One reason for this is found in that general effort of nations . . . to procure from their own soils, the articles of prime necessity requisite to their own consumption and use, and which serves to render their demand for a foreign supply of such articles, in a great degree occasional and contingent. . . .

Another circumstance which gives a superiority of commercial advantages to states that manufacture as well as cultivate, consists in the more numerous attractions, which a more diversified market offers to foreign Customers, and in the greater scope which it affords to mercantile enterprise. . . .

From these circumstances collectively—two important inferences are to be drawn, one, that there is always a higher probability of a favorable balance of Trade, in regard to countries in which manufactures founded on the basis of a thriving Agriculture flourish, than in regard to those, which are confined wholly or almost wholly to Agriculture; the other (which is also a consequence of the first), that countries of the former description are likely to possess more pecuniary wealth, or money, than those of the latter.

. . . . [T]he uniform appearance of an abundance of specie, as the concomitant of a flourishing state of manufactures, and of the reverse, where they do not prevail, afford a strong presumption of their favorable operation upon the wealth of a Country.

Not only the wealth, but the independence and security of a country, appear to be materially connected with the prosperity of manufactures. Every nation, with a view to those great objects, ought to endeavour to possess within itself all the essentials of national supply. These comprise the means of *Subsistence, habitation, clothing,* and *defence.*

The possession of these is necessary to the perfection of the body politic; to the safety as well as to the welfare of the society; the want of either is the want of an important Organ of political life and Motion; and in the various crises which await a state, it must severely feel the effects of any such deficiency. The extreme embarrassments of the United States during the late War, from an incapacity of supplying themselves, are still matter of keen recollection: A future war might be expected again to exemplify the mischiefs and dangers of a situation to which that incapacity is still in too great a degree applicable, unless changed by timely and vigorous exertion. To effect this change, as fast as shall be prudent, merits all the attention and all the Zeal of our Public Councils; it is the next great work to be accomplished.

The want of a Navy, to protect our external commerce, as long as it shall Continue, must render it a peculiarly precarious reliance, for the supply of essential articles, and must serve to strengthen prodigiously the arguments in favour of manufactures.

In order to a better judgment of the Means proper to be resorted to by the United States, it will be of use to Advert to those which have been employed with success in other Countries. The principal of these are—

1) Protecting Duties—Or Duties On Those Foreign Articles Which Are The Rivals Of The Domestic Ones Intended To Be Encouraged

Duties of this nature evidently amount to a virtual bounty on the domestic fabrics since by enhancing the charges on foreign articles, they enable the National Manufacturers to undersell all their foreign Competitors. . . .

2) Prohibitions Of Rival Articles, Or Duties Equivalent To Prohibitions

This is another and an efficacious mean of encouraging national manufactures but in general it is only fit to be employed when a manufacture, has made such progress and is in so many hands as to insure a due competition, and an adequate supply on reasonable terms. . . .

3) Prohibitions Of The Exportation Of The Materials Of Manufactures

The desire of securing a cheap and plentiful supply for the national workmen, and where the article is either peculiar to the Country, or of peculiar quality there, the jealousy of enabling foreign workmen to rival those of the nation with its own Materials, are the leading motives to this species of regulation. It ought not to be affirmed, that it is in no instance proper, but it is, certainly one which ought to be adopted with great circumspection, and only in very plain Cases. . . .

4) Pecuniary Bounties

This has been found one of the efficacious means of encouraging manufactures, and, is in some views, the best. . . .

Bounties have not, like high protecting duties, a tendency to produce scarcity. An increase of price is not always the immediate, though, where the progress of a domestic Manufacture does not counteract a rise, it is commonly the ultimate effect of an additional duty. In the interval, between the laying of the duty and the proportional increase of price, it may discourage importation, by interfering with the profits to be expected from the sale of the article.

It cannot escape notice, that the duty upon the importation of an article can no otherwise aid the domestic production of it, than by giving the latter greater advantages in the home market. It can have no influence upon the advantageous sale of the article produced in foreign markets; no tendency, therefore, to promote its exportation.

The true way to conciliate these two interests is to lay a duty on foreign *manufactures* of the material, the growth of which is desired to be encouraged, and to apply the produce of that duty, by way of bounty, either upon the production of the material itself or upon its manufacture at home, or upon both. . . .

5) Premiums

These are of a nature allied to bounties, though distinguishable from them in some important features.

Bounties are applicable to the whole quantity of an article produced, or manufactured, or exported, and involve a correspondent expense. Premiums serve to reward some particular excellence or superiority, some extraordinary exertion or skill, and are dispensed only in a small number of cases. . . .

6) The Exemption Of The Materials Of Manufactures From Duty

The policy of that Exemption as a general rule particularly in reference to new Establishments is obvious. It can hardly ever be advisable to add the obstructions of fiscal burthens to the difficulties which naturally embarrass a new manufacture; and where it is matured and in condition to become an object of revenue it is generally speaking better that the fabric than the Material should be the subject of Taxation. . . .

7) Drawbacks Of The Duties Which Are Imposed On The Materials Of Manufactures

It has already been observed as a general rule that duties on those materials ought with certain exceptions, to be forborne. Of these exceptions, three cases occur, which may serve as examples—one, where the material is itself an object of general or extensive consumption, and a fit and productive source of revenue: Another, where a manufacture of a simpler kind, the competition of which with a like domestic article is desired to be restrained, partakes of the Nature of a raw material, from being capable, by a further process to be converted into a manufacture of a different kind, the introduction or growth of which is desired to be encouraged; a third where the Material itself is a production of the country, and in sufficient abundance to furnish a cheap and plentiful supply to the national Manufacturers.

8) The Encouragement Of New Inventions And Discoveries, At Home, And Of The Introduction Into The United States Of Such As May Have Been Made In Other Countries; Particularly Those Which Relate To Machinery

. . . . The usual means of that encouragement are pecuniary rewards, and, for a time, exclusive privileges. The first must be employed according to the occasion, and the utility of the invention, or discovery. For the last, so far as respects "authors and inventors," provision has been made by Law. . . .

It is customary with manufacturing nations to prohibit, under severe penalties, the exportation of implements and machines, which they have either invented or improved. There are already objects for a similar regulation in the United States; and others may be expected to occur from time to time. The adoption of it seems to be dictated by the principle of reciprocity. Greater liberality, in such respects, might better comport with the general spirit of the country; but a selfish exclusive policy, in other quarters, will not always permit the free indulgence of a spirit which would place us upon an unequal footing. As far as prohibitions tend to prevent foreign competitors from deriving the benefit of the improvements made at home, they tend to increase the advantages of those by whom they may have been introduced, and operate as an encouragement to exertion.

9) Judicious Regulations For The Inspection Of Manufactured Commodities

. . . . Contributing to prevent frauds upon consumers at home and exporters to foreign countries, to improve the quality & preserve the character of the national manufactures, it cannot fail to aid the expeditious and advantageous sale of them, and to serve as a guard against successful competition from other quarters. . . .

10) The Facilitating Of Pecuniary Remittances From Place To Place

—is a point of considerable moment to trade in general, and to manufactures in particular; by rendering more easy the purchase of raw materials and provisions and the payment for manufactured supplies. A general circulation of Bank paper, which is to be expected from the institution lately established will be a most valuable mean to this end. . . .

11) The Facilitating Of The Transportation Of Commodities

The great copiousness of the subject of this Report has insensibly led to a more lengthy preliminary discussion than was originally contemplated, or intended. It appeared proper to investigate principles, to consider objections, and to endeavour to establish the utility of the thing proposed to be encouraged, previous to a specification of the objects which might occur, as meriting or requiring encouragement, and of the measures, which might be proper, in respect to each. The first purpose having been fulfilled, it remains to pursue the second.

In the selection of objects, five circumstances seem entitled to particular attention, the capacity of the Country to furnish the raw material—the degree in which the nature of the manufacture admits of a substitute for manual labour in machinery—the facility of execution—the extensiveness of the uses, to which the article can be applied—its subserviency to other interests, particularly the great one of national defence. There are however objects, to which these circumstances are little applicable, which for some special reasons, may have a claim to encouragement.

In countries where there is great private wealth, much may be effected by the voluntary contributions of patriotic individuals; but in a community situated like that of the United States, the public purse must supply the deficiency of private resource. In what can it be so useful, as in prompting and improving the efforts of industry?

Political and Cosmopolitical Economy

FRIEDRICH LIST

Before Quesnay and the French economists there existed only a *practice* of political economy which was exercised by the State officials, administrators, and authors who wrote about matters of administration, occupied themselves exclusively with the agriculture, manufactures, commerce, and navigation of those countries to which they belonged, without analysing the causes of wealth, or taking at all into consideration the interests of the whole human race.

Quesnay (from whom the idea of universal free trade originated) was the first who extended his investigations to the whole human race, without taking into consideration the idea of the nation. He calls his work "Physiocratie, ou du Gouvernement le plus avantageux au Genre Humain," his demands being that we must imagine that *the merchants of all nations formed one commercial republic.* Quesnay undoubtedly speaks of cosmopolitical economy, i.e., of that science which teaches how the entire human race may attain prosperity; in opposition to political economy, or that science which limits its teaching to the inquiry how a *given nation* can obtain (under the existing conditions of the world) prosperity, civilisation, and power, by means of agriculture, industry, and commerce.

Adam Smith treats his doctrine in a similarly extended sense, by making it his task to indicate the cosmopolitical idea of the absolute freedom of the commerce of the whole world in spite of the gross mistakes made by the physiocrates against the very nature of things and against logic. Adam Smith

This is a reprint of the 1885 edition of Friedrich List's "Political and Cosmopolitical Economy," in *The National System of Political Economy* by Reprints of Economic Classics. (New York: Augustus M. Kelley, 1966.)

concerned himself as little as Quesnay did with true political economy, i.e., that policy which each separate nation had to obey in order to make progress in its economical conditions. He entitles his work, "The Nature and Causes of the Wealth of Nations" (i.e., of all nations of the whole human race). He speaks of the various systems of political economy in a separate part of his work solely for the purpose of demonstrating their non-efficiency, and of proving that "political" or *national* economy must be replaced by "cosmopolitical or world-wide economy." Although here and there he speaks of wars, this only occurs incidentally. The idea of a perpetual state of peace forms the foundation of all his arguments. Moreover . . . his investigations from the commencement are based upon the principle that "most of the State regulations for the promotion of public prosperity are unnecessary, and a nation in order to be transformed from the lowest state of barbarism into a state of the highest possible prosperity needs nothing but bearable taxation, fair administration of justice, and *peace.*" . . .

J.B. Say openly demands that we should imagine the existence of a *universal republic* in order to comprehend the idea of general free trade. This writer, whose efforts were mainly restricted to the formation of a system out of the materials which Adam Smith had brought to light, says explicitly in the sixth volume (p. 288) of his "Economie politique pratique:" "We may take into our consideration the economical interests of the family with the father at its head; the principles and observations referring thereto will constitute *private economy.* Those principles, however, which have reference to the interests of whole nations, whether in themselves or in relation to other nations, form *public economy* (l'économie publique). *Political Economy,* lastly, relates to the interests of all nations, to *human society in general.*"

It must be remarked here, that in the first place Say recognises the existence of a national economy or political economy, under the name "économie publique," but that he nowhere treats of the latter in his works; secondly, that he attributes the name *political* economy to a doctrine which is evidently of *cosmopolitical* nature; and that in this doctrine he invariably merely speaks of an economy which has for its sole object the interests of the whole human society, without regard to the separate interests of distinct nations.

This substitution of terms might be passed over if Say, after having explained what he calls political economy (which, however, is nothing else but cosmopolitical or world-wide economy, or economy of the whole human race), had acquainted us with the principles of the doctrine which he calls "économie publique," which however is, properly speaking, nothing else but the economy of given nations, or true political economy.

In defining and developing this doctrine he could scarcely forbear to proceed from the idea and the nature of the nation, and to show what material modifications the "economy of the whole human race" must undergo by the fact that at present that race is still separated into distinct nationalities each held together by common powers and interests, and distinct from other societies of the same kind which in the exercise of their natural liberty are opposed to one another. However, by giving his cosmopolitical economy the name *political,* he dispenses with this explanation, effects by means of a transposition of terms also a transposition of meaning, and thereby masks a series of the gravest theoretical errors.

All later writers have participated in this error. Sismondi also calls political economy explicitly, "La science qui se charge du bonheur de l'espéce humaine." Adam Smith and his followers teach us from this mainly nothing more than what Quesnay and his followers had taught us already, for the article of the "Revue Méthodique" treating of the physiocratic school states, in almost the same words: "*The well-being of the individual is dependent altogether on the well-being of the whole human race.*"

The first of the North American advocates of free trade, as understood by Adam Smith—Thomas Cooper, President of Columbia College—denies even the existence of nationality; he calls the nation "a grammatical invention," created only to save periphrases, a nonentity, which has no actual existence save in the heads of politicians. Cooper is moreover perfectly consistent with respect to this, in fact much more consistent than his predecessors and instructors, for it is evident that as soon as the existence of nations with their distinct nature and interests is recognised, it becomes necessary to modify the economy of human society in accordance with these special interests, and that if Cooper intended to represent these modifications as errors, it was very wise on his part from the beginning to disown the very existence of nations.

For our own part, we are far from rejecting the theory of *cosmopolitical* economy, as it has been perfected by the prevailing school; we are, however, of opinion that political economy, or as Say calls it "économie publique," should also be developed scientifically, and that it is always better to call things by their proper names than to give them significations which stand opposed to the true import of words.

If we wish to remain true to the laws of logic and of the nature of things, we must set the economy of individuals against the economy of societies, and discriminate in respect to the latter between true political or national economy (which, emanating from the idea and nature of the nation, teaches how a given *nation* in the present state of the world and its own special national relations can maintain and improve its economical conditions) and cosmopolitical economy, which originates in the assumption that all nations of the earth form but one society living in a perpetual state of peace.

If, as the prevailing school requires, we assume a universal union or confederation of all nations as the guarantee for an everlasting peace, the principle of international free trade seems to be perfectly justified. The less every individual is restrained in pursuing his own individual prosperity, the greater the number and wealth of those with whom he has free intercourse, the greater the area over which his individual activity can exercise itself, the easier it will be for him to utilise for the increase of his prosperity the properties given him by nature, the knowledge and talents which he has acquired, and the forces of nature placed at his disposal. As with separate individuals, so is it also the case with individual communities, provinces, and countries. A simpleton only could maintain that a union for free commercial intercourse between themselves is not as advantageous to the different states included in the United States of North America, to the various departments of France, and to the various German allied states, as would be their separation by internal provincial customs tariffs.

In the union of the three kingdoms of Great Britain and Ireland the world witnesses a great and irrefragable example of the immeasurable efficacy of free trade between united nations. Let us only suppose all other nations of the earth to be united in a similar manner, and the most vivid imagination will not be able to picture to itself the sum of prosperity and good fortune which the whole human race would thereby acquire.

A true principle, therefore, underlies the system of the popular school, but a principle which must be recognised and applied by science if its design to enlighten practice is to be fulfilled, an idea which practice cannot ignore without getting astray; only the school has omittted to take into consideration the nature of nationalities and their special interests and conditions, and to bring these into accord with the idea of universal union and an everlasting peace.

The popular school has assumed as being actually in existence a state of things which has yet to come into existence. It assumes the existence of a universal union and a state of perpetual peace, and deduces therefrom the great benefits of free trade. In this manner it confounds effects with causes. Among the provinces and states which are already politically united, there exists a state of perpetual peace; from this political union originates their commercial union, and it is in consequence of the perpetual peace thus maintained that the commercial union has become so beneficial to them. All examples which history can show are those in which the political union has led the way, and the commercial union has followed. Not a single instance can be adduced in which the latter has taken the lead, and the former has grown up from it. That, however, under the existing conditions of the world, the result of general free trade would not be a universal republic, but, on the contrary, a universal subjection of the less advanced nations to the supremacy of the predominant manufacturing, commercial, and naval power, is a conclusion for which the reasons are very strong and, according to our views, irrefragable. A universal republic (in the sense of Henry IV, and of the Abbé St. Pierre), i.e. a union of the nations of the earth whereby they recognise the same conditions of right among themselves and renounce self-redress, can only be realised if a large number of nationalities attain to as nearly the same degree as possible of industry and civilisation, political cultivation, and power. Only with the gradual formation of this union can free trade be developed, only as a result of this union can it confer on all nations the same great advantages which are now experienced by those provinces and states which are politically united. The system of protection, inasmuch as it forms the only means of placing those nations which are far behind in civilisation on equal terms with the one predominating nation (which, however, never received at the hands of Nature a perpetual right to a monopoly of manufacture, but which merely gained an advance over others in point of time), the system of protection regarded from this point of view appears to be the most efficient means of furthering the final union of nations, and hence also of promoting true freedom of trade. And national economy appears from this point of view to be that science which, correctly appreciating the existing interests and the individual circumstances of nations, teaches how *every separate nation* can be raised to that stage of industrial development in which union with other nations equally well developed, and consequently freedom of trade, can become possible and useful to it.

The popular school, however, has mixed up both doctrines with one another; it has fallen into the grave error of judging of the conditions of nations according to purely cosmopolitical principles, and of ignoring from merely political reasons the cosmopolitical tendency of the productive powers.

Only by ignoring the cosmopolitical tendency of the productive powers could Malthus be led into the error of desiring to restrict the increase of population, or Chalmers and Torrens maintain more recently the strange idea that augmentation of capital and unrestricted production are evils the restriction of which the welfare of the community imperatively demands, or Sismondi declare that manufactures are things injurious to the community. Their theory in this case resembles Saturn, who devours his own children— the same theory which allows that from the increase of population, of capital and machinery, division of labour takes place, and explains from this the welfare of society, finally considers these forces as monsters which threaten the prosperity of nations, because it merely regards the present conditions of individual nations, and does not take into consideration the conditions of the whole globe and the future progress of mankind.

It is not true that population increases in a larger proportion than production of the means of subsistence; it is at least foolish to assume such disproportion, or to attempt to prove it by artificial calculations or sophistical arguments, so long as on the globe a mass of natural forces still lies inert by means of which ten times or perhaps a hundred times more people than are now living can be sustained. It is mere narrow-mindedness to consider the present extent of the productive forces as the test of how many persons could be supported on a given area of land. . . . The culture of the potato and of food-yielding plants, and the more recent improvements made in agriculture generally, have increased tenfold the productive powers of the human race for the creation of the means of subsistence. In the Middle Ages the yield of wheat of an acre of land in England was fourfold, to-day it is ten to twenty fold, and in addition to that five times more land is cultivated. In many European countries (the soil of which possesses the same natural fertility as that of England) the yield at present does not exceed fourfold. Who will venture to set further limits to the discoveries, inventions, and improvements of the human race? Agricultural chemistry is still in its infancy; who can tell that to-morrow, by means of a new invention or discovery, the produce of the soil may not be increased five or ten fold? . . .

If in a nation the population increases more than the production of the means of subsistence, if capital accumulates at length to such an extent as no longer to find investment, if machinery throws a number of operatives out of work and manufactured goods accumulate to a large excess, this merely proves, that nature will not allow industry, civilisation, wealth, and power to fall exclusively to the lot of a single nation, or that a large portion of the globe suitable for cultivation should be merely inhabited by wild animals, and that the largest portion of the human race should remain sunk in savagery, ignorance, and poverty.

We have shown into what errors the school has fallen by judging the productive forces of the human race from a political point of view; we have now also to point out the mistakes which it has committed by regarding the separate interests of nations from a cosmopolitical point of view.

If a confederation of all nations existed in reality, as is the case with the separate states constituting the Union of North America, the excess of population, talents, skilled abilities, and material capital would flow over from England to the Continental states, in a similar manner to that in which it travels from the eastern states of the American Union to the western, provided that in the Continental states the same security for persons and property, the same constitution and general laws prevailed, and that the English Government was made subject to the united will of the universal confederation. Under these suppositions there would be no better way of raising all these countries to the same stage of wealth and cultivation as England than free trade. This is the argument of the school. But how would it tally with the actual operation of free trade under the existing conditions of the world?

The Britons as an independent and separate nation would henceforth take their national interest as the sole guide of their policy. The Englishman, from predilection for his language, for his laws, regulations, and habits, would wherever it was possible devote his powers and his capital to develop his own native industry, for which the system of free trade, by extending the market for English manufactures over all countries, would offer him sufficient opportunity; he would not readily take a fancy to establish manufactures in France or Germany. All excess of capital in England would be at once devoted to trading with foreign parts of the world. If the Englishman took it into his head to emigrate, or to invest his capital elsewhere than in England, he would as he now does prefer those more distant countries where he would find already existing his language, his laws, and regulations, rather than the benighted countries of the Continent. All England would thus be developed into one immense manufacturing city. Asia, Africa, and Australia would be civilised by England, and covered with new states modelled after the English fashion. In time a world of English states would be formed, under the presidency of the mother state, in which the European Continental nations would be lost as unimportant, unproductive races. By this arrangement it would fall to the lot of France, together with Spain and Portugal, to supply this English world with the choicest wines, and to drink the bad ones herself: at most France might retain the manufacture of a little millinery. Germany would scarcely have more to supply this English world with than children's toys, wooden clocks, and philological writings, and sometimes also an auxiliary corps, who might sacrifice themselves to pine away in the deserts of Asia or Africa, for the sake of extending the manufacturing and commercial supremacy, the literature and language of England. It would not require many centuries before people in this English world would think and speak of the Germans and French in the same tone as we speak at present of the Asiatic nations.

True political science, however, regards such a result of universal free trade as a very unnatural one; it will argue that had universal free trade been introduced at the time of the Hanseatic League, the German nationality instead of the English would have secured an advance in commerce and manufacture over all other countries.

It would be most unjust, even on cosmopolitical grounds, now to resign to the English all the wealth and power of the earth, merely because by them the political system of commerce was first established and the cosmopolitical principle for the most part ignored. In order to allow freedom of trade to operate naturally, the less advanced nations must first be raised by artificial measures to that stage of cultivation to which the English nation has been artificially elevated. In order that, through that cosmopolitical tendency of the powers of production to which we have alluded, the more distant parts of the world may not be benefited and enriched before the neighboring European countries, those nations which feel themselves to be capable, owing to their moral, intellectual, social, and political circumstances, of developing a manufacturing power of their own must adopt the system of protection as the most effectual means for this purpose. The effects of this system for the purpose in view are of two kinds; in the first place, by gradually excluding foreign manufactured articles from our markets, a surplus would be occasioned in foreign nations, of workmen, talents, and capital, which must seek employment abroad; and secondly, by the premium which our system of protection would offer to the immigration into our country of workmen, talents, and capital, that excess of productive power would be induced to find employment with us, instead of emigrating to distant parts of the world and to colonies. Political science refers to history, and inquires whether England has not in former times drawn from Germany, Italy, Holland, France, Spain, and Portugal by these means a mass of productive power. She asks: Why does the cosmopolitical school, when it pretends to weigh in the balance the advantages and the disadvantages of the system of protection, utterly ignore this great and remarkable instance of the results of that system?

Classic Liberalism

2

Liberal theorists redefined political economy. By focusing on the logic and consequences of economic action, they undermined mercantilist theory. The early liberals did not wholly separate economics from politics, as is often done by contemporary neoclassical economists. They understood that economic policy was infused with particularistic interests. Liberals argued, however, that economic development and transformation could not be attained if entrenched political interests continued to subvert market forces. Moreover, if markets were allowed to function freely, then the broader political interest of the many, if not the entire community, would be better served. Liberalism thus reversed the mercantilist formula and suggested that economic reason could ultimately resolve conflicting political interests.

Adam Smith (1723–1790), drawing upon emergent liberal themes as well as his own insights, led the way in attacking mercantilist orthodoxy and creating a new approach to political economy. Although mercantilist theory was losing its vitality, it still dominated economic policies of his day—and would continue to for long after. Smith therefore had to begin with a thoroughgoing critique of mercantilism. He went right to the heart of the matter, analyzing the nature of wealth. For Smith, wealth is not merely a function of the amount of gold and silver in state coffers. Rather, wealth flows from the general productive capacity of an economy. National wealth, and with it power, increases only through comprehensive economic growth. To gain this end, the state need not intervene in the market. Productive gains are best secured by rational egoists freely pursuing individual material interests. Internationally, Smith suggests that such productive gains are not necessarily zero–sum. If the inherent productivity rewards of a free market are

55

allowed to spread around the world via free trade, the wealth of all nations is ensured.

Smith further elaborates the rationale for free trade. Domestically, efficient production and wealth rest upon a division of labor and economic interdependence. These principles also apply to the world economy: "what is prudent in the conduct of every private family, can scarce be folly in that of a great kingdom." Just as government agents cannot effectively manage the myriad economic interrelations of the national economy, so too, states should not interfere in world markets. If placed in an unregulated international economy, each nation would discover a productive niche, an absolute or comparative advantage. The division of labor can, and should, be replicated globally. Smith is not Panglossian in outlook, however. He realizes that vested interests, especially merchants, benefit from protectionism and will fight to retain their advantages. But these specific interests should not be confused with the broader national interest, which is better served by the prosperity flowing from free trade.

Smith does not call for unilateral and unconditional free trade. He offers four qualifications to his argument. First, free trade may be limited by the exigencies of national security. Smith sympathizes with the Navigation Acts in this regard: "the wisest of all commercial regulations of England." Second, duties should be imposed on foreign goods equal to domestic taxes on national products in order to avoid offering undue advantage to imports. Third, duties can be imposed as retaliation for unfair restrictions in foreign markets but only as a means of forcing other states to rescind their duties. Retaliation in and of itself is more harmful than good. Finally, free trade should be phased in gradually so that domestic industry and labor have time to make necessary adjustments to heightened international competition. Smith thus tempers his argument with an understanding of prevailing mercantilist practice and domestic political realities.

David Ricardo (1772–1823) builds upon, and moves away from, Smith. He, too, sees political interests behind existing economic policies. Yet where Smith argues against mercantilist businessmen, Ricardo regards landed interests as more subversive to economic progress. His reasoning is bound up with his concepts of rent, wages, and profits. Accepting Thomas Malthus's notion of finite resources (one of the few things on which these two friends agreed), Ricardo foresaw rising food prices that would push up rents accruing to landlords. Higher food prices would also cause wages to rise, undermining profits for the fledgling bourgeoisie. The landlord's gain was the industrialist's loss. Without adequate profits, businessmen could not invest and economic development would suffer. World markets offer a means of overcoming the agricultural obstacle to development. Ricardo, therefore, opens the chapter on foreign trade in his *Principles of Political Economy and Taxation* with a discussion of the relationship of trade to domestic profits and wages. Foreign trade is nationally beneficial only insofar as it contributes to lower wages, which in turn will allow profits to rise.

To gain the most from foreign trade, however, nations should concentrate on comparative advantage. Ricardo's famous example of British cloth and Portuguese wine makes a powerful case for economic specialization based on comparative costs and open world markets. He is careful to consider this argument in light of international payments imbalances. Monetary forces, he finds, do not endanger comparative advantage because of the self-correcting specie flow mechanism (the forerunner of the quantity theory of money). If there is a flaw in this enduring argument, it may be the assumption of immobile capital and labor, conditions that have changed in the era of the transnational corporation and modern transportation.

For Ricardo, international economics is not like domestic economics. A national economy is constrained by finite resources and conflicting interests; the world economy offers untapped avenues of growth and expansion. He does not ponder global exhaustion, a remote possibility in his day. In sum, although they differ in methodology—Ricardo's abstract theory contrasting sharply with Smith's narrative style—they agree on the positive results of free trade.

Of the Principle of the Commercial or Mercantile System

ADAM SMITH

That wealth consists in money, or in gold and silver, is a popular notion which naturally arises from the double function of money, as the instrument of commerce, and as the measure of value. In consequence of its being the instrument of commerce, when we have money we can more readily obtain whatever else we have occasion for, than by means of any other commodity. The great affair, we always find, is to get money. When that is obtained, there is no difficulty in making any subsequent purchase. In consequence of its being the measure of value, we estimate that of all other commodities by the quantity of money which they will exchange for. We say of a rich man that he is worth a great deal, and of a poor man that he is worth very little money. A frugal man, or a man eager to be rich, is said to love money; and a careless, a generous, or a profuse man, is said to be indifferent about it. To grow rich is to get money; and wealth and money, in short, are, in common language, considered as in every respect synonymous.

A rich country, in the same manner as a rich man, is supposed to be a country abounding in money; and to heap up gold and silver in any country is supposed to be the readiest way to enrich it. . . .

Mr. Locke remarks a distinction between money and other moveable goods. All other moveable goods, he says, are of so consumable a nature that the wealth which consists in them cannot be much depended on, and a nation which abounds in them one year may, without any exportation, but merely by their own waste and extravagance, be in great want of them the next. Money,

Reprinted from Adam Smith, "Of the Principle of the Commercial or Mercantile System," *The Wealth of Nations.* (New York: Modern Library, 1937.)

on the contrary, is a steady friend, which, though it may travel about from hand to hand, yet if it can be kept from going out of the country, is not very liable to be wasted and consumed. Gold and silver, therefore, are, according to him, the most solid and substantial part of the moveable wealth of a nation, and to multiply those metals ought, he thinks, upon that account, to be the great object of its political economy.

Others admit that if a nation could be separated from all the world, it would be of no consequence how much, or how little money circulated in it. The consumable goods which were circulated by means of this money, would only be exchanged for a greater or a smaller number of pieces; but the real wealth or poverty of the country, they allow, would depend altogether upon the abundance or scarcity of those consumable goods. But it is otherwise, they think, with countries which have connections with foreign nations, and which are obliged to carry on foreign wars, and to maintain fleets and armies in distant countries. This, they say, cannot be done, but by sending abroad money to pay them with; and a nation cannot send much money abroad, unless it has a good deal at home. Every such nation, therefore, must endeavour in time of peace to accumulate gold and silver, that, when occasion requires, it may have wherewithal to carry on foreign wars.

In consequence of these popular notions, all the different nations of Europe have studied, though to little purpose, every possible means of accumulating gold and silver in their respective countries. Spain and Portugal, the proprietors of the principal mines which supply Europe with those metals, have either prohibited their exportation under the severest penalties, or subjected it to a considerable duty. The like prohibition seems anciently to have made a part of the policy of most other European nations. . . .

When those countries became commercial, the merchants found this prohibition, upon many occasions, extremely inconvenient. They could frequently buy more advantageously with gold and silver than with any other commodity, the foreign goods which they wanted, either to import into their own, or to carry to some other foreign country. They remonstrated, therefore, against this prohibition as hurtful to trade.

They represented, first, that the exportation of gold and silver in order to purchase foreign goods, did not always diminish the quantity of those metals in the kingdom. That, on the contrary, it might frequently increase that quantity; because, if the consumption of foreign goods was not thereby increased in the country, those goods might be re-exported to foreign countries, and, being there sold for a large profit, might bring back much more treasure than was originally sent out to purchase them. . . .

They represented, secondly, that this prohibition could not hinder the exportation of gold and silver, which, on account of the smallness of their bulk in proportion to their value, could easily be smuggled abroad. That this exportation could only be prevented by a proper attention to, what they called, the balance of trade. That when the country exported to a greater value than it imported, a balance became due to it from foreign nations, which was necessarily paid to it in gold and silver, and thereby increased the quantity of those metals in the kingdom. But that when it imported to a greater value than it exported, a contrary balance became due to foreign nations, which was necessarily paid to them in the same manner, and thereby diminished that quantity. . . .

Those arguments were partly solid and partly sophistical. They were solid so far as they asserted that the exportation of gold and silver in trade might frequently be advantageous to the country. They were solid too, in asserting that no prohibition could prevent their exportation, when private people found any advantage in exporting them. But they were sophistical in supposing, that either to preserve or to augment the quantity of those metals required more the attention of government, than to preserve or to augment the quantity of any other useful commodities, which the freedom of trade, without any such attention, never fails to supply in the proper quantity. They were sophistical too, perhaps, in asserting that the high price of exchange necessarily increased, what they called, the unfavourable balance of trade, or occasioned the exportation of a greater quantity of gold and silver. . . . The high price of exchange . . . would naturally dispose the merchants to endeavour to make their exports nearly balance their imports, in order that they might have this high exchange to pay upon as small a sum as possible. The high price of exchange, besides, must necessarily have operated as a tax, in raising the price of foreign goods, and thereby diminishing their consumption. It would tend, therefore, not to increase, but to diminish, what they called, the unfavourable balance of trade, and consequently the exportation of gold and silver.

Such as they were, however, those arguments convinced the people to whom they were addressed. They were addressed by merchants to parliaments, and to the councils of princes, to nobles, and to country gentlemen; by those who were supposed to understand trade, to those who were conscious to themselves that they knew nothing about the matter. That foreign trade enriched the country, experience demonstrated to the nobles and country gentlemen, as well as to the merchants; but how, or in what manner, none of them well knew. The merchants knew perfectly in what manner it enriched themselves. It was their business to know it. But to know in what manner it enriched the country, was no part of their business. This subject never came into their consideration, but when they had occasion to apply to their country for some change in the laws relating to foreign trade. It then became necessary to say something about the beneficial effects of foreign trade, and the manner in which those effects were obstructed by the laws as they then stood. To the judges who were to decide the business, it appeared a most satisfactory account of the matter, when they were told that foreign trade brought money into the country, but that the laws in question hindered it from bringing so much as it otherwise would do. Those arguments therefore produced the wished-for effect. . . . The attention of government was turned away from guarding against the exportation of gold and silver, to watch over the balance of trade, as the only cause which could occasion any augmentation or diminution of those metals. From one fruitless care it was turned away to another care much more intricate, much more embarrassing, and just equally fruitless. . . .

A country that has no mines of its own must undoubtedly draw its gold and silver from foreign countries, in the same manner as one that has no vineyards of its own must draw its wines. It does not seem necessary, however, that the attention of government should be more turned towards the one than towards the other object. A country that has wherewithal to buy wine, will always get the wine which it has occasion for; and a country that has wherewithal to buy gold and silver, will never be in want of those metals.

They are to be bought for a certain price like all other commodities, and as they are the price of all other commodities, so all other commodities are the price of those metals. We trust with perfect security that the freedom of trade, without any attention of government, will always supply us with the wine which we have occasion for: and we may trust with equal security that it will always supply us with all the gold and silver which we can afford to purchase or to employ, either in circulating our commodities, or in other uses.

The quantity of every commodity which human industry can either purchase or produce, naturally regulates itself in every country according to the effectual demand, or according to the demand of those who are willing to pay the whole rent, labour and profits which must be paid in order to prepare and bring it to market. But no commodities regulate themselves more easily or more exactly according to this effectual demand than gold and silver; because, on account of the small bulk and great value of those metals, no commodities can be more easily transported from one place to another, from the places where they are cheap, to those where they are dear, from the places where they exceed, to those where they fall short of this effectual demand. . . .

When the quantity of gold and silver imported into any country exceeds the effectual demand, no vigilance of government can prevent their exportation. . . . If, on the contrary, in any particular country their quantity fell short of the effectual demand, so as to raise their price above that of the neighboring countries, the government would have no occasion to take any pains to import them. If it were even to take pains to prevent their importation it would not be able to effectuate it. . . .

If, not withstanding all this, gold and silver should at any time fall short in a country which has wherewithal to purchase them, there are more expedients for supplying their place, than that of almost any other commodity. If the materials of manufacture are wanted, industry must stop. If provisions are wanted, the people must starve. But if money is wanted, barter will supply its place, though with a good deal of inconveniency. Buying and selling upon credit, and the different dealers compensating their credits with one another, once a month or once a year, will supply it with less inconveniency. A well-regulated paper money will supply it, not only without any inconveniency, but, in some cases, with some advantages. Upon every account, therefore, the attention of government never was so unnecessarily employed, as when directed to watch over the preservation or increase of the quantity of money in any country.

It would be too ridiculous to go about seriously to prove, that wealth does not consist in money, or in gold and silver; but in what money purchases, and is valuable only for purchasing. Money, no doubt, makes always a part of the national capital; but . . . it generally makes but a small part, and always the most unprofitable part of it.

It is not because wealth consists more essentially in money than in goods, that the merchant finds it generally more easy to buy goods with money, than to buy money with goods; but because money is the known and established instrument of commerce, for which every thing is readily given in exchange, but which is not always with equal readiness to be got in exchange for every thing. . . . Goods can serve many other purposes besides purchasing money, but money can serve no other purpose besides purchasing goods. Money, therefore, necessarily runs after goods, but goods do not always or necessarily run after money. The man who buys, does not always mean to sell again, but frequently to use or to consume; whereas he who sells, always means to buy again. The one may frequently have done the whole, but the other can never have done more than the one-half of his business. It is not for its own sake that men desire money, but for the sake of what they can purchase with it.

. . . Gold and silver, whether in the shape of coin or plate, are utensils, it must be remembered, as much as the furniture of the kitchen. Increase the use for them, increase the consumable commodities which are to be circulated, managed, and prepared by means of them, and you will infallibly increase the quantity; but if you attempt, by extraordinary means, to increase the quantity, you will as infallibly diminish the use and even the quantity too, which in those metals can never be greater than what the use requires. Were they ever to be accumulated beyond this quantity, their transportation is so easy, and the loss which attends their lying idle and unemployed so great, that no law could prevent their being immediately sent out of the country.

It is not always necessary to accumulate gold and silver, in order to enable a country to carry on foreign wars, and to maintain fleets and armies in distant countries. Fleets and armies are maintained, not with gold and silver, but with consumable goods. The nation which, from the annual produce of its domestic industry, from the annual revenue arising out of its lands, labour, and consumable stock, has wherewithal to purchase those consumable goods in distant countries, can maintain foreign wars there.

A nation may purchase the pay and provisions of an army in a distnat country three different ways; by sending abroad either, first, some part of its accumulated gold and silver; or secondly, some part of the annual produce of its manufactures; or last of all, some part of its annual rude produce.

The gold and silver which can properly be considered as accumulated or stored up in any country, may be distinguished into three parts; first, the circulating money; secondly, the plate of private families; and last of all, the money which may have been collected by many years parsimony, and laid up in the treasury of the prince.

The funds which maintained the foreign wars of the present century, the most expensive perhaps which history records, seem to have had little dependency upon the exportation either of the circulating money, or of the plate of private families, or of the treasure of the prince. . . .

The enormous expense of the late war, therefore, must have been chiefly defrayed, not by the exportation of gold and silver, but by that of British commodities of some kind or other. . . .

The commodities most proper for being transported to distant countries, in order to purchase there, either the pay and provisions of an army, or some part of the money of the mercantile republic to be employed in purchasing them, seem to be the finer and more improved manufactures; such as contain a great value in a small bulk, and can, therefore, be exported to a great distance at little expense. A country whose industry produces a great annual surplus of such manufactures, which are usually exported to foreign countries, may carry on for many years a very expensive foreign war, without either exporting any considerable quantity of gold and silver, or even having any such quantity to export. . . .

No foreign war of great expense or duration could conveniently be carried on by the exportation of the rude produce of the soil. The expense of sending such a quantity of it to a foreign country as might purchase the pay and provisions of an army, would be too great. Few countries too produce much more rude produce than what is sufficient for the subsistence of their own inhabitants. To send abroad any great quantity of it, therefore, would be to send abroad a part of the necessary subsistence of the people. It is otherwise with the exportation of manufactures. The maintenance of the people employed in them is kept at home, and only the surplus part of their work is exported. . . .

The importation of gold and silver is not the principal, much less the sole benefit which a nation derives from its foreign trade. Between whatever places foreign trade is carried on, they all of them derive two distinct benefits from it. It carries out that surplus part of the produce of their land and labour for which there is no demand among them, and brings back in return for it something else for which there is a demand. It gives a value to their superfluities, by exchanging them for something else, which may satisfy a part of their wants, and increase their enjoyments. By means of it, the narrowness of the home market does not hinder the division of labour in any particular branch of art or manufacture from being carried to the highest perfection. By opening a more extensive market for whatever part of the produce of their labour may exceed the home consumption, it encourages them to improve its productive powers, and to augment its annual produce to the utmost, and thereby to increase the real revenue and wealth of the society. These great and important services foreign trade is continually occupied in performing, to all the different countries between which it is carried on. They all derive great benefit from it, though that in which the merchant resides generally derives the greatest, as he is generally more employed in supplying the wants, and carrying out the superfluities of his own, than of any other particular country. To import the gold and silver which may be wanted, into the countries which have no mines, is, no doubt, a part of the business of foreign commerce. It is, however, a most insignificant part of it. A country which carried on foreign trade merely upon this account, could scarce have occasion to freight a ship in a century.

I thought it necessary, though at the hazard of being tedious, to examine at full length this popular notion that wealth consists in money, or in gold and silver. Money in common language, as I have already observed, frequently signifies wealth; and this ambiguity of expression has rendered this popular notion so familiar to us, that even they, who are convinced of its absurdity, are very apt to forget their own principles, and in the course of their reasonings to take it for granted as a certain and undeniable truth. Some of the best English writers upon commerce set out with observing, that the wealth of a country consists, not in its gold and silver only, but in its lands, houses, and consumable goods of all different kinds. In the course of their reasonings, however, the lands, houses, and consumable goods seem to slip out of their memory, and the strain of their argument frequently supposes that all wealth consists in gold and silver, and that to multiply those metals is the great object of national industry and commerce.

The two principles being established, however, that wealth consisted in gold and silver, and that those metals could be brought into a country which had no mines only by the balance of trade, or by exporting to a greater value than it imported; it necessarily became the great object of political economy to diminish as much as possible the importation of foreign goods for home consumption, and to increase as much as possible the exportation of the produce of domestic industry. Its two great engines for enriching the country, therefore, were restraints upon importation, and encouragements to exportation.

Of Restraints Upon the Importation from Foreign Countries of Such Goods as Can Be Produced at Home

ADAM SMITH

By restraining, either by high duties, or by absolute prohibitions, the importation of such goods from foreign countries as can be produced at home, the monopoly of the home market is more or less secured to the domestic industry employed in producing them. . . .

That this monopoly of the home-market frequently gives great encouragement to that particular species of industry which enjoys it, and frequently turns towards that employment a greater share of both the labour and stock of the society than would otherwise have gone to it, cannot be doubted. But whether it tends either to increase the general industry of the society, or to give it the most advantageous direction, is not, perhaps, altogether so evident.

The general industry of the society never can exceed what the capital of the society can employ. As the number of workmen that can be kept in employment by any particular person must bear a certain proportion to his capital, so the number of those that can be continually employed by all the members of a great society, must bear a certain proportion to the whole capital of that society, and never can exceed that proportion. No regulation of commerce can increase the quantity of industry in any society beyond what its capital can maintain. It can only divert a part of it into a direction into which it might not otherwise have gone; and it is by no means certain that this artificial direction is likely to be more advantageous to the society than that into which it would have gone of its own accord.

Every individual is continually exerting himself to find out the most advantageous employment for whatever capital he can command. It is his own advantage, indeed, and not that of the society, which he has in view. But the study of his own advantage naturally, or rather necessarily leads him to prefer that employment which is most advantageous to the society.

First, every individual endeavours to employ his capital as near home as he can, and consequently as much as he can in the support of domestic industry; provided always that he can thereby obtain the ordinary, or not a great deal less than the ordinary profits of stock.

Thus, upon equal or nearly equal profits, every wholesale merchant naturally prefers the home-trade to the foreign trade of consumption, and the foreign trade of consumption to the carrying trade. In the home-trade his capital is never so long out of his sight as it frequently is in the foreign trade of consumption. He can know better the character and situation of the persons whom he trusts, and if he should happen to be deceived, he knows better the laws of the country from which he must seek redress. In the carrying trade, the capital of the merchant is, as it were, divided between two foreign countries, and no part of it is ever necessarily brought home, or placed under his own immediate view and command. . . . But a capital employed in the home-trade, it has already been shown, necessarily puts into motion a greater quantity of domestic industry, and gives revenue and employment to a greater number of the inhabitants of the country, than an equal capital employed in the foreign trade of consumption: and one employed in the foreign trade of consumption has the same advantage over an equal capital employed in the carrying trade. Upon equal, or only nearly equal profits, therefore, every individual naturally inclines to employ his capital in the manner in which it is likely to afford the greatest support to domestic industry, and to give revenue and employment to the greatest number of people of his own country.

Secondly, every individual who employs his capital in the support of domestic industry, necessarily endeavours so to direct that industry, that its produce may be of the greatest possible value.

The produce of industry is what it adds to the subject or materials upon which it is employed. In proportion as the value of this produce is great or small, so will likewise be the profits of the employer. But it is only for the sake of profit that any man employs a capital in the support of industry; and he will always, therefore, endeavour to employ it in the support of that industry of which the produce is likely to be of the greatest value, or to exchange for the greatest quantity either of money or of other goods.

But the annual revenue of every society is always precisely equal to the exchangeable value of the whole annual produce of its industry, or rather is precisely the same thing with that exchangeable value. As every individual, therefore, endeavours as much as he can both to employ his capital in the support of domestic industry, and so to direct that industry that its produce may be of the greatest value; every individual necessarily labours to render the annual revenue of the society as great as he can. He generally, indeed, neither intends to promote the public interest, nor knows how much he is promoting it. By preferring the support of domestic to that of foreign industry, he intends only his own security; and by directing that industry in such a manner as its produce may be of the greatest value, he intends only his own gain, and he is in this, as in many other cases, led by an invisible hand to promote an end which was no part of his intention. Nor is it always the worse for the society that it was no part of it. By pursuing his own interest he frequently promotes that of the society more effectually than when he really intends to promote it. I have never known much good done by those who affected to trade for the public good. It is an affectation, indeed, not very common among merchants, and very few words need be employed in dissuading them from it.

What is the species of domestic industry which his capital can employ, and of which the produce is likely to be of the greatest value, every individual, it is evident, can, in his local situation, judge much better than any statesman or lawgiver can do for him. The statesman, who should attempt to direct private people in what manner they ought to employ their capitals, would not only load himself with a most unnecessary attention, but assume an authority which could safely be trusted, not only to no single person, but to no council or senate whatever, and which would nowhere be so dangerous as in the hands of a man who had folly and presumption enough to fancy himself fit to exercise it.

To give the monopoly of the home-market to the produce of domestic industry, in any particular art or manufacture, is in some measure to direct private people in what manner they ought to employ their capitals, and must, in almost all cases, be either a useless or a hurtful regulation. If the produce of domestic can be brought there as cheap as that of foreign industry, the regulation is evidently useless. If it cannot, it must generally be hurtful. It is the maxim of every prudent master of a family, never to attempt to make at home what it will cost him more to make than to buy. The taylor does not attempt to make his own shoes, but buys them of the shoemaker. The shoemaker does not attempt to make his own clothes, but employs a taylor. The farmer attempts to make neither the one nor the other, but employs those different artificers. All of them find it for their interest to employ their whole industry in a way in which they have some advantage over their neighbours, and to purchase with a part of its produce, or what is the same thing, with the price of a part of it, whatever else they have occasion for.

What is prudence in the conduct of every private family, can scarce be folly in that of a great kingdom. If a foreign country can supply us with a commodity cheaper than we ourselves can make it, better buy it of them with some part of the produce of our own industry, employed in a way in which we have some advantage. The general industry of the country, being always in proportion to the capital which employs it, will not thereby be diminished, no more than that of the above-mentioned artificers; but only left to find out the way in which it can be employed with the greatest advantage. It is certainly not employed to the greatest advantage, when it is thus directed towards an object which it can buy cheaper than it can make. The value of its annual produce is certainly more or less diminished, when it is thus turned away from producing commodities evidently of more value than the commodity which it is directed to produce. According to the supposition, that commodity could be purchased from foreign countries cheaper than it can be made at home. It could, there-fore, have been purchased with a part only of the commodities, or, what is the same thing, with a part only of the price of the commodities, which the industry employed by an equal capital would have produced at home, had it been left to follow its natural course. The industry of the country, therefore, is thus turned away from a more, to a less advantageous employment, and the exchangeable value of its annual produce, instead of being increased, accord-ing to the intention of the lawgiver, must necessarily be diminished by every such regulation.

By means of such regulations, indeed, a particular manufacture may some-times be acquired sooner than it could have been otherwise, and after a certain time may be made at home as cheap or cheaper than in the foreign country. But though the industry of the society may be thus carried with advantage into a particular channel sooner than it could have been otherwise, it will by no means follow that the sum total, either of its industry, or of its revenue, can ever be augmented by any such regulation. The industry of the society can augment only in proportion as its capital augments, and its capital can augment only in proportion to what can be gradually saved out of its revenue. But the immediate effect of every such regulation is to diminish its revenue, and what diminishes its revenue is certainly not very likely to aug-ment its capital faster than it would have augmented of its own accord, had both capital and industry been left to find out their natural employments.

Though for want of such regulations the society should never acquire the proposed manufacture, it would not, upon that account, necessarily be the poorer in any one period of its duration. In every period of its duration its whole capital and industry might still have been employed, though upon different objects, in the manner that was most advantageous at the time. In every period its revenue might have been the greatest which its capital could afford, and both capital and revenue might have been augmented with the greatest possible rapidity.

The natural advantages which one country has over another in producing particular commodities are sometimes so great, that it is acknowledged by all the world to be in vain to struggle with them. . . . Whether the advantages which one country has over another, be natural or acquired, is in this respect of no consequence. As long as the one country has those advantages, and the other wants them, it will always be more advantageous for the latter, rather to buy of the former than to make. It is an acquired advantage only, which one artificer has over his neighbour, who exercises another trade; and yet they both find it more advantageous to buy of one another, than to make what does not belong to their particular trades.

There seem, however, to be two cases in which it will generally be advanta-geous to lay some burden upon foreign, for the encouragement of domestic industry.

The first is, when some particular sort of industry is necessary for the reference of the country. The defence of Great Britain, for example, depends very much upon the number of its sailors and shipping. The act of navigation, therefore, very properly endeavours to give the sailors and shipping of Great Britain the monopoly of the trade of their own country, in some cases, by absolute prohibitions, and in others by heavy burdens upon the shipping of foreign countries. . . .

The act of navigation is not favourable to foreign commerce, or to the growth of that opulence which can arise from it. The interest of a nation in its commercial relations to foreign nations is, like that of a merchant with regard to the different people with whom he deals, to buy as cheap and to sell as dear as possible. But it will be most likely to buy cheap, when by the most perfect freedom of trade it encourages all nations to bring to it the goods which it has occasion to purchase; and, for the same reason, it will be most likely to sell dear, when its markets are thus filled with the greatest number of buyers. The act of navigation, it is true, lays no burden upon foreign ships that come to export the produce of British industry. Even the ancient aliens duty, which used to be paid upon all goods exported as well as imported, has, by several subsequent acts, been taken off from the greater part of the articles of exportation. But if foreigners, either by prohibitions or high duties, are hindered from coming to sell, they cannot always afford to come to buy; because coming without a cargo, they must lose the freight from their own country to Great Britain. By diminishing the number of sellers, therefore, we necessarily diminish that of buyers, and are thus likely not only to buy foreign goods dearer, but to sell our own cheaper, than if there was a more perfect freedom of trade. As defence, however, is of much more importance than opulence, the act of navigation is, perhaps, the wisest of all the commercial regulations of England.

The second case, in which it will generally be advantageous to lay some burden upon foreign for the encouragement of domestic industry, is, when some tax is imposed at home upon the produce of the latter. In this case, it seems reasonable that an equal tax should be imposed upon the like produce of the former. This would not give the monopoly of the home market to domestic industry, nor turn towards a particular employment a greater share of the stock and labour of the country, than what would naturally go to it. It would only hinder any part of what would naturally go to it from being turned away by the tax, into a less natural direction, and would leave the competition between foreign and domestic industry, after the tax, as nearly as possible upon the same footing as before it. . . .

This second limitation of the freedom of trade according to some people should, upon some occasions, be extended much farther than to the precise foreign commodities which could come into competition with those which had been taxed at home. When the necessaries of life have been taxed in any country, it becomes proper, they pretend, to tax not only the like necessaries of life imported from other countries, but all sorts of foreign goods which can come into competition with any thing that is the produce of domestic industry. Subsistence, they say, becomes necessarily dearer in consequence of such taxes; and the price of labour must always rise with the price of the labourers' subsistence. Every commodity, therefore, which is the produce of domestic industry, though not immediately taxed itself, becomes dearer in consequence of such taxes, because the labour which produces it becomes so. Such taxes, therefore, are really equivalent, they say, to a tax upon every particular commodity produced at home. In order to put domestic upon the same footing with foreign industry, therefore, it becomes necessary, they think, to lay some duty upon every foreign commodity, equal to this enhancement of the price of the home commodities with which it can come into competition.

Such taxes, when they have grown up to a certain height, are a curse equal to the barrenness of the earth and the inclemency of the heavens; and yet it is in the richest and most industrious countries that they have been most generally imposed. No other countries could support so great a disorder. As the strongest bodies only can live and enjoy health, under an unwholesome regimen; so the nations only, that in every sort of industry have the greatest natural and acquired advantages, can subsist and prosper under such taxes. Holland is the country in Europe in which they abound most, and which from peculiar circumstances continues to prosper, not by means of them, as has been most absurdly supposed, but in spite of them.

As there are two cases in which it will generally be advantageous to lay some burden upon foreign, for the encouragement of domestic industry; so there are two others in which it may sometimes be a matter of deliberation; in the one, how far it is proper to continue the free importation of certain foreign goods; and in the other, how far, or in what manner, it may be proper to restore that free importation after it has been for some time interrupted.

The case in which it may sometimes be a matter of deliberation how far it is proper to continue the free importation of certain foreign goods, is, when some foreign nation restrains by high duties or prohibitions the importation of some of our manufactures into their country. Revenge in this case naturally dictates retaliation, and that we should impose the like duties and prohibitions upon the importation of some or all of their manufactures into ours. Nations accordingly seldom fail to retaliate in this manner. . . .

There may be good policy in retaliations of this kind, when there is a probability that they will procure the repeal of the high duties or prohibitions complained of. The recovery of a great foreign market will generally more than compensate the transitory inconveniency of paying dearer during a short time for some sorts of goods . . . When there is no probability that any such repeal can be procured, it seems a bad method of compensating the injury done to certain classes of our people, to do another injury ourselves, not only to those classes, but to almost all the other classes of them. . . .

The case in which it may sometimes be a matter of deliberation, how far, or in what manner, it is proper to restore the free importation of foreign goods, after it has been for some time interrupted, is, when particular manufactures, by means of high duties or prohibitions upon all foreign goods which can come into competition with them, have been so far extended as to employ a great multitude of hands. Humanity may in this case require that the freedom of trade should be restored only by slow gradations, and with a good deal of reserve and circumspection. Were those high duties and prohibitions taken away all at once, cheaper foreign goods of the same kind might be poured so fast into the home market, as to deprive all at once many thousands of our people of their ordinary employment and means of subsistence. The disorder which this would occasion might no doubt be very considerable. It would in all probability, however, be much less than is commonly imagined. . . .

To expect, indeed, that the freedom of trade should ever be entirely restored in Great Britain, is as absurd as to expect that an Oceana or Utopia should ever be established in it. Not only the prejudices of the public, but what is much more unconquerable, the private interests of many individuals, irresistibly oppose it. Were the officers of the army to oppose with the same zeal and unanimity any reduction in the number of forces, with which master manufacturers set themselves against every law that is likely to increase the number of their rivals in the home market; were the former to animate their soldiers, in the same manner as the latter enflame their workmen, to attack with violence and outrage the proposers of any such regulation; to attempt to reduce the army would be as dangerous as it has now become to attempt to diminish in any respect the monopoly which our manufacturers have obtained against us. This monopoly has so much increased the number of some particular tribes of them, that, like an overgrown standing army, they have become formidable to the government, and upon many occasions intimidate the legislature. The member of parliament who supports every proposal for strengthening this monopoly, is sure to acquire not only the reputation of understanding trade, but great popularity and influence with an order of men whose numbers and wealth render them of great importance. If he opposes them, on the contrary, and still more if he has authority enough to be able to thwart them, neither the most acknowledged probity, nor the highest rank, nor the greatest public services, can protect him from the most infamous abuse and detraction, from personal insults, nor sometimes from real danger, arising from the insolent outrage of furious and disappointed monopolists.

On Foreign Trade

DAVID RICARDO

No extension of foreign trade will immediately increase the amount of value in a country, although it will very powerfully contribute to increase the mass of commodities, and therefore the sum of enjoyments. As the value of all foreign goods is measured by the quantity of the produce of our land and labour, which is given in exchange for them, we should have no greater value, if by the discovery of new markets, we obtained double the quantity of foreign goods in exchange for a given quantity of ours. . . .

It has indeed been contended, that the great profits which are sometimes made by particular merchants in foreign trade, will elevate the general rate of profits in the country, and that the abstraction of capital from other employments, to partake of the new and beneficial foreign commerce, will raise prices generally, and thereby increase profits. It has been said, by high authority, that less capital being necessarily devoted to the growth of corn, to the manufacture of cloth, hats, shoes, & c., while the demand continues the same, the price of these commodities will be so increased, that the farmer, hatter, clothier, and shoemaker, will have an increase of profits, as well as the foreign merchant.

They who hold this argument agree with me, that the profits of different employments have a tendency to conform to one another; to advance and recede together. Our variance consists in this: They contend that the equality of profits will be brought about by the general rise of profits; and I am of opinion, that the profits of the favoured trade will speedily subside to the general level.

Reprinted from David Ricardo, "On Foreign Trade," *The Principles of Political Economy and Taxation* (New York: E. P. Dutton & Co. Inc., 1960).

For, first, I deny that less capital will necessarily be devoted to the growth of corn, to the manufacture of cloth, hats, shoes, & c., unless the demand for these commodities be diminished; and if so, their price will not rise. In the purchase of foreign commodities, either the same, a larger, or a less portion of the produce of the land and labour of England will be employed. If the same portion be so employed, then will the same demand exist for cloth, shoes, corn, and hats as before, and the same portion of capital will be devoted to their production. If, in consequence of the price of foreign commodities being cheaper, a less portion of the annual produce of the land and labour of England is employed in the purchase of foreign commodities, more will remain for the purchase of other things. If there be a greater demand for hats, shoes, corn, & c., than before, which there may be, the consumers of foreign commodities having an additional portion of their revenue disposable, the capital is also disposable with which the greater value of foreign commodities was before purchased; so that with the increased demand for corn, shoes, & c., there exists also the means of procuring an increased supply, and therefore neither prices nor profits can permanently rise. If more of the produce of the land and labour of England be employed in the purchase of foreign commodities, less can be employed in the purchase of other things, and therefore fewer hats, shoes, & c., will be required. At the same time that capital is liberated from the production of shoes, hats, & c., more must be employed in manufacturing those commodities with which foreign commodities are purchased; and, consequently, in all cases the demand for foreign and home commodities together, as far as regards value, is limited by the revenue and capital of the country. If one increases the other must diminish. If the quantity of wine, imported in exchange for the same quantity of English commodities, be doubled, the people of England can either consume double the quantity of wine that they did before, or the same quantity of wine and a greater quantity of English commodities. If my revenue had been 1000£, with which I purchased annually one pipe of wine for 100£, and a certain quantiy of English commodities for 900£; when wine fell to 50£ per pipe, I might buy out the 50£ saved, either in the purchase of an additional pipe of wine, or in the purchase of more English commodities. If I bought more wine, and every wine-drinker did the same, the foreign trade would not be in the least disturbed; the same quantity of English commodities would be exported in exchange for wine, and we should receive double the quantity, though not double the value of wine. But if I, and others, contented ourselves with the same quantity of wine as before, fewer English commodities would be exported, and the wine-drinkers might either consume the commodities which were before exported, or any others for which they had an inclination. The capital required for their production would be supplied by the capital liberated from the foreign trade.

It is not, therefore, in consequence of the extension of the market that the rate of profit is raised, although such extension may be equally efficacious in increasing the mass of commodities, and may thereby enable us to augment the funds destined for the maintenance of labour, and the materials on which labour may be employed. It is quite as important to the happiness of mankind, that our enjoyments should be increased by the better distribution of labour, by each country producing those commodities for which by its situation, its climate, and its other natural or artificial advantages, it is adapted, and by their exchanging them for the commodities of other countries, as that they should be augmented by a rise in the rate of profits.

It has been my endeavour to show throughout this work, that the rate of profits can never be increased but by a fall in wages, and that there can be no permanent fall of wages but in consequence of a fall of the necessaries on which wages are expended. If, therefore, by the extension of foreign trade, or by improvements in machinery, the food and necessaries of the labourer can be brought to market, at a reduced price, profits will rise. If, instead of growing our own corn, or manufacturing the clothing and other necessaries of the labourer, we discover a new market from which we can supply ourselves with these commodities at a cheaper price, wages will fall and profits rise; but if the commodities obtained at a cheaper rate, by the extension of foreign commerce, or by the improvement of machinery, be exclusively the commodities consumed by the rich, no alteration will take place in the rate of profits. The rate of wages would not be affected, although wine, velvets, silks, and other expensive commodities should fall 50 per cent., and consequently profits would continue unaltered.

Foreign trade, then, though highly beneficial to a country, as it increases the amount and variety of the objects on which revenue may be expended, and affords, by the abundance and cheapness of commodities, incentives to saving, and to the accumulation of capital, has no tendency to raise the profits of stock, unless the commodities imported be of that description on which the wages of labour are expended.

The remarks which have been made respecting foreign trade, apply equally to home trade. The rate of profits is never increased by a better distribution of labour, by the invention of machinery, by the establishment of roads and canals, or by any means of abridging labour either in the manufacture or in the conveyance of goods. These are causes which operate on price, and never fail to be highly beneficial to consumers; since they enable them, with the same labour, or with the value of the produce of the same labour, to obtain in exchange a greater quantity of the commodity to which the improvement is applied; but they have no effect whatever on profit. On the other hand, every diminution in the wages of labour raises profits, but produces no effect on the price of commodities. One is advantageous to all classes, for all classes are consumers; the other is beneficial only to producers; they gain more, but every thing remains at its former price. In the first case they get the same as before; but every thing on which their gains are expended, is diminished in exchangeable value.

The same rule which regulates the relative value of commodities in one country, does not regulate the relative value of the commodities exchanged between two or more countries.

Under a system of perfectly free commerce, each country naturally devotes its capital and labour to such employments as are most beneficial to each. This pursuit of individual advantage is admirably connected with the universal good of the whole. By stimulating industry, by rewarding ingenuity, and by using most efficaciously the peculiar powers bestowed by nature, it distributes labour most effectively and most economically: while, by increasing the general mass of productions, it diffuses general benefit, and binds together, by one common tie of interest and intercourse, the universal society of nations throughout the civilized world. It is this principle which determines that wine shall be made in France and Portugal, that corn shall be grown in America and Poland, and that hardware and other goods shall be manufactured in England.

In one and the same country, profits are, generally speaking, always on the same level; or differ only as the employment of capital may be more or less secure and agreeable. It is not so between different countries. If the profits of capital employed in Yorkshire, should exceed those of capital employed in London, capital would speedily move from London to Yorkshire, and an equality of profits would be effected; but if in consequence of the diminished rate of production in the lands of England, from the increase of capital and population, wages should rise, and profits fall, it would not follow that capital and population would necessarily move from England to Holland, or Spain, or Russia, where profits might be higher.

If Portugal had no commercial connexion with other countries, instead of employing a great part of her capital and industry in the production of wines, with which she purchases for her own use the cloth and hardware of other countries, she would be obliged to devote a part of that capital to the manufacture of those commodities, which she would thus obtain probably inferior in quality as well as quantity.

The quantity of wine which she shall give in exchange for the cloth of England, is not determined by the respective quantities of labour devoted to the production of each, as it would be, if both commodities were manufactured in England, or both in Portugal.

England may be so circumstanced, that to produce the cloth may require the labour of 100 men for one year; and if she attempted to make the wine, it might require the labour of 120 men for the same time. England would therefore find it her interest to import wine, and to purchase it by the exportation of cloth.

To produce the wine in Portugal, might require only the labour of 80 men for one year, and to produce the cloth in the same country, might require the labour of 90 men for the same time. It would therefore be advantageous for her to export wine in exchange for cloth. This exchange might even take place, notwithstanding that the commodity imported by Portugal could be produced there with less labour than in England. Though she could make the cloth with the labour of 90 men, she would import it from a country where it required the labour of 100 men to produce it, because it would be advantageous to her rather to employ her capital in the production of wine, for which she would obtain more cloth from England, than she could produce by diverting a portion of her capital from the cultivation of vines to the manufacture of cloth.

Thus England would give the produce of the labour of 100 men, for the produce of the labour of 80. Such an exchange could not take place between the individuals of the same country. The labour of 100 Englishmen cannot be given for that of 80 Englishmen, but the produce of the labour of 100 English-men may be given for the produce of the labour of 80 Portuguese, 60 Russians, or 120 East Indians. The difference in this respect, between a single country and many, is easily accounted for, by considering the difficulty with which capital moves from one country to another, to seek a more profitable employment, and the activity with which it invariably passes from one province to another in the same country.

It would undoubtedly be advantageous to the capitalists of England, and to the consumers in both countries, that under such circumstances, the wine and the cloth should both be made in Portugal, and therefore that the capital and labour of England employed in making cloth, should be removed to Portugal for that purpose. In that case, the relative value of these commodities would be regulated by the same principle, as if one were the produce of Yorkshire, and the other of London: and in every other case, if capital freely flowed towards those countries where it could be most profitably employed, there could be no difference in the rate of profit, and no other difference in the real or labour price of commodities, than the additional quantity of labour required to convey them to the various markets where they were to be sold.

Experience, however, shows, that the fancied or real insecurity of capital, when not under the immediate control of its owner, together with the natural disinclination which every man has to quit the country of his birth and connexions, and intrust himself, with all his habits fixed, to a strange government and new laws, check the emigration of capital. These feelings, which I should be sorry to see weakened, induce most men of property to be satisfied with a low rate of profits in their own country, rather than seek a more advantageous employment for their wealth in foreign nations.

Gold and silver having been chosen for the general medium of circulation, they are, by the competition of commerce, distributed in such proportions amongst the different countries of the world, as to accommodate themselves to the natural traffic which would take place if no such metals existed, and the trade between countries were purely a trade of barter.

Thus, cloth cannot be imported into Portugal, unless it sell there for more gold than it cost in the country from which it was imported; and wine cannot be imported into England, unless it will sell for more there than it cost in Portugal. If the trade were purely a trade of barter, it could only continue whilst England could make cloth so cheap as to obtain a greater quantity of wine with a given quantity of labour, by manufacturing cloth than by growing vines; and also whilst the industry of Portugal were attended by the reverse effects. Now suppose England to discover a process for making wine, so that it should become her interest rather to grow it than import it; she would naturally divert a portion of her capital from the foreign trade to the home trade; she would cease to manufacture cloth for exportation, and would grow wine for herself. The money price of these commodities would be regulated accordingly; wine would fall here while cloth continued at its former price, and in Portugal no alteration would take place in the price of either commodity. Cloth would continue for some time to be exported from this country, because its price would continue to be higher in Portugal than here; but money instead of wine would be given in exchange for it, till the accumulation of money here, and its diminution abroad, should so operate on the relative value of cloth in the two countries, that it would cease to be profitable to export it. If the improvement in making wine were of a very important description, it might become profitable for the two countries to exchange employments; for England to make all the wine, and Portugal all the cloth consumed by them; but this could be effected only by a new distribution of the precious metals, which should raise the price of cloth in England, and lower it in Portugal. The relative price of wine would fall in England in consequence of the real advantage from the improvement of its manufacture; that is to say, its natural price would fall; the relative price of cloth would rise there from the accumulation of money.

But the diminution of money in one country, and its increase in another, do not operate on the price of one commodity only, but on the prices of all, and therefore the price of wine and cloth will be both raised in England, and both lowered in Portugal. . . .

It is thus that the money of each country is apportioned to it in such quantities only as may be necessary to regulate a profitable trade of barter. England exported cloth in exchange for wine, because, by so doing, her industry was rendered more productive to her; she had more cloth and wine than if she had manufactured both for herself; and Portugal imported cloth and exported wine, because the industry of Portugal could be more beneficially employed for both countries in producing wine. Let there be more difficulty in England in producing cloth, or in Portugal in producing wine, or let there be more facility in England in producing wine, or in Portugal in producing cloth, and the trade must immediately cease.

No change whatever takes place in the circumstances of Portugal; but England finds that she can employ her labour more productively in the manufacture of wine, and instantly the trade of barter between the two countries changes. Not only is the exportation of wine from Portugal stopped, but a new distribution of the precious metals takes place, and her importation of cloth is also prevented.

Both countries would probably find it their interest to make their own wine and their own cloth; but this singular result would take place: in England, though wine would be cheaper, cloth would be elevated in price, more would be paid for it by the consumer; while in Portugal the consumers, both of cloth and of wine, would be able to purchase those commodities cheaper. In the country where the improvement was made, prices would be enhanced; in that where no change had taken place, but where they had been deprived of a profitable branch of foreign trade, prices would fall.

This, however, is only a seeming advantage to Portugal, for the quantity of cloth and wine together produced in that country would be diminished, while the quantity produced in England would be increased. Money would in some degree have changed its value in the two countries; it would be lowered in England and raised in Portugal. Estimated in money, the whole revenue of Portugal would be diminished; estimated in the same medium, the whole revenue of England would be increased.

Thus, then, it appears that the improvement of a manufacture in any country tends to alter the distribution of the precious metals amongst the nations of the world: it tends to increase the quantity of commodities, at the same time that it raises general prices in the country where the improvement takes place.

To simplify the question, I have been supposing the trade between two countries to be confined to two commodities—to wine and cloth; but it is well known that many and various articles enter into the list of exports and imports. By the abstraction of money from one country, and the accumulation of it in another, all commodities are affected in price, and consequently encouragement is given to the exportation of many more commodities besides money, which will therefore prevent so great an effect from taking place on the value of money in the two countries as might otherwise be expected.

Beside the improvements in arts and machinery, there are various other causes which are constantly operating on the natural course of trade, and which interfere with the equilibrium, and the relative value of money. Bounties on exportation or importation, new taxes on commodities, sometimes by their direct, and at other times by their indirect operation, disturb the natural trade of barter, and produce a consequent necessity of importing or exporting money, in order that prices may be accommodated to the natural course of commerce; and this effect is produced not only in the country where the disturbing cause takes place, but, in a greater or less degree, in every country of the commercial world.

This will in some measure account for the different value of money in different countries; it will explain to us why the prices of home commodities, and those of great bulk, though of comparatively small value, are, independently of other causes, higher in those countries where manufactures flourish. Of two countries having precisely the same population, and the same quantity of land of equal fertility in cultivation, with the same knowledge too of agriculture, the prices of raw produce will be highest in that where the greater skill, and the better machinery is used in the manufacture of exportable commodities. The rate of profits will probably differ but little; for wages, or the real reward of the labourer, may be the same in both; but those wages, as well as raw produce, will be rated higher in money in that country, into which, from the advantages attending their skill and machinery, an abundance of money is imported in exchange for their goods.

Of these two countries, if one had the advantage in the manufacture of goods of one quality, and the other in the manufacture of goods of another quality, there would be no decided influx of the precious metals into either; but if the advantage very heavily preponderated in favour of either, that effect would be inevitable.

In the former part of this work, we have assumed, for the purpose of argument, that money always continued of the same value; we are now endeavouring to show that, besides the ordinary variations in the value of money, and those which are common to the whole commercial world, there are also partial variations to which money is subject in particular countries; and to the fact, that the value of money is never the same in any two countries, depending as it does on relative taxation, on manufacturing skill, on the advantages of climate, natural productions, and many other causes.

Although, however, money is subject to such perpetual variations, and consequently the prices of the commodities which are common to most countries, are also subject to considerable difference, yet no effect will be produced on the rate of profits, either from the influx or efflux of money. Capital will not be increased, because the circulating medium is augmented. If the rent paid by the farmer to his landlord, and the wages to his labourers, be 20 per cent. higher in one country than another, and if at the same time the nominal value of the farmer's capital be 20 per cent. more, he will receive precisely the same rate of profits, although he should sell his raw produce 20 per cent. higher.

Profits, it cannot be too often repeated, depend on wages; not on nominal, but real wages; not on the number of pounds that may be annually paid to the labourer, but on the number of days' work necessary to obtain those pounds. Wages may therefore be precisely the same in two countries; they may bear, too, the same proportion to rent, and to the whole produce obtained from the land, although in one of those countries the labourer should receive ten shillings per week, and in the other twelve.

In the early states of society, when manufactures have made little progress, and the produce of all countries is nearly similar, consisting of the bulky and most useful commodities, the value of money in different countries will be chiefly regulated by their distance from the mines which supply the precious metals; but as the arts and improvements of society advance, and different nations excel in particular manufactures, although distance will still enter into the calculation, the value of the precious metals will be chiefly regulated by the superiority of those manufactures.

Suppose all nations to produce corn, cattle, and coarse clothing only, and that it was by the exportation of such commodities that gold could be obtained from the countries which produced them, or from those who held them in subjection; gold would naturally be of greater exchangeable value in Poland than in England, on account of the greater expense of sending such a bulky commodity as corn the more distant voyage, and also the greater expense attending the conveying of gold to Poland.

This difference in the value of gold, or, which is the same thing, this difference in the price of corn in the two countries, would exist, although the facilities of producing corn in England should far exceed those of Poland, from the greater fertility of the land, and the superiority in the skill and implements of the labourer.

If, however, Poland should be the first to improve her manufactures, if she should succeed in making a commodity which was generally desirable, including great value in little bulk, or if she should be exclusively blessed with some natural production, generally desirable, and not possessed by other countries, she would obtain an additional quantity of gold in exchange for this commodity, which would operate on the price of her corn, cattle, and coarse clothing. The disadvantage of distance would probably be more than compensated by the advantage of having an exportable commodity of great value, and money would be permanently of lower value in Poland than in England. If, on the contrary, the advantage of skill and machinery were possessed by England, another reason would be added to that which before existed, why gold should be less valuable in England than in Poland, and why corn, cattle, and clothing, should be at a higher price in the former country.

These I believe to be the only two causes which regulate the comparative value of money in the different countries of the world; for although taxation occasions a disturbance of the equilibrium of money, it does so by depriving the country in which it is imposed of some of the advantages attending skill, industry and climate.

It has been my endeavour carefully to distinguish between a low value of money, and a high value of corn, or any other commodity with which money may be compared. These have been generally considered as meaning the same thing; but it is evident, that when corn rises from five to ten shillings a bushel, it may be owing either to a fall in the value of money, or to a rise in the value of corn. Thus we have seen, that from the necessity of having recourse successively to land of a worse and worse quality, in order to feed an increasing population, corn must rise in relative value to other things. If therefore money continue permanently of the same value, corn will exchange for more of such money, that is to say, it will rise in price. The same rise in the price of corn will be produced by such improvement of machinery in manufactures, as shall enable us to manufacture commodities with peculiar advantages: for the influx of money will be the consequence; it will fall in value, and therefore exchange for less corn. But the effects resulting from a high price of corn when produced by the rise in the value of corn, and when caused by a fall in the value of money, are totally different. In both cases the money price of wages will rise, but if it be in consequence of the fall in the value of money, not only wages and corn, but all other commodities will rise. If the manufacturer has more to pay for wages, he will receive more for his manufactured goods, and the rate of profits will remain unaffected. But when the rise in the price of corn is the effect of the difficulty of production, profits will fall; for the manufacturer will be obliged to pay more wages, and will not be enable to remunerate himself by raising the price of his manufactured commodity.

Any improvement in the facility of working the mines, by which the precious metals may be produced with a less quantity of labour, will sink the value of money generally. It will then exchange for fewer commodities in all countries; but when any particular country excels in manufactures, so as to occasion an influx of money towards it, the value of money will be lower, and the prices of corn and labour will be relatively higher in that country than in any other.

This higher value of money will not be indicated by the exchange; bills may continue to be negotiated at par, although the prices of corn and labour should be 10, 20, or 30 percent. higher in one country than another. Under the circumstances supposed, such a difference of prices is the natural order of things, and the exchange can only be at par, when a sufficient quantity of money is introduced into the country excelling in manufactures, so as to raise the price of its corn and labour. If foreign countries should prohibit the exportation of money, and could successfully enforce obedience to such a law, they might indeed prevent the rise in the prices of the corn and labour of the manufacturing country; for such rise can only take place after the influx of the precious metals, supposing paper money not to be used; but they could not prevent the exchange from being very unfavourable to them. If England were the manufacturing country, and it were possible to prevent the importation of money, the exchange with France, Holland, and Spain, might be 5, 10, or 20 per cent. against those countries.

Whenever the current of money is forcibly stopped, and when money is prevented from settling at its just level, there are no limits to the possible variations of the exchange. The effects are similar to those which follow, when a paper money, not exchangeable for specie at the will of the holder, is forced into circulation. Such a currency is necessarily confined to the country where it is issued: it cannot, when too abundant, diffuse itself generally amongst other countries. The level of circulation is destroyed, and the exchange will inevitably be unfavourable to the country where it is excessive in quantity: just so would be the effects of a metallic circulation, if by forcible means, by laws which could not be evaded, money should be detained in a country, when the stream of trade gave it an impetus towards other countries.

When each country has precisely the quantity of money which it ought to have, money will not indeed be of the same value in each, for with respect to many commodities it may differ 5, 10, or even 20 per cent., but the exchange will be at par. One hundred pounds in England, or the silver which is in 100£, will purchase a bill of 100£, or an equal quantity of silver in France, Spain, or Holland.

In speaking of the exchange and the comparative value of money in different countries, we must not in the least refer to the value of money estimated in commodities, in either country. The exchange is never ascertained by estimating the comparative value of money in corn, cloth, or any commodity whatever, but by estimating the value of the currency of one country, in the currency of another.

. . . How is it to be ascertained whether English money has fallen, or Hamburg money has risen? There is no standard by which this can be determined. It is a plea which admits of no proof, and can neither be positively affirmed, nor positively contradicted. The nations of the world must have been early convinced, that there was no standard of value in nature, to which they might unerringly refer, and therefore chose a medium, which on the whole appeared to them less variable than any other commodity.

To this standard we must conform till the law is changed, and till some other commodity is discovered, by the use of which we shall obtain a more perfect standard than that which we have established. While gold is exclusively the standard in this country, money will be depreciated, when a pound sterling is not of equal value with 5 dwts. and 3 grs. of standard gold, and that, whether gold rises or falls in general value.

3

Marx and the Early Marxists

Karl Marx (1818–1883) was not primarily interested in international political economy. His greatest work examined the genesis and internal dynamics of the capitalist mode of production. He commented upon the expansion of capital internationally, especially British colonialism, but his thoughts on the subject were not rigorously integrated into his general theory of capital. Marx's episodic writing on IPE centers on two themes: the dialectical interaction of international forces and the development of capitalism; and the consequences of the internationalization of capital.

Marx has been interpreted as holding an underconsumptionist theory of imperialism. An often-quoted passage from the *Communist Manifesto* appears to bear this out: "The need of a constantly expanding market for its products chases the bourgeoisie over the whole surface of the globe." This has been taken to mean that as capitalism develops, and the working class becomes more and more impoverished, domestic demand decreases. In such circumstances, the accumulation of capital, which is dependent upon the realization of surplus value through the sale of commodities, is undermined. Thus, if accumulation is to continue, and the capitalist mode of production is to survive, capitalists must seek overseas markets to sell their goods. Underconsumption at home forces capital to expand abroad. This argument implies that expansion is necessary for a relatively well-developed capitalist mode of production, one in which class contradictions between bourgeoisie and proletariat have matured to the point of underconsumption.

In other writings, however, Marx makes quite a different argument. His analysis of the "Rise of Manufactures" in the *German Ideology* illustrates how capital is not pushed overseas by internal contradictions; it is pulled by new opportunities.

Marx posits three phases in the development of manufacturing industry. The first period, running from the advent of a manufacturing division of labor in roughly the fifteenth century to the early sixteenth century, is transitionary in nature. Feudal class structures and economic practices are extant, but some manufacturers are beginning to break away from the medieval guild system. This process of socioeconomic transformation is promoted by, and itself promotes, international trade. In creating new sources of wealth, foreign trade promotes the rise of the bourgeoisie. New domestic conditions, in turn, transform international economic relations. Where once trade was "inoffensive exchange," it is now highly competitive, marked by mercantilism and colonization. This competitiveness cannot be explained by underconsumption; the capitalist mode of production is hardly established. Interestingly, Marx suggests that early mercantilism is due to state interests: "The state, which was daily less and less able to do without money, now retained the ban on the export of gold and silver out of fiscal considerations." Although this ultimately serves the interests of capital, as manufacturing grows behind protectionist barriers, it opens the possibility of relatively autonomous state action.

The second phase in the development of manufacturing is mature mercantilism and the rise of the "big bourgeoisie," extending from the mid-seventeenth to the late eighteenth century. The merchant class, taking greatest advantage of protectionism, forms the most powerful sector of the bourgeoisie, while manufacturers are small-scale and possessed of "an extreme petty-bourgeois outlook." The concentration of trade and manufacturing in Britain at this time, however, is of pivotal importance. British interests create a world market for their goods, building "a demand for the manufactured products of this country, which could no longer be met by the industrial productive forces hitherto existing." In short, demand is greater than supply, and this stimulates the further development of domestic industry and international trade. Again, industrial capital has yet to fully mature; therefore, the underconsumptionist argument does not adequately explain these phenomena.

The expansion of international demand ushers in the third phase of manufacturing development. This period, covering the nineteenth century, is charcterized by universalized international competition and the ascendance of manufacturers over merchants. Protectionism becomes merely a rearguard action against the onslaught of free trade. During this time, the full maturation of industrial capital occurs and, presumably, underconsumption comes into play, though Marx does not argue this explicitly. In sum, the relationship of the emergence of capital and foreign economic relations is dialectical and interactive.

Marx also analyzes the consequences of the internationalization of capital. In both the *Communist Manifesto* and the *German Ideology,* he suggests that capitalism will ultimately expand and dominate the world: "The cheap prices of its commodities are the heavy artillery with which it batters down all Chinese walls." His discussion of India provides greater detail to this point.

Domestic economic, social, and political conditions in India are very different from the European experience. The indigenous "village system," which Marx elsewhere refers to as the Asiatic mode of production, is composed of a powerful centralized state perched above, and largely autonomous from, an atomized collection of self-reliant agricultural towns. The lack of organic connections among the towns, and between state and society, rob this peculiar amalgam of the developmental dynamism of European modes of production. Asia is simply resistant to social change from within. But British colonialism destroys the structural foundation of the Asiatic mode of production. India will industrialize and class relations will be restructured. Even "changeless" Asia cannot resist the transforming power of capital. Although this is a brutal process, selfishly serving the interests of the British bourgeoisie, it is inevitable and necessary to create conditions for further development in India.

Vladimir Lenin (1870–1924) agrees with Marx's conclusion that capital will expand and dominate the world. However, Lenin's discussion of the causes of capitalist expansion differs somewhat from Marx's broad historical analysis. Writing in the twentieth century, Lenin stresses the uneven nature of capitalist development that leads him to an underconsumptionist position: "The necessity of exporting capital arises from the fact that in a few countries capitalism has become "overripe" and (owing to the backward state of agriculture and the impoverished state of the masses) capital cannot field 'profitable' investment." From this premise, Lenin argues that imperialism is a distinct stage, indeed the "highest stage," of capitalism. Building upon Rudolf Hilferding's concept of "finance capital," Lenin illustrates how concentration and centralization eventually require the internationalization of capital. This has crucial political consequences, as the imperialist powers first "divide the world" among themselves, and are finally driven to war among themselves. Although Lenin's discussion of imperialism is derived from Marx's general analysis of capital, and has greatly influenced succeeding generations of Marxists, its underconsumptionist inclination does not fully capture the complexity of Marx's examination of the ways in which international economic forces shaped the earlier rise of capitalism.

The Communist Manifesto

KARL MARX AND FRIEDRICH ENGELS

I. Bourgeois and Proletarians

The history of all hitherto existing society is the history of class struggles.

The modern bourgeois society that has sprouted from the ruins of feudal society, has not done away with class antagonisms. It has but established new classes, new conditions of oppression, new forms of struggle in place of the old ones.

Our epoch, the epoch of the bourgeoisie, possesses, however, this distinctive feature: It has simplified the class antagonisms. Society as a whole is more and more splitting up into two great hostile camps, into two great classes directly facing each other—bourgeoisie and proletariat.

From the serfs of the Middle Ages sprang the chartered burghers of the earliest towns. From these burgesses the first elements of the bourgeoisie were developed.

The discovery of America, the rounding of the Cape, opened up fresh ground for the rising bourgeoisie. The East Indian and Chinese markets, the colonization of America, trade with the colonies, the increase in the means of exchange and in commodities generally, gave to commerce, to navigation, to industry, an impulse never before known, and thereby, to the revolutionary element in the tottering feudal society, a rapid development.

The feudal system of industry, in which industrial production was monopolized by closed guilds, now no longer sufficed for the growing wants of the new markets. The manufacturing system took its place. The guild-masters were

Reprinted from *The Communist Manifesto* by Karl Marx and Friedrich Engels, "Bourgeois and Proletarians," by permission of International Publishers, NY. (c) 1948.

pushed aside by the manufacturing middle class; division of labour between the different corporate guilds vanished in the face of division of labour in each single workshop.

Meantime the markets kept ever growing, the demand ever rising. Even manufacture no longer sufficed. Thereupon, steam and machinery revolutionized industrial production. The place of manufacture was taken by the giant, modern industry, the place of the industrial middle class, by industrial millionaires—the leaders of whole industrial armies, the modern bourgeois.

Modern industry has established the world market, for which the discovery of America paved the way. This market has given an immense development to commerce, to navigation, to communication by land. This development has, in its turn, reacted on the extension of industry; and in proportion as industry, commerce, navigation, railways extended, in the same proportion the bourgeoisie developed, increased its capital, and pushed into the background every class handed down from the Middle Ages.

We see, therefore, how the modern bourgeoisie is itself the product of a long course of development, of a series of revolutions in the modes of production and of exchange.

Each step in the development of the bourgeoisie was accompanied by a corresponding political advance of that class. An oppressed class under the sway of the feudal nobility, it became an armed and self-governing association in the medieval commune; here independent urban republic (as in Italy and Germany), there taxable "third estate" of the monarchy (as in France); afterwards, in the period of manufacture proper, serving either the semi-feudal or the absolute monarchy as a counterpoise against the nobility, and, in fact, cornerstone of the great monarchies in general—the bourgeoisie has at last, since the establishment of modern industry and of the world market, conquered for itself, in the modern representative state, exclusive political sway. The executive of the modern state is but a committee for managing the common affairs of the whole bourgeoisie.

The bourgeoisie has played a most revolutionary role in history.

The bourgeoisie, wherever it has got the upper hand, has put an end to all feudal, patriarchal, idyllic relations. It has pitilessly torn asunder the motley feudal ties that bound man to his "natural superiors," and has left no other bond between man and man than naked self-interest, than callous "cash payment." It has drowned the most heavenly ecstasies of religious fervor, of chivalrous enthusiasm, of philistine sentimentalism, in the icy water of egotistical calculation. It has resolved personal worth into exchange value, and in place of the numberless indefeasible chartered freedoms, has set up that single, unconscionable freedom—Free Trade. In one word, for exploitation, veiled by religious and political illusions, it has substituted naked, shameless, direct, brutal exploitation.

The bourgeoisie cannot exist without constantly revolutionizing the instruments of production, and thereby the relations of production, and with them the whole relations of society. Conservation of the old modes of production in unaltered form, was, on the contrary, the first condition of existence for all

earlier industrial classes. Constant revolutionizing of production, uninterrupted disturbance of all social conditions, everlasting uncertainty and agita-
tion distinguish the bourgeois epoch from all earlier ones. All fixed, fast-
frozen relations, with their train of ancient and venerable prejudices and
opinions, are swept away, all new-formed ones become antiquated before
they can ossify. All that is solid melts into air, all that is holy is profaned, and
man is at last compelled to face with sober senses his real conditions of life and
his relations with his kind.

The need of a constantly expanding market for its products chases the
bourgeoisie over the whole surface of the globe. It must nestle everywhere,
settle everywhere, establish connections everywhere.

The bourgeoisie has through its exploitation of the world market given a
cosmopolitan character to production and consumption in every country. To
the great chagrin of reactionaries, it has drawn from under the feet of industry
the national ground on which it stood. All old-established national industries
have been destroyed or are daily being destroyed. They are dislodged by new
industries, whose introduction becomes a life and death question for all civilized nations, by industries that no longer work up indigenous raw material,
but raw material drawn from the remotest zones; industries whose products
are consumed, not only at home, but in every quarter of the globe. In place of
the old wants, satisfied by the production of the country, we find new wants,
requiring for their satisfaction the products of distant lands and climes. In
place of the old local and national seclusion and self-sufficiency, we have
intercourse in every direction, universal inter-dependence of nations. And as
in material, so also in intellectual production. The intellectual creations of
individual nations become common property. National one-sidedness and
narrow-mindedness become more and more impossible, and from the numerous national and local literatures there arises a world literature.

The bourgeoisie, by the rapid improvement of all instruments of production, by the immensely facilitated means of communication, draws all nations,
even the most barbarian, into civilization. The cheap prices of its commodities
are the heavy artillery with which it batters down all Chinese walls, with which
it forces the barbarians' intensely obstinate hatred of foreigners to capitulate.
It compels all nations, on pain of extinction, to adopt the bourgeois mode of
production; it compels them to introduce what it calls civilization into their
midst, i.e., to become bourgeois themselves. In a word, it creates a world
after its own image.

The bourgeoisie has subjected the country to the rule of the towns. It has
created enormous cities, has greatly increased the urban population as compared with the rural, and has thus rescued a considerable part of the population from the idiocy of rural life. Just as it has made the country dependent on
the towns, so it has made barbarian and semi-barbarian countries dependent
on the civilized ones, nations of peasants on nations of bourgeois, the East on
the West.

More and more the bourgeoisie keeps doing away with the scattered state
of the population, of the means of production, and of property. It has agglom-

erated population, centralized means of production, and has concentrated property in a few hands. The necessary consequence of this was political centralization. Independent, or but loosely connected provinces, with separate interests, laws, governments, and systems of taxation, became lumped together into one nation, with one government, one code of laws, one national class interest, one frontier, and one customs tariff.

The German Ideology:
The Rise of Manufactures

KARL MARX

With the advent of manufactures, the various nations entered into a competitive relationship, the struggle for trade, which was fought out in wars, protective duties and prohibitions, whereas earlier the nations, insofar as they were connected at all, had carried on an inoffensive exchange with each other. Trade had from now on a political significance.

Manufacture and the movement of production in general received an enormous impetus through the extension of commerce which came with the discovery of America and the sea-route to the East Indies. The new products imported thence, particularly the masses of gold and silver which came into circulation and totally changed the position of the classes towards one another, dealing a hard blow to feudal landed property and to workers; the expeditions of adventurers, colonisation; and above all the extension of markets into a world market, which has now become possible and was daily becoming more and more a fact, called forth a new phase of historical development, into which in general we cannot here enter further. Through the colonisation of the newly discovered countries the commercial struggle of the nations amongst one another was given new fuel and accordingly greater extension and animosity.

The expansion of trade and manufacture accelerated the accumulation of movable capital, while in the guilds, which were not stimulated to extend their production, natural capital remained stationary or even declined. Trade and manufacture created the big bourgeoisie; in the guilds was concentrated the petty bourgeoisie, which no longer was dominant in the towns as formerly, but

Karl Marx, *The German Ideology* (New York: International Publishers, 1947).

had to bow to the might of the great merchants and manufacturers. Hence the decline of the guilds, as soon as they came into contact with manufacture.

The intercourse of nations took on, in the epoch of which we have been speaking, two different forms. At first the small quantity of gold and silver in circulation involved the ban on the export of these metals; and industry, for the most part imported from abroad and made necessary by the need for employing the growing urban population, could not do without those privileges which could be granted not only, of course, against home competition, but chiefly against foreign. The local guild privilege was in these original prohibitions extended over the whole nation. Customs duties originated from the tributes which the feudal lords exacted as protective levies against robbery from merchants passing through their territories, tributes later imposed likewise by the towns, and which, with the rise of the modern states, were the Treasury's most obvious means of raising money.

The appearance of American gold and silver on the European markets, the gradual development of industry, the rapid expansion of trade and the consequent rise of the non-guild bourgeoisie and of money, gave these measures another significance. The State, which was daily less and less able to do without money, now retained the ban on the export of gold and silver out of fiscal considerations; the bourgeois, for whom these masses of money which were hurled on to the market became the chief object of speculative buying, were thoroughly content with this; privileges established earlier became a source of income for the government and were sold for money; in the customs legislation there appeared the export duty, which, since it only [placed] a hindrance in the way of industry, had a purely fiscal aim.

The second period began in the middle of the seventeenth century and lasted almost to the end of the eighteenth. Commerce and navigation had expanded more rapidly than manufacture, which played a secondary role; the colonies were becoming considerable consumers; and after long struggles the separate nations shared out the opening world market among themselves. This period begins with the Navigation Laws and colonial monopolies. The competition of the nations among themselves was excluded as far as possible by tariffs, prohibitions and treaties; and in the last resort the competitive struggle was carried on and decided by wars (especially naval wars). The mightiest maritime nation, the English, retained preponderance in trade and manufacture. Here, already, we find concentration in one country.

Manufacture was all the time sheltered by protective duties in the home market, by monopolies in the colonial market, and abroad as much as possible by differential duties. The working-up of home-produced material was encouraged (wool and linen in England, silk in France), the export of home-produced raw material forbidden (wool in England), and the [working-up] of imported material neglected or suppressed (cotton in England). The nation dominant in sea trade and colonial power naturally secured for itself also the greatest quantitative and qualitative expansion of manufacture. Manufacture could not be carried on without protection, since, if the slightest change takes place in other countries, it can lose its market and be ruined; under reasonably favourable conditions it may easily be introduced into a country, but for this very reason can easily be destroyed. At the same time through the mode in which it is carried on, particularly in the eighteenth century, in the country-side, it is to such an extent interwoven with the vital relationships of a great mass of individuals, that no country dare jeopardise its existence by permitting free competition. Insofar as it manages to export, it therefore depends entirely on the extension or restriction of commerce, and exercises a relatively very small reaction [on the latter]. Hence its secondary [importance] and the influence of [the merchants] in the eighteenth century. It was the merchants and especially the shippers who more than anybody else pressed for State protection and monopolies; the manufacturers also demanded and indeed received protection, but all the time were inferior in political importance to the merchants. The commercial towns, particularly the maritime towns, became to some extent civilised and acquired the outlook of the big bourgeoisie, but in the factory towns an extreme petty-bourgeois outlook persisted.

This period is also characterised by the cessation of the bans on the export of gold and silver and the beginning of the trade in money; by banks, national debts, paper money, by speculation in stocks and shares and stockjobbing in all articles; by the development of finance in general. Again capital lost a great part of the natural character which had still clung to it.

The concentration of trade and manufacture in one country, England, developing irresistibly in the seventeenth century, gradually created for this country a relative world market, and thus a demand for the manufactured products of this country, which could no longer be met by the industrial productive forces hitherto existing. This demand, outgrowing the productive forces, was the motive power which, by producing big industry—the application of elemental forces to industrial ends, machinery and the most complex division of labour—called into existence the third period of private ownership since the Middle Ages. There already existed in England the other pre-conditions of this new phase: freedom of competition inside the nation, the development of theoretical mechanics, etc. (Indeed, the science of mechanics perfected by Newton was altogether the most popular science in France and England in the eighteenth century.) (Free competition inside the nation itself had everywhere to be conquered by a revolution—1640 and 1688 in England, 1789 in France.) Competition soon compelled every country that wished to retain its historical role to protect its manufactures by renewed customs regulations (the old duties were no longer any good against big industry) and soon after to introduce big industry under protective duties. Big industry universalised competition in spite of these protective measures (it is practical free trade; the protective duty is only a palliative, a measure of defence *within* free trade), established means of communication and the modern world market, subordinated trade to itself, transformed all capital into industrial capital, and thus produced the rapid circulation (development of the financial system) and the centralisation of capital. By universal competition it forced all individuals to strain their energy to the utmost. It destroyed as far as possible ideology, religion, morality, etc., and where it could not do this, made them into a palpable lie. It produced world history for the first time, insofar as it made all civilised nations and every individual member of them dependent for the satisfaction of their wants on the whole world, thus destroying the former natural exclusiveness of separate nations. It made natural science subservient to capital and took from the division of labour the last semblance of its natural character. It destroyed natural growth in general, as far as this is possible while labour exists, and resolved all natural relationships into money relationships. In the place of naturally grown towns it created the modern, large industrial cities which have sprung up overnight. Wherever it penetrated, it destroyed the crafts and all earlier stages of industry. It completed the victory of the commerical town over the countryside. Generally speaking, big industry created everywhere the same relations between the classes of society, and thus destroyed the peculiar individuality of the various nationalities. And finally, while the bourgeoisie of each nation still retained separate national interests, big industry created a class, which in all nations has the same interest and with which nationality is already dead; a class which is really rid of all the old world and at the same time stands pitted against it. Big industry makes for the worker not only the relation to the capitalist, but labour itself, unbearable.

It is evident that big industry does not reach the same level of development in all districts of a country. This does not, however, retard the class movement of the proletariat, because the proletarians created by big industry assume leadership of this movement and carry the whole mass along with them, and because the workers excluded from big industry are placed by it in a still worse situation than the workers in big industry itself. The countries in which big industry is developed act in a similar manner upon the more or less non-industrial countries, insofar as the latter are swept by universal commerce into the universal competitive struggle.

On Imperialism In India

KARL MARX

Hindostan is an Italy of Asiatic dimensions, the Himalayas for the Alps, the Plains of Bengal for the Plains of Lombardy, the Deccan for the Appenines, and the Isle of Ceylon for the Island of Sicily. The same rich variety in the products of the soil, and the same dismemberment in the political configuration. Just as Italy has, from time to time, been compressed by the conqueror's sword into different national masses, so do we find Hindostan, when not under the pressure of the Mohammedan, or the Mogul, or the Briton, dissolved into as many independent and conflicting States as it numbered towns, or even villages. Yet, in a social point of view, Hindostan is not the Italy, but the Ireland of the East. And this strange combination of Italy and of Ireland, of a world of voluptuousness and of a world of woes, is anticipated in the ancient traditions of the religion of Hindostan. That religion is at once a religion of sensualist exuberance, and a religion of self-torturing asceticism. . . .

There cannot, however, remain any doubt but that the misery inflicted by the British on Hindostan is of an essentially different and infinitely more intensive kind than all Hindostan had to suffer before.

All the civil wars, invasions, revolutions, conquests, famines, strangely complex, rapid and destructive as the successive action in Hindostan may appear, did not go deeper than its surface. England had broken down the entire framework of Indian society, without any symptoms of reconstitution yet appearing. This loss of his old world, with no gain of a new one, imparts a particular kind of melancholy to the present misery of the Hindoo, and sepa-

Reprinted from Robert C. Tucker, *The Marx-Engels Reader* (New York: Norton, 1978).

rates Hindostan, ruled by Britain, from all its ancient traditions, and from the whole of its past history.

There have been in Asia, generally, from immemorial times, but three departments of Government: that of Finance, or the plunder of the interior; that of War, or the plunder of the exterior; and, finally, the department of Public Works. Climate and territorial conditions, especially the vast tracts of desert, extending from the Sahara, through Arabia, Persia, India and Tartary, to the most elevated Asiatic highlands, constituted artificial irrigation by canals and waterworks the basis of Oriental agriculture. As in Egypt and India, inundations are used for fertilising the soil of Mesopotamia, Persia, etc.; advantage is taken of a high level for feeding irrigative canals. This prime necessity of an economical and common use of water, which, in the Occident, drove private enterprise to voluntary association, as in Flanders and Italy, necessitated, in the Orient where civilisation was too low and the territorial extent too vast to call into life voluntary association, the interference of the centralising power of Government. Hence an economical function devolved upon all Asiatic Governments the function of providing public works. This artificial fertilisation of the soil, dependent on a Central Government, and immediately decaying with the neglect of irrigation and drainage, explains the otherwise strange fact that we now find whole territories barren and desert that were once brilliantly cultivated, as Palmyra, Petra, the ruins in Yemen, and large provinces of Egypt, Persia and Hindostan; it also explains how a single war of devastation has been able to depopulate a country for centuries, and to strip it of all its civilisation.

Now, the British in East India accepted from their predecessors the department of finance and of war, but they have neglected entirely that of public works. Hence the deterioration of an agriculture which is not capable of being conducted on the British principle of free competition, of *laissez-faire* and *laissez-aller*. But in Asiatic empires we are quite accustomed to see agriculture deteriorating under one government and reviving again under some other government. There the harvests correspond to good or bad government, as they change in Europe with good or bad seasons. Thus the oppression and neglect of agriculture, bad as it is, could not be looked upon as the final blow dealt to Indian society by the British intruder, had it not been attended by a circumstance of quite different importance, a novelty in the annals of the whole Asiatic world. However changing the political aspect of India's past must appear, its social condition has remained unaltered since its remotest antiquity, until the first decennium of the 19th century. The hand-loom and the spinning-wheel, producing their regular myriads of spinners and weavers, were the pivots of the structure of that society. From immemorial times, Europe received the admirable textures of Indian labour, sending in return for them her precious metals, and furnishing thereby his material to the gold-smith, that indispensable member of Indian society, whose love of finery is so great that even the lowest class, those who go about nearly naked, have commonly a pair of golden ear-rings and a gold ornament of some kind hung round their necks. Rings on the fingers and toes have also been common.

Women as well as children frequently wore massive bracelets and anklets of gold or silver, and statuettes of divinities in gold and silver were met with in the households. It was the British intruder who broke up the Indian hand-loom and destroyed the spinning wheel. England began with driving the Indian cottons from the European market; it then introduced twist into Hindostan and in the end inundated the very mother country of cotton with cottons. From 1818 to 1836 the export of twist from Great Britain to India rose in the proportion of 1 to 5,200. In 1824 the export of British muslins to India hardly amounted to 1,000,000 yards while in 1837 surpassed 64,000,000 yards. But at the same time the population of Decca decreased from 150,000 inhabitants to 20,000. This decline of Indian towns celebrated for their fabrics was by no means the worst consequence. British steam and science uprooted, over the whole surface of Hindostan, the union between agricultural and manufacturing industry.

These two circumstances—the Hindoo, on the one hand, leaving, like all Oriental peoples, to the central government the care of the great public works, the prime condition of his agriculture and commerce, dispersed, on the other hand over the surface of the country, and agglomerated in small centers by the domestic union of agricultural and manufacturing pursuits—these two circumstances had brought about, since the remotest times, a social system of particular features—the so-called *village system,* which gave to each of these small unions their independent organisation and distinct life. . . .

These small stereotype forms of social organism have been to the greater part dissolved, and are disappearing, not so much through the brutal interference of the British tax-gatherer and the British soldier, as to the working of English steam and English free trade. Those family-communities were based on domestic industry, in that peculiar combination of hand-weaving, hand-spinning and hand-tilling agriculture which gave them self-supporting power. English interference having placed the spinner in Lancashire and the weaver in Bengal, or sweeping away both Hindoo spinner and weaver, dissolved these small semi-barbarian, semi-civilised communities, by blowing up their economical basis, and thus produced the greatest, and, to speak the truth, the only social revolution ever heard of in Asia.

Now, sickening as it must be to human feeling to witness those myriads of industrious patriarchal and inoffensive social organisations disorganised and dissolved into their units, thrown into a sea of woes, and their individual members losing at the same time their ancient form of civilisation, and their hereditary means of subsistence, we must not forget that these idyllic village communities, inoffensive though they may appear, had always been the solid foundation of Oriental despotism, that they restrained the human mind within the smallest possible compass, making it the unresisting tool of superstition, enslaving it beneath traditional rules, depriving it of all grandeur and historical energies. We must not forget the barbarian egotism which, concentrating on some miserable patch of land, had quietly witnessed the ruin of empires, the perpetration of unspeakable cruelties, the massacre of the population of large towns, with no other consideration bestowed upon them than on natural events, itself the helpless prey of any aggressor who deigned to notice it at all. We must not forget that this undignified, stagnatory, and vegetative life, that this passive sort of existence evoked on the other part, in contradistinction, wild, aimless, unbounded forces of destruction and rendered murder itself a religious rite in Hindostan. We must not forget that these little communities were contaminated by distinctions of caste and by slavery, that they subjugated man to external circumstances instead of elevating man to be the sovereign of circumstances, that they transformed a self-developing social state into never changing natural destiny, and thus brought about a brutalising worship of nature, exhibiting its degradation in the fact that man, the sovereign of nature, fell down on his knees in adoration of *Hunuman,* the monkey, and *Sabbala,* the cow.

England, it is true, in causing a social revolution in Hindostan, was actuated only by the vilest interests, and was stupid in her manner of enforcing them. But that is not the question. The question is, can mankind fulfill its destiny without a fundamental revolution in the social state of Asia? If not, whatever may have been the crimes of England she was the unconscious tool of history in bringing about that revolution.

The Export Of Capital

V. I. LENIN

Under the old capitalism, when free competition prevailed, the export of *goods* was the most typical feature. Under modern capitalism, when monopolies prevail, the export of *capital* has become the typical feature.

Capitalism is commodity production at the highest stage of development, when labour power itself becomes a commodity. The growth of internal exchange, and particularly of international exchange, is the characteristic distinguishing feature of capitalism. The uneven and spasmodic character of the development of individual enterprises, of individual branches of industry and individual countries, is inevitable under the capitalist system. England became a capitalist country before any other, and in the middle of the nineteenth century, having adopted free trade, claimed to be the "workshop of the world," the great purveyor of manufactured goods to all countries, which in exchange were to keep her supplied with raw materials. But in the last quarter of the nineteenth century, *this* monopoly was already undermined. Other countries, protecting themselves by tariff walls, had developed into independent capitalist states. On the threshold of the twentieth century, we see a new type of monopoly coming into existence. Firstly, there are monopolist capitalist combines in all advanced capitalist countries; secondly, a few rich countries, in which the accumulation of capital reaches gigantic proportions, occupy a monopolist position. An enormous "superabundance of capital" has accumulated in the advanced countries.

It goes without saying that if capitalism could develop agriculture, which

Reprinted from *Imperialism: The Highest State of Capitalism* by V. I. Lenin, "The Export of Capital," "Imperialism as a Special Stage of Capitalism," by permission of International Publishers, NY. (c) 1939.

today lags far behind industry everywhere, if it could raise the standard of living of the masses, who are everywhere still poverty-stricken and underfed, in spite of the amazing advance in technical knowledge, there could be no talk of a superabundance of capital. This "argument" the petty-bourgeois critics of capitalism advance on every occasion. But if capitalism did these things it could not be capitalism; for uneven development and wretched conditions of the masses are fundamental and inevitable conditions and premises of this mode of production. As long as capitalism remains what it is, surplus capital will never be utilised for the purpose of raising the standard of living of the masses in a given country, for this would mean a decline in profits for the capitalist; it will be used for the purpose of increasing those profits by exporting capital abroad to the backward countries. In these backward countries profits are usually high, for capital is scarce, the price of land is relatively low, wages are low, raw materials are cheap. The possibility of exporting capital is created by the fact that numerous backward countries have been drawn into international capitalist intercourse; main railways have either been built or are being built there; the elementary conditions for industrial development have been created, etc. The necessity for exporting capital arises from the fact that in a few countries capitalism has become "over-ripe" and (owing to the backward state of agriculture and the impoverished state of the masses) capital cannot field "profitable" investment.

The export of capital greatly affects and accelerates the development of capitalism in those countries to which it is exported. While, therefore, the export of capital may tend to a certain extent to arrest development in the countries exporting capital, it can only do so by expanding and deepening the further development of capitalism throughout the world.

The countries which export capital are nearly always able to obtain "advantages," the character of which throws light on the peculiarities of the epoch of finance capital and monopoly. . . .

Finance capital has created the epoch of monopolies, and monopolies introduce everywhere monopolist methods: the utilisation of "connections" for profitable transactions takes the place of competition on the open market. The most usual thing is to stipulate that part of the loan that is granted shall be spent on purchases in the country of issue, particularly on orders for war materials, or for ships, etc. In the course of the last two decades (1890–1910), France often resorted to this method. The export of capital abroad thus becomes a means for encouraging the export of commodities. In these circumstances transactions between particularly big firms assume a form "bordering on corruption," as Schilder "delicately" puts it. Krupp in Germany, Schneider in France, Armstrong in England are instances of firms which have close connections with powerful banks and governments and cannot be "ignored" when arranging a loan.

Thus, finance capital, almost literally, one might say, spreads its net over all countries of the world. Banks founded in the colonies or their branches, play an important part in these operations. German imperialists look with envy on the "old" colonising nations which are "well established" in this respect. In 1904, Great Britain had 50 colonial banks with 2,279 branches (in 1910 there were 72 banks with 5,449 branches); France had 20 with 136 branches; Holland 16 with 68 branches; and Germany had a "mere" 13 with 70 branches. The American capitalists, in their turn, are jealous of the English and German: "In South America," they complained in 1915, "five German banks have forty branches and five English banks have seventy branches. . . . England and Germany have invested in Argentina, Brazil, and Uruguay in the last twenty-five years approximately four thousand million dollars, and as a result enjoy together 46 per cent of the total trade of these three countries."

The capital exporting countries have divided the world among themselves in the figurative sense of the term. But finance capital has also led to the *actual* division of the world.

Imperialism as a Special Stage of Capitalism

V. I. LENIN

We must now try to sum up and put together what has been said above on the subject of imperialism. Imperialism emerged as the development and direct continuation of the fundamental attributes of capitalism in general. But capitalism only became capitalist imperialism at a definite and very high stage of its development when certain of its fundamental attributes began to be transformed into their opposites, when the features of a period of transition from capitalism to a higher social and economic system began to take shape and reveal themselves all along the line. Economically, the main thing in this process is the substitution of capitalist monopolies for capitalist free competition. Free competition is the fundamental attribute of capitalism, and of commodity production generally. Monopoly is exactly the opposite of free competition; but we have seen the latter being transformed into monopoly before our very eyes, creating large-scale industry and eliminating small industry, replacing large-scale industry by still larger-scale industry, finally leading to such a concentration of production and capital that monopoly has been and is the result: cartels, syndicates and trusts, and merging with them, the capital of a dozen or so banks manipulating thousands of millions. At the same time monopoly, which has grown out of free competition, does not abolish the latter, but exists over it and alongside of it, and thereby gives rise to a number of very acute, intense antagonisms, frictions and conflicts. Monopoly is the transition from capitalism to a higher system.

If it were necessary to give the briefest possible definition of imperialism we should have to say that imperialism is the monopoly stage of capitalism. Such a definition would include what is most important, for, on the one hand, finance capital is the bank capital of a few big monopolist banks, merged with the capital of the monopolist combines of manufacturers; and, on the other hand, the division of the world is the transition from a colonial policy which has extended without hindrance to territories unoccupied by any capitalist power, to a colonial policy of monopolistic possession of the territory of the world which has been completely divided up.

But very brief definitions, although convenient, for they sum up the main points, are nevertheless inadequate, because very important features of the phenomenon that has to be defined have to be especially deduced. And so, without forgetting the conditional and relative value of all definitions, which can never include all the concatenations of a phenomenon in its complete development, we must give a definition of imperialism that will embrace the following five essential features:

1) The concentration of production and capital developed to such a high stage that it created monopolies which play a decisive role in economic life.

2) The merging of bank capital with industrial capital, and the creation, on the basis of this "finance capital," of a "financial oligarchy."

3) The export of capital, which has become extremely important, as distinguished from the export of commodities.

4) The formation of international capitalist monopolies which share the world among themselves.

5) The territorial division of the whole world among the greatest capitalist powers is completed.

Imperialism is capitalism in that stage of development in which the dominance of monopolies and finance capital has established itself; in which the export of capital has acquired pronounced importance; in which the division of the world among the international trusts has begun; in which the division of all territories of the globe among the great capitalist powers has been completed.

In this matter of defining imperialism, however, we have to enter into controversy, primarily, with K. Kautsky, the principal Marxian theoretician of the epoch of the so-called Second International—that is, of the twenty-five years between 1889 and 1914.

Kautsky, in 1915 and even in November 1914, very emphatically attacked the fundamental ideas expressed in our definition of imperialism. Kautsky said that imperialism must not be regarded as a "phase" or stage of economy, but as a policy; a definite policy "preferred" by finance capital; that imperialism cannot be "identified" with "contemporary capitalism"; that if imperialism is to be understood to mean "all the phenomena of contemporary capitalism"—cartels, protection, the domination of the financiers and colonial policy—then the question as to whether imperialism is necessary to capitalism becomes reduced to the "flattest tautology"; because, in that case, "imperialism is naturally a vital necessity for capitalism," and so on. The best way to present Kautsky's ideas is to quote his own definition of imperialism, which is diametrically opposed to the substance of the ideas which we have set forth. . . .

Kautsky's definition is as follows:

> Imperialism is a product of highly developed industrial capitalism. It consists in the striving of every industrial capitalist nation to bring under its control and to annex increasingly big *agrarian*" (Kautsky's italics) "regions irrespective of what nation inhabit those regions."

This definition is utterly worthless because it one-sidedly, i.e., arbitrarily, brings out the national question alone (although this is extremely important in itself as well as in its relation to imperialism), it arbitrarily and *inaccurately* relates this question *only* to industrial capital in the countries which annex other nations, and in an equally arbitrary and inaccurate manner brings out the annexation of agrarian regions.

Imperialism is a striving for annexations—this is what the *political* part of Kautsky's definition amounts to. It is correct, but very incomplete, for politically, imperialism is, in general, a striving towards violence and reaction. For the moment, however, we are interested in the *economic* aspect of the question, which Kautsky *himself* introduced into *his* definition. The inaccuracy of Kautsky's definition is strikingly obvious. The characteristic feature of imperialism is *not* industrial capital, *but* finance capital. It is not an accident that in France it was precisely the extraordinarily rapid development of *finance* capital, and the weakening of industrial capital, that, from 1880 onwards, gave rise to the extreme extension of annexationist (colonial) policy. The characteristic feature of imperialism is precisely that it strives to annex *not only* agricultural regions, but even highly industrialised regions (German appetite for Belgium; French appetite for Lorraine), because 1) the fact that the world is already divided up obliges those contemplating a *new* division to reach out for *any kind* of territory, and 2) because an essential feature of imperialism is the rivalry between a number of great powers in the striving for hegemony, i.e., for the conquest of territory, not so much directly for themselves as to weaken the adversary and undermine *his* hegemony. (Belgium is chiefly necessary to Germany as a base for operations against England; England needs Bagdad as a base for operations against Germany, etc.)

Kautsky refers especially—and repeatedly—to English writers who, he alleges, have given a purely political meaning to the word "imperialism" in the sense that Kautsky understands it. We take up the work by the Englishman Hobson, *Imperialism,* which appeared in 1902, and therein we read:

> The new imperialism differs from the older, first, in substituting for the ambition of a single growing empire the theory and the practice of competing empires, each motivated by similar lusts of political aggrandisement and commercial gain; secondly, in the dominance of financial or investing over mercantile interests.

We see, therefore, that Kautsky is absolutely wrong in referring to English writers generally (unless he meant the vulgar English imperialist writers, or the avowed apologists for imperialism). We see that Kautsky, while claiming that he continues to defend Marxism, as a matter of fact takes a step backward compared with the *social-liberal* Hobson, who *more correctly* takes into account two "historically concrete" (Kautsky's definition is a mockery of historical concreteness) features of modern imperialism: 1) the competition between *several* imperialisms, and 2) the predominance of the financier over the merchant. If it were chiefly a question of the annexation of agrarian countries by industrial countries, the role of the merchant would be predominant.

Kautsky's definition is not only wrong and un-Marxian. It serves as a basis for a whole system of views which run counter to Marxian theory and Marxian practice all along the line. We shall refer to this again later. The argument about words which Kautsky raises as to whether the modern stage of capitalism should be called "imperialism" or "the stage of finance capital" is of no importance. Call it what you will, it matters little. The fact of the matter is that Kautsky detaches the politics of imperialism from its economics, speaks of annexations as being a policy "preferred" by finance capital, and opposes to it another bourgeois policy which, he alleges, is possible on this very basis of finance capital. According to his argument, monopolies in economics are compatible with non-monopolistic, non-violent, non-annexationist methods in politics. According to his argument, the territorial division of the world, which was completed precisely during the period of finance capital, and which constitutes the basis of the present peculiar forms of rivalry between the biggest capitalist states, is compatible with a non-imperialist policy. The result is a slurring-over and a blunting of the most profound contradictions of the latest stage of capitalism, instead of an exposure of their depth; the result is bourgeois reformism instead of Marxism.

Kautsky writes: "from the purely economic point of view it is not impossible that capitalism will yet go through a new phase: that of the extension of the policy of the cartels to foreign policy, the phase of ultra-imperialism," i.e., of a super-imperialism, a union of world imperialisms and not struggles among imperialisms: a phase of "the joint exploitation of the world by internationally combined finance capital."

We shall have to deal with this "theory of ultra-imperialism" later on in order to show in detail how definitely and utterly it departs from Marxism. In keeping with the plan of the present work, we shall examine the exact economic data on this question. Is "ultra-imperialism" possible "from the purely economic point of view" or is it ultra-nonsense?

If, by purely economic point of view a "pure" abstraction is meant, then all that can be said reduces itself to the following proposition: evolution is proceeding towards monopoly; therefore the trend is towards a single world monopoly, to a universal trust. This is indisputable, but it is also as completely meaningless as is the statement that "evolution is proceeding" towards the manufacture of foodstuffs in laboratories. In this sense the "theory" of ultra-imperialism is no less absurd than a "theory of ultra-agriculture" would be.

If, on the other hand, we are discussing the "purely economic" conditions of the epoch of finance capital as an historically concrete epoch which opened at the beginning of the twentieth century, then the best reply that one can make to the lifeless abstractions of "ultra-imperialism" . . . is to contrast them with the concrete economic realities of present-day world economy. Kautsky's utterly meaningless talk about ultra-imperialism encourages, among other things, that profoundly mistaken idea which only brings grist to the mill of the apologists of imperialism, *viz.,* that the rule of finance capital *lessens* the unevenness and contradictions inherent in world economy, where in reality it *increases* them.

R. Calwer, in his little book, *An Introduction to World Economics,* attempted to compile the main, purely economic, data required to understand in a concrete way the internal relations of world economy at the end of the nineteenth and beginning of the twentieth centuries. He divides the world into five "main economic areas," as follows: 1) Central Europe (the whole of Europe with the exception of Russia and Great Britain); 2) Great Britain; 3) Russia; 4) Eastern Asia; 5) America; he includes the colonies in the "areas" of the state to which they belong and "leaves out" a few countries not distributed according to areas, such as Persia, Afghanistan and Arabia in Asia; Morocco and Abyssinia in Africa, etc.

We notice three areas of highly developed capitalism with a high development of means of transport, of trade and of industry, the Central European, the British and the American areas. Among these are three states which dominate the world: Germany, Great Britain, the United States. Imperialist rivalry and the struggle between these countries have become very keen because Germany has only a restricted area and few colonies (the creation of "Central Europe" is still a matter for the future; it is being born in the midst of desperate struggles). For the moment the distinctive feature of Europe is political disintegration. In the British and American areas, on the other hand, political concentration is very highly developed, but there is a tremendous disparity between the immense colonies of the one and the insignificant colonies of the other. In the colonies, capitalism is only beginning to develop. The struggle for South America is becoming more and more acute.

There are two areas where capitalism is not strongly developed: Russia and Eastern Asia. In the former, the density of population is very low, in the latter it is very high; in the former political concentration is very high, in the latter it does not exist. The partition of China is only beginning, and the struggle between Japan, U.S.A., etc., in connection therewith is continually gaining in intensity.

Compare this reality, the vast diversity of economic and political conditions, the extreme disparity in the rate of development of the various countries, etc., and the violent struggles of the imperialist states, with Kautsky's silly little fable about "peaceful" ultra-imperialism. Is this not the reactionary attempt of a frightened philistine to hide from stern reality? Are not the international cartels which Kautsky imagines are the embryos of "ultra-imperialism" . . . an example of the division and the *redivision* of the world, the transition from peaceful division to non-peaceful division and *vice versa?* Is not American and other finance capital, which divided the whole world peacefully, with Germany's participation, for example, in the international rail syndicate, or in the international mercantile shipping trust, now engaged in *redividing* the world on the basis of a new relation of forces, which has been changed by methods *by no means* peaceful?

Finance capital and the trusts are increasing instead of diminishing the differences in the rate of development of the various parts of world economy. When the relation of forces is changed, how else, *under capitalism,* can the solution of contradictions be found, except by resorting to *violence?* Railway statistics provide remarkably exact data on the different rates of development of capitalism and finance capital in world economy. . . .

. . . . [T]he development of railways has been more rapid in the colonies and in the independent (and semi-dependent) states of Asia and America. Here, as we know, the finance capital of the four or five biggest capitalist states reigns undisputed. Two hundred thousand kilometers of new railways in the colonies and in the other countries of Asia and America represent more than 40,000,000,000 marks in capital, newly invested on particularly advantageous terms, with special guarantees of a good return and with profitable orders for steel works, etc., etc.

Capitalism is growing with the greatest rapidity in the colonies and in overseas countries. Among the latter, *new* imperialist powers are emerging (e.g., Japan). The struggle of world imperialism is becoming more acute. The tribute levied by finance capital on the most profitable colonial and overseas enterprises is increasing. In sharing out this "booty," an exceptionally large part goes to countries which, as far as the development of productive forces is concerned, do not always stand at the top of the list. . . .

. . . . [A]bout 80 per cent of the total existing railways are concentrated in the hands of the five Great Powers. But the concentration of the *ownership* of these railways, of finance capital is much greater still: French and English millionaires, for example, own an enormous amount of stocks and bonds in American, Russian and other railways.

Thanks to her colonies, Great Britain has increased the length of "her" railways by 100,000 kilometers, four times as much as Germany. And yet, it is well known that the development of productive forces in Germany, and especially the development of the coal and iron industries, has been much more rapid during this period than in England—not to mention France and Russia. In 1892, Germany produced 4,900,000 tons of pig iron and Great Britain produced 6,800,000 tons; in 1912, Germany produced 17,600,000 tons and Great Britain 9,000,000 tons. Germany, therefore, had an overwhelming superiority over England in this respect. We ask, is there *under capitalism* any means of removing the disparity between the development of productive forces and the accumulation of capital on the one side, and the division of colonies and "spheres of influence" for finance capital on the other side— other than by resorting to war?

4

Revisions of Liberalism:
Interdependence Theory

Modern liberalism has both affirmed and denied the theoretical project of international political economy. Neoclassical analysis essentially ignores the problem of how economics and politics interact, focusing exclusively on "pure economics." On the other hand, John Maynard Keynes, with his ideas of macroeconomic aggregates and countercyclical state intervention, lays the analytic groundwork for a revised liberal IPE theory. Although Keynes himself did not fully develop the political side of the argument, his ideas have been incorporated and extended by interdependence theorists.

Keynesianism resonates in the work of Richard Cooper, one of the first to popularize the notion of interdependence. Cooper suggests that advances in transportation, communications, technology transfer, and the like have fundamentally altered the conditions of international economics. Most importantly, differences in comparative costs appear to be diminishing. This implies that the gains from trade seen by Smith and Ricardo may not be as obvious as they once were. Furthermore, global economic integration may thwart equilibrating world market forces: "in normal periods prospective imbalances in international payments . . . are likely to be more frequent and of larger amplitude than they have been in the past." In a manner similar to Keynes's discussion of the difficulties of achieving domestic equilibrium, Cooper argues that new policies are needed to address the unprecedented conditions of international interdependence.

Although diminishing comparative cost differentials in an interdependent world may tempt national leaders to return to mercantilist practice, Cooper vigorously opposes such a course. Invoking Keynes, he argues that economic nationalism invites policy competition that is doomed to fail: "like members of a crowd rising to their tip-toes to see a parade better but in the end merely standing uncomfortably on their tip-toes." National economic independence is further constrained by contemporary international conventions, such as the General Agreement on Tariffs and Trade, that limit policy instruments (e.g., quantitative trade restrictions) available to state leaders. Cooper concludes that international policy coordination is virtually the only means to achieve national economic goals in an interdependent world.

Cooper thus defines the challenges of interdependence and prescribes cooperation as the best response. He, again like Keynes, does not consider how political conditions may promote or undermine international cooperation. Presumably, state leaders will realize the irrationalities of policy competition and state interests will come to be defined in terms of cooperation. Robert Keohane and Joseph Nye go a step further and analyze how international politics is transformed by interdependence.

Keohane and Nye are engaged in a conversation with international relations realists. Out of their critique of realism, they construct an ideal typical vision of IPE, complex interdependence, that falls within the purview of the liberal tradition. Realism, they suggest, is based on two key assumptions: the preeminence of states as world actors and the centrality of military force as international power. Keohane and Nye argue that global economic interdependence has cast doubt upon these assumptions. Transnational corporations and organizations born of economic integration now vie with states for global influence. Military power is essentially useless in a wide variety of significant issue-areas; firepower has little relevance in international monetary negotiations among regional allies. Moreover, the advent of nuclear weapons has dramatically raised the cost of employing military force, reducing its utility. Traditional realism, Keohane and Nye contend, does not take account of these changing world conditions.

In situations of interdependence, new power relationships are established, based upon mutual asymmetrical dependencies. Keohane and Nye hold that the politics of interdependence are best understood in terms of sensitivity and vulnerability. Sensitivity applies when costs imposed from without can be minimized by a change in existing policy. If costs cannot be significantly reduced even with a change in policy, then the situation is one of vulnerability. The costliness of alternative courses of action will vary from issue area to issue area; a state may be vulnerable to sudden changes in world oil prices, but be only sensitive to fluctuations in the supply of certain strategic minerals. Moreover, within a given issue area, one actor may be sensitive to changing conditions while others are vulnerable. In political terms, vulnerabilities are most important, as they may provide sources of power that realism fails to elucidate.

The politics of interdependence is also influenced by international regimes. Keohane and Nye define regimes as "networks of rules, norms, and procedures that regularize behavior" in a given issue-area. Regimes are affected by the distribution of power among states, but regimes, in turn, may critically influence the bargaining process among states. The point here is that realist analysis of systemic balances of power is insufficient to comprehend the modern world. Moreover, state interests may be constrained by regimes. In some instances, regimes are the "rules of the game" that limit even the most powerful actors. International regimes are therefore important loci of the politics of interdependence. Keohane and Nye are modest in generalizing about regime creation and maintenance, pointing out that further research is necessary to explain such processes. They offer a prolegomenon to interdependence theory that inspired many students of IPE in the 1970s and 1980s.

Keohane and Nye agree with Cooper that interdependence has transformed international relations. They also agree that interdependence offers new opportunities for cooperation. States exposed to interdependence vulnerabilities may seek compromises on many issues. Keohane and Nye, however, argue against an overly optimistic attitude toward global harmony, which they label the "modernist" position. Although they are somewhat more circumspect toward potential cooperation, they are, in the final analysis, consistent with general liberal orientations. Their interpretation of interdependence assumes a world in which politics, while not wholly transformed, is fundamentally shaped by economic forces.

National Economic Policy
in an Interdependent World Economy

RICHARD COOPER

During the past decade [1960s] there has been a strong trend toward economic interdependence among the industrial countries. This growing interdependence makes the successful pursuit of national economic objectives much more difficult. Broadly speaking, increasing interdependence complicates the successful pursuit of national economic objectives in three ways. First, it increases the number and magnitude of the disturbances to which each country's balance of payments is subjected, and this in turn diverts policy attention and instruments of policy to the restoration of external balance. Second, it slows down the process by which national authorities, each acting on its own, are able to reach domestic objectives. Third, the response to greater integration can involve the community of nations in counteracting motions which leave all countries worse off than they need be. These difficulties are in turn complicated by the fact that the objective of greater economic integration involves international agreements which reduce the number of policy instruments available to national authorities for pursuit of their economic objectives. This chapter touches on all of these facets of higher economic interdependence among industrial nations, both as fact and as objective, but its principal focus is on the third complication—the process of mutually damaging competition among national policies.

     . . . . [B]oth institutional and economic changes have increased economic interdependence among the industrial countries since the late 1940s. Import quotas in industrial countries have been virtually abolished on trade in manu-

Reprinted from *The Economics of Interdependence: Economic Policy in the Atlantic Community* by Richard Cooper, "National Economic Policy in an Interdependent World Economy," by permission of McGraw-Hill Publishing Company.

facture products; tariffs have been reduced; and transportation costs have fallen relative to the value of goods. At the same time, the accumulation of capital and the spread of technology have made national economies more similar in their basic characteristics of production; comparative cost differences have apparently narrowed, suggesting that imports can be replaced by domestic production with less loss in national income than heretofore. Whether a country imports a particular good or exports it thus becomes less dependent on the basic characteristics of the economy, more dependent on historical development and on relatively accidental and transitory features of recent investment decisions at home and abroad. An invention in one country may lead to production there for export, but the new product will relatively quickly be produced abroad—or supplanted by a still newer product—and possibly even exported to the original innovating country.

Enlargement of the decision-making domain of the world's great producing firms results in the rapid movement of capital and technical knowledge across national frontiers, thereby contributing to the narrowing of comparative cost differences; but their activity will also quicken the speed with which trade adjusts to new sales opportunities because they have direct knowledge of foreign markets and access to distribution channels.

Monetary disturbances, too, are likely to be much more quickly translated into changes in the volume of exports and imports than they were formerly. Under fixed exchange rates, greater than average monetary inflation in one country will invite a more rapid deterioration in the balance on goods and services than was true in the past.

Finally, as financial markets become more closely integrated, relatively small differences in yields on securities will induce large flows of funds between countries. Banks will increasingly number "foreign" firms among their prime customers; the advantages of inexpensive credit to firms in countries with ample savings and well-functioning financial markets, such as the United States, will be shared increasingly with firms elsewhere.

All these changes in the characteristics of the international economy during the past decade—and it should be emphasized again that economic integration is still far from complete—are crucial to the functioning of the international payments system and the autonomy which it permits in the formation of national economic policy. These changes mean that in normal periods prospective imbalances in international payments—imbalances that would arise if countries did not respond to reduce them or did not adjust policy measures to forestall them—are likely to be more frequent and of larger amplitude than they have been in the past. "Disturbances" arising from new innovations, from generous wage settlements leading to price increases, and from excess or deficient domestic demand will affect the balance of payments more perceptibly. Whether or not imbalances also last longer depends upon the relationship among the "disturbances"; if they are well distributed among countries and tend equally toward deficit or surplus, the duration of imbalances may well be less than in the past; otherwise it may be longer.

These changes suggest that prospective balance-of-payments difficulties are likely to be more common, and that they will worsen as the structural changes continue in their recent trend. By the same token, however, correction of imbalances in international payments should be easier in the future. Trade flows will respond more sharply to small "disturbances;" but the flows should also respond more quickly to policy measures designed to influence them. If a small relative increase in the price level will lead it into greater balance-of-payments difficulties than before, a relatively small decrease should undo the difficulties. Similarly, international capital flows will respond more readily to small differences in national credit conditions; but small differences in national credit conditions directed to correcting the imbalance can induce equilibrating flows of capital. Thus if the national authorities can recognize disturbances early, are willing to use some of the tools at their disposal for correcting imbalances in international payments, and can act reasonably quickly in doing so, then the increased sensitivity of payments to various disturbances need cause no undue difficulty, provided that policy instruments are properly chosen and adequately coordinated among countries.

Interdependence before 1914

There is a natural inclination to compare the international economy of today, especially in the claim that it is becoming more integrated, with the international economy before 1914, when, it is often said, the world economy was highly integrated. In the four decades before World War I, most of the major countries were customarily on the gold standard (implying fixed exchange rates), capital was free to move into or out of most countries, trade was impeded only by comparatively moderate tariffs, and quotas were generally absent. Even labor was generally free to migrate from country to country without visas, security checks, and immigration quotas.

In one important sense, however, the comparison is not at all apt. Today national governments are much more ambitious about the objectives of national economic policy than they were in the nineteenth century. . . . Governments have taken on the responsibility for assuring high levels of employment and, increasingly, a rapid rate of growth; and they attempt actively to influence the allocation of resources and the distribution of income to a much greater degree. These new tasks place greater burdens on the available instruments of policy. Before 1914, by contrast, preoccupation with "defending the currency" was dominant, and the (admittedly more limited) policy instruments at hand were more willingly devoted to that end. Thus, the intrusions of international economic integration on national economic policy was more readily accepted because national economic policy was far less ambitious in its aims.

In addition to this important difference, economic relations among industrial countries are probably potentially much closer today than they were even before 1914, despite the characteristics of the pre-1914 world noted above. True, British and French capital moved overseas readily and British investors built railroads around the world. The proportion of Britain's annual savings which went abroad was, in fact, staggering by modern standards. Nonetheless, communications were far less perfect than they were today and foreign investors ran greater commercial risks arising from imperfect knowledge (except in the case of colonial bonds that in effect had the sponsorship of the home government).

Despite the freedom of capital to move, it did not in fact move in sufficient volume even to erase differences in short-term interest rates. Over the period 1876–1914, short-term interest rates in New York averaged more than one percentage point higher than corresponding rates in London, and there was only a weak correspondence in movement between short-term rates in the two financial centers. Short-term interest rates in London and Paris were much closer together and the correspondence in their movement was higher but still far from perfect. Long-term interest rates showed similar divergence in their levels and movement. Response to new investment opportunities, when it came at all, was often slow.

While tariffs were generally low, barriers to trade in the form of transportation costs were very substantial, although they declined sharply after the introduction of the ocean steamship. Large differences in comparative costs meant trade was socially very profitable, but the composition and level of trade was correspondingly less sensitive to small changes in costs, prices, and quality. Finally, business organizations, far from being international, became truly national corporations in the United States only with the approach of World War I, and the process was even slower in many European countries.

Thus, the integration of the pre-1914 world economy was something of an illusion. While the pre-1914 world was integrated in the sense that government-imposed barriers to the movement of goods, capital and people were minimal, those imposed by nature were much greater and economic integration was not high in the sense used here: quick responsiveness to differential earning opportunities resulting in a sharp reduction in differences in factor rewards.

Countries today are gradually entering a new environment, not merely returning to a condition that once existed. They confront new problems arising from the combination of more ambitious national and international economic objectives and a potentially higher degree of economic interdependence than has ever existed before. . . . It is now necessary to specify more precisely how conflicts may arise and to indicate some of the ways in which governments have responded to those conflicts.

Economic Objectives and Policy Instruments

A well known proposition in the theory of economic policy requires that the number of policy instruments be at least as great as the number of objectives (target variables) if all objectives are to be achieved. If the number of instruments is fewer than the number of targets, it will not be possible to reach all of the targets; in that case at least some targets must be given up, and the authorities must choose among them.

A simple example can illustrate the need to have at least as many instruments as targets. Suppose the government of an isolated country has two economic objectives: it would like to assure full employment of its labor forces at all times, and it would like its national product to grow at a specified rate each year. It can vary the over-all size of the budget deficit or surplus (fiscal policy) to assure full employment. But full employment of resources can be met with a variety of combinations of investment, consumption, and government expenditure. Without some other instrument, the desired growth rate cannot be assured. If, however, investment is stimulated by a low rate of interest and higher investment leads to more growth, then monetary policy and fiscal policy together can be manipulated to achieve the two objectives. The higher the growth rate desired, the lower should be the rate of interest. Fiscal policy can then be adjusted to assure full employment. This very simple model apparently influenced thinking in the early years of the Kennedy administration.

Viewing economic policy as a problem in specifying targets and finding sufficient instruments to reach them helps to illuminate many policy problems confronting national authorities . . . The objective of greater economic integration has led many officials to reject both flexible exchange rates and frequent variations in fixed exchange rates as instruments for maintaining balance-of-payments equilibrium. A number of other instruments of policy have been ruled out by international agreement on the same grounds, or on the grounds that their use was likely to lead to retaliation and counter-retaliation that would leave countries worse off than they were at the outset. Most types of export subsidy, tariff discrimination among countries, increases in tariffs, and discriminatory exchange regulations fall into this category. A number of provisions of the GATT are devoted to these exclusions and prohibitions; with specified exceptions, such as the formation of customs unions or free trade areas, trade discrimination is proscribed, as are many types of export subsidies and discrimination in domestic taxation between home and foreign goods. The IMF Articles of Agreement make similar prohibitions with respect to currency arrangements. . . . The extensive use of these measures in the past, especially in the 1930s, led to widespread retaliation and mutual recriminations, and they acquired a bad name among outward looking officials. But the price of international rules of good behavior as set forth in the GATT and the IMF Articles has been a reduction in the range of instrument available to national policy-makers.

Some policy instruments may be used, as a practical matter, only within a limited range. In the United States, changes in the discount rate of the Federal Reserve System and (since 1962) deliberate deficits or surpluses in the government budget are both regarded as legitimate tools of economic policy; but in normal times the public is not likely to countenance a discount rate of 20 per cent or a budget deficit of $50 billion. These exceed the range of acceptability; policy instruments have "boundary conditions." In the abnormal situations when such limits become operative, an instrument is withdrawn from use.

Sometimes these limits are not fully known until they are tested; then we discover that we have more targets (or fewer instruments) than were previously apparent.

It goes without saying that to be attainable, economic objectives must be consistent. If they are not consistent, no number of policy instruments will suffice to reach the objectives. One illustration in the forefront of discussion in most industrial countries involves the relationship between employment and price stability. Given the institution of private collective bargaining, is the target of "full employment" (4 per cent unemployment in the United States, under 2 per cent in the United Kingdom, according to the standards and definitions accepted by each) consistent with "price stability," defined, say, as stability in the consumer price index? Many economists would find a conflict.

This kind of inconsistency can perhaps be overcome by developing new policy instruments. Another kind of inconsistency, especially important to national economies linked through international trade and capital movements, cannot be eliminated through the development of new instruments. Examples are objectives regarding the balance of payments and the trade balance. Since one country's trade surplus is another country's trade deficit, it is impossible for all countries to succeed in running trade surpluses. The same is true for balance of payments, taking into account capital movements. If there are n countries, only $n-1$ of them can succeed in reaching their independent balance-of-payments targets; at least one must accept defeat or else fail to target values for its trade position and its balance-of-payments position, thereby acting as an international residual. It has been suggested that the United States played this role until the late 1950s, by taking a relatively passive position toward its payments position after the termination of Marshall Plan aid.

The requirement of consistency is not merely theoretical. In 1962, for instance, all of the major industrial countries wanted simultaneously to improve their payments positions on current account. While mutual success was logically possible in this case, it did imply a correspondingly sharp deterioration in the current account position of the less developed countries taken together, which in turn would require ample financing from the industrial countries in the form of grants or loans. No such increase in capital outflows was targeted. Thus, national targets were inconsistent.

The Speed of Adjustment

In summary, successful economic policy requires an adequate number of policy instruments for the number of economic objectives, and it requires that these objectives be consistent with one another. If either of these conditions fails, policy-makers are bound to be frustrated in their efforts. Before turning to how these frustrations become manifest, however, one further point should be made: growing interdependence can slow down greatly the process by which independently acting national authorities reach their economic objectives, even when all the targets are consistent and there are sufficient policy instruments at hand to reach them. Thus, in practice, nations may find themselves farther from their objectives than would be true with less independence.

High interdependence slows the speed of adjustment to disturbances if national policy-makers do not take the interdependence into account. This is because the economic authorities in one country may be working at cross purposes with those in another. An investment boom in one country may raise interest rates both at home and, by attracting internationally mobile funds, in neighboring countries. The first country may temporarily welcome the high interest rates to help curb the boom and may also tighten fiscal policy to keep inflationary pressures in check. But other countries may fear that higher interest rates will deter investment at home and take steps to lower interest rates. Unless this monetary relaxation is taken into account in framing fiscal policy in the first country, its authorities will find that fiscal policy has not been sufficiently contractionary. But more contractionary fiscal policy will tend to hold interest rates up, so that the monetary authorities in the neighboring countries will find they have only been partially successful in lowering their rates. Even if in the end the whole process settles to a point where the various national authorities are satisfied, it will have taken longer than if there had been close coordination between the authorities in the several countries involved. The greater the interaction between the countries, the longer convergence will take if countries act solely on their own.

If policy decisions are truly decentralized among nations, in the sense that the authorities in each nation pursue only their own objectives with their own instruments without taking into account the interactions with other countries, then the more interdependent the international economy is, the less successful countries are likely to be in reaching and maintaining their economic objectives. This is due to the greater impact of domestic measures on foreign economies, calling forth correspondingly greater offsetting responses which in turn affect the first country. Under these circumstances, countries must either reconcile themselves to prolonged delays in reaching their objectives or they must coordinate their policies more closely with those of other nations.

International Competition in Economic Policy

In an interdependent economy, governments do not have full control over the instrument variables needed to influence the trade balance or the balance of payments. Each government can affect the domestic interest rate in an attempt to influence international capital movements or can set tariffs on imports and subsidies on exports to influence the trade balance. But success in influencing capital movements or trade flows depends on what other countries are doing. It is interest rate *differentials,* not the absolute level of interest rates, which induce the movement of capital. And it is domestic tariffs *less* foreign subsidies which influence the level of imports. There are many instruments of economic policy for which relative differences affect international transactions, but the absolute value may continue to exert a strong influence on purely domestic decisions. This is true, for example, not only of short- and long-term interest rates, but also of liberal tax benefits to investment, generous depreciation allowances, lax regulation of corporate activities and a host of other measures designed to influence corporate location. It is also true of foreign trade: generous credit arrangements or credit-risk guarantees for exports may encourage total exports without improving the trade balance if other countries are pursuing similar measures.

This feature of policy instruments—that the absolute level of the instrument may have important effects domestically, but that only the level relative to that in other countries influence the balance of trade or payments—raises the question: where do the values of these instruments finally settle? International capital movements between two otherwise isolated countries will presumably be roughly the same whether interest rates are at 7 per cent in one and 5 per cent in the other or at 4 per cent in the first country and 2 per cent in the second. In each case, the differential is two percentage points. But what determines whether "community" interest rates settle at the higher level or the lower one? The effects on other objectives may be very different. Economic growth will be inhibited more in the first case than in the second.

The values that policy instruments take on in the community of nations, and the process by which those values are reached, are of strong interest to the individual nations. They may not have sufficient domestic flexibility to offset the damaging effects of policy instruments that are forced to an inappropriate level by international competition among governments. As a result, greater international integration can force choices among national objectives, all of which might otherwise be attainable.

There are situations in which most or even all members of the international community will find themselves worse off. The competitive devaluations and tariff wars of the interwar period offer the most striking example; many of the proscriptions in the GATT and the IMF Articles of Agreement are designed to avoid a repetition of those events.

But competition among policies was not thereby banished on all fronts. For example, interest rates shot upward in 1965 and 1966 to levels one to two percentage points higher than those which had prevailed in most countries in 1964. Some of the increases were designed to curb domestic demand; others were defensive, to limit capital outflow. Even after domestic economies had cooled down, it took a dramatic meeting of finance ministers at Checquers, England, in early 1967, to reverse the process.

Four other types of policy instruments having these characteristics have been used in the effort to strengthen the balance of payments of various countries: restrictions on government procurement, government-sponsored export promotion, tax incentives to domestic investment, and changes in domestic tax structure. The United States, faced with large payments deficits during the early 1960s, made or considered moves in all of these areas. In each case there was ample precedent abroad for doing so.

Government purchases for government use are specifically excluded from coverage by the GATT rules governing international trade. The result is that a conspicuously small proportion of government purchases, by any government, is from foreign suppliers who compete with domestic producers. In the United States the "Buy American" provision, which after 1954 officially gave preferential treatment of 6 to 12 per cent (in addition to tariffs) to domestic over foreign competitors, has existed since the 1930s. But in 1962, a number of government agencies, including most importantly the Department of Defense, raised the preference accorded to domestic supplies as high as 50 per cent. Foreign aid expenditures by the American government are even more restricted. Starting with development loans in 1959, such expenditures were tied increasingly to purchases in the United States, until only a limited class of expenditures was not so tied, regardless of the price advantages offered by foreign suppliers.

The government procurement practices of other countries are more difficult to document, since most governments do not require open bidding on government purchases with well-publicized preferences to domestic producers, such as are found in the "Buy American" provisions. Many countries follow the practice of tying foreign assistance, either by law or by skillful selection of projects and recipient countries, to purchases from the donor country. This is as true for those donors with fully employed economies as for those with excess capacity and unemployment, even though tying is far less effective in the former case, and merely stimulates additional imports; and it is as true for donor countries in balance-of-payments surplus as for those in deficit. . . .

Many of these practices, of course, arise not only from balance-of-payments considerations but also from protectionist sentiment. Domestic producers apply strong political pressures on their governments to buy at home, especially when the goods are to be "given away." But weakness in the balance of payments often strengthens their arguments and increases public acceptibility of such restrictive measures.

Government activities are not solely restrictive of trade. On the contrary, a second range of practices involves all kinds of schemes, except direct subsidies proscribed by GATT, to promote exports of goods and services. Governments sponsor trade fairs, product exhibitions, and other advertisements for the products of their exporters; they insure commercial and so-called noncommercial risks involved in exporting; and they often help to finance exports directly. No major industrial trading nation can be found without a government or government-sponsored agency for insuring and/or extending credit for exports. Some countries, such as France and Italy, give especially favorable treatment to export paper in their banking systems or at their central banks. Export credit is often exempt from general credit limitations to restrict domestic demand. All of these measures really subsidize exports, although it is often impossible to identify the amount of the subsidy in any particular sale.

Subsidies to domestic investment is another area in which governments have moved to improve their international payments positions. Investment subsidies for manufacturing and agriculture improve the competitiveness of a country's products in world markets. Some countries give direct fiscal incentives to new investment in plant and equipment, such as the investment tax credit of 7 per cent adopted by the United States in 1962 and the 25 per cent investment grants in the United Kingdom. . . .

Under a regime of fixed exchange rates, government subsidy for domestic investment is similar to a devaluation of the currency in that it improves the cost competitiveness both of the country's export products and of its products which compete with imports.

Subsidies to investment are obviously motivated by considerations extending well beyond the balance of payments; economic growth has become a target of economic policy in its own right, partly for political and strategic reasons (arising in part from the "economic race" with the Soviet bloc), partly because rising standards of living are universally desired. But balance-of-payments considerations do play an important role in the decision to inaugurate investment incentives. Britain for years has emphasized the need to enlarge and improve its capital stock to compete more effectively in world markets. . . .

Changes in the structure of domestic taxation, and in particular the "mix" between direct and indirect taxes, constitutes another area in which governments have moved, or have been tempted to move, to improve their national trade positions. GATT rules prohibiting export subsidies have been interpreted to preclude remission of direct taxes on exports but to permit remission of indirect taxes. Thus taxes on corporate profits arising from export cannot be rebated, but manufacturers' excise taxes or turnover taxes can be. Similarly, countries are permitted to levy indirect taxes, but not direct taxes, on imports. Because of this asymmetry in border tax adjustment, it is possible under fixed exchange rates for a country to stimulate exports and to impede imports by shifting its tax structure from direct taxes to indirect taxes, provided that direct taxes affect prices.

All of these policy measures have a common characteristic. Taken by one country alone, each represents a concealed devaluation of the currency, at least with respect to a selected class of transactions. But like devaluation, these measures are effective only if other countries do not respond in kind. To each country, tying foreign aid and giving preference to domestic producers in government procurement may appear to offer a means to improve the balance of payments; indeed, in the short run it may do so. But if all countries follow the same practices, the benefit to each is much reduced and some countries will have their payments positions worsened as a result. In the meantime, the total real value of foreign aid has been reduced by reliance on high cost suppliers, and inefficient production has been fostered.

The same thing is true of the other measures discussed. General adoption of export promotion schemes and government-sponsored tourist publicity will surely have a much greater effect on the total level of world exports and tourism than on the payments position of any one country, since the measures will largely cancel one another and leave only residual effects on the balance of payments. Similarly, if all countries adopt special tax incentives for domestic investment, the net improvement in competitiveness—which depends as much on incentives abroad as on those at home—will be haphazard and unpredictable. The principal effect may well be not on any one country's balance-of-payments position but on the total investment and the rate of growth in the world economy at large—so long as these effects are not nullified by a competitive rise in long-term interest rates! Finally, an effort to raise exports and impede imports through changes in domestic tax structure may have little overall effect on foreign trade and leave countries with tax structures which many would prefer not to have.

At any point in time, there are often cogent and persuasive arguments for introducing one or more of these measures to improve the balance of payments. If other countries did not respond in kind, the desired improvement would be forthcoming. But if other countries act likewise, the measures largely cancel out. Not only is the purpose of the move nullified, but all countries may find themselves worse off in terms of their other objectives. As a rule, individual countries cannot act unilaterally without inviting reaction. If they are successful, they are quickly emulated by their neighbors, so that the initial gains are transitory at best. Countries often must act in self-defense, in response to the behavior of their trading partners. This is particularly so when measures to reduce one country's deficit do not reduce the surpluses of the surplus countries but increase the deficit of another deficit country or move countries in balance into deficit. These third countries then feel compelled to respond defensively and their actions in turn increase the deficit of the initial deficit country. Moreover, many of the measures thus taken are difficult to reverse; countries do not readily contract export credit programs or lengthen the period of depreciation allowable for tax purposes.

In Summary

Contemporary competition among policies is not obvious, as it was in the round of tariff increases in the late 1920s and the competitive depreciations of the early 1930s. But more subtle and sophisticated methods can substitute, albeit imperfectly, for currency depreciation. Taken in sequence by different countries, these measures produce a kind of ratchet effect. We then have a series of competitive depreciations in disguise.

This chapter has focused on how balance-of-payments difficulties, actual or feared, can give rise to undesirable competition in policies. . . .

These developments are understandable, and can be expected to become more common. In a highly integrated economic area which surpasses in size the jurisdiction of governments, each group of policy-makers is subject to such strong interactions with the surrounding area that the constraints on its actions become very severe. Indeed, in the hypothetically limiting case, these constraints determine entirely the course of action each jurisdiction must take. The region, or the nation, in a highly integrated economy becomes analogous to the perfect competitor—or at best the oligopolist—in market economy. The range of choice it has, consistent with economic survival, is very small; for the most part it simply adapts its behavior to stimuli from outside. Awareness of the high interactions will eventually inhibit action.

A. C. Pigou and John Maynard Keynes pointed out long ago that the sum of individual decisions by consumers and producers may not always be optimal for society as a whole (and hence for its members), even though its members may be acting individually on entirely rational grounds. Some kind of collective action is therefore required to produce an optimal outcome.

The same can be true among nations or among regions within a nation, if the interactions among their decisions are sufficiently strong. One jurisdiction gropes around for new instruments in an attempt to improve its position. If it succeeds, others follow and there is a competition in policies which defeats everyone's objectives and in fact can even lead all participants *away* from their national or local objectives, like the members of a crowd rising to their tip-toes to see a parade better but in the end merely standing uncomfortably on their tip-toes.

An invisible hand seems to be working in the area of economic policy as well as in the market place. Competition in the market place is alleged to lead to the most efficient allocation of resources. Whatever the merits of this claim, we can be much less confident that competition among policies will be optimal. Governments seek many ends, not the efficient allocation of resources alone; and the process of policy competition can certainly thwart some of those objectives.

Existing rules of international behavior as set forth in GATT and in the Bretton Woods Agreement do limit the use of direct and straightforward means of policy competition such as open export subsidies and multiple exchange rates, and they therefore slow the process of policy competition since the more subtle and sophisticated methods—loopholes in GATT and the Bretton Woods Agreement—usually involve strong domestic considerations which delay their implementation. But existing rules do not fully accomplish the aim of preventing self-defeating policy competition and of freeing domestic policy measures to purse largely domestic objectives. Moreover, the pressures on domestic policy are likely to become greater as the world economy becomes more interdependent. Freedom of action in economic policy formation can be lost through the need for each country to compete in policies with its competitors in commerce.

 . . . . Countries can coordinate closely their national economic policies, attempting to define and reach an optimum combination of policies for the community as a whole. This route involves extensive "internationalization" of the process of economic policy-making, transferring this government function to the larger integrated area.

Alternatively, countries can attempt to remove the major source of pressure on their actions—their unfavorable international payments positions— by providing each country with ample liquidity to finance any deficit and allowing it to go its own way. Or this goal can be achieved by reversing the growth in interdependence, by artificially breaking down or reducing the numerous economic links between countries. . . .

Interdependence in World Politics

ROBERT O. KEOHANE AND JOSEPH S. NYE

We live in an era of interdependence. This vague phrase expresses a poorly understood but widespread feeling that the very nature of world politics is changing. The power of nations—that age-old touchstone of analysts and statesmen—has become more elusive. . . .

How profound are the changes? A modernist school sees telecommunications and jet travel as creating a "global village" and believes that burgeoning social and economic transactions are creating a "world without borders." To greater or lesser extent, a number of scholars see our era as one in which the territorial state, which has been dominant in world politics for the four centuries since feudal times ended, is being eclipsed by nonterritorial actors such as multinational corporations, transnational social movements, and international organizations. As one economist put it, "the state is about through as an economic unit."

Traditionalists call these assertions unfounded "globaloney." They point to the continuity in world politics. Military interdependence has always existed, and military power is still important in world politics—witness nuclear deterrence; the Vietnam, Middle East, and India-Pakistan wars; and Soviet influence in Eastern Europe or American influence in the Caribbean. Moreover, as the Soviet Union has shown, authoritarian states can, to a considerable extent, control telecommunications and social transactions that they consider disruptive. Even poor and weak countries have been able to nationalize multinational corporations, and the prevalence of nationalism casts doubt on the proposition that the nation-state is fading away.

Neither the modernists nor the traditionalists have an adequate framework for understanding the politics of global interdependence. Modernists point correctly to the fundamental changes now taking place, but they often assume without sufficient analysis that advances in technology and increases in social and economic transactions will lead to a new world in which states, and their control of force, will no longer be important. Traditionalists are adept at showing flaws in the modernist vision by pointing out how military interdependence continues, but find it very difficult accurately to interpret today's multi-dimensional economic, social, and ecological interdependence.

Our task . . . is not to argue either the modernist or traditionalist position. Because our era is marked by both continuity and change, this would be fruitless. Rather, our task is to provide a means of distilling and blending the wisdom in both positions by developing a coherent theoretical framework for the political analysis of interdependence. We shall develop several different but potentially complementary models, or intellectual tools, for grasping the reality of interdependence in contemporary world politics. Equally important, we shall attempt to explore the *conditions* under which each model will be most likely to produce accurate predictions and satisfactory explanations. . . .

Interdependence As An Analytic Concept

In common parlance, *dependence* means a state of being determined or significantly affected by external forces. *Interdependence,* most simply defined, means *mutual* dependence. Interdependence in world politics refers to situations characterized by reciprocal effects among countries or among actors in different countries.

These effects often result from international transactions—flows of money, goods, people, and messages across international boundaries. Such transactions have increased dramatically since World War II: Yet this interconnectedness is not the same as interdependence. The effects of transactions on interdependence will depend on the constraints, or costs, associated with them. A country that imports all of its oil is likely to be more dependent on a continual flow of petroleum than a country importing furs, jewelry, and perfume (even of equivalent monetary value) will be on uninterrupted access to these luxury goods. Where there are reciprocal (although not necessarily symmetrical) costly effects of transactions, there is interdependence. Where interactions do not have significant costly effects, there is simply interconnectedness. The distinction is vital if we are to understand the *politics* of interdependence.

Costly effects may be imposed directly and intentionally by another actor—as in Soviet–American strategic interdependence, which derives from the mutual threat of nuclear destruction. But some costly effects do not come directly or intentionally from other actors. For example, collective action may be necessary to prevent disaster for an alliance (the members of which are interdependent), for an international economic system (which may face chaos because of the absence of coordination, rather than through the malevolence of any actor), or for an ecological system threatened by a gradual increase of industrial effluent.

We do not limit the term *interdependence* to situations of mutual benefit. Such a definition would assume that the concept is only useful analytically where the modernist view of the world prevails: where threats of military force are few and levels of conflict are low. It would exclude from interdependence cases of mutual dependence, such as the strategic interdependence between the United States and the Soviet Union. Furthermore, it would make it very ambiguous whether relations between industrialized countries and less developed countries should be considered interdependent or not. Their inclusion would depend on an inherently subjective judgment about whether the relationships were "mutually beneficial."

Because we wish to avoid sterile arguments about whether a given set of relationships is characterized by interdependence or not, and because we seek to use the concept of interdependence to integrate rather than further to divide modernist and traditional approaches, we choose a broader definition. Our perspective implies that interdependent relationships will always involve costs, since interdependence restricts autonomy; but it is impossible to specify *a priori* whether the benefits of a relationship will exceed the costs. This will depend on the values of the actors as well as on the nature of the relationship. Nothing guarantees that relationships that we designate as "interdependent" will be characterized by mutual benefits.

Two different perspectives can be adopted for analyzing the costs and benefits of an interdependent relationship. The first focuses on the joint gains or joint losses to the parties involved. The other stresses *relative* gains and distributional issues. Classical economists adopted the first approach in formulating their powerful insight about comparative advantage: that undistorted international trade will provide overall net benefits. Unfortunately, an exclusive focus on joint gain may obscure the second key issue: how those gains are divided. Many of the crucial political issues of interdependence revolve around the old question of politics, "who gets what?"

It is important to guard against the assumption that measures that increase joint gain from a relationship will somehow be free of distributional conflict. Governments and nongovernmental organizations will strive to increase their shares of gains from transactions, even when they both profit enormously from the relationship. Oil-exporting governments and multinational oil companies, for instance, share an interest in high prices for petroleum; but they have also been in conflict over shares of the profits involved.

We must therefore be cautious about the prospect that rising interdependence is creating a brave new world of cooperation to replace the bad old world of international conflict. As every parent of small children knows, baking a larger pie does not stop disputes over the size of the slices. An optimistic approach would overlook the uses of economic and even ecological interdependence in competitive international politics.

The difference between traditional international politics and the politics of economic and ecological interdependence is *not* the difference between a world of "zero–sum" (where one side's gain is the other side's loss) and "nonzero–sum" games. Military interdependence need not be zero–sum. Indeed, military allies actively seek interdependence to provide enhanced security for all. Even balance of power situations need not be zero–sum. If one side seeks to upset the status quo, then its gain is at the expense of the other. But if most or all participants want a stable status quo, they can jointly gain by preserving the balance of power among them. Conversely, the politics of economic and ecological interdependence involve competition even when large net benefits can be expected from cooperation. There are important continuities, as well as marked differences, between the traditional politics of military security and the politics of economic and ecological interdependence.

We must also be careful not to define interdependence entirely in terms of situations of *evenly balanced* mutual dependence. It is *asymmetries* in dependence that are most likely to provide sources of influence for actors in their dealings with one another. Less dependent actors can often use the interdependent relationship as a source of power in bargaining over an issue and perhaps to affect other issues. At the other extreme from pure symmetry is pure dependence (sometimes disguised by calling the situation interdependence); but it too is rare. Most cases lie between these two extremes. And that is where the heart of the political bargaining process of interdependence lies.

Power and Interdependence

Power has always been an elusive concept for statesmen and analysts of international politics; now it is even more slippery. The traditional view was that military power dominated other forms, and that states with the most military power controlled world affairs.

But the resources that produce power capabilities have become more complex . . . Hans Morgenthau, author of the leading realist text on international politics, went so far in his reaction to the events of the early 1970s as to announce an historically unprecedented severing of the functional relationship between political, military, and economic power shown in the possession by militarily weak countries of "monopolistic or quasi-monopolistic control of raw materials essential to the operation of advanced economies."

Power can be thought of as the ability of an actor to get others to do something they otherwise would not do (and at an acceptable cost to the actor). Power can also be conceived in terms of control over outcomes. In either case, measurement is not simple. We can look at the initial power resources that give an actor a potential ability; or we can look at that actor's actual influence over patterns of outcomes. When we say that asymmetrical interdependence can be a source of power we are thinking of power as control over resources, or the *potential* to affect outcomes. A less dependent actor in a relationship often has a significant political resource, because changes in the relationship (which the actor may be able to initiate or threaten) will be less costly to that actor than to its partners. This advantage does not guarantee, however, that the political resources provided by favorable asymmetries in interdependence will lead to similar patterns of control over outcomes. There is rarely a one-to-one relationship between power measured by any type of resources and power measured by effects on outcomes. Political bargaining is the usual means of translating potential into effects, and a lot is often lost in the translation.

To understand the role of power in interdependence, we must distinguish between two dimensions, *sensitivity* and *vulnerability.* Sensitivity involves degrees of responsiveness within a policy framework—how quickly do changes in one country bring costly changes in another, and how great are the costly effects? It is measured not merely by the volume of flows across borders but also by the costly effects of changes in transactions on the societies or governments. Sensitivity interdependence is created by interactions within a framework of policies. Sensitivity assumes that the framework remains unchanged. The fact that a set of policies remains constant may reflect the difficulty in formulating new policies within a short time, or it may reflect a commitment to a certain pattern of domestic and international rules.

An example of sensitivity dependence is the way the United States, Japan, and Western Europe were affected by increased oil prices in 1971 and again in 1973–74 and 1975. In the absence of new policies, which could take many years or decades to implement, the sensitivity of these economies was a function of the greater costs of foreign oil and the proportion of petroleum they imported. The United States was less sensitive than Japan to petroleum price rises, because a smaller proportion of its petroleum requirements was accounted for by imports, but as rapid price increases and long lines at gasoline stations showed, the United States was indeed sensitive to the outside change. . . .

Sensitivity interdependence can be social or political as well as economic. For example, there are social "contagion effects," such as . . . the way in which the development of radical student movements during the late 1960s was reinforced by knowledge of each other's activities. The rapid growth of transnational communications has enhanced such sensitivity. Television, by vividly presenting starvation in South Asia to Europeans and Americans about to sit down to their dinners, is almost certain to increase attention to and concern about the issue in European and American societies. Sensitivity to such an issue may be reflected in demonstrations or other political action, even if no action is taken to alleviate the distress (and no economic sensitivity thereby results).

Using the word *interdependence,* however, to refer only to sensitivity obscures some of the most important political aspects of mutual dependence. We must also consider what the situation would be if the framework of policies could be changed. If more alternatives were available, and new and very different policies were possible, what would be the costs of adjusting to the outside change? In petroleum, for instance, what matters is not only the proportion of one's needs that is imported, but the alternatives to imported energy and the costs of pursuing those alternatives. Two countries, each importing 35 percent of their petroleum needs, may seem equally sensitive to price rises; but if one could shift to domestic sources at moderate cost, and the other had no such alternative, the second state would be more *vulnerable* than the first. The vulnerability dimension of interdependence rests on the relative availability and costliness of the alternative that various actors face.

Under the Bretton Woods monetary regime during the late 1960s, both the United States and Great Britain were sensitive to decisions by foreign speculators or central banks to shift assets out of dollars or sterling, respectively. But the United States was less vulnerable than Britain because it had the option (which it exercised in August 1971) of changing the rules of the system at what it considered tolerable costs. The underlying capabilities of the United States reduced its vulnerability, and therefore made its sensitivity less serious politically.

In terms of the costs of dependence, sensitivity means liability to costly effects imposed from outside before policies are altered to try to change the situation. Vulnerability can be defined as an actor's liability to suffer costs imposed by external events even after policies have been altered. Since it is usually difficult to change policies quickly, immediate effects of external changes generally reflect sensitivity dependence. Vulnerability dependence can be measured only by the costliness of making effective adjustments to a changed environment over a period of time.

Vulnerability is particularly important for understanding the political structure of interdependence relationships. In a sense, it focuses on which actors are "the definers of the *ceteris paribus* clause," or can set the rules of the game. Vulnerability is clearly more relevant than sensitivity, for example, in analyzing the politics of raw materials such as the supposed transformation of power after 1973. All too often, a high percentage of imports of a material is taken as an index of vulnerability, when by itself it merely suggests that sensitivity may be high. The key question for determining vulnerability is how effectively altered policies could bring into being sufficient quantities of this, or a comparable, raw material, and at what cost. The fact that the United States imports approximately 85 percent of its bauxite supply does not indicate American vulnerability to actions by bauxite exporters, until we know what it would cost (in time as well as money) to obtain substitutes.

How does this distinction help us understand the relationship between interdependence and power? Clearly, it indicates that sensitivity interdependence will be less important than vulnerability interdependence in providing power resources to actors. If one actor can reduce its costs by altering its policy, either domestically or internationally, the sensitivity patterns will not be a good guide to power resources.

Consider trade in agriculatural products between the United States and the Soviet Union from 1972 to 1975. Initially, the American economy was highly sensitive to Soviet grain purchases: prices of grain rose dramatically in the United States. The Soviet Union was also sensitive to the availability of surplus American stocks, since its absence could have internal political as well as economic implications. The vulnerability asymmetries, however, ran strongly in favor of the United States, since its alternatives to selling grain to the USSR (such as government storage, lower domestic prices, and more food aid abroad) were more attractive than the basic Soviet alternative to buying grain from the United States (slaughtering livestock and reducing meat consumption). Thus, as long as the United States government could retain coherent control of the policy—that is, as long as interest groups with a stake in expanded trade did not control it—agricultural trade could be used as a tool in political bargaining with the Soviet Union.

Vulnerability interdependence includes the strategic dimension that sensitivity interdependence omits, but this does not mean that sensitivity is politically unimportant. Rapidly rising sensitivity often leads to complaints about interdependence and political efforts to alter it, particularly in countries with pluralistic political systems. Textile and steel workers and manufacturers, oil consumers, and conservatives suspicious of radical movements originating abroad are all likely to demand government policies to protect their interests. Policymakers and policy analysts, however, must examine underlying patterns of vulnerability interdependence when they decide on strategies. What can they do, at what cost? And what can other actors do, at what cost, in response? Although patterns of sensitivity interdependence may explain where the shoe pinches or the wheel squeaks, coherent policy must be based on an analysis of actual and potential vulnerabilities. An attempt to manipulate asymmetrical sensitivity interdependence without regard for underlying patterns of vulnerability is likely to fail.

Manipulating economic or sociopolitical vulnerabilities, however, also bears risks. Strategies of manipulating interdependence are likely to lead to counterstrategies. It must always be kept in mind, furthermore, that military power dominates economic power in the sense that economic means alone are likely to be ineffective against the serious use of military force. Thus, even effective manipulation of asymmetrical interdependence within a nonmilitary area can create risks of military counteraction. When the United States exploited Japanese vulnerability to economic embargo in 1940–41, Japan countered by attacking Pearl Harbor and the Philippines. Yet military actions are usually very costly; and for many types of actions, these costs have risen steeply during the last thirty years.

Table 1 shows the three types of asymmetrical interdependence that we have been discussing. The dominance ranking column indicates that the power resources provided by military interdependence dominate those provided by nonmilitary vulnerability, which in turn dominate those provided by asymmetries in sensitivity. Yet exercising more dominant forms of power brings higher costs. Thus, *relative to cost,* there is no guarantee that military means will be more effective than economic ones to achieve a given purpose. We can expect, however, that as the interests at stake become more important, actors will tend to use power resources that rank higher in both dominance and cost.

A movement from one power resource to a more effective, but more costly, resource, will be most likely where there is a substantial *incongruity*

Table 1. Asymmetrical Interdependence and its Uses

Source of Interdependence	Dominance ranking	Cost ranking	Contemporary use
Military (costs of using military force)	1	1	Used in extreme situations or against weak foes when costs may be slight.
Nonmilitary vulnerability (costs of pursuing alternative policies)	2	2	Used when normative constraints are low, and international rules are not considered binding (including nonmilitary relations between adversaries, and situations of extremely high conflict between close partners and allies).
Nonmilitary sensitivity (costs of change under existing policies)	3	3	A power resource in the short run or when normative constraints are high and international rules are binding. Limited, since if high costs are imposed, disadvantaged actors may formulate new policies.

between the distribution of power resources on one dimension and those on another. In such a situation, the disadvantaged actor's power position would be improved by raising the level at which the controversy is conducted. For instance, in a concession agreement, a multinational oil company may seem to have a better bargaining position than the host government. The agreement may allow the company to set the level of output, and the price, of the petroleum produced, thus making government revenues sensitive to company decisions. Yet such a situation is inherently unstable, since the government may be stronger on the vulnerability dimension. Once the country has determined that it can afford to alter the agreement unilaterally, it may have the upper hand. Any attempt by the company to take advantage of its superior position on the sensitivity dimension, without recognizing its weakness at the vulnerability level (much less at the level of military force) is then likely to end in disaster.

We conclude that a useful beginning in the political analysis of international interdependence can be made by thinking of asymmetrical interdependencies as sources of power among actors. Such a framework can be applied to relations between transnational actors (such as multinational corporations) and governments as well as interstate relations. Different types of interdependence lead to potential political influence, but under different constraints. Sensitivity interdependence can provide the basis for significant political influence only when the rules and norms in effect can be taken for granted, or when it would be prohibitively costly for dissatisfied states to change their policies quickly. If one set of rules puts an actor in a disadvantageous position, that actor will probably try to change those rules if it can do so at reasonable cost. Thus influence deriving from favorable asymmetries in sensitivity is very limited when the underlying asymmetries in vulnerability are unfavorable. Likewise, if a state chafes at its economic vulnerabilities, it may use military force to attempt to redress that situation as Japan did in 1941; or, it may subtly threaten to use force, as did the United States in 1975, when facing the possibility of future oil boycotts. But in many contemporary situations, the use of force is so costly, and its threat so difficult to make credible, that a military strategy is an act of desperation.

Yet this is not the whole story of power and interdependence. Just as important as understanding the way that manipulation of interdependence can be an instrument of power is an understanding of that instrument's limits. Asymmetrical interdependence by itself cannot explain bargaining outcomes, even in traditional relations among states. As we said earlier, power measured in terms of resources or potential may look different from power measured in terms of influence over outcomes. We must also look at the "translation" in the political bargaining process. One of the most important reasons for this is that the commitment of a weaker state may be much greater than that of its stronger partner. The more dependent actor may be (or appear to be) more willing to suffer. At the politico-military level, the United States' attempt to coerce North Vietnam provides an obvious example.

Yet the point holds even in more cooperative interstate relations. In the Canadian-American relationship, for example, the use or threat of force is virtually excluded from consideration by either side. The fact that Canada has less military strength than the United States is therefore not a major factor in the bargaining process. The Canadians can take advantage of their superior position on such economic issues as oil and natural gas exports without fearing military retaliation or threat by the United States. Moreover, other conditions of contemporary international interdependence tend to limit the abilities of statesmen to manipulate asymmetrical interdependence. In particular, the smaller state may have greater internal political unity than the larger one. Even though the more powerful state may be less dependent in aggregate terms, it may be more fragmented internally and its coherence reduced by conflicts of interest and difficulties of coordination within its own government.

. . . . What we have said is sufficient to indicate that we do not expect a measure of potential power, such as asymmetrical interdependence, to predict perfectly actors' successes or failures at influencing outcomes. It merely provides a first approximation of initial bargaining advantages available to either side. Where predictions based on patterns of asymmetrical interdependence are incorrect, one must look closely for the reasons. They will often be found in the bargaining process that translates power resources into power over outcomes.

International Regime Change

Understanding the concept of interdependence and its relevance to the concept of power is necessary to answering the first major question of this book— what are the characteristics of world politics under conditions of extensive interdependence? Yet as we have indicated, relationships of interdependence often occur within, and may be affected by, networks of rules, norms, and procedures that regularize behavior and control its effects. We refer to the sets of governing arrangements that affect relationships of interdependence as *international regimes*. Although not so obvious as the political bargaining process, equally important to understanding power and interdependence is our second major question: How and why do regimes change?

In world politics rules and procedures are neither so complete nor so well enforced as in well-ordered domestic political systems, and the institutions are neither so powerful nor so autonomous. The weakness of international organizations and the problems of enforcing international law sometimes mislead observers into thinking that international regimes are insignificant, or into ignoring them entirely. Yet although overall global integration is weak, specific international regimes often have important effects on interdependent relationships that involve a few countries, or involve many countries on a specific issue. Since World War II, for instance, specific sets of rules and procedures have been developed to guide states and transnational actors in a wide variety of areas, including aid to less developed countries, environmental protection, fisheries conservation, international food policy, international meteorological coordination, international monetary policy, regulation of multinational corporations, international shipping policy, international telecommunications policy, and international trade. In some cases these regimes have been formal and comprehensive; in others informal and partial. Their effectiveness has varied from issue-area to issue-area and from time to time. On a more selective or regional level, specific groups of countries such as those in the European Community or the Organization for Economic Cooperation and Development (OECD) have developed regimes that affect several aspects of their countries' relationships with each other.

International regimes may be incorporated into interstate agreements or treaties, as were the international monetary arrangements developed at Bretton Woods in 1944, or they may evolve from proposed formal arrangements that were never implemented, as was the General Agreement on Tariffs and Trade (GATT), which derived from the International Trade Organization proposed after World War II. Or they may be merely implicit, as in the postwar Canadian–American relationship. They vary not only in their extensiveness but in the degree of adherence they receive from major actors. When there are no agreed norms and procedures or when the exceptions to the rules are more important than the instances of adherence, there is a *nonregime* situation.

To understand the international regimes that affect patterns of interdependence, one must look . . . at structure and process in international systems, as well as at how they affect each other. The *structure* of a system refers to the distribution of capabilities among similar units. In international political systems the most important units are states, and the relevant capabilities have been regarded as their power resources. There is a long tradition of categorizing the distribution of power in interstate systems according to the number and importance of major actors (for instance, as unipolar, bipolar, multipolar, and dispersed) just as economists describe the structure of market systems as monopolistic, duopolistic, oligopolistic, and competitive. Structure is therefore distinguished from *process,* which refers to allocative or bargaining behavior within a power structure. To use the analogy of a poker game, at the process level analysts are interested in how the players play the hands they have been dealt. At the structural level they are interested in how the cards and chips were distributed as the game started.

International regimes are intermediate factors between the power structure of an international system and the political and economic bargaining that takes place within it. The structure of the system (the distribution of power resources among states) profoundly affects the nature of the regime (the more or less loose set of formal and informal norms, rules, and procedures relevant to the system). The regime, in turn, affects and to some extent governs the political bargaining and daily decision-making that occurs within the system.

Changes in international regimes are very important. In international trade, for example, an international regime including nondiscriminatory trade practices was laid down by the General Agreement on Tariffs and Trade (GATT) in 1947. For almost three decades, the GATT arrangements have constituted a relatively effective international regime. But the last decade, particularly since the first United Nations Conference on Trade and Development in 1964, has been marked by the partly successful efforts of less developed countries to change this regime. More broadly, by the mid-1970s, the demands of less developed countries for a New International Economic Order involved struggles over what international regimes should govern trade in raw materials and manufactures as well as direct foreign investment.

In the two issue areas . . . —money and oceans—some regime changes have been rapid and dramatic whereas others have been gradual. Dramatic changes took place in international monetary policy in 1914 (suspension of the gold standard); 1931 (abandonment of the gold-exchange standard); 1944 (agreement on the "Bretton Woods System"); and 1971 (abandonment of the convertibility of dollars into gold). Rules governing the uses of the world's oceans changed more slowly, but with significant turning points in 1945 and after 1967. Yet we have no theory in the field of international relations that adequately explains such changes. Indeed, most of our theories do not focus on this question at all.

. . . . Since world politics varies, over time and from place to place, there is no reason to believe that a single set of conditions will always and everywhere apply, or that any one model is likely to be universally applicable. Thus, before examining the explanatory models, we shall establish the conditions under which they can be expected to apply. . . .

Realism and Complex Interdependence

ROBERT O. KEOHANE AND JOSEPH S. NYE

One's assumptions about world politics profoundly affect what one sees and how one constructs theories to explain events. We believe that the assumptions of political realists, whose theories dominated the postwar period, are often an inadequate basis for analyzing the politics of interdependence. The realist assumptions about world politics can be seen as defining an extreme set of conditions or ideal type. One could also imagine very different conditions. In this chapter, we shall construct another ideal type, the opposite of realism. We call it complex interdependence. After establishing the differences between realism and complex interdependence, we shall argue that complex interdependence sometimes comes closer to reality than does realism. When it does, traditional explanations of change in international regimes become questionable and the search for new explanatory models becomes more urgent.

For political realists, international politics, like all other politics, is a struggle for power but, unlike domestic politics, a struggle dominated by organized violence. . . . Three assumptions are integral to the realist vision. First, states as coherent units are the dominant actors in world politics. This is a double assumption: states are predominant; and they act as coherent units. Second, realists assume that force is a usable and effective instrument of policy. Other instruments may also be employed, but using or threatening force is the most effective means of wielding power. Third, partly because of their second assumption, realists assume a hierarchy of issues in world politics, headed by questions of military security: the "high politics" of military security dominates the "low politics" of economic and social affairs.

These realist assumptions define an ideal type of world politics. They allow us to imagine a world in which politics is continually characterized by

133

active or potential conflict among states, with the use of force possible at any time. Each state attempts to defend its territory and interests from real or perceived threats. Political integration among states is slight and lasts only as long as it serves the national interests of the most powerful states. Transnational actors either do not exist or are politically unimportant. Only the adept exercise of force or the threat of force permits states to survive, and only while statesmen succeed in adjusting their interests, as in a well-functioning balance of power, is the system stable.

Each of the realist assumptions can be challenged. If we challenge them all simultaneously, we can imagine a world in which actors other than states participate directly in world politics, in which a clear hierarchy of issues does not exist, and in which force is an ineffective instrument of policy. Under these conditions—which we call the characteristics of complex interdependence—one would expect world politics to be very different than under realist conditions.

The Characteristics of Complex Interdependence

Complex interdependence has three main characteristics:

1. *Multiple channels* connect societies, including: informal ties between governmental elites as well as formal foreign office arrangements; informal ties among nongovernmental elites (face-to-face and through telecommunications); and transnational organizations (such as multinational banks or corporations). These channels can be summarized as interstate, transgovernmental, and transnational relations. *Interstate* relations are the normal channels assumed by realists. *Transgovernmental* applies when we relax the realist assumption that states act coherently as units; *transnational* applies when we relax the assumption that states are the only units.

2. The agenda of interstate relationships consists of multiple issues that are not arranged in a clear or consistent hierarchy. This *absence of hierarchy among issues* means, among other things, that military security does not consistently dominate the agenda. Many issues arise from what used to be considered domestic policy, and the distinction between domestic and foreign issues becomes blurred. These issues are considered in several government departments (not just foreign offices), and at several levels. Inadequate policy coordination on these issues involves significant costs. Different issues generate different coalitions, both within governments and across them, and involve different degrees of conflict. Politics does not stop at the waters' edge.

3. Military force is not used by governments toward other governments within the region, or on the issues, when complex interdependence prevails. It may, however, be important in these governments' relations with governments outside that region, or on other issues. Military force could, for instance, be irrelevant to resolving disagreements on economic issues among members of an alliance, yet at the same time be very important for that alliance's political and military relations with a rival bloc. For the former

relationships this condition of complex interdependence would be met; for the latter, it would not.

Traditional theories of international politics implicitly or explicitly deny the accuracy of these three assumptions. Traditionalists are therefore tempted also to deny the relevance of criticisms based on the complex interdependence ideal type. We believe, however, that our three conditions are fairly well approximated on some global issues of economic and ecological interdependence and that they come close to characterizing the entire relationship between some countries. . . .

The Political Processes of Complex Interdependence

The three main characteristics of complex interdependence give rise to distinctive political processes, which translate power resources into power as control of outcomes. As we argued earlier, something is usually lost or added in the translation. Under conditions of complex interdependence the translation will be different than under realist conditions, and our predictions about outcomes will need to be adjusted accordingly.

In the realist world, military security will be the dominant goal of states. It will even affect issues that are not directly involved with military power or territorial defense. Nonmilitary problems will not only be subordinated to military ones; they will be studied for their politico-military implications. Balance of payments issues, for instance, will be considered at least as much in the light of their implications for world power generally as for their purely financial ramifications. . . .

In a world of complex interdependence, however, one expects some officials, particularly at lower levels, to emphasize the *variety* of state goals that must be pursued. In the absence of a clear hierarchy of issues, goals will vary by issue, and may not be closely related. Each bureaucracy will pursue its own concerns; and although several agencies may reach compromises on issues that affect them all, they will find that a consistent pattern of policy is difficult to maintain. Moreover, transnational actors will introduce different goals into various groups of issues.

Linkage Strategies

Goals will therefore vary by issue area under complex interdependence, but so will the distribution of power and the typical political processes. Traditional analysis focuses on *the* international system, and leads us to anticipate similar political processes on a variety of issues. Militarily and economically strong states will dominate a variety of organizations and a variety of issues, by linking their own policies on some issues to other states' policies on other issues. By using their overall dominance to prevail on their weak issues, the strongest states will, in the traditional model, ensure a congruence between the overall structure of military and economic power and the pattern of outcomes on any one issue area. Thus world politics can be treated as a seamless web.

Under complex interdependence, such congruence is less likely to occur. As military force is devalued, militarily strong states will find it more difficult to use their overall dominance to control outcomes on issues in which they are weak. And since the distribution of power resources in trade, shipping, or oil, for example, may be quite different, patterns of outcomes and distinctive political processes are likely to vary from one set of issues to another. If force were readily applicable, and military security were the highest foreign policy goal, these variations in the issue structures of power would not matter very much. The linkages drawn from them to military issues would ensure consistent dominance by the overall strongest states. But when military force is largely immobilized, strong states will find that linkage is less effective. They may still attempt such links, but in the absence of a hierarchy of issues, their success will be problematic.

Dominant states may try to secure much the same result by using overall economic power to affect results on other issues. If only economic objectives are at stake, they may succeed: money, after all, is fungible. But economic objectives have political implications, and economic linkage by the strong is limited by domestic, transnational, and transgovernmental actors who resist having their interests traded off. Furthermore, the international actors may be different on different issues, and the international organizations in which negotiations take place are often quite separate. Thus it is difficult, for example, to imagine a militarily or economically strong state linking concessions on monetary policy to reciprocal concessions in oceans policy. . . .

Thus as the utility of force declines, and as issues become more equal in importance, the distribution of power within each issue will become more important. If linkages become less effective on the whole, outcomes of political bargaining will increasingly vary by issue area.

Agenda Setting

Our second assumption of complex interdependence, the lack of clear hierarchy among multiple issues, leads us to expect that the politics of agenda formation and control will become more important. Traditional analyses lead statesmen to focus on politico-military issues and to pay little attention to the broader politics of agenda formation. Statesmen assume that the agenda will be set by shifts in the balance of power, actual or anticipated, and by perceived threats to the security of states. Other issues will only be very important when they seem to affect security and military power. In these cases, agendas will be influenced strongly by considerations of the overall balance of power.

Yet, today, some nonmilitary issues are emphasized in interstate relations at one time, whereas others of seemingly equal importance are neglected or quietly handled at a technical level. International monetary politics, problems of commodity terms of trade, oil, food, and multinational corporations have all been important during the last decade; but not all have been high on interstate agendas throughout that period.

Traditional analysts of international politics have paid little attention to agenda formation: to how issues come to receive sustained attention by high officials. The traditional orientation toward military and security affairs implies that the crucial problems of foreign policy are imposed on states by the actions or threats of other states. These are high politics as opposed to the low politics of economic affairs. Yet, as the complexity of actors and issues in world politics increases, the utility of force declines and the line between domestic policy and foreign policy becomes blurred: as the conditions of complex interdependence are more closely approximated, the politics of agenda formation becomes more subtle and differentiated.

Under complex interdependence we can expect the agenda to be affected by the international and domestic problems created by economic growth and increasing sensitivity interdependence. . . . Discontented domestic groups will politicize issues and force more issues once considered domestic onto the interstate agenda. Shifts in the distribution of power resources within sets of issues will also affect agendas. During the early 1970s the increased power of oil-producing governments over the transnational corporations and the consumer countries dramatically altered the policy agenda. Moreover, agendas for one group of issues may change as a result of linkages from other groups in which power resources are changing; for example, the broader agenda of North–South trade issues changed after the OPEC price rises and the oil embargo of 1973–74. Even if capabilities among states do not change, agendas may be affected by shifts in the importance of transnational actors. . . .

Transnational and Transgovernmental Relations

Our third condition of complex interdependence, multiple channels of contact among societies, further blurs the distinction between domestic and international politics. The availability of partners in political coalitions is not necessarily limited by national boundaries as traditional analysis assumes. The nearer a situation is to complex interdependence, the more we expect the outcomes of political bargaining to be affected by transnational relations. Multinational corporations may be significant both as independent actors and as instruments manipulated by governments. The attitudes and policy stands of domestic groups are likely to be affected by communications, organized or not, between them and their counterparts abroad.

The multiple channels of contact found in complex interdependence are not limited to nongovernmental actors. Contacts between governmental bureaucracies charged with similar tasks may not only alter their perspectives but lead to transgovernmental coalitions on particular policy questions. To improve their chances of success, government agencies attempt to bring actors from other governments into their own decision-making processes as allies. Agencies of powerful states such as the United States have used such coalitions to penetrate weaker governments in such countries as Turkey and Chile. They have also been used to help agencies of other governments penetrate the United States bureaucracy. . . .

The existence of transgovernmental policy networks leads to a different interpretation of one of the standard propositions about international politics—that states act in their own interest. Under complex interdependence, this conventional wisdom begs two important questions: which self and which interest? A government agency may pursue its own interests under the guise of the national interest; and recurrent interactions can change official perceptions of their interests. . . .

The ambiguity of the national interest raises serious problems for the top political leaders of governments. As bureaucracies contact each other directly across national borders (without going through foreign offices), centralized control becomes more difficult. There is less assurance that the state will be united when dealing with foreign governments or that its components will interpret national interests similarly when negotiating with foreigners. The state may prove to be multifaceted, even schizophrenic. National interests will be defined differently on different issues, at different times, and by different governmental units. States that are better placed to maintain their coherence (because of a centralized political tradition such as France's) will be better able to manipulate uneven interdependence than fragmented states that at first glance seem to have more resources in an issue area.

Role of International Organizations

Finally, the existence of multiple channels leads one to predict a different and significant role for international organizations in world politics. Realists in the tradition of Hans J. Morgenthau have portrayed a world in which states, acting from self-interest, struggle for "power and peace." Security issues are dominant; war threatens. In such a world, one may assume that international institutions will have a minor role, limited by the rare congruence of such interests. International organizations are then clearly peripheral to world politics. But in a world of multiple issues, perfectly linked, in which coalitions are formed transnationally and transgovernmentally, the potential role of international institutions in political bargaining is greatly increased. In particular, they help set the international agenda, and act as catalysts for coalition-formation and as arenas for political initiatives and linkage by weak states.

Complex interdependence therefore yields different political patterns than does the realist conception of the world (Table 2 summarizes these differences.) Thus, one would expect traditional theories to fail to explain international regime change in situations of complex interdependence. But, for a situation that approximates realist conditions, traditional theories should be appropriate. . . .

Table 2. Political Processes Under Conditions of Realism and Complex Interdependence

	Realism	Complex Interdependence
Goals of actors	Military security will be the dominant goal.	Goals of states will vary by issue area. Transgovernmental politics will make goals difficult to define. Transnational actors will pursue their own goals.
Instruments of state policy	Military force will be most effective, although economic and other instruments will also be used.	Power resources specific to issue areas will be more relevant. Manipulation of interdependence, international organizations, and transnational actors will be major instruments.
Agenda formation	Potential shifts in the balance of power and security threats will set agenda in high politics and will strongly influence other agendas.	Agenda will be affected by changes in the distribution of power resources within issue areas; the status of international regimes; changes in the importance of transnational actors; linkages from other issues and politicization as a result of rising sensitivity interdependence.
Linkages of issues	Linkages will reduce differences in outcomes among issue areas and reinforce international hierarchy.	Linkages by strong states will be more difficult to make since force will be ineffective. Linkages by weak states through international organizations will erode rather than reinforce hierarchy.
Roles of international organizations	Roles are minor, limited by state power and the importance of military force.	Organizations will set agendas, induce coalition-formation, and act as arenas for political action by weak states. Ability to choose the organizational forum for an issue and to mobilize votes will be an important political resource.

5

Contemporary Marxist Currents

Marxism after Marx is replete with lively disagreements and creative tension. Neo-Marxists contend among themselves, as well as with post-Marxists and non-Marxists, on many questions: the formation of "late capitalism," the possibilities of economic development in the periphery of the world-economy, the nature of the state, to name but a few. Of the many strands of thought, two that have been especially influential in recent IPE theory are the world-systems perspective, here represented by the writing of Christopher Chase-Dunn, and the Gramscian view of Robert Cox.

Chase-Dunn begins with a theoretical critique of two interpretations of how politics and economics relate internationally. He argues against "economism," the simplistic assumption that economics determines politics and he finds fault with "historicism," which denies the possibility of underlying social laws and is a failing of those who "focus on exclusively political relations." Economics and politics, while in some ways discrete processes, are interactive and linked by one common logic: the accumulation of capital. Thus, Chase-Dunn constructs a "holistic" IPE theory that views an economic process, capital accumulation, as a crucial integrating force. Immanuel Wallerstein's discussion of capitalism as a world-system, is, for Chase-Dunn, the most promising framework for IPE theory precisely because it avoids the pitfalls of both economism and historicism.

Chase-Dunn explores Wallerstein's reconceptualization of capitalism as a global mode of production. Where other neo-Marxist theories, most notably dependency theory, are based largely upon economic forces, Wallerstein's capitalist world-system is composed of two complementary subsystems: a world-economy driven by the exigencies of accumulation, and an "interstate system"

141

based upon the distribution of politico-military power among states in a formally anarchic environment. Chase-Dunn sees the two as "part of the same interactive socioeconomic system." How are they related to one another? The interstate system provides the political context for the world market. A balance of power among a number of leading states inhibits the development of a single overarching political authority that could subvert international production and exchange. In short, the economic vigor of capitalism depends upon a competitive interstate system.

The interstate system, in turn, is critically influenced by world economic forces. The process of accumulation is responsible for the longevity of the international political system, elements of which can be traced back to early Renaissance Italy. Chase-Dunn argues that unequal economic development favors some countries at some times (i.e., hegemonic core powers), but such advantages are ephemeral in the long term because technology diffuses globally and offers new economic opportunities to other countries. This economic dynamic prevents any one state from growing into a permanent world-imperial power, thus promoting the maintenance of a competitive interstate system. In addition, contradictions among internationalist and nationalist fractions of the bourgeoisie within a hegemonic core power undermine that state's rise to permanent world domination. Economic forces also work against attempts by second-rank powers to impose a new international political order. The Hapsburgs, Louis IV, Napoleon, and Hitler all were unable to harness the changing fortunes of uneven development and failed in their bids for world-empire.

Chase-Dunn foresees continuing interimperial rivalry, contending national identities and interests of the economically most powerful countries, as both inevitable, due to uneven development, and essential for the maintenance of the system as a whole. On this point Robert Cox disagrees.

Cox's Gramscian analysis highlights cooperation and consensus among the most powerful global economic actors. Gramsci's notion of a "historic bloc," a combination of the objective (i.e., productive forces) and subjective (i.e., ideas and culture) elements of capitalism at a particular time and place, is used by Cox to describe post–World War II international political economy. At present, transnational production and finance enable national elites to merge into a *nebuleuse*, "governance without government," a shared worldview of neoclassical economic orthodoxy that narrows differences of national policies and leads ultimately to the "internationalizing of the state." The result is "global *perestroika*," a concerted worldwide effort to reduce state intervention in markets, which allows accumulation to proceed unfettered by social and political concerns. Cox thus sees the centers of global capital growing closer together.

He does not ignore uneven development but sees it as working itself out on regional, both micro- and macro-, levels and less in terms of nation-states. Macroregions—the European Community is perhaps the best example—are concrete examples of the internationalizing of the state, and function to rationalize economic management in the core of the world-economy; poorer countries have little to gain from integration of the rich. Microregions represent a more complex distribution of global wealth: certain areas within rich countries benefit more than others. Uneven development therefore doubly undermines state power, simultaneously dissolving it into internationalized macroregions and fragmenting it into particularistic microregions. State sovereignty is increasingly constrained, and state capacity to smooth out distributional differences is gradually declining.

Cox also foresees greater possibility for alternative political action or, in Gramscian terms, counterhegemony. World-systems analysis, in emphasizing global economic dynamics, tends to discount the possibility of genuine liberation from capitalism, except on a world-systemic level. Cox, drawing on Gramsci's less deterministic view of politics, suggests that "new social movements," mobilized around specific issues and identities, have the potential to coalesce into a new historic bloc that might challenge the power of capital in certain localities. Although Cox would agree with much of Chase-Dunn's theorizing, especially the general explication of capital as a global mode of production, he differs from the world-systems approach by seeing greater variation and flexibility within contemporary capitalism.

Interstate System and Capitalist World-Economy: One Logic or Two?

CHRISTOPHER CHASE-DUNN

This article attempts to clarify a number of issues arising from the critique of Immanuel Wallerstein's (1979) world-system perspective, which is a reinterpretation of the theory of capitalist development inspired by dependency theory. In this perspective, capitalism as a mode of production has always been "imperialistic" in the sense that it constitutes a hierarchical division of labor between core areas and peripheral areas. Wallerstein (1974) has traced the emergence of this capitalist world economy from European feudalism in the long sixteenth century. Viewed as a whole, the modern world-system has exhibited cyclical patterns and secular trends as it has expanded to include the entire globe. . . .

The elaboration of this perspective has raised anew the issue of the relationship between economic and political processes in the capitalist mode of production, and this has occurred in the context of a renaissance of Marxist theories of the state. This burgeoning Marxist literature has, as a response to the so-called "economism" of the Stalinist Third International, emphasized the autonomy of political processes and the "relative autonomy of the state." Though most of this literature has focused on the capitalist state and its relationship to the power of social classes, this emphasis on the autonomy of political factors has spilled over to the more recent critiques of Wallerstein's alleged "economism." These critiques advance claims about the relative autonomy of the interstate system and the processes of geopolitics.

In addition to the neo-Marxist argument a number of non-Marxist political

Reprinted from *International Studies Quarterly,* Vol. 25, No. 1, March 1981, "Interstate System and Capitalist World-Economy: One Logic or Two?" Christopher Chase-Dunn by permission of *International Studies Quarterly.* © 1981.

scientists have made similar criticisms. All these authors claim that Wallerstein has reduced the operation of the state system (or "international" system) to a consequence of the process of capital accumulation. Indeed, some have contended that geopolitics and state building are themselves the main motors of the modern world-system. Here I will argue that the capitalist mode of production exhibits a single logic in which both political–military power and the appropriation of surplus value through production and sale on the world market play an integrated role. This article will raise a number of methodological and metatheoretical issues, argue for a redefinition of the capitalist mode of production, and discuss evidence for the interdependence of the interstate system and the capital accumulation process.

Metatheoretical and Methodological Issues

In this article, rather than argue at the philosophical level about economics, politics, and political economy in general, I shall ground the discussion in the particular processes which have been operating in the capitalist world economy since the sixteenth century. However, before I advance my arguments that the state system and the capital accumulation process are part of the same interactive socioeconomic system, I should like to discuss briefly a number of methodological problems raised by this issue.

Why have many theorists who focus on politics tended to adopt a narrowly historicist approach to capitalist development? Marx made a broad distinction between the growth of the forces of production (technology), which occurs in the capital accumulation process, and the reorganization of social relations of production (class relations, forms of property, and other institutions which structure exploitation and the accumulation process). The widening of the world market and the deepening of commodity production to more and more spheres of life have occurred in a series of semiperiodic waves which Kondratieff called "longwaves." These and other economic phenomena seem to be associated with "noneconomic" political events such as wars, revolutions, and so on. This has caused some economists to argue that long waves are not really *economic* cycles at all, but are set off by "exogenous" political events.

The causality and interrelationship among wars, revolutions, and long business cycles is not precisely understood, but the accumulation process expands within a certain political framework to the point where that framework is no longer adequate to the scale of world commodity production and distribution. Thus world wars and the rise and fall of hegemonic core powers (Netherlands, Britain, and the United States) can be understood as the violent reorganization of production relations on a world scale, which allows the accumulation process to adjust to its own contradictions and to begin again on a new scale. Political relations among core powers and the colonial empires which are the formal political structure of core-periphery relations are reorganized in a way which allows the increasing internationalization of capitalist production. Wallerstein's observation that capitalism has always been "international" (and transnational) does not contradict the existence of a long-run increase in the proportion of all production decisions and commodity chains which cross state boundaries.

The above discussion does not establish causal priority between accumulation and political reorganization, but it indicates that these are truly interdependent processes. The tendency toward narrow historicism by those who focus on political events may be due to the greater irregularity of politics and the apparently more direct involvement of human collective rationality in political movements. On the other hand, the overemphasis on determinism and mechanical models of development by those who focus exclusively on "economic" processes may be due to the greater regularity of these phenomena and their lawlike market aggregation of many individual wills uncontrolled by rational collective action. Politics seems less systematic and predictable because human freedom is involved, while economic patterns seem more systematic and determined by forces beyond human will.

These perceptions are correct to a considerable extent precisely because capitalism as a system mystifies the social nature of investment decisions by separating the calculation of profit to the enterprise from the calculation of more general social needs. Anticapitalist movements have tried to reintegrate economics and politics in practice, but up to now the scale of the commodity economy has evaded them. Even the "socialist" states have not succeeded in creating a collectively rational and democratic mode of production. The interstate system itself is the fundamental basis of the competitive commodity economy at the system level. Thus the interaction of world market and state system is fundamental to an understanding of capitalist development and its potential transformation into a more collectively rational system. Neither mechanical determinism nor narrow historicism is useful in this project.

Capitalism as a Mode of Production

The critiques of Wallerstein contain implicit assumptions about the nature of capitalism which tend to conceptualize it as an exclusively "economic" process. Skocpol (1979:22) formulates the issue by arguing that Wallersteinians "assume that individual nation-states are instruments used by economically dominant groups to pursue world-market oriented development at home and international economic advantages abroad." She continues, explaining her own position:

> But a different perspective is adopted here, one which holds that nation-states are, more fundamentally, organizations geared to maintain control of home territories and populations and to undertake actual or potential military competition with other states in the international system. The international states system as a transnational structure of military competition was not originally created by capitalism. Throughout modern world history, it represents an analytically autonomous level of transnational reality—*interdependent* in its structure and dynamics with world capitalism, but not reducible to it.

[Other scholars] argue even more strongly for the autonomy of the state system in opposition to what they see as Wallerstein's economic reductionism. These authors raise the important question about the extent to which it is theoretically valuable to conceptualize economic and political processes as independent sub-systems, but in so doing they oversimplify Wallerstein's perspective. Wallerstein's work suggests a reconceptualization of the capitalist mode of production itself, such that references to capitalism do not point simply to market-oriented strategies for accumulating surplus value. According to Wallerstein, the capitalist mode of production is a system in which groups pursue both political–military and profitable strategies, and the winners are those who effectively combine the two. Thus the state system, state building, and geopolitics are the political side of the capitalist mode of production.

This mode of production is a feature of the whole world-system, not its parts. Wallerstein distinguishes between world empires and world economies. A world empire is a socioeconomic system in which the economic division of labor is incorporated within a single overarching state apparatus. A world economy is an economic division of labor which is overlaid by a multicentric system of states. The political system of capitalism is not the state, but the larger competitive state system. Particular states exhibit more or fewer tendencies toward politicomilitary aggrandizement or free market accumulation depending on their position in the larger system, and the system as a whole goes through periods in which state power is more generally employed versus periods in which a relatively free world market of commodity exchange comes to the fore.

Hegemonic core states with a clear competitive advantage in production advocate free trade. Similarly, peripheral states in the control of peripheral capitalist producers of low-wage goods for export to the core support the "open economy" of free international exchange. Smaller core states heavily dependent on international trade tend to support a liberal economic order. Semi-peripheral states and core states contending for hegemony utilize protectionism and mercantilist monopoly to protect and expand their access to world surplus value. Periods of rapid worldwide economic growth are characterized by a relatively unobstructed world market of commodity exchange as the interests of consumers in low prices come to outweigh the interests of producers in protection. In periods of stagnation, political power is more frequently utilized to protect shares of a diminishing pie.

How does this conceptualization of the capitalist mode of production differ from that of Marx? Marx's model of capital accumulation assumed an institutional basis in which the state played no direct role in production, but maintained the class relations necessary for private accumulation to proceed. His abstract model, explicated in Volume 1 of *Capital,* assumed this "caretaker" state, and also a class structure composed of only two classes, capitalists and proletarians. The world-system perspective, in attempting to come to grips with the realities of capitalist development which have become apparent since Marx's time, seeks to integrate the state and class relations into the accumulation model. Class structures and states are not now seen as merely "historical" forms, the product of impossibly complex processes, but as related in a systematic way to the process of accumulation.

The world-system perspective revises Marx's definition of the capitalist mode of production as follows. The mode of production is thought to be a characteristic of the whole effective division of labor, that is, the world economy. Therefore, the capitalist mode of production includes commodity producers employing wage labor in the core areas and coerced labor in the peripheral areas. Peripheral areas are not seen as "precapitalist" but rather as integrated, exploited, and essential parts of the larger system. Capitalist production relations, in this view, are not limited to wage labor (which is nevertheless understood to be very important to the expanded reproduction of the core areas), but rather are composed of the combination of wage labor with coerced labor in the periphery. This combination is accomplished, not only by the world market exchange of commodities, but also by the forms of political coercion which the core powers often exercise over peripheral areas. The state, and the system of competing states which compose the world polity, constitute the basic structural support for capitalist production relations. Marx saw that the state stood behind the opaque capital/wage-labor relationship in nineteenth-century England. The more direct involvement of the state in the extraction of surplus product with slave labor or serf labor is but a more obvious example of the way in which the state stands behind production relations.

If the state is often directly involved in extraction of surplus product, what is the difference between capitalist production relations and labor extraction in precapitalist agrarian empires? The difference is that the capitalist world economy has no overarching single state which encompasses the entire arena of economic competition. Rather than a world state, there is the "international system" of competing states operating within the world market. Thus state power is used to extract labor power (more directly in the periphery than in the core) but the competitive nature of the state system prevents any single state from maintaining a systemwide monopoly and subjects producers to the necessity of increasing productivity in order to maintain or increase their shares of the world product.

The state system enforces the capital/wage-labor relationship in the core, the coerced labor extraction in the periphery, and the shifting forms of extraction between the core and the periphery, and constitutes the basis of production relations for the capitalist system. States are organizations within the arena of competition which are often utilized by the classes that control them to expropriate shares of the world surplus product. Market forces are either supported or distorted depending on the world market position of the classes controlling a particular state. Thus hegemonic core states and peripheral states (controlled by classes producing raw materials for export to the core) implement, and try to influence others to implement, free trade policies. States in which producers are seeking to protect home markets against cheap foreign goods erect tariff barriers and other political controls on the world market forces. Thus both political organizations and economic producers are subjected to a long-run "competing down" process, whereas in the ancient empires the monopoly of violence held by a single center minimized both market and political competition among different organizational forms.

In the capitalist world economy, state structures themselves are submitted to a political version of the "competing down" process which occurs in the realm of the market. Inefficient state structures, ones that tax their producers too heavily or do not spend their revenues in ways which facilitate politico-economic competition in the world economy, lose the struggle for domination. In Marxist theoretical terms, the state system produces an equalization of surplus profits, the profits which return because political coercion enforces monopolies. There are no complete long-run monopolies. Even the largest organizations (both states and firms) are subjected to the pressures of politico-economic competition.

It has been pointed out that not all precapitalist modes of production were world empires. Indeed, it was European feudalism's "parcellization of sovereignty" which allowed the capitalist mode of production to become dominant. The possibilities for political competition and the space for new departures in social relations which such a decentralized political structure allowed were a fertile context for the emergence of capitalism. Classical European feudalism, although somewhat integrated culturally, and sharing a common political matrix, did not have more than a rudimentary division of labor across the manors and towns. The growth of commodity production, merchant capital and "industrial" capital producing manufactures for the emerging local and long-distance markets transformed the "stateless" classical feudalism into the capitalist world economy and interstate system of the sixteenth century. The dynamic of mercantile competition between both public and private enterprises in the long sixteenth century, together with the emergence of a core-periphery hierarchy, led Wallerstein to argue that the capitalist system was then born. . . .

Most social theorists have correctly identified the differentiation between economic and political institutions as a key feature of capitalism, but, since Adam Smith, this separation has been primarily identified with the separation between private and public spheres within nation-states. The contemporary growth of state capitalism, and Wallerstein's reinterpretation of seventeenth- and eighteenth-century mercantilism, imply that the main locus of the differentiation between economic and political institutions is at the level of the world economy as a whole—that is, the distinction between the state system and the world division of labor. The public-private separation was an important political issue for the triumph of industrial capital over the state-institutionalized interests of older agrarian capital in the eighteenth and nineteenth centuries, especially in the core states. But the more direct role of the state in fostering national economic development in most of the world economy belies the exclusive identification of capitalism with private ownership.

In the competitive state system it has been impossible for any single state to monopolize the entire world market, and to maintain hegemony indefinitely. Hegemonic core powers, such as Britain and the United States, have, in the long run, lost their relative domination to more efficient producers. This means that, unlike the agrarian empires, success in the capitalist world-system is based on a combination of effective state power and competitive advantage in production. The extraction of surplus product is based on two legs: the ability to use political power for the appropriation of surplus product; and the ability to produce efficiently for the competitive world market. This is not the state-centric system which some analysts describe, because states cannot escape, for long, the competitive forces of the world economy. States that attempt to cut themselves off or who overtax their domestic producers condemn themselves to marginality. On the other hand, the system is not simply a free world market of competing producers. The interaction between political power and competitive advantage is a delicate balance.

Skocpol (1977) has argued that Wallerstein is wrong in contending that core states are strong states. She correctly points out that the most successful core states have been those that combined a relatively strong world-economy-oriented bourgeoisie with a relatively decentralized state. . . . This problem can best be handled by observing that there is a certain differentiation among core states in the type of development path followed. Some rely more on geopolitical military advantage and centralized and effective fiscal structures, while others—the more successful ones—rely on low over-head decentralized states which act efficiently to protect and extend the vital business interests of their national capitalists. . . .

Thus, core states are strong relative to peripheral states, but some are stronger vis-à-vis their own internal capitalist class fractions than others. The most successful core nations have achieved their hegemony by having strong and convergent business class interests which unified state policy behind a drive for successful commodity production and trade with the world market. Second-runners have often achieved some centrality in the world economy by relying on a more state-organized attempt to catch up with the "caretaker" states in terms of political and economic hegemony. Skocpol's (1977) emphasis on the less autocratic form of development in the most successful states does not lend support to the contention that geopolitics and capital accumulation are autonomous from one another, although success is perhaps not the best criterion for determining the nature of capitalism as a system. For this we need to focus on the dynamics and relationships operating in the system as a whole, not in its parts, the national societies.

It may be argued that the existence of states which successfully follow an exclusively political–military development path is evidence in favor of the thesis that geopolitical and economic processes operate independently. The existence of such a development path is unquestionable (for example, Prussia, Sweden, Japan, U.S.S.R.), but the upward mobility of these states was certainly conditioned by their context, a world economy in which commodity production and capitalist accumulation were becoming general. If all states had followed such a path, the modern world-system would be a very different kind of entity. It is argued below that the reproduction and expansion of the kind of interstate system which emerged in Europe requires the institutional forms and dynamic processes which are associated with commodity production and capitalist accumulation. First, though, let us discuss the ways in which the interstate system helps to preserve the dynamics of the capitalist process of accumulation.

The Reproduction of Capitalist Accumulation

The competitive state system serves several functions which allow the capitalist accumulation process to overcome temporarily the contradictions it creates, and to expand. The balance of power in the interstate system prevents any single state from controlling the world economy, and from imposing a political monopoly over accumulation. This means that "factors of production" cannot be constrained to the degree that they could be if there were an overarching world state. Capital is subjected to controls by states, but it can still flow from areas where profits are low to areas where profits are higher. This allows capital to escape the political claims which exploited classes attempt to impose on it. If workers are successful in creating organizations which enable them to demand higher wages, or if communities demand that corporations spend more money on pollution controls, capital can usually escape these demands by moving to areas where there is less opposition. This process can also be seen to operate within federal nation-states. Class struggles are most often oriented toward and constrained within particular territorial state structures.

Thus the state system provides the political underpinning of the mobility of capital, and also the institutional basis for the continuing expansion of capitalist development. States which successfully prevent capital from migrating do not necessarily solve this problem, because capital from other sources may take advantage of the less costly production opportunities outside the national boundaries, and push the domestic products out of the world market.

This implies that capitalism is not possible in the context of a single world state, or rather that such a system would eventually develop a political regulation of resource allocation which would more regularly and fully include social desiderata in the calculation of investment decisions. The dynamic of the present system, in which profit criteria and national power are the main controllers of resource use, would be transformed into a system which balances development according to a calculation of the individual and collective use values of human society. This system, which we can call socialism, would not constitute a utopia in which the problem of production has been completely solved, but in political struggles for resources, which would be oriented toward a single overarching world government, would exhibit a very different long-run dynamic of political change and economic development than that which has characterized the capitalist world economy.

Reproduction of the Interstate System

Thus I am arguing that the interstate system is important for the continued viability of the capital accumulation process. But is the accumulation process equally as important for the generation and reproduction of the interstate system? First, what do I mean by reproduction of the interstate system? . . . By an interstate system, I mean a system of unequally powerful and competing states in which no single state is capable of imposing control on all others. These states are in interaction with one another in a set of shifting alliances and wars, and changes in the relative power of states upsets any temporary set of alliances, leading to a restructuring of the balance of power. If such a system disintegrates due to the dissolution of the states, or due to the complete elimination of economic exchanges between the national territories, or as a result of the imposition of domination by a single overarching state, the system can be said to have fundamentally changed (that is, to be transformed, not reproduced). . . .

Skocpol contends that the state system predates the emergence of capitalism and implies that this is evidence of its relative autonomy. It is clearly the case that multistate systems exhibiting some of the tendencies of the European balance of power existed prior to the emergence of the capitalist mode of production. These state systems were unstable, however, and tended either to become world empires or to disintegrate. The multicentric "international system" which developed among the Italian city-states and their trade partners in the East and West invented many of the institutions of diplomacy and shifting alliance which were later adopted by the European states. . . .

Many of the capitalistic financial and legal institutions later elaborated in the European capitalist world economy were invented in the Italian city-states. Wallerstein contends that the Christian Mediterranean constituted a kind of interstitial proto-capitalist world economy. Analogous to Marx's analysis of merchant capitalism, the Mediterranean world economy—though developing the seeds of capitalist production with labor as a commodity—was primarily based on the exchange of preciosities among social systems which were not integrated into a single-commodity economy. Nevertheless this proto-capitalist world economy succeeded in developing several institutional features which were only later fully articulated in the capitalist mode of production that emerged in Europe and Latin America in the sixteenth century. One of these was the state system, which . . . only became stabilized after its emergence in Europe.

Does the continuity of the Italian state system, its failure to develop into a world empire, constitute a case for the independence of the state system? No—its incorporation into the emerging capitalist world economy allowed the Italian system to evade this fate.

Skocpol's contention that nation-states predated the dominance of capitalism is clearly correct. Medieval states were present in precapitalist England and France. However, the emergence of the interstate system is another matter. The balance-of-power system defined above emerged first among the

Italian city-states and later in the Europe of the long sixteenth century, contemporaneous with the emerging dominance of capitalism as a world economy.

One clue to the dependence or independence of the state system is its ability to reproduce itself, or to weather crises without either becoming transformed into a world empire, or experiencing disintegration of its division of labor and network of economic exchange. Wallerstein's analysis of the Habsburg failure to transform the still shaky sixteenth century capitalist world economy into a world empire is asserted to demonstrate the strength of capitalism in reproducing the state system. I will discuss the later points at which such challenges to the state system were mounted (Louis XIV's, the Napoleonic wars, and the twentieth-century world wars) and the causes of continuity of the state system. . . .

The European world-system became the global capitalist system in a series of expanding waves which eventually incorporated all the territories and peoples of the earth. Although political–military alliances with states external to the system occurred after the sixteenth century, they were never again so crucial to the survival and development of the system. But the system continued to face challenges of survival based on its internal contradictions. Uneven economic development and the vast expansion of productive forces outstripped the structures of political power, causing violent reorganizations of the state system (hegemonic wars) to accommodate new levels of economic development. This process can be seen in the cycles of core competition, the rise and fall of hegemonic core states, which have accompanied the expansion and deepening of the capitalist mode of production.

After the failure of the Habsburgs there have been three other attempts to impose a world empire on the capitalist world economy: those of France under Louis XIV and Napoleon, and that of Germany and its allies in the twentieth-century world wars. Each of these came in a period when the hegemonic core power was weak. Louis XIV attempted to expand his monarchy over the whole of the core powers during the decline of Dutch hegemony. Napoleon's attempt came while Britain was still emerging as the hegemonic power. The German attempts came after Britain's decline and before the full emergence of the United States. In these three instances we may see a threat to the state system and to the existence of the capitalist world economy.

One striking thing about these events is that they were not perpetrated by the hegemonic core powers themselves, but by emerging second runners among the competing core states. This raises the question of why hegemonic core powers do not try to impose imperium when it becomes obvious that their competitive advantage in production is waning. Similarly we may ask, why opposing forces were able to prevent the conversion of the system into a single empire. To both of these questions I would answer that the transitional structures associated with the capitalist commodity economy operated to tip the balance in favor of preserving the state system.

Hegemonic core states often use state power to enforce the interests of their "own" producers, although typically they do not rely on it as heavily as other competing core states. However, a hegemonic core power begins to lose its competitive edge in production with the spread of production techniques and the equalization of labor costs which accompany the growth of new core production in other areas. The profit rate differentials change such that capital is exported from the hegemonic core state to areas where profit rates are higher. This reduces the level at which the capitalists of the hegemonic core state will support the "economic nationalism" of their home state. Their interests come to be spread across the core. In other words, hegemonic core states develop fractions of their capitalist classes having different interests. There evolves a fraction of "international capitalists" who support peace and supranational federation, and "national" capitalists who seek protection and politicomilitary expansion. This explains the ambivalent and contradictory policies of hegemonic core powers during the periods of their decline.

Why have the second-running core powers who seek to impose imperium on the world economy failed? Most theorists of the state system have not addressed this question as such. The balance-of-power idea explains why, in a multicentric system, alliances between the most powerful actors weaken. Coalitions in a triad, for example, balance the two weakest actors against the strongest. However, this alliance falls apart when the stronger of the partners gains enough to become the strongest single actor, because the ally can gain more by allying with the declining former power than by sticking to the original alliance. This simple game theory is extended to the state system by the theorists of equilibrium, but it does not answer our question substantively. Again, it is not the most powerful actor that tries to impose imperium, but upwardly mobile second runners with less than their "fair" share of political influence over weaker areas of the globe. . . .

Of course, we are not considering strictly historical explanations which make use of uniquely historical factors: such a theoretical maneuver (or rather an atheoretical maneuver) is easy to accomplish when one is explaining only four "events." Here we seek an explanation of what seems to be a regularity of the system from our understanding of the logic of the system itself.

Morganthau invokes the notion of a normatively organized liberal world culture which successfully mobilizes counterforce against the threat to the balance-of-power system. This conceptualization of the world-system as a normatively integrated system is shared by more recent authors who seek to extend modernization theory to the world-system. Wallerstein's perspective emphasizes that the capitalist world economy is not primarily a normatively integrated system. In Wallerstein's broad typology of social systems, social systems based on normatively regulated reciprocal exchange (termed "minisystems" by Wallerstein) no longer exist except in vestigial form in the family and as symbolic subsystems of the present world economy, which are not determinant of its developmental tendencies. While Wallerstein does not deny that some normative patterns are generalized across the system, he focuses on the fact that culture tends to follow state boundaries so that the system remains primarily multicultural.

The linguistic boundaries of the world culture are formed and reformed primarily by the process of nation building and associated state formation. These processes are somewhat similar across the system, and the national cultures which come to exist have an isomorphic character. These facts do not contradict the main point that normative integration at the system level remains weak, although growing. From this perspective it is farfetched to explain the failure of empire in terms of commitment to shared norms. The ideologies employed by the second runners undoubtedly played some part in their inability to mobilize support, but this is unlikely to have been the most important factor.

I argue that both the attempts and the failures of imperium can be understood as responses to the pressures of uneven development in the world economy, albeit somewhat reactive responses. We have already noted that the attempts were fomented, not by the most powerful states in the system, but by emerging second-running core powers contending for hegemony. One striking aspect of all four cases is their appearance, in retrospect, of wild irrationality in terms of their attempt to use military power to conquer areas much too vast to subdue, let alone to exploit effectively. In this we may see the weakness of the strategy of politicomilitary domination unaccompanied by a strategy of competitive production for sale on the market. The countries that adopted the strategy of aggrandizement reached far beyond their own capacities and failed to generate sufficient support from allied countries. This second condition bears further examination. Why did the French and German imperiums not receive more support? Potential allies, in part, doubted the extent to which their interests would be protected under the new imperium, and the path of capitalist growth in the context of the multicentric system appeared preferable to the emerging bourgeoisies of potential allied states.

If I am correct, the interstate system is dependent on the institutions and opportunities presented by the world market for its survival. There are two main characteristics of the interstate system which need to be sustained: the division of sovereignty in the core (interimperial rivalry) and the maintenance of a network of exchange among the states. The nature of the world economy assures that states will continue to exchange due to natural and socially created comparative advantages in production. Withdrawal from the world market can be accomplished for short periods of time, but it is costly and unstable. Even the "socialist" states which have tried to establish a separate mode of production have eventually returned to production for, and exchange with, larger commodity markets.

The maintenance of interimperial rivalry is facilitated by a number of institutional processes. At any point in time national sentiments, language, and cultural differences make supranational integration difficult, as is well illustrated by the EEC. These "historical" factors may be traced back to the long-run processes of state formation and nation building, and these processes have themselves been conditioned by the emergence of the commodity economy over the past 500 years.

The main institutional feature of the world economy which maintains interimperial rivalry is the uneven nature of capitalist economic development.

As discussed above, hegemonic core powers lose their competitive advantage in production to other areas. This causes the export of capital, which restrains the hegemonic power from attempting to impose political imperium. Second-running challengers, who do try to impose imperium, cannot gain sufficient support from other core allies to win, or at least, historically, they have not been able to do so. This is in part because the potential for further expansion and deepening of the commodity economy, and growth and development in the context of a decentralized interstate system, appears greater to potential allies than the potential for political and economic power within the proposed imperium. It is the very success of capitalist development in the past which preserves the interstate system. Success stories in the uneven development history of the world economy are frequent enough to prevent imperium.

Despite the contentions of many Marxists that the increased size of firms has led to a new stage of "monopoly" capitalism, the conception of capitalism proposed here—which incorporates state capitalism and political control of home markets as normal instances of capitalist competition for shares of the world market—implies that the basic tendencies of the accumulation of capital have been with us since the sixteenth century. This does not deny the increased political density of controls on accumulation which has accompanied the secular increase in the power of states over the process of production. However, this increased density of political control, including the resistance of peripheral states to unbridled exploitation by the core, has not altered the basic nature of the larger system.

The transformation of capitalism cannot be accomplished by the emergence of state control as long as the interstate system remains unregulated by a world government. Proponents of the relative autonomy thesis might point to the bickering and bloody competition among the "socialist" states as evidence of the independence of the interstate system from the capitalist mode of production. My position is that these states remain part of the larger capitalist world-system. This does not mean that the institutional experiments in the "socialist" states have no meaning for the transformation of capitalism, but that they, themselves, do not constitute that transformation.

The current return to mercantilist international economic policy and the rising nationalism and conflict among states can be understood primarily in terms of the repetition of earlier cyclical phases of the world-system. The capitalist mode of production with its logic, including the logic of the interstate system, remains very much the dominant source of developmental tendencies in the contemporary world-system.

The conclusion I wish to reach here is by no means definitive. The usefulness of theorizing about the modern world-system in terms of a single logic versus political and economic subsystems can be decided only when competing theories have been formulated with enough clarity to allow them to be systematically subjected to evidence. My goal has been to present an alternative way of conceptualizing capitalist development in order to stimulate further discussion and research. The attempt to create a reintegrated interdisciplinary science of political economy is a necessary step in the project to understand (and influence) the directions and potentialities of our present collective history.

Bibliography

Skocpol, Theda. "Wallerstein's World Capitalist System. A Theoretical and Historical Critique." *American Journal of Sociology* 82:5 (March 1977): 1075–90.
———. *States and Social Revolutions.* New York: Cambridge University Press, 1979.
Wallerstein, I. *The Modern World System.* New York: Academic Press, 1974, 1980.
———. *The Capitalist World Economy.* Cambridge: Cambridge University Press, 1979.

Global *Perestroika*

ROBERT W. COX

Mikhail Gorbachev's *perestroika* was a revolution from above, a decision by political leadership to undertake a reform of the economic organization of "real socialism" which, once initiated, got out of control and spun into entropy. Underlying that decision was a vague idea that some kind of socialism could be rebuilt in the context of market forces. No one had a clear strategy based upon real social forces as to how this result could be achieved. The consequence has been a devastating destruction of the real economy, i.e., the productive capacity and the economic organization of real (albeit ailing) socialism, and a disarticulation of social forces. Soviet *perestroika* aggravated the decay of public services, created large-scale unemployment, polarized new wealth and new poverty, generated inflation, and made a former superpower dependent upon foreign relief. Those who gained from the "market" were preeminently well-placed members of the former nomenklatura, speculators, and gangsters. The market is the mafia.

Perestroika in the now defunct Soviet empire is perhaps the worst case of what has become a global phenomenon—worst not in an absolute sense but in the most dramatic descent from production to entropy. Global *perestroika*, more euphemistically called *globalization*, is not the consequence of a conscious decision of political leadership. It is a result of structural changes in capitalism, in the actions of many people, corporate bodies, and states, that cumulatively produce new relationships and patterns of behavior. The project of global *perestroika* is less the conscious will of an identifiable group than the latent consequence of these structural changes. These consequences form a coherent, interrelated pattern; but this pattern contains within itself contradictions that threaten the persistence of this structural whole in formation. Those of us who abhor the social and political implications of the globalization project must study its contradictions in order to work for its eventual replacement.

Sources of Globalization

It has been fashionable, especially in the Anglo-Saxon tradition, to distinguish states and markets in the analysis of economic forces and economic change. Where this distinction leads to the privileging of one to the exclusion of the other, it always departs from historical reality. States and political authorities have had a variety of relationships to economic activity, even when proclaiming nonintervention, and the market is a power relationship. . . . Where the distinction serves to assess the relative weight of the visible hand of political authority and of the latent outcome of an infinity of private actions, it has some analytical merit.

In the capitalist core of the world-economy, the balance has shifted over time from the mercantilism that went hand in hand with the formation of the modern state, to the liberalism of *les bourgeois conquerants* and back again to a more state-regulated economic order, first in the age of imperialism and then, after a postwar interlude of aborted liberalism, during the Great Depression of the 1930s. The state during the 1930s had to assume the role of agent of economic revival and defender of domestic welfare and employment against disturbances coming from the outside world. Corporatism, the union of the state with productive forces at the national level, became, under various names, the model of economic regulation.

Following World War II, the Bretton Woods system attempted to strike a balance between a liberal world market and the domestic responsibilities of states. States became accountable to agencies of an international economic order—the International Monetary Fund, World Bank, and the General Agreement on Tariffs and Trade—as regards trade liberalization and exchange-rate stability and convertibility, and were granted facilities and time to make adjustments in their national economic practices so as not to have to sacrifice the welfare of domestic groups. Keynesian demand management, along with varieties of corporatism, sustained this international economic order through the ups and downs of the capitalist business cycle. Moderate inflation, attributable to the fine-tuning of national economies, stimulated a long period of economic growth. War and arms production played a key role: World War II pulled the national economies out of the Depression; the Korean War and the Cold War underpinned economic growth of the 1950s and 1960s.

The crisis of this postwar order can be traced to the years 1968–75. During this period, the balanced compromise of Bretton Woods shifted toward subordination of domestic economies to the perceived exigencies of a global economy. States willy-nilly became more effectively accountable to a *nebuleuse* personified as the global economy; and they were constrained to mystify this external accountability in the eyes and ears of their own publics through the new vocabulary of globalization, interdependence, and competitiveness.

How and why did this happen? It is unlikely that any fully adequate explanation can be given now. The matter will be long debated. It is, however, possible to recognize this period as a real turning point in the structural sense of the weakening of old and the emergence of new structures. Some key elements of the transformation can be identified.

The Structural Power of Capital Inflation, which hitherto had been a stimulus to growth, beneficent alike to business and organized labor, now, at higher rates and with declining profit margins, became perceived by business as inhibiting investment. Discussions among economists as to whether the fault lay in demand pull or in cost push were inconclusive. Business blamed unions for raising wages and governments for the cycle of excessive spending, borrowing, and taxing. Governments were made to understand that a revival of economic growth would depend upon business confidence to invest, and that this confidence would depend upon 'discipline' directed at trade unions and government fiscal management. The investment strike and capital flight are powerful weapons that no government can ignore with impunity. . . .

The Structuring of Production Insofar as government policies did help restore business confidence, new investment was by and large of a different type. The crisis of the postwar order accelerated the shift from Fordism to post-Fordism—from economies of scale to economies of flexibility. The large integrated plant employing large numbers of semiskilled workers on mass production of standardized goods became an obsolete model of organization. The new model was based on a core-periphery structure of production, with a relatively small core of relatively permanent employees handling finance, research and development, technological organization, and innovation, and a periphery consisting of dependent components of the production process.

While the core is integrated with capital, the fragmented components of the periphery are much more loosely linked to the overall production process. They can be located partly within the core plant, for example, as maintenance services, and partly spread among different geographical sites in many countries. Periphery components can be called into existence when they are needed by the core and disposed of when they are not. Restructuring into the core-periphery model has facilitated the use of a more precariously employed labor force segmented by ethnicity, gender, nationality, or religion. It has weakened the power of trade unions and strengthened that of capital within the production process. It has also made business less controllable by any single state authority. Restructuring has thereby accelerated the globalizing of production.

The Role of Debt Both corporations and governments have relied increasingly on debt financing rather than on equity investment or taxation. Furthermore, debt has to an increasing extent become foreign debt. There was a time when it could be said that the extent of public debt did not matter "because we owed it to ourselves." However plausible that attitude may have been, it no longer applies. Governments now have to care about their international credit ratings. They usually have to borrow in currencies other than their own and face the risk that depreciation of their own currency will raise the costs of debt service.

As the proportion of state revenue going into debt service rises, governments have become more effectively accountable to external bond markets than to their own publics. Their options in exchange rate policy, fiscal policy, and trade policy have become constrained by financial interests linked to the global economy. In Canada, among the very first acts of the heads of the Parti Quebecois government elected in Quebec in 1976 and of the New Democratic Party government elected in Ontario in 1990, both of them appearing as radical challenges to the preexisting political order, was to go to New York to reassure the makers of the bond market. In Mexico, the government had to abandon an agricultural reform designed to expand medium-sized farming for local consumption goods, and revert to large-scale production of luxury export crops in order to earn dollars to service the country's debt.

Corporations are no more autonomous than governments. The timing of an announcement by General Motors just prior to Christmas 1991 that it was going to close 21 plants and cut 74,000 jobs was hardly prompted by a particularly Scrooge-like malevolence. By informed accounts, it was intended, by appearing as a token of the corporation's intention to increase competitiveness, to deter a downgrading of its bond rating, which would have increased the corporation's cost of borrowing. A large corporation, flagship of the U.S. economy, is shown to be tributary to the financial manipulators of Wall Street. Finance has become decoupled from production to become an independent power, an autocrat over the real economy.

And what drives the decision making of the financial manipulators? The short-range thinking of immediate financial gain, not the long-range thinking of industrial development. The market mentality functions synchronically; development requires a diachronic mode of thought. Financial markets during the 1980s were beset by a fever of borrowing, leveraged takeovers, junk bonds, and savings and loan scandals—a roller coaster of speculative gains and losses that Susan Strange called "casino capitalism." The result of financial power's dominance over the real economy was as often as not the destruction of jobs and productive capital. This is Western capitalism's counterpart to *perestroika*'s destruction of the residual productive powers of real socialism.

The Structures of Globalization

The crisis of the postwar order has expanded the breadth and depth of a global economy that exists alongside and incrementally supersedes the classical international economy. The global economy is the system generated by globalizing production and global finance. Global production is able to make use of the territorial divisions of the international economy, playing off one territorial jurisdiction against another so as to maximize reductions in costs, savings in taxes, avoidance of antipollution regulation, control over labor, and guarantees of political stability and favor. Global finance has achieved a virtually unregulated and electronically connected 24-hour-a-day network. The collective decision making of global finance is centered in world cities rather than states—New York, Tokyo, London, Paris, Frankfurt—and extends by computer terminals to the rest of the world.

The two components of the global economy are in potential contradiction. Global production requires a certain stability in politics and finance in order to expand. Global finance has the upper hand because its power over credit creation determines the future of production; but global finance is in a parlously fragile condition. A calamitous concatenation of accidents would bring it down. . . . For now, governments, even the combined governments of the G-7, have not been able to devise any effectively secure scheme of regulation for global finance that could counter such a collapse.

There is, in effect, no explicit political or authority structure for the global economy. There is, nevertheless, something there that remains to be deciphered, something that could be described by the French word *nebuleuse* or by the notion of "governance without government."

There is a transnational process of consensus formation among the official caretakers of the global economy. This process generates consensual guidelines, underpinned by an ideology of globalization, that are transmitted into the policy-making channels of national governments and big corporations. Part of this consensus-formation process takes place through unofficial forums like the Trilateral Commission, the Bilderberg conferences, or the more esoteric Mont Pelerin Society. Part of it goes on through official bodies like the OECD, the Bank of International Settlements, the International Monetary Fund, and the G-7. These shape the discourse within which policies are defined, the terms and concepts that circumscribe what can be thought and done. They also tighten the transnational networks that link policy-making from country to country.

The structural impact on national governments of this global centralization of influence over policy can be called the internationalizing of the state. Its common feature is to convert the state into an agency for adjusting national economic practices and policies to the perceived exigencies of the global economy. The state becomes a transmission belt from the global to the national economy, where heretofore it had acted as the bulwark defending domestic welfare from external disturbances. Power within the state becomes concentrated in those agencies in closest touch with the global economy—the offices of presidents and prime ministers, treasuries, central banks. The agencies that are more closely identified with domestic clients—ministries of industries, labor ministries, etc.—become subordinated. This phenomenon, which has become so salient since the crisis of the postwar order, needs much more study.

Different forms of states facilitate this tightening of the global/local relationship for countries occupying different positions in the global system. At one time, the military-bureaucratic form of state seemed to be optimum in countries of peripheral capitalism for the enforcement of monetary discipline. Now IMF-inspired 'structural adjustment' is pursued by elected presidential regimes (Argentina, Brazil, Mexico, Peru) that manage to retain a degree of insulation from popular pressures. India, formerly following a more auto-centric or self-reliant path, has moved closer and closer toward integration into the global economy. Neoconservative ideology has sustained the transformation of the state in Britain, the United States, Canada, and Australasia in the direction of globalization. Socialist party governments in France and in Spain have adjusted their policies to the new orthodoxy. The states of the former Soviet empire, insofar as their present governments have any real authority, seem to have been swept up into the globalizing trend.

In the European Community (EC), the unresolved issue over the social charter indicates a present stalemate in the conflict over the future nature of the state and of the regional authority. There is a struggle between two kinds of capitalism: the hyperliberal, globalizing capitalism of Thatcherism, and a capitalism more rooted in social policy and territorially balanced development. The latter stems from the social democratic tradition and also from an older conservatism that thinks of society as an organic whole rather than in the contractual individualism of so-called neoconservatism.

In Japan, the guiding and planning role of the state retains initiative in managing the country's relationship with the world outside its immediate sphere, and will likely be of increasing significance in lessening that economy's dependence upon the U.S. market and the U.S. military. The EC and Japan are now the only possible counterweights to total globalization at the level of states.

Globalization and Democracy

The issues of globalization have an important implication for the meaning of democracy. The ideologues of globalization are quick to identify democracy with the free market. There is, of course, very little historical justification for this identification. It derives almost exclusively from the coincidence of liberal parliamentary constitutionalism in Britain with the industrial revolution and the growth of a market economy. This obscured, in a way, the necessity of state force to establish and maintain the conditions for a workable market—a new kind of police force internally and sea power in the world market. It also ignored the fact that the other European states following the British lead in the nineteenth century, for example, the French Second Empire, were not notably liberal in the political sense. In our own time, the case of Pinochet's Chile preconfigured the role of military-bureaucratic regimes in installing the bases for liberal economic policies. Ideological mystification has obscured the fact that a stronger case can probably be made for the pairing of political authoritarianism with market economics. It is perhaps worth reflecting upon this point when undertaking the task of constructing the socialist alternative for the future.

Since the crisis of the postwar order, democracy has been quietly redefined in the centers of world capitalism. The new definition is grounded in a revival of the nineteenth-century separation of economy and politics. Key aspects of economic management are therefore to be shielded from politics, that is to say, from popular pressures. This is achieved by confirmed practices, by treaty, by legislation, and by formal constitutional provisions. By analogy to the constitutional limitations on royal authority called limited monarchy, the late-twentieth-century redefinition of pluralist politics can be called 'limited democracy." . . .

During . . . 1975, three ideologues of the Trilateral Commission produced a report to the commission that addressed the issue of the "ungovernability" of democracies. The thesis of the report was that a "democratic surge" in the 1960s had increased demands on government for services, challenged and weakened governmental authority, and generated inflation. The Trilateral governments, and especially the United States, were suffering from an "excess of democracy," the report argued; and this overloading of demands upon the state could only be abated by a degree of political demobilization of those 'marginal' groups that were pressing new demands.

The underlying ideology here propounded became expressed in a variety of measures intended to insulate economic policy-making from popular pressures. Cynicism, depoliticization, a sense of the inefficacy of political action, and a disdain for the political class are current in the old democracies.

Although the tendency toward limited democracy remains dominant, it has not gone unchallenged. Prime Minister Brian Mulroney of Canada sold the Free Trade Agreement with the United States in the oil-producing region of Alberta with the argument that it would forevermore prevent the introduction of a new national energy policy; but opposition to free trade, though defeated in the elections of 1988, did mobilize many social groups in Canada more effectively than ever before. In Europe, the 'democratic deficit' in the EC is at the center of debate. Business interests are, on the whole, pleased with the existing bureaucratic framework of decision making, remote from democratic pressures—apart, of course, from the more paranoid hyper-liberals who see it as risking socialism through the back door. But advocates of the social charter and of more powers for the European parliament are sensitive to the long-term need for legitimation of a European form of capitalism.

One can question the long-term viability of the new limited or exclusionary democracies of peripheral capitalism. They must continue to administer an austerity that polarizes rich and poor in the interests of external debt relationships. Very likely, they will be inclined to resort to renewed repression, or else face an explosion of popular pressures. Nowhere is this dramatic alternative more apparent than in the former Soviet empire. Whereas *glasnost* has been a resounding success, *perestroika* has been a disastrous failure. The race is between the constitution of pluralist regimes grounded in the emergence of a broadly inclusionary civil society, and new fascist-type populist authoritarianism.

The Changing Structure of World Politics

Out of the crisis of the postwar order, a new global political structure is emerging. The old Westphalian concept of a system of sovereign states is no longer an adequate way of conceptualizing world politics. Sovereignty is an ever looser concept. The old legal definitions conjuring visions of ultimate and fully autonomous power are no longer meaningful. Sovereignty has gained meaning as an affirmation of cultural identity and lost meaning as power over the economy. It means different things to different people.

The affirmation of a growing multitude of 'sovereignties' is accompanied by the phenomena of macroregionalism and microregionalism. Three macroregions are defining themselves respectively in a Europe centered on the EC, an East Asian sphere centered on Japan, and a North American sphere centered on the United States and looking to embrace Latin America. It is unlikely that these macroregions will become autarkic economic blocs reminiscent of the world of the Great Depression. Firms based in each of the regions have too much involvement in the economies of the other regions for such exclusiveness to become the rule. Rather, the macroregions are political–economic frameworks for capital accumulation and for organizing inter-regional competition for investment and shares of the world market. They also allow for the development, through internal struggles, of different forms of capitalism. Macroregionalism is one facet of globalization, one aspect of how a globalizing world is being restructured.

These macroregions are definable primarily in economic terms, but they also have important political and cultural implications. The EC, for instance, poses a quandary for Switzerland, whose business elites see their future economic welfare as linked to integration in the EC, but many of whose people, including many in the business elites, regret the loss of local control upon which Swiss democracy has been based. On the other hand, people in Catalonia, Lombardy, and Scotland look to the EC as an assurance of greater future autonomy or independence in relation to the sovereign states of which they now form apart. And there have been no more fervent advocates of North American free trade than the Quebec *independentistes*. Globalization encourages macroregionalism, which, in turn, encourages microregionalism.

For the relatively rich microregions, autonomy or independence means keeping more of their wealth for themselves. The *lega* in Lombardy would jealously guard northern wealth against redistribution to the south of Italy. Such motivations in other relatively wealthy regions are less overtly proclaimed. An institutionalized process of consultation (an incipient intermicroregional organization) among the 'four motors' of Europe—Catalonia, Lombardy, Rhone-Alpes, and Baden-Wurtemberg—has been joined by Ontario.

Microregionalism among the rich will have its counterpart, surely, among poorer microregions. Indeed, some of the richer microregions have, as a gesture of solidarity, 'adopted' poor microregions. Microregionalism in poor areas will be a means not only of affirming cultural identities but of claiming payoffs at the macroregional level for maintaining political stability and economic good behavior. The issues of re-distribution are thereby raised from the sovereign state level to the macroregional level, while the manner in which redistributed wealth is used becomes decentralized to the microregional level.

At the base of the emerging structure of world order are social forces. The old social movements—trade unions and peasant movements—have suffered setbacks under the impact of globalization; but the labor movement, in particular, has a background of experience in organization and ideology that can still be a strength in shaping the future. If it were to confine itself to its traditional clientele of manual industrial workers, while production is being restructured on a world scale so as to diminish this traditional base of power, the labor movement would condemn itself to a steadily weakening influence. Its prospect for revival lies in committing its organizational and ideologically mobilizing capability to the task of building a broader coalition of social forces.

New social movements, converging around specific sets of issues—environmentalism, feminism, and peace—have grown to a different extent in different parts of the world. More amorphous and vaguer movements—'people power' and democratization—are present wherever political structures are seen to be both repressive and fragile. These movements evoke particular identities—ethnic, nationalist, religious, gender. They exist within states but are transnational in essence. The indigenous peoples' movement affirms rights prior to the existing state system.

The newly affirmed identities have in a measure displaced class as the focus of social struggle; but like class, they derive their force from resentment against exploitation. There is a material basis for their protest, a material basis that is broader than the particular identities affirmed. Insofar as this common material basis remains obscured, the particular identities now reaffirmed can be manipulated into conflict with one another. The danger of authoritarian populism, or reborn fascism, is particularly great where political structures are crumbling and the material basis of resentment appears to be intractable. Democratization and "people power" can move to the right as well as to the left.

Openings for a Countertrend: The Clash of Territorial and Interdependence Principles

The emerging world order thus appears as a multilevel structure. At the base are social forces. Whether they are self-conscious and articulated into what Gramsci called a historic bloc, or are depoliticized and manipulatable, is the key issue to the making of the future. The old state system is resolving itself into a complex of political–economic entities: microregions, traditional states, and macroregions with institutions of greater or lesser functional scope and formal authority. World cities are the keyboards of the global economy. Rival transnational processes of ideological formation aim respectively at hegemony and counterhegemony. Institutions of concertation and coordination bridge the major states and macroregions. Multilateral processes exist for conflict management, peacekeeping, and regulation and service provision in a variety of functional areas (trade, communications, health, etc.). The whole picture resembles the multilevel order of medieval Europe more than the Westphalian model of a system of sovereign independent states that has heretofore been the paradigm of international relations.

The multilevel image suggests the variety of levels at which intervention becomes possible, indeed necessary, for any strategy aiming at transformation into an alternative to global *perestroika*. It needs to be completed with a depiction of the inherent instability of this emerging structure. This instability arises from the dialectical relationship of two principles in the constitution of order: the principle of interdependence and the territorial principle.

The interdependence principle is nonterritorial in essence, geared to competition in the world market, to global finance unconstrained by territorial boundaries, and to global production. It operates in accordance with the thought processes of what Susan Strange has called the "business civilization." The territorial principle is state-based, grounded ultimately in military–political power.

Some authors have envisaged the rise of the interdependence principle as implying a corresponding decline of the territorial principle; but the notion of a reciprocal interactive relationship of the two principles is closer to reality. The myth of the free market is that it is self-regulating. As Karl Polanyi demonstrated, it required the existence of military or police power for enforcement of market rules. The fact that this force may rarely have to be applied helps to sustain the myth but does not dispense with the necessity of the force in reserve. Globalization in the late twentieth century also depends upon the military–territorial power of an enforcer.

The counterpart today to nineteenth-century British sea power, and Britain's ability through much of that century to manage the balance of power in Europe, is U.S. ability to project military power on a world scale. The U.S. world role in the period 1975–1991, however, contrasts markedly with its role in the period 1945–1960. In the earlier period, U.S. hegemonic leadership provided the resources and the models to revive the economies of other noncommunist industrial countries, allies and former enemies alike, and from the 1950s also to incorporate part of what came to be called the Third World into an expanding global economy. U.S. practices in industrial organization and productivity-raising were emulated far and wide. The United States also led in the formation of international "regimes" to regulate multilateral economic relations. This postwar order was based upon a power structure in which the United States was dominant, but its dominance was expressed in universal principles of behavior through which, though consistent with the dominant interests in U.S. society, others also stood to gain something. In that sense the U.S. role was hegemonic.

From the mid–1960s, the United States began to demand economic benefits from others as a quid pro quo for its military power. This mainly took the form of pressing other industrial countries to accept an unlimited flow of U.S. dollars. General Charles de Gaulle was the first to blow the whistle, by converting French dollar reserves into gold and denouncing U.S. practice as a ploy to have others finance an unwanted U.S. war in Vietnam and aggressive U.S. corporate takeovers and penetration into Europe. West Germany was initially more tractable than France, perceiving itself as more dependent upon the U.S. military presence in Europe.

By the 1980s, the rules of the Bretton Woods system, which had some potential for restraint on U.S. policy, ceased to be operative. With Bretton Woods, one of the principal consensual 'regimes' failed. The link of the dollar to gold was severed in the summer of 1971, and from 1973 the exchange rates of the major world currencies were afloat. Management of the dollar became a matter of negotiation among the treasuries and central banks of the chief industrial powers, and in these negotiations U.S. military power and its world role could not be a factor. Under the Reagan presidency, the buildup of U.S. military strength contributed to growing budget deficits. A U.S. trade deficit also appeared during the 1970s and continued to accumulate during this period. The U.S. economy was consuming far in excess of its ability to pay, and the difference was extracted from foreigners. The hegemonic system of the postwar period was becoming transformed into a tributary system. At the end of 1981, the United States was in a net world creditor position of $141 billion. By the end of 1987, the United States had become the world's biggest debtor nation to the tune of some $400 billion, and the debt has continued to grow ever since. Japan became the chief financier of the U.S. deficit.

There is a striking contrast between the U.S. situation as the greatest debtor nation and that of other debtor nations. While the United States has been able to attract, cajole, or coerce other nations' political leaders, central bankers, and corporate investors into accepting its IOUs, other countries become subject to the rigorous discipline imposed by the agencies of the world economy, notably the IMF. Under the euphemistic label of "structural adjustment," other states are required to impose domestic austerity with the effect of raising unemployment and domestic prices, which fall most heavily on the economically weaker segments of the population. Through the financial mechanism, these debtor states are constrained to play the role of instruments of the global economy, opening their national economies more fully to external pressures. By acquiescing, they contribute to undermining the territorial principle, i.e., the possibility of organizing collective national self-defense against external economic forces. Any show of resistance designed to opt for an alternative developmental strategy can be countered by a series of measures beginning with a cutoff of credit, progressing through political destabilization, and culminating in covert and ultimately overt military attack.

The Gulf War revealed the structure and modus operandi of the new world order. The conflict began as a challenge from forces based on the territorial principle—Saddam Hussein's project to use regional territorial–military power to secure resources for Iraq's recovery from the Iran–Iraq war and for consolidation of a strong regional territorial power that could control resources (oil) required by the world-economy, and thereby to extract from the world-economy a rent that could be used to further his developmental and military ambitions. Kuwait, Saudi Arabia, and the other Gulf states are fully integrated into the interdependent world-economy. Indeed, these states are more analogous to large holding companies than to territorial states. The revenues they derive from oil are invested by their rulers through transnational banks into debt and equities around the world. Within the territories of these countries, the workforce is multinational and highly vulnerable.

The United States responded to the perceived Iraqi threat in its role as guarantor and enforcer of the world economic order; and, consistent with that role, rallied support from other states concerned about the security of the global economy. The United States made on its own the decision to go to war, had it ratified by the United Nations Security Council, and demanded and obtained payment for the war from Japan, Germany, Saudi Arabia, and Kuwait.

The role of enforcer is, however, beset by a contradiction. U.S. projection of military power on the world scale has become more salient, monopolistic, and unilateral while the relative strength of U.S. protective capacity has declined. This rests upon the other contradiction already noted: that the United States consumes more than its own production can pay for, because foreigners are ready to accept a flow of depreciating dollars. Part of the debt-causing U.S. deficit is attributable to military expenditure (or military-related, i.e., payments to client states that provide military staging grounds like Egypt or the Philippines); and part is attributable to domestic payments (statutory entitlement payments, not to mention the savings and loan scandal bail-out), which by and large benefit the American middle and upper middle class.

Deficit and failing productivity result less from willful policy than from a structural inability of the American political system to effect a change. Domestic political resistance to cuts in the entitlement programs is on a par with resistance to tax increases. American politicians will not confront their electors with the prospect of a necessary, even if modest, reduction in living standards to bring consumption (military and civilian) into balance with production. With no relief in the deficit, there can be no prospect of the United States undertaking the massive investment in human resources that would be needed in the long run to raise U.S. productivity by enabling the marginalized quarter or third of the nation's population to participate effectively in the economy. Only thus could the United States gradually move out of its dependence on foreign subsidies sustained by military power. All elements of the military/debt syndrome conspire to obstruct an American initiative to escape from it.

Structural obstacles to change exist also outside the United States, though perhaps not quite so obstinately. Those foreigners who hold U.S. debt are increasingly locked in as the exchange rate of the dollar declines. They would suffer losses by shifting to other major currencies; and their best immediate prospect may be to exchange debt for equity by purchase of U.S. assets. In the longer run, however, foreigners may weigh seriously the option of declining to finance the U.S. deficit; and if this were to happen, it would force the United States into a painful domestic readjustment. Indeed, it is probably the only thing that could precipitate such an adjustment.

There are, however, serious risks for the rest of the world in forcing the world's preeminent military power into such a painful course. They are the risks inherent in assessing self-restraint in the use of military power. Whether or not openly discussed, this has to be the salient issue for Japanese in thinking about their future relations with the United States and with the world. The new world order of global *perestroika* is weak at the top. The next few years will likely make this weakness more manifest. There is a kind of utopian optimism abroad that sees the United Nations as coming to play its "originally intended" role in the world. But the United Nations can only be the superstructure or the architectural facade of an underlying global structure of power. It could never sustain a breakdown of that structure, nor should it be asked to do so. The United Nations, for all its recent achievements in the realm of regional conflicts . . . is probably today at greater risk than it was during the years of the Cold War and the North–South impasse when it was substantially sidelined. If the United Nations is to become strengthened as an institution of world order, it will have to be by constructing that order on surer foundations than those presently visible.

Terrains of Struggle for an Alternative World Order

Global *perestroika* penetrates the totality of structures constituting world order. It can be countered effectively only by a challenge at several levels, by a Gramscian war of position, probably of long duration.

The basic level is the level of social forces. The globalizing economy is polarizing advantaged and disadvantaged while it fragments the disadvantaged into distinct and often rival identities. The challenge here is to build a coherent coalition of opposition. Such a coalition must, most likely, be built at local and national levels among groups that are aware of their day-to-day coexistence and are prepared to work to overcome what keeps them apart. Labor movements have experience in organizing capability and ideological work that can be used in this task, provided they are able to transcend narrow corporative thinking to comprehend the requirements of a broader-based social movement.

A new discourse of global socialism that could become a persuasive alternative to the now dominant discourse of globalizing capitalism remains to be created. It is the task of organic intellectuals of the countertendency not just to deconstruct the reigning concepts of competitiveness, structural adjustment, etc., but to offer alternative concepts that serve to construct a coherent alternative order. This goes beyond the strictly economic to include the political foundations of world order. An alternative future world order implies a new intersubjective understanding of the nature of world order and its basic entities and relationships.

Part of this intersubjectivity to be created will be an alternative model of consumption. Consumerism has been the driving force of capitalist *perestroika*, not only in the advanced capitalist societies but in the ex-Soviet east and in the Third World. Perhaps the greatest failure of 'real socialism' was its failure, in its fixation upon 'overtaking' capitalism, to generate alternative aspirations to those of capitalist consumerism. This paralleled real socialism's failure to envisage alternative ways of organizing production to those of the hierarchical capitalist factory system. An alternative model of consumption would be one in balance with global ecology, minimizing energy and resources consumption and pollution, and maximizing emancipatory and participatory opportunities for people.

The local basis for political and ideological action, while indispensable, will by itself be ineffective. Since the globalizing tendency extends everywhere, the countertendency could be rather easily snuffed out if it were isolated in one or a few places. Many locally based social forces will have to build transnational arrangements for mutual support. The alternative to capitalist globalization will need to build upon the productive forces created by capitalism by converting them to the service of society. The counterforce to capitalist globalization will also be global, but it cannot be global all at once.

The macroregional level offers a prospectively favorable terrain, most of all in Europe. It is at the macroregional level that the confrontation of rival forms of capitalism is taking place. Those who are looking beyond that phase of struggle have to be aware of the ideological space that is opened by this confrontation of hyperliberal and state-capitalist or corporatist forms of capitalism. A similar kind of confrontation is developing between Japanese and American forms of capitalism. The long-term strategic view has to take account of opportunities in the medium-term encounter of forces.

Another major source of conflict lies in the rising power of Islamism (or what Western journalists like to call Islamic fundamentalism). Islam, in this context, can be seen as a metaphor for the rejection of Western capitalist penetration in many peripheral societies. Some of its aspects—the penal code, the place of women in society, the concept of jihad—are incomprehensible or abhorrent to Western progressives. Yet Islam has superseded socialism as the force rallying the disadvantaged of much of the populations in North Africa, the Middle East, and parts of Asia. One of the more difficult challenges in building a global counterforce is for Western "progressives" to be able to come to terms, on a basis of mutual comprehension, with the progressive potential in contemporary Islam.

The fragility of the existing global structure is felt particularly at two points: military and financial. These are the instruments of power that shape the behavior of states today both structurally and instrumentally. They need to be more fully understood in their relationship to the goal of a future world social order.

On the military side, the struggle is bound to be asymmetrical against a concentrated monopoly of high technology military power. Strategies that rely upon a different kind of power will be required. Experience has been gained with relatively nonviolent methods of opposition, for example, the intifada.

Finally, rather more thought needs to be devoted to financial strategies that could be brought into play in the event of a global financial crisis. A financial crisis is the most likely way in which the existing world order could begin to collapse. A new financial mechanism would be needed to seize the initiative for transcending the liberal separation of economy from polity and for reembedding the economy in a society imbued with the principles of equity and solidarity.

6

The Return to Statist Theories of International Political Economy

In the 1970s, disillusionment with liberal and Marxist approaches to IPE led some theorists back to mercantilist themes. Their primary concern was how political action, centering on the definition of state interests and the use of state power, influences international economic relations. These state-oriented arguments discard a number of classic mercantilist ideas, such as the importance of specie, and they do not always accept the normative superiority of economic nationalism. A link to the mercantilist past can be found, however, in the definition of politics as potentially autonomous from class interests and market forces.

Robert Gilpin is instrumental in the revival of state-power analyses of the IPE. He situates himself in opposition to liberal and Marxist perspectives, arguing vigorously against "transnational ideologists," who are overly optimistic in their assessment of interdependence, and "revisionist" theories of U.S. foreign policy, which explain strategic actions as extensions of economic interests. Instead, he posits an interactive IPE theory which, in contradistinction to Chase-Dunn's position, emphasizes the importance of political and security interests in shaping economic outcomes. He sees transnational actors, such as multinational corporations, as dependent upon the political context created by the most powerful states. To make this point he examines British and American moments of international preeminence.

In his discussion of the United States, Gilpin argues that the Cold War was not simply a result of the expanding power of the U.S. bourgeoisie. He illustrates how, at times, U.S. state action contradicted national capitalist interests, particularly in regard to the trade discrimination U.S. leaders accepted as a cost for the political benefits of an economically integrated Europe. Moreover, he suggests that particular strategic circumstances, the reliance on air and sea power as opposed to a large standing army, critically influenced postwar U.S. international economic policy. Security interests of the state, not economic interests of major corporations, motivated U.S. policy toward Europe and Japan.

How do transnational corporations influence international politics? Gilpin holds that the global corporation is an American phenomenon which has, ironically, inspired an even greater amount of political regulation in world markets. In response to the American challenge, European states have promoted internationalization of their national corporations and have attempted to limit the power of U.S. firms. This does not mean that economic forces are irrelevant to international relations. Gilpin recognizes that economic and technological dynamics, which have given rise to transnational corporations, are not wholly determined by political conditions. His primary concern, however, is to illustrate how global economics is constrained by the structure of international politics. In looking to the future, he suggests that changes in the political environment could undermine transnationalism: "the determining consideration will be the diplomatic and strategic interests of the dominant powers."

Alice Amsden also argues that politics, in this case the domestic power and practices of the Taiwan state, shape economic outcomes. With her careful analysis of the extensive and multifaceted interventions by Guomindang (Nationalist Party) planners, she dispels the notion that unfettered market forces have been the source of East Asian economic success.

In agriculture, Taiwan is noteworthy for its land reform of the early 1950s, which created conditions for rapid industrialization with relatively low levels of income inequality. How is it that the Guomindang state, which was notorious for its failure to carry out effective land reform during its reign on the mainland (1927–1949), was able to implement it shortly after its arrival on Taiwan? Amsden notes that the changed political context, in which the Guomindang was no longer beholden to landlords and could redistribute land without undermining its social support, enabled what became a very successful agricultural policy.

Amsden details how the Guomindang state took nothing for granted but continued to carefully plan and guide Taiwan's economy throughout its industrial transformation. When land reform was complete, the state was closely linked to the countryside through Farmers' Associations and the rice/fertilizer barter system, which was a key mechanism for drawing surplus out of agriculture and directing it to industry. As the early industrial policy of import-substitution began to run out of steam in the late 1950s, due to the limited size of the domestic market, state managers prudently orchestrated the transition to export promotion, all the while protecting sectors of the national economy for state-owned enterprises and local entrepreneurs. As Taiwan has become more closely integrated with world markets, the state has overseen economic adjustment to maintain the island's competitiveness. At each step along the way, political institutions have played key roles in economic development.

Politics could have been an obstacle to economic growth: military leaders could have clung to mercantilist autarky and prohibited economic liberalization. They did not, as it turned out, because their cherished defense production was protected; and over time, they came to see that national interest was best served by capital accumulation. As economic performance gradually became the benchmark of national strength and political legitimacy, the old military core of the state was overshadowed by a technocratic elite responsible for economic planning and policy. Although it is beyond the scope of Amsden's article, the most recent product of Taiwan's political economy is the emergence of democracy, a remarkable reconstruction of state power. In a manner similar to Gilpin, Amsden's analysis of Taiwan illustrates how politics and economics are interactive: "The state, in short, can be said both to have transformed Taiwan's economic structure and to have been transformed by it."

The Politics of Transnational Economic Relations

ROBERT GILPIN

I

. . . . International society, we are told, is increasingly rent between its economic and its political organization. On the one hand, powerful economic and technical forces are creating a highly integrated transnational economy, blurring the traditional significance of national boundaries. On the other hand, the nation-state continues to command men's loyalties and to be the basic unit of political decision.

. . . . In specific terms the issue is whether the multinational corporation has become or will become an important actor in international affairs, supplanting, at least in part, the nation-state. If the multinational corporation is indeed an increasingly important and independent international actor, what are the factors that have enabled it to break the political monopoly of the nation-state? What is the relationship of these two sets of political actors, and what are the implications of the multinational corporation for international relations? Finally, what about the future? If the contemporary role of the multinational corporation is the result of a peculiar configuration of political and economic factors, can one foresee the continuation of its important role in the future?

Fundamental to these rather specific issues is a more general one raised by the growing contradiction between the economic and political organiza-

Reprinted from *International Organization,* Vol. XXV, No. 3, Summer 1971, Robert Gilpin, "The Politics of Transnational Economic Relations" by permission of The MIT Press, Cambridge, MA.

tion of contemporary international society. This is the relationship between economic and political activities. While the advent of the multinational corporation puts it in a new guise, the issue is an old one. It was, for example, the issue which in the nineteenth century divided classical liberals like John Stuart Mill and the German Historical School represented by Georg Friedrich List. Whereas the former gave primacy to economics and the production of wealth, the latter emphasized the political determination of economic relations. As this issue is central to the contemporary debate on the implications of the multinational corporation for international relations, I would like to discuss it in brief outline.

The classical position was, of course, first set forth by Adam Smith in *The Wealth of Nations*. While Smith appreciated the importance of power, his purpose was to inquire into the nature and causes of wealth. Economic growth, Smith argued, is primarily a function of the extent of the division of labor which in turn is dependent upon the scale of the market. Much of his attack, therefore, was directed at the barriers erected by feudal principalities and mercantilist states against the free exchange of goods and the enlargement of markets. If men are to multiply their wealth, Smith argued, the contradiction between political organization and economic rationality had to be resolved in favor of the latter.

Marxism, the rebellious ideological child of classical liberalism, erected the concept of the contradiction between economic and political relations into a historical law. Whereas classical liberalism held that the requirements of economic rationality *ought* to determine political relations, the Marxist position was that the mode of production *does* determine the superstructure of political relations. History can be understood as the product of the dialectical process—the contradiction between evolving economic forces and the sociopolitical system.

Although Karl Marx and Friedrich Engels wrote amazingly little on the subject of international economies, Engels in his famous polemic, *Anti-Dühring*, dealt explicitly with the question of whether economics or politics was primary in determining the structure of international relations. Karl Dühring's anti-Marxist theory maintained that property relations resulted less from the economic logic of capitalism than from extraeconomic political factors. Engels, on the other hand, using the example of the unification of Germany in his attack on Dühring, argued that economic factors were primary.

Engels argued that when contradictions arise between economic and political structures, political power adapts itself to changes in the balance of economic forces and yields to the dictates of economic development. Thus, in the case of nineteenth-century Germany, the requirements of industrial production had become incompatible with feudal, politically fragmented Germany. Though political reaction was victorious in 1815 and again in 1848, it was unable to prevent the growth of large-scale industry in Germany and the growing participation of German commerce in the world market. In summary, Engles argued that "German unity had become an economic necessity."

In the view of both Smith and Engels the nation-state represented a progressive stage in human development because it enlarged the political realm of economic activity. In each successive economic epoch the advancing technology and scale of production necessitates an enlargement of political organization. Because the city-state and feudalism were below the optimum for the scale of production and the division of labor required by the Industrial Revolution, they prevented the efficient utilization of resources and were superseded by larger political units. Smith considered this to be a desirable objective; for Engels it was a historical necessity.

In contrast to the position of liberals and Marxists alike who stress the primacy of economic relations nationalists and the so-called realist school of political science have emphasized the primacy of politics. Whereas the liberal or Marxist emphasizes the production of wealth as the basic determinant of social and political organization, the realist stresses power, security, and national sentiment. . . .

Although himself a proponent of economic liberalism, the late Jacob Viner made one of the best analyses of the relationship of economic and political factors in determining the structure of international relations and concluded that political and security considerations are primary. In his classic study, *The Customs Union Issue,* Viner analyzed all known cases of economic and political unification from the perspective of whether the basic motivation was political or economic. Thus, whereas Engels interpreted the formation of the Zollverein as a response to the industrialization of Germany and the economic necessity of larger markets, Viner argued "that Prussia engineered the customs union primarily for political reasons, in order to gain hegemony or at least influence over the lesser German states. It was largely in order to make certain that the hegemony should be Prussian and not Austrian that Prussia continually opposed Austrian entry into the Union, either openly or by pressing for a customs union tariff lower than highly protectionist Austria could stomach." In pursuit of this strategic interest it was "Prussian might, rather than a common zeal for political unification arising out of economic partnership, [that] had played the major role."

Whereas liberalism and Marxism foresee economic factors leading to the decline of political boundaries and eventually to political unification, Viner argued that economic and political boundaries need not coincide and may actually be incompatible with one another. The tendency today, he pointed out, to take the identity of political and economic frontiers for granted is in fact a quite modern phenomenon and is even now not universal. With respect to tariffs, the concern of his study, the general rule until recently was that political unification was greater than the area of economic unification. Furthermore, any attempt to further economic unification might undermine political unification; this was the case with respect to the American Civil War and is the case today in Canada.

Viner concluded his argument that economic factors are of secondary importance to political unification with the following observation, which is highly relevant for the concerns of this essay:

> The power of nationalist sentiment can override all other considerations; it can dominate the minds of a people, and dictate the policies of government, even when in every possible way and to every conceivable degree it is in sharp conflict with what seem to be and are in fact the basic economic interests of the people in question. To accept as obviously true the notion that the bonds of allegiance must necessarily be largely economic in character to be strong, or to accept unhesitatingly the notion that where economic entanglements are artificially or naturally strong the political affections will also necessarily become strong, is to reject whatever lessons past experience has for us in this field.

The contemporary argument that interstate relations will recede in face of contemporary technological developments and will be replaced by transnational relations between large multinational corporations was anticipated in the 1930s by Eugene Staley. In a fascinating book, *World Economy in Transition,* Staley posed the issue which is our main concern: "A conflict rages between technology and politics. Economics, so closely linked to both, has become the major battlefield. Stability and peace will reign in the world economy only when, somehow, the forces on the side of technology and the forces on the side of politics have once more been accommodated to each other."

While Staley believed, along with many present-day writers, that politics and technology must ultimately adjust to one another, he emphasized, in contrast to contemporary writers, that it was not inevitable that politics adjust to technology. Reflecting the intense economic nationalism of the 1930s, Staley pointed out that the adjustment may very well be the other way around. . . .

II

This . . . discussion of the relationship between economics and politics argues the point that, although the economic and technical substructure partially determines and interacts with the political superstructure, political values and security interests are crucial determinants of international economic relations. Politics determines the framework of economic activity and channels it in directions which tend to serve the political objectives of dominant political groups and organizations. Throughout history each successive hegemonic power has organized economic space in terms of its own interests and purposes.

Following in this vein, the thesis of this essay is that transnational actors and processes are dependent upon peculiar patterns of interstate relations. Whether one is talking about the merchant adventurers of the sixteenth century, nineteenth-century finance capitalists, or twentieth-century multinational corporations, transnational actors have been able to play an important role in world affairs because it has been in the interest of the predominant power(s) for them to do so. As political circumstances have changed due to the rise and decline of nation-states, transnational processes have also been altered or ceased altogether. Thus, . . . the world economy did not develop as result of competition between equal partners but through the emergence and influence of great national economies that successively became dominant.

From this perspective the multinational corporation exists as a trans-national actor today because it is consistent with the political interest of the world's dominant power, the United States. This argument does not deny the analyses of economists who argue that the multinational corporation is a response to contemporary technological and economic developments. The argument is rather that these economic and technological factors have been able to exercise their profound effects because the United States—sometimes with the cooperation of other states and sometimes over their opposition—has created the necessary political framework. By implication, a diminution of the Pax Americana and the rise of powers hostile to the global activities of the multinational corporations would bring their reign over international eco-nomic relations to an end.

Perhaps the most effective way to defend the thesis that the pattern of international economic relations is dependent upon the structure of the inter-national political system is to review the origins of the Pax Britannica, its demise with the First World War, and the eventual rise of a Pax Americana after the Second World War. What this history clearly reveals is that trans-national economic processes are not unique to our own age and that the pattern of international economic activity reflects the global balance of eco-nomic and military power.

Each successive international system that the world has known is the consequence of the territorial, diplomatic, and military realignments that have followed history's great wars. The origins of the Pax Britannica lie in the complicated series of negotiations that followed the great upheavals of the Napoleonic wars. The essential features of the system which were put into place at that time provided the general framework of international economic relations until the collapse of the system under the impact of the First World War.

The first essential feature of the Pax Britannica was the territorial settle-ment and the achievement of a balance of power among the five Great Powers. This territorial realignment can be divided into two parts. In the first place, on the continent of Europe the territorial realignments checked the ambitions of Russia in the east and France in the west. Second, the overseas conquests of the continental powers were reduced at the same time that Great Britain acquired a number of important strategic overseas bases. As a result the four major powers on the Continent were kept in check by their own rivalries and by offshore Britain which played a balancing and mediating role.

British naval power, the second essential feature of the Pax Britannica, was able to exercise a powerful and pervasive influence over global politics due to a fortunate juncture of circumstances. Great Britain's geographical position directly off the coast of continental Europe and its possession of several strategic naval bases enabled it to control Europe's access to the outside world and to deny overseas colonies to continental governments. As a consequence, from 1825, when Great Britain warned France not to take advantage of the revolt of the Spanish colonies in America, to the latter part of the century, the greater part of the non-European world was either independent or under British rule. Moreover, the maintenance of this global military hegemony was remarkably inexpensive; it thus permitted Great Britain to utilize its wealth and energies in the task of economic development.

Third, using primarily the instruments of free trade and foreign investment in this political-strategic framework, Great Britain was able, in effect, to restructure the international economy and to exercise great influence over the course of international affairs. As the world's first industrial nation, Great Britain fashioned an international division of labor which favored its own industrial strengths at the same time that it brought great benefits to the world at large. Exchanging manufactured goods for the food and raw materials of other nations, Great Britain was the industrial and financial center of a highly interdependent international economy.

One may reasonably argue, I believe, that in certain respects the regime of the Pax Britannica was the Golden Age of transnationalism. The activities of private financiers and capitalists enmeshed the nations in a web of interdependencies which certainly influenced the course of international relations. In contrast to our own era, in which the role of the multinational corporation in international economic relations is unprecedented, the private institutions of the City of London under the gold standard and the regime of free trade had a strategic and central place in world affairs unmatched by any transnational organization today. Prior to 1914 the focus of much of international relations was the City of London and the private individuals who managed the world's gold, traded in commodities, and floated foreign loans. Though this interdependence differs radically in kind from the internationalization of production and the immense trade in manufactured goods which characterize our own more industrialized world economy, this earlier great age of transnationalism should not be overlooked. . . .

The foundations underlying the Pax Britannica and the transnational processes it fostered began to erode in the latter part of the nineteenth century. On the Continent the industrialization and unification of Germany profoundly altered the European balance of power. France, too, industrialized and began to challenge Great Britain's global supremacy. Overseas development of equal or potentially greater magnitude were taking place. The rapid industrialization of Japan and the United States and their subsequent creation of powerful navies ended British control of the seas. No longer could Great Britain use its naval power to deny rivals access to the globe. With the decline of British supremacy the imperial struggle for the division of Africa and Asia began, leading eventually to the outbreak of the First World War.

The war completed the destruction of the pre-1914 system. As a consequence of the duration and intensity of the conflict one sector after another of economic life was nationalized and brought into the service of the state. The role of the state in economic affairs became pervasive, and economic nationalism largely replaced the laissez-faire traditions upon which so much of pre-war transnationalism had rested. Not until the Second World War would political relations favor the reemergence of extensive transnational activity.

The failure to revive the international economy after the First World War was due to many causes: the policies of economic revenge against Germany; the ill-conceived attempt to reestablish the gold standard; the nationalistic "beggar-thy-neighbor" policies pursued by most states, etc. In terms of our primary concern in this essay one factor in particular needs to be stressed, namely, the failure of the United States to assume leadership of the world economy, a role Great Britain could no longer perform. Whereas before the war the City of London provided order and coordinated international economic activities, now London was unable and New York was unwilling to restructure the international economy disrupted by the First World War. The result was a leadership vacuum which contributed in part to the onset of the Great Depression and eventually the Second World War.

For our purposes two developments during this interwar period hold significance. The first was the Ottawa Agreement of 1932 which created the sterling area of imperial preference and reversed Great Britain's traditional commitment to multinational free trade. The purpose of the agreement between Great Britain and the Commonwealth, an action whose intellectual roots went back to the nineteenth century, was to establish a regional trading bloc effectively isolated from the rest of the world economy. Germany in central Europe and Japan in Asia followed suit, organizing under their hegemonies the neighboring areas of strategic and economic importance. "This development of trading blocs led by great powers," one authority writes, "was the most significant economic development of the years immediately preceding the Second World War. As always the breakdown of international law and economic order gave opportunity to the ruthless rather than to the strong."[1] Such a system of law and order the international gold standard had provided. Under this system transnational actors could operate with little state interference. With its collapse nation-states struggled to create exclusive spheres of influence, and trade relations became instruments of economic warfare.

The second important development from the perspective of this essay was the passage of the Reciprocal Trade Agreements Act in June 1934. The purpose of this act was to enable the United States government to negotiate reductions in tariff barriers. Followed in 1936 by the Tripartite Monetary Agreement, the act not only reflected the transformation of the United States into a major industrial power but also represented the first step by the United States to assert its leadership of the world economy. Furthermore, it demonstrated the potential of bilateral negotiation as a method to achieve the expansion of multinational trade even though the immediate impact of the act was relatively minor. World trade continued to be dominated by preference systems, especially the sterling area, from which the United States was excluded. The importance of this prewar situation and the determination of the United States to overcome this discrimination cannot be too greatly emphasized. The reorganization of the world economy was to be the keynote of American postwar planning.

III

American plans for the postwar world were based on several important assumptions. In the first place, American leadership tended to see the origins of the Second World War as largely economic. The failure to revive the international economy after the First World War and the subsequent rise of rival trading blocs were regarded as the underlying causes of the conflict. Second, it was assumed that peace would be best promoted by the establishment of a system of multinational trade relations which guaranteed to all states equal access to the world's resources and markets. Third, the main obstacles to the achievement of such a universal system, Americans believed, were the nationalistic and discriminatory measures adopted in the 1930s by various European countries—trade preferences, exchange controls, quantitative restrictions, competitive currency depreciations, etc.

The importance of economic considerations in American postwar planning has led in recent years to a spate of writings by revisionist historians who interpret these efforts as part of a large imperial design. While this literature does serve to correct the simple-minded orthodox position that the cold war originated as a Communist plot to achieve world domination, it goes much too far and distorts the picture in another direction.

There is no question that the creation of a system of multilateral trade relations was in the interests of the United States. Preference systems ran directly counter to American basic interests as the world's dominant economic power and a major trading nation. It does not follow from this fact, however, that American efforts to achieve such a system were solely self-serving and unmotivated by the sincere belief that economic nationalism and competition were at the root of the Second World War. Nor does it follow that what is good for the United States is contrary to the general welfare of other nations.

The American emphasis on postwar economic relations represented a long tradition in American thought on international relations. The American liberal ideal since the founding of the Republic has been the substitution of commercial for political relations between states. In the best free trade tradition, trade relations between nations are considered to be a force for peace. Furthermore, as a nation which felt it had been discriminated against by the more powerful European states, the United States wanted a world in which it would have equal access to markets. Universal equality of opportunity, not imperial domination, was the motif of American postwar foreign economic planning.

This naïve American faith in the beneficial effects of economic intercourse was reflected in the almost complete absence of attention to strategic matters in American postwar plans. In contrast to the prodigious energies devoted to the restructuring of the international economy, little effort was given to the strategic and territorial balance of the postwar world. This neglect is explainable in large part, however, by the prevailing American assumption that a universal system based on an integrated world economy and on the United Nations would replace the traditional emphasis on spheres of influence and the balance of power.

If one accepts the revisionist argument that imperial ambition underlay American postwar plans, then the cold war should have been between the United States and Western Europe, particularly the United Kingdom, rather than between the Union of Soviet Socialist Republics and the United States. The bete noir of American planners was European discrimination, and especially the imperial preference which encompassed a high percentage of world trade and exercised considerable discrimination against American goods. American plans for the postwar era were directed against the British in particular. Beginning with the framing of the Atlantic Charter in 1941 and continuing through the negotiation of the Lend-Lease Act (1941), the Bretton Woods Agreement (1944), and the British Loan (1945), the thrust of American policy was directed against Commonwealth discrimination.

In light of the intensity of these American efforts to force the United Kingdom and other European countries to accept a multilateral system it is important to appreciate that they were abandoned in response to growth of Soviet–American hostility. As American leadership came to accept the Soviet diplomatic-military challenge as the major postwar problem, the United States attitude toward international economic relations underwent a drastic reversal. In contrast to earlier emphases on multilateralism and nondiscrimination the United States accepted discrimination in the interest of rebuilding the shattered West European economy.

The retort of revisionists to this argument is that the American–Soviet struggle originated in the American desire to incorporate Eastern Europe, particularly Poland, into the American scheme for a global empire. This effort, it is claimed, clashed with the legitimate security concerns of the Soviet Union, and the cold war evolved as the Soviet defensive response to the American effort to expand economically into the Soviet sphere of influence. If the United States had not been driven by the greed of its corporations, American and Soviet interests could easily have been accommodated.

There are sufficient grounds for this interpretation to give it some plausibility. Certainly, American efforts to incorporate Eastern Europe and even the Soviet Union into the world capitalistic economy raised Soviet suspicions. Although the American view was that the withdrawal of the Soviet Union from the world economy following the Bolshevik Revolution had been a contributing factor to the outbreak of the Second World War and that a peaceful world required Soviet reintegration, the Russians could easily interpret these efforts as an attempt to undermine communism. No doubt in part they were. But it is a long jump from these American efforts to trade in an area of little historical interest to the United States to a conflict so intense and durable that it has on several occasions taken the world to the brink of thermonuclear holocaust.

A more realistic interpretation, I believe, is that the origins of the cold war lie in the unanticipated consequences of the Second World War. The collapse of German power in Europe and of Japanese power in Asia created a power vacuum which both the United States and the Soviet Union sought to fill to their own advantage. One need not even posit aggressive designs on either side to defend this interpretation, although my own position is that the Soviet Union desired (and still desires) to extend its sphere of influence far beyond the glacis of Eastern Europe. To support this political interpretation of the cold war it is sufficient to argue that the power vacuums in Central Europe and the northwestern Pacific created a security dilemma for both powers. In terms of its own security neither power could afford to permit the other to fill this vacuum, and the efforts of each to prevent this only increased the insecurity of the other, causing it to redouble its own efforts. Each in response to the other organized its own bloc, freezing the lines of division established by the victorious armies and wartime conferences.

One cannot understand, however, the pattern of the cold war and its significance for international economic relations unless one appreciates the asymmetric situations of the United States and the Soviet Union. Whereas the Soviet Union is a massive land power directly abutting Western Europe and the northwestern Pacific (primarily Korea and Japan), the United States in principally a naval and air power separated from the zones of contention by two vast oceans. As a consequence, while the Soviet Union has been able with relative ease to bring its influence to bear on its periphery at relatively much less cost in terms of its balance of payments, the United States has had to organize a global system of bases and alliances involving an immense drain on its balance of payments. Moreover, while the Soviet system has been held together largely through the exercise of Soviet military power, economic relations have been an important cement holding the American bloc together.

These economic and strategic differences between the two blocs have been crucial determinants of the postwar international economy and the patterns of transnational relations which have emerged. For this reason some attention must be given to the interplay of economic and political factors in the evolution of relations between the three major components of the contemporary international economy: the United States, Western Europe, and Japan.

Contrary to the hopes of the postwar economic planners who met at Bretton Woods in 1944, the achievement of a system of multilateral trade was soon realized to be an impossibility. The United Kingdom's experience with currency convertibility, which had been forced upon it by the United States, had proven to be a disaster. The United Kingdom and the rest of Europe were simply too weak and short of dollars to engage in a free market. A further weakening of their economies threatened to drive them into the arms of the Soviet Union. In the interest of preventing this the United States, in cooperation with Western Europe, had to rebuild the world economy in a way not envisaged by the postwar planners.

The reconstruction of the West European economy involved the solution of three problems. In the first place, Europe was desperately short of the dollars required to meet immediate needs and to replenish its capital stock. Second, the prewar European economies had been oriented toward colonial markets. Now the colonies were in revolt, and the United States strongly opposed the revival of a world economy based on a colonial preference system. Third, the practices of economic nationalism and closed preference systems between European states and their overseas colonies had completely fragmented the European economy.

The problem of rehabilitating the economy of the Federal Republic of Germany (West Germany) was particularly difficult. The major trading nation on the Continent, its division into Soviet and Western zones and the Soviet occupation of Eastern Europe had cut industrial West Germany off from its natural trading partners in the agricultural German Democratic Republic (East Germany) and the East. The task therefore was to integrate the industrial Western zones into a larger West European economy comprising agricultural France and Italy. The failure to reintegrate industrial Germany into the larger world economy was regarded to have been one of the tragic errors after World War I. A repetition of this error would force West Germany into the Soviet Camp.

The American response to this challenge is well known. Through the Marshall Plan, the Organization for European Economic Cooperation (OEEC), and the European Coal and Steel Community (ECSC) the European economy was revived and radically transformed. For our purposes one point is significant. In the interest of security the United States tolerated, and in fact promoted, the creation of a preference area in Western Europe which discriminated against American goods. At first the mechanism of discrimination was the nonconvertibility of European currencies; then, after the establishment of the European Economic Community (EEC) in 1958, discrimination took the form of one common external tariff.

The economic impact of economic regionalism in Western Europe was not, however, completely detrimental to United States–European trade. One can in fact argue that regionalism gave Europe the courage and security to depart from traditions of economic nationalism and colonialism. The establishment of a large trading area in Europe turned out to be more trade-creating than trade-diverting. As a consequence American and European economic ties increased and the United States continued to enjoy a favorable balance of trade with its European partners.

With respect to Japan the United States faced a situation similar to that presented by West Germany. Although Japan was not severely damaged by the war, it was a densely populated major trading nation exceptionally dependent upon foreign sources of raw materials, technology, and agricultural products. With the victory of the communists on the Chinese mainland Japan's major prewar trading partner came under the control of the Soviet bloc. Furthermore, Japan suffered from discrimination by other industrialized states both in their home markets and in their overseas colonial empires. The exclusion of the Japanese from South and Southeast Asia practiced by the Dutch, French, and British had been a major cause of Japan's military aggression, and the continued existence of these preference systems threatened its economic well-being. Separated from the Soviet Union by a small body of water and economically isolated, Japan's situation was a highly precarious one.

As in the case of West Germany, the task of American foreign policy was to integrate Japan into the larger world economy and lessen the attraction of markets controlled by the Communist bloc. While this history of American efforts to restructure Japan's role in the world economy is less well known than is the history of its European counterpart, the basic aspects deserve to be emphasized. In the first place, the United States brought pressures to bear against Dutch, French, and British colonialism in South and Southeast Asia and encouraged the integration of these areas into a larger framework of multilateral trade. Second, over the strong opposition of Western Europe, the United States sponsored Japanese membership in the International Monetary Fund (IMF), the General Agreement on Tariffs and Trade (GATT), and other international organizations. Third, and most significant, the United States in the negotiations leading to the Treaty of Peace with Japan granted Japan privileged access to the American home market.

At the same time that these developments in the economic realm were taking place, through the instrumentalities of the North Atlantic Treaty Organization (NATO) and the Treaty of Peace with Japan, Western Europe and Japan were brought under the protection of the American nuclear umbrella. In Europe, Japan, and around the periphery of the Soviet Union and the People's Republic of China (Communist China), the United States erected a base system by which to counter the Soviet advantage of geographical proximity. Thus, with their security guaranteed by this Pax Americana, Japan, Western Europe, and, to a lesser extent, the United States have been able to devote the better part of their energies to the achievement of high rates of economic growth within the framework of a highly interdependent transnational economy.

Just as the Pax Britannica provided the security and political framework for the expansion of transnational economic activity in the nineteenth century, so this Pax Americana has fulfilled a similar function in the mid-twentieth century. Under American leadership the various rounds of GATT negotiations have enabled trade to expand at an unprecedented rate, far faster than the growth of gross national product in the United States and Western Europe. The United States dollar has become the basis of the international monetary system, and, with the rise of the Eurodollar market, governments have lost almost all control over a large segment of the transnational economy. Finally, the multinational corporation has found the global political environment a highly congenial one and has been able to integrate production across national boundaries.

The corollary of this argument is, of course, that just as a particular array of political interests and relations permitted this system of transnational economic relations to come into being, so changes in these political factors can profoundly alter the system and even bring it to an end. If, as numerous writers argue, there is a growing contradiction between the nation-state and transnational activities, the resolution may very well be in favor of the nation-state or, more likely, of regional arrangements centered on the dominant industrial powers: Japan, the United States, and Western Europe.

I V

This argument that contemporary transnational processes rest on a peculiar set of political relationships can be substantiated, I believe, if one analyzes the two most crucial relationships which underlie the contemporary international economy. The first is the relationship between the United States and West Germany, the second is that between the United States and Japan.

While the American–West German special relationship is based on a number of factors including that of mutual economic advantage, from the perspective of transnational activities one factor is of crucial importance. In simplest terms this is the exchange of American protection of West Germany against the Soviet Union for guaranteed access to EEC markets for American products and direct investment. . . . With respect to direct investment the subsidiaries of American corporations have been able to establish a very powerful position in Western Europe since the beginning of the EEC in 1958.

Without . . . West German willingness to hold dollars, the American balance-of-payments situation might, the West Germans fear, force the United States to reduce its troop strength in West Germany. As such a move could lessen the credibility of the American nuclear deterrent, the West Germans are very reluctant to make any moves which would weaken the American presence in Western Europe. Consequently, while the significance of American direct investment in Europe for the American balance of payments is unclear, the West Germans are unwilling to take any action regarding this investment which might alienate American opinion and lessen the American commitment to Western Europe.

Turning to the other pillar of the contemporary transnational economy the American–Japanese special relationship, mutual economic interest is an important bond, but the primary factor in this relationship has been the security issue. In contrast to the American–West German situation, however, this relationship involves American protection and a special position for the Japanese in the American market in exchange for United States bases in Japan and Okinawa. The asymmetry of this relationship compared with that between the United States and West Germany reflects the differences in the economic and military situations.

As mentioned earlier the basic problem for American foreign policy with respect to Japan was how to reintegrate this highly industrialized and heavily populated country into the world economy. Given communist control of mainland Asia and the opposition of European countries to opening their markets to the Japanese, this meant throwing open the American economy to Japanese exports. As a consequence of this favored treatment, the Japanese have enjoyed an exceptionally favorable balance of trade with the United States. . . .

In contrast to the situation prevailing in Europe, the purpose of American military base structure in Japan is not merely to deter local aggression against the Japanese; rather, it is essential for the maintenance of American power and influence throughout the western Pacific and Southeast Asia. Without access to Japanese bases the United States could not have fought two wars in Asia . . . and could not continue its present role in the area. . . .

In the case of both the American–European and the American–Japanese relationships, new forces are now at work which threaten to undermine the foundations of contemporary transnational relations. In the case of United States–European relations, the most dramatic change is the decreased fear of the Soviet Union by both partners. As a consequence, both Americans and Europeans are less tolerant of the price they have to pay for their special relationship. The Europeans feel less dependent upon the United States for their security and are more concerned with the detrimental aspects of close economic, military, and diplomatic ties with the United States. The United States, for its part, is increasingly sensitive to European discrimination against American exports and feels threatened by EEC moves toward the creation of a preference system encompassing much of Western Europe, the Middle East, and Africa. . . .

With respect to the relationship of Japan to the United States, strategic and economic changes are undermining the foundations of transnationalism. At the same time that Communist China is receding as a security threat to the United States and Japan, economic strains are beginning to aggravate relations between the two countries. In the eyes of the United States Japan's economy is no longer weak and vulnerable, necessitating special consideration by the United States. As a consequence, the demands of American interests for import curb against Japanese goods and for the liberalization of Japanese policies on foreign direct investment are beginning to take precedence over foreign policy and strategic considerations. Nor does the United States continue to accept the fact that the defense burden should rest so heavily on it alone. Underlying the Nixon Doctrine of American retrenchment in Asia is the appreciation that a greater Japanese military effort would not only reduce American defense costs but would also cause the Japanese to divert resources from their export economy and relieve Japanese pressures in the American market.

The Japanese for their part resent the fact that they are almost totally dependent upon the United States for their security and economic well-being. While they of course want to maintain a strong position in the American market and feel particularly threatened by protectionist sentiment in the United States, they are growing increasingly concerned about the price they must pay for their close association with the United States. Moreover, they feel especially vulnerable to American economic pressures such as those that have been exerted to induce Japan to permit direct investment by American corporations. But the dominant new factor is the Japanese desire to play a more independent role in the world and to enjoy the prestige that is commensurate with their powerful and expanding economy.

In the cases of both American–European and American–Japanese relations, new strains have appeared which threaten to undermine the political framework of transnational economic activity. Diplomatic and military bonds tying Europe and Japan to the United States have weakened at the same time that economic conflicts have intensified and have become less tolerable to all three major parties. As a result, the favorable political factors that have facilitated the rapid expansion of transnational processes over the past several decades are receding. In their stead, new political forces have come into play that are tending to isolate the United States and to favor a more regional organization of the international economy.

On the other hand, one must readily acknowledge that the multinational corporation and transnational processes have achieved tremendous momentum. It is not without good reason that numerous authorities have predicted the demise of the nation-state and the complete reordering of international life by 200 or 300 "megafirms." Perhaps, as these authorities argue, the multinational corporation as an institution has sufficiently taken root in the vested interests of all major parties that it can survive the vicissitudes of political change. History, however, does not provide much comfort for this train of thought. As Staley and Viner have suggested, the contradiction between the economic and political organization of society is not always resolved in favor of economic rationality. Moreover, whatever the outcome—the preservation of multilateral transnational processes, a reversion to economic nationalism, or the division of the globe by economic regionalism—the determining consideration will be the diplomatic and strategic interests of the dominant powers.

V

Prior to concluding this essay, one crucial question remains to be treated: What, after all, has been the impact of transnational economic activities, especially the multinational corporation, on international politics? In answer to this question both Marxists and what one might call the transnational ideologists see these transnational processes and actors as having had a profound impact on international relations. Some go much further. By breaking the monopoly of the nation-state over international economic relations, the multi-national corporation is claimed to have altered the very nature of international relations.

Under certain circumstances, and in relation to particular states, there can be little doubt that the multinational corporation has, and can, exercise considerable influence over domestic and international relations. One could mention in this connection the international petroleum companies, for example. But in general, there is little evidence to substantiate the argument that the multinational corporation as an independent actor has had a significant impact on international politics. As Staley has convincingly shown in his study of foreign investment prior to World War II, where business corporations have exercised an influence over political developments they have tended to do so as intruments of their home governments rather than as independent actors.

Contemporary studies on the multinational corporation indicate that Staley's conclusion continues to hold true. While the evidence is indisputable that the multinational corporation is profoundly important in the realm of international economic relations, its political significance is largely confined to its impact on domestic politics where it is an irritant to nationalistic sentiments. In part the resentment has been due to the unwarranted interference by foreign-owned corporations in domestic affairs; this has especially been the case in less developed countries. More frequently, nationalistic feelings have been aroused by the predominant positions multinational corporations may hold in the overall economy or in particularly sensitive sectors.

Despite all the polemics against multinational corporations, there is little evidence to support the view that they have been very successful in replacing the nation-state as the primary actor in international politics. Where these business enterprises have influenced international political relations, they have done so, like any interest group, by influencing the policies of their home governments. Where they have tried to influence the foreign and economic policies of host governments, they have most frequently been acting in response to the laws of their home countries and as agents of their home governments. . . .

Contrary to the argument that the multinational corporation will somehow supplant the nation-state, I think it is closer to the truth to argue that the role of the nation-state in economic as well as in political life is increasing and that the multinational corporation is actually a stimulant to the further extension of state power in the economic realm. One should not forget that the multinational corporation is largely an American phenomenon and that in response to this American challenge other governments are increasingly intervening in their domestic economies in order to counterbalance the power of American corporations and to create domestic rivals of equal size and competence.

The paradox of the contemporary situation is that the increasing interdependence among national economies, for which the multinational corporation is partially responsible, is accompanied by increased governmental interference in economic affairs. What this neo-mercantilism constitutes, of course, is one response to the basic contradiction between the economic and political organization of contemporary international society. But in contrast to the opinion of a George Ball who sees this conflict resolved in favor of transnational processes, the internationalization of production, and actors like the multinational corporation, nationalists in Canada, Western Europe, and the less developed world favor upholding more powerful states to counterbalance large multinational corporations.

Similarly, the impetus today behind the EEC, Japan's effort to build an economic base less dependent on the United States, and other moves toward regionalism reflects in part a desire to lessen the weight of American economic power; in effect, these regional undertakings are essentially economic alliances between sovereign governments. Although they are altering the political framework within which economic forces will increasingly have to operate, the basic unit is and will remain the nation-state. For better or for worse, it continues to be the most powerful object of man's loyalty and affection.

Notes

1. J. B. Condliffe, *The Commerce of Nations* (New York: W. W. Norton & Co. 1950), p. 502.

The State and Taiwan's Economic Development

ALICE H. AMSDEN

Two features of Taiwan's post–World War II history are striking. First, it is one of the few nonsocialist economies since Japan to rise from the grossest poverty and to enter the world of the "developed." Second, the state in Taiwan has played a leading role in the process of capital accumulation. It has positioned itself to prevail on key economic parameters such as the size of the surplus extracted from agriculture and the rate of profit in industry. To understand Taiwan's economic growth, therefore, it is necessary to understand its potent state.

The challenge of understanding the role of the state in Taiwan's economic development is increased by the fact that the state's initial aims were so clearly military and geopolitical rather than economic. When Taiwan was occupied by the vanquished Nationalist government in 1949, the Guomindang [the Nationalist Party] was obsessed with one objective: military buildup in order to retake the Mainland. As Edwin Winckler bluntly put it, "The Jiang Jie-Shi forces, if they had had their own way, wouldn't have spent one penny on economic development." Given that militarism and economic development must to some extent operate at cross-purposes, competing for the same scarce resources, Taiwan's success must seem somewhat paradoxical.

If the role of the state is critical to economic development, why should an economy under the heel of the military end up with a "good claim to be ranked as the most successful of the developing countries"? One of the obvious factors mitigating the negative consequences of militarism in the Taiwan case was American aid, which diminished the extent of resource competition. I shall try to show, however, that this was not the only, or necessarily even the most important, factor in allowing economic growth to arise out of militarism.

Rather, I shall argue that the reality of economic development itself both seduced the military away from its initial orientation and changed its position within the state apparatus, which then freed up the process of capital accumulation still further.

Although the Guomindang state in Taiwan's "economic miracle" is our central focus, it is necessary to take into account other factors that favored the island's economic development after World War II. One of the most important of these is the legacy of the Japanese colonial period. We shall begin, then, with a discussion of the colonial period and from there look at the Guomindang state itself, its role in agriculture and industry, and its gradual transformation from a state in which the preeminence of military aims was overwhelming to one in which military aims came to coexist with an ever more absorbing interest in economic growth.

The Colonial Heritage

It is a misconception that the Taiwan miracle commenced with the export of labor-intensive manufactures and a reduction of government management of trade and monetary matters in the decade of the 1960s. Taiwan already enjoyed a relatively fast-rising real gross domestic product (GDP) in the 1950s. Agriculture was then the dominant sector, and the economic regime in industry, as in many other underdeveloped countries, was one of protection of infant industries. Growth was also rapid during the years of Japanese domination (1895–1945). Excluding the war years of 1941–45, the per capita income of the agricultural sector almost doubled in half a century. This is a rather impressive figure given that the population rose by approximately 43 percent.

The economy that the Japanese fashioned in Taiwan was achieved by means of deliberate planning and government ownership of major resources (in partnership with private Japanese capitalists). The dominance of the Japanese colonial administration in Taiwan's economy mirrored the dominant role of the Meiji government in Japan proper, which distinguished it in important respects from the colonial offices of England and France. The Jiang Jie-Shi forces benefited enormously from their inheritance of Japanese state monopolies, and the whole interventionist approach taken by the Japanese to the development of an occupied territory was not lost on the Guomindang.

From the start, Taiwan was regarded as an agricultural appendage to be developed as a complement to Japan. A two-crop economy (sugar and rice) was encouraged much in the classical imperial pattern. But one aspect that sets Taiwan's colonial experience apart from the rest is that primary production was not confined to a foreign enclave with limited spillover into subsistence agriculture. Many farmers with access to arable land produced rice for market to meet the ever-escalating needs of Japanese consumers. Although sugarcane is frequently cultivated on large plantations in some Third World countries, in Taiwan it was grown by small owner-operators and tenants as well as on large land tracts owned by Japanese sugar manufacturers. Thus, agriculture in Taiwan was quickly and generally commercialized. . . .

An elaborate network of agricultural associations, under the aegis of the government and rich landlords, provided peasants with extensive education, the cooperative purchase of fertilizers, warehousing, and other services. When persuasion failed, the police were employed to force modern techniques onto rural communities that resisted change. The experience that small tenants gained in experimenting with new seed strains and their familiarization with scientific farming would also prove to be of immense usefulness to the later land reform efforts of the Chinese Nationalists. The extensive network of agricultural associations that the Japanese introduced was created to facilitate police surveillance and control over the local population. . . .

In the 1930s, Japan reshaped its policy of transforming Taiwan into a source of food supply for the home market. The shift in policy can be understood only in the context of Japan's increasing militarism and expansionism in the Pacific. Belatedly and frantically, Japan sought to refashion Taiwan as an industrial adjunct to its own war preparations and ambitions in Southeast Asia and South China.

From a few industries with strong locational advantages before 1930 (e.g., sugar and cement), industry in Taiwan expanded in the 1930s to include the beginnings of chemical and metallurgical sectors, and as World War II cut off the flow of duty-free goods, some import substitution began. Japanese hopes of building Taiwan into an industrial bridgehead to Southeast Asia and South China, however, never materialized. The policy was in effect for too short a time before it was halted by World War II. Although the last-minute efforts to construct transport and harbor facilities suited to military and industrial needs proved highly beneficial in postwar years, many projects remained on the drawing board when war erupted.

Thus, economic growth in Taiwan under Japanese rule went about as far as it could go, given the internal contradictions of imperialism. Growth included a rise in per capita income; indeed, the welfare of Taiwanese peasants in the first half of the twentieth century may have exceeded that of Japanese peasants. . . . The most enduring legacy of the Japanese occupation, however, was less the betterment of living standards than a relatively well educated population and the building of a foundation for subsequent development. Whereas much of the gain in per capita income was lost as a consequence of war and an influx of Mainlanders following the Communist victory in China (and was not regained until the 1950s and 1960s), a relatively high level of literacy and the economic structure implanted by the Japanese survived. The major lesson of the Japanese interlude, however, was that to exploit the economic potential of Taiwan required much more than a reliance on inexorable market forces. It required deliberate state policies, something that the invading force from the Mainland seemed very unlikely to be able to provide.

The Nature of the Guomindang State

The state that took over Taiwan from the Japanese was a highly militaristic bureaucracy dominated by a single leader, Jiang Jie-Shi. On this there is much agreement. But the internal structure of the state, the relative power of different groups within it, and even the extent to which it was a real bureaucracy in the positive Weberian sense are open to debate. . . .

. . . Those who would try to examine the state's role have, of course, no choice but to sift through the available evidence and make the inferences that seem the most reasonable. The problem we are presently interested in exploring is the relationship between militarism and economic development. Hence, we are interested in the Taiwan state's military and technocratic dimensions. Concerning the latter, one view holds that Taiwan's new rulers were a competent group. Another view, rooted in an earlier historical period, is far less flattering. . . .

[However,] we can speak of the existence fairly early on of an economic technocracy in Taiwan—albeit an embryonic one—and not make fools of ourselves, for the technocrats need not be equated with the rascals they once were in prewar Mainland China.

Nevertheless, the development-oriented technocracy was overshadowed in the early postwar period by the military. Most of the Nationalist cliques of the prewar period had disintegrated with the Communist victory, save one: the Whampoa military cadets. Studies of the Taiwan state in the early and late 1960s discuss the power plays centered around the then security administrator (Jiang Jie-Shi's son). For the purposes of understanding the policy orientation of the Taiwan state in the immediate postwar period, however, it is sufficient to note a consensus in the literature about Jiang Jie-Shi's unchallenged political supremacy and the fact that he, "more than any other person . . . was responsible for asserting and perpetuating the concept of mainland recovery. . . . He insisted on tighter authoritarian controls and a greater diversion of resources to military and security purposes."

On the basis of this admittedly sketchy picture of the Guomindang state apparatus, the possibilities of the state serving as an effective instrument of economic development would seem bleak. Yet from the beginning of its reign, the Guomindang bureaucracy embarked on a set of policies that, though they appear to have been chosen for political as much as, or more than, for economic reasons, were crucial to the island's eventual economic growth. Nowhere is this more evident than in agriculture.

Agriculture

When the Guomindang regime arrived on Taiwan, agriculture was by far the most important sector economically. Its share of GDP was twice that of industry, and it accounted for 90 percent of exports. It was, in addition, important politically. The potential threat of an impoverished peasantry had been driven home to the Nationalists on the Mainland, and they were concerned with restructuring agriculture accordingly. From the beginning, Guomindang policy toward agriculture had two faces. On the one hand, state action was the key to increasing agricultural output. On the other hand, agriculture was consistently squeezed to provide the surplus necessary to finance the growth of other sectors. The cornerstone of both sides of state policy was the land reform initiated in 1949 and completed in 1953.

Agriculture was reformed in three stages. First, farm rent was limited to a maximum of 37.5 percent of the total main crop yield. Second, public land formerly owned by Japanese nationals was distributed on easy terms, with preference given to the tenant claimants. Third, landlords were obliged to divest themselves of their holdings above a minimal size and to sell out to their tenants under the Land-to-the-Tiller Act. This end to landlordism and the creation of a class of small holders was the inspiration of Dr. Sun Yat-Sen. The Guomindang's Land-to-the-Tiller Program amounted to sheer rhetoric in China during the 1930s and 1940s because would-be expropriated landlords were stalwarts of the Nationalists. In Taiwan, by contrast, the Mainlander government was under no obligation to the rural Taiwanese elite. Although both were of Chinese origin, they were as different ethnically and socially as the French and the Americans. Landlords were given land bonds in kind and stocks in public enterprise in exchange for the compulsory divestiture of their holdings. Some landlords profited from their stock ownership and became successful industrialists. Others went into bankruptcy. The landlord class, however, sank into social oblivion. . . .

Thus, almost overnight the countryside in Taiwan ceased to be oppressed by a small class of large landlords and became characterized by a large number of owner-operators with extremely small holdings. By 1973, almost 80 percent of the agricultural population consisted of owner-cultivators and another tenth of part owners. Only 6 percent of farm income accrued to landlords and money lenders. This undoubtedly underscores the fact that income distribution (by household) in Taiwan is far less inequitable than in most other Third World countries and is more like the pattern in advanced capitalist countries, which is not to say, however, that income distribution is equitable.

The years 1953–68 witnessed annual growth rates in agricultural output that were impressive by any standard. Equally impressive was the spillover effect on industry, for however tight the squeeze on agriculture under Japanese rule, it was even tighter under the Jiang Jie-Shi administration. Whereas net real capital outflow from agriculture had increased at a rate of 3.8 percent annually between 1911 and 1940, it rose on average by 10 percent annually between 1951 and 1960. Fast growth and a transfer of agricultural resources to the towns, however, were neither the outcome of free market forces nor the automatic result of purely technical phenomena—the green revolution. Rather, they reflected the structure of ownership in the countryside and state management of almost every conceivable economic activity.

It is well known that in developing countries there have been substantial gains in income among the few (i.e., the bigger farmers) when the new technology associated with the green revolution has been introduced. By contrast, the green revolution in Taiwan has transformed the life of almost every peasant. Furthermore, such an extensive application of science appears to hinge on government control over capital accumulation. The state distributes resources equally among all peasants, as the market mechanism might not do. Hence, there have been large gains among the many. A small class of big landowners has not yet resurfaced (nor, consequently, has a potentially cohesive source of opposition to the state). It is, then, a defining characteristic of Taiwan's agriculture that a multiplicity of small peasant proprietors exists in conformity with the bourgeois model of individualistic family farming, whereas directing this drama is a highly centralized government bureaucracy. . . .

In 1965, government agencies or related credit institutions supplied 65 percent of all agricultural loans. Before land reform, private moneylenders accounted for 82 percent of credit. With respect to such activities as agricultural education and marketing, the government exerts its control through the elaborate network of agricultural associations laid down by the Japanese. The state monopoly on fertilizers was perhaps the most important element both in stimulating production and in extracting the surplus from agriculture. . . .

. . . [T]he fertilizer monopoly was the key to extracting surplus from agriculture. Fertilizer was bartered for rice, and the barter ratio was highly unfavorable to farmers. The price that Taiwanese farmers paid for 100 kilograms of ammonium sulfate in 1964–65 was higher by almost 40 percent than the price that Japanese, Dutch, Belgian, American, or Indian farmers paid. . . .

Thus, a self-exploitative peasantry, working long hours to maximize production per hectare, and a superexploitative state, ticking along effectively to exact the fruits of the peasantry's labor, operated hand in hand in Taiwan to great advantage until the late 1960s.

The only question that remains is, to whose advantage in particular? For Taiwan is not a classless entity, and the state acted in the interests of an elite when it squeezed the countryside. Unfortunately, whereas a voluminous amount of statistical information is available about Taiwan, very little class analysis has been published. Clearly, however, the historical roots of the Guomindang's *étatisme* and its class affiliations are traceable not only to Japanese colonialism but also to events on the Mainland. We may hypothesize that the system of "bureaucratic capitalism" of late imperial China, with its total interpenetration of public and private interests, was transplanted into Taiwan, along with the Mainlanders. Although historical conditions were unpropitious for economic development under bureaucratic capitalism in China, they were favorable in Taiwan. The 1953 land reform and subsequent agricultural development breathed new life into the Guomindang apparatus, and the bureaucratic capitalism of the Guomindang regime sustained the life of the reform and small-scale farming.

In summary, agriculture in Taiwan gave industrial capital a labor force, a surplus, and foreign exchange. Even during the immediate postwar years of economic chaos and a world record rate of population growth, agriculture managed to produce a food supply sufficient to meet minimum domestic consumption requirements as well as a residual for export. Good rice harvests have been a major factor behind Taiwan's stunning price (and real wage) stability. The foreign exchange saved as a result of high productivity in agriculture has been equally important. Agriculture also managed to provide an important source of demand for Taiwan's industrial output, particularly chemicals and tools, and a mass market for consumption goods. The agrarian structure provided a degree of political stability sufficient to draw the most timid of foreign firms to the island. Agriculture has even been sufficiently productive to set a floor on industrial wages. Factory women who returned home to the farm during the sharp depression of 1974–75 subsequently refused to return to wage employment at prevailing rates. A labor shortage symbolizes Taiwan's introduction to the problems of capitalist development rather than underdevelopment, and it is to industrialization that attention is now turned.

Industrialization

Taiwan's industrialization has often been falsely characterized as exhibiting the efficacy of a "laissez-faire" strategy. It has been alleged that Taiwan's success is due to the fact that it, unlike most Third World countries, resisted the temptations of infant industry protection. A study published by the Organization for Economic Cooperation and Development (OECD) in 1970, comparing industrialization in Brazil, Mexico, Argentina, India, Pakistan, the Philippines, and Taiwan, made a start toward dispelling this illusion. The study showed that a regime of import substitution preceded the export of labor-intensive manufactures in Taiwan. Nor was infant industry protection a trivial episode in Taiwan's economic history. The protection afforded to sales on the home market in 1966, the year under examination in the OECD report, far exceeded that which prevailed in Mexico, a country reputed to be highly protectionist.

In the period from 1956 to 1961, the government introduced a package of reforms to reorient the Taiwan economy toward export-led growth. Monetary and fiscal policies were redesigned, the exchange rate was devalued and unified, inflation was brought under control, and exports were made highly profitable. These changes have earned the title "liberalization" and have been responsible for Taiwan's reputation for successful development with sound formulas. Nevertheless, what is not appreciated is that protection in Taiwan of key import substitutes never appears to have abated. Whereas exporters were allowed to import their inputs duty free after "liberalization," critical second-stage import-substitute items continue to be shielded from foreign competition. . . .

Inward-oriented growth in Taiwan was introduced in 1949 partly by default (traditional agricultural exports no longer found protected or preferential markets in Japan and China) and partly by design (it was politically expedient to aid the class of small capitalists that had acquired a portion of the old Japanese facilities). Small enterprises were in serious trouble by 1949 as a result of the loss of the Mainland market and the reappearance of competitive Japanese goods. Import, foreign exchange, and licensing controls were introduced by the government to salvage small establishments from extinction and to ease the critical balance of payments situation.

Inward-oriented growth in Taiwan's small domestic market, however, soon stalled. Although it conferred high profits on some, it conferred inflation, monopoly, excess capacity, a reliance on American donations of hard currency, and corruption on all. It was only after manufacturing had made a fair start, however, that the Taiwan government hesitantly charted a new course in the direction of export-led growth. Two points are worth stressing in this regard. First, "liberalization" should in no way be interpreted as a restoration in Taiwan of a "market economy." Government management of capital accumulation has continued, as evidenced, if by nothing else, by tariff protection. Second, although economists have viewed a regime of export-led growth as one that is more in keeping with liberal economic principles, the Taiwan government has not been guided by any theoretical orthodoxy to turn a profit. . . .

Cartels, in whatever variation, have been encouraged by the government and, at one time or another, have covered most of Taiwan's major exports: textiles, canned mushrooms and asparagus, rubber, steel, paper products, and cement. The government has tried to get the marketing of all exports into Taiwanese hands because both bureaucrats and businesspersons alike are sensitive to the inroads in overseas marketing made by large Japanese trading companies; this is in spite of the efficacy of these trading companies and the lackluster track record of those of Taiwan.

At issue is not merely the quibble that the government of Taiwan has intervened far more in the Taiwan economy than liberal economists who champion export-led growth acknowledge. The point, rather, is that the government of Taiwan has never been guided by free-market principles as such; so to attribute Taiwan's success to a commitment to such principles, whether in theory or in practice, is misleading. What has obsessed the Guomindang state since its defeat in China is economic stability. . . .

To achieve stability, the government of Taiwan appears to have thought it prudent sometimes to shield the economy as much as possible from market forces and at other times to use them, but never to embrace them as a rule of thumb out of conviction.

Foreign Aid, Foreign Capital, and State Enterprises

Flows of U.S. aid in the 1950s and 1960s and, more recently, flows of foreign direct investment played a critical role in capital formation in Taiwan. These flows, particularly the initial deluge of U.S. aid, obviously had implications for policies and politics in addition to providing capital. The magnitude of the aid cannot be denied. In 1955, when aid reached its peak, it amounted to over half of gross investment, and it was not until 1964 that it fell below 20 percent.

Politically, aid was critically important: It kept the state in power by helping to bring inflation down from 3400 percent in 1949 to 9 percent in 1953 by means of the arrival of large quanties of both consumer goods and producer goods at a desperate moment.

In terms of long-run economic growth, the impact of aid was minor. Most aid went for military purposes and the remainder for infrastructure broadly defined. . . . Thus, the effects of aid may be said to have been felt in perpetuity only in terms of a multiplication of civil engineering projects and know-how and improvements in the administrative capability of the Taiwan technocracy. The extent to which Taiwan's turn to export-led growth can be attributed to U.S. pressures is difficult to say. Now, all parties concerned are eager to take credit for it. All that is certain is that freer trade and freer enterprise (including freer foreign enterprise) were preached by the American Aid Mission. In view of the preferences of its major benefactor, the extent to which the Guomindang government persisted in its *étatisme* is all the more impressive. To appreciate this fully, we must focus on public sector production as well as on policy making.

In 1952, as much as 57 percent of total industrial production (value added at 1966 prices) and 56.7 percent of manufacturing output were accounted for by public corporations. Since then, the government has repeatedly been under pressure either to freeze or to reduce the size of its holdings. Partly under the persuasion of the U.S. Agency for International Development, majority or 100 percent equity in four public corporations (one highly profitable, two others distinctly less so) was transferred to landlords in 1954 as partial compensation for confiscations carried out under the 1953 land reform. There has also been sporadic pressure for denationalization from local capitalists, who want less crowding out in credit markets or who want a greater share of the action in lucrative state enterprises (in 1982, however, fourteen of fifteen state enterprises were in the red). Finally, there has been pressure from what may be termed the liberalization lobby to reduce both tariff protection and the scope of public corporations. . . .

The government has been slow to divest itself of its holdings for two basic reasons. From the beginning, public enterprise has served to consolidate the power of the Mainlander bureaucracy. In recent years, public enterprise has also allowed the Guomindang to buttress its own power vis-à-vis foreign capital. One of the fundamental consequences of public enterprise has been the control by the state rather than by multinationals of key sectors in the economy. This is not to belittle the power of the multinationals, nor to suggest the absence of an organic solidarity between the productive activities of the state and foreign investors. Recently, in the case of automobiles, they have tried to ally to form a nucleus of expansion. But the state has held its own in several crucial respects. The government did not abandon its traditionally conservative attitude toward foreign investment until the export boom of the late 1960s had gotten underway. Only then did foreign firms begin arriving in Taiwan in significant numbers.

By 1971, overseas Chinese and other foreign investments amounted to roughly one-seventh of total registered capital (about the same as in Brazil), although statistics on foreign investment are problematic. Foreign investments, however, have been concentrated in electronics, chemicals, and textiles destined for export. Foreign investments have not mushroomed with the government's turn to heavy industry. According to one account, between 1973 and 1980, foreign firms were responsible for as much as half of total investment and as much as 20 percent of total exports in the electronics sector, but they were responsible for only 10 percent of total investment in manufacturing. Finally, Taiwan has not become highly indebted to international banks to finance its heavy industry. As discussed shortly, a relatively low reliance on foreign credit is due to a high domestic propensity to save. Moreover, although Taiwan has been a sizable international borrower by the standards of less developed countries, its international debt service/export ratio is very low—ranging between 5 percent and 10 percent—as a consequence of its very rapid growth of exports.

The Jiang Jie-Shi government, therefore, cannot be said to have delivered Taiwan into foreign hands, either by letting foreign banks dominate credit or by letting foreign firms dominate manufacturing. Nor can the government be said to have been overwhelmed by its own technocracy (mostly American-educated), which has lobbied for lower tariffs and a privatization of state enterprises. The voice of the military has remained audible even as its visibility within the state apparatus has diminished (e.g., in the 1950s, an army general served as economics minister). The voice has remained audible to the extent that it appears to speak for continued state control of the economy for purposes of defense and social order, much as in the old Guomindang tradition. . . .

The public sector in Taiwan is also still very important as far as capital formation is concerned. Although the state's share of gross domestic investment has fallen from a high of 62 percent in 1958, it still amounted in 1980 to as much as 50 percent. State spending has gone largely to finance ten major development projects in infrastructure, integrated steel, shipbuilding, and petrochemicals, which contributes to the fact that manufacturing in Taiwan has progressed in breadth (the percentage of manufacturing in GDP) and in depth (the percentage of "sophisticated" products and processes in total manufacturing output). . . .

Nor has manufacturing been confined to "wigs and wallets," as myth once held. In the course of six "plan periods," which incidentally can be described, at most, only as "indicative," important structural changes have occurred within manufacturing. Textiles and food processing were the leading sectors during the first two plan periods (1953–56 and 1957–60). During the second plan period, however, the relative contribution of nondurable consumer goods, particularly food processing, declined, whereas that of intermediate goods (cement and paper) expanded. Chemicals (fertilizer, soda ash, plastics, and pharmaceuticals) assumed major importance during the third plan period (1961–64). Capital and the production of durable goods (electrical and non-electrical machinery, such as radios and sewing machines, and transport equipment, such as bicycles and ships) as well as petroleum products grew enormously during the fourth and fifth plan periods (1965–68 and 1969–72). The seventh plan period (1976–81) saw large increases in heavy industry. . . . The percentage of so-called light industry in manufacturing output was still 48 percent in 1977, down, however, from 54 percent in 1970 and 60 percent in 1960.

Exploiting the World Market

The nineteen-point reform program introduced by the government between 1956 and 1961 made exporting highly profitable. Not only were exporters wined on tax and credit subsidies; they were also dined on tariff reductions from prewar China heights. This allowed them to take advantage simultaneously of advanced levels of world productivity for their inputs and exotic Taiwan wage levels for their outputs. In what follows, we discuss the supply-side factors that permitted Taiwan to profit from the world market, directing attention to the role of the state.

Taiwan exports (90 percent of them manufactures) are highly competitive in world markets for reasons of low costs and rising productivity. There appears to have been a substantial fall in Taiwan's wage costs per unit of output relative to those of competitors in the period spanning 1954–71, although there is a great deal of uncertainty about the figures. After the energy crisis in 1973, when the dust had settled, Taiwan could still be seen to have a cost advantage due to lower wage rates, by comparison not only with Japan but also with South Korea, Hong Kong, and Singapore. . . .

Apart from the noise of exchange-rate distortions, wage levels remain relatively low because the rate of increase in wages has been modest. What is more, the movement of wages in relation to labor productivity has been favorable for unit labor costs. In both regards, one detects the arm of the state. Labor unions are virtually nonexistent and strikes are prohibited, because Taiwan is still technically at war. One key to the advance in productivity is the enormous emphasis placed on public education, financed by a tax system that is highly regressive. . . . The rapid rise in labor productivity has not been autonomous and may be understood as emerging out of the cumulative process of fast growth itself. As growth has accelerated, throughput time has decreased, profitability has risen, and investments have skyrocketed in foreign technology (both embodied in machinery imports and disembodied in the form of services). The scale of production has mounted and, with it, specialization and the division of labor; and, finally, the time required for the accumulation of experience has been telescoped, opportunities to use such experience to improve process and product have multiplied, and firm-level increments in productivity have been realized.

That Taiwan has assimilated foreign technology as effectively as it has in no small part harks to its highly educated population. It was thought to be the most educated in all of Asia, with the exception of Japan, when the Japanese occupation of Taiwan ended after World War II. High investments in education continued thereafter, increasingly in the technical fields. By the early 1970s, Taiwan had more engineers per 1,000 persons engaged in manufacturing than all other developing countries for which data are available, with the exception of Singapore. Since then, investments in education have soared in tandem with the rate of growth of output; the number of engineering students studying abroad almost doubled between 1975 and 1976, and the number of engineering students studying in Taiwan doubled between 1968–69 and 1972–73 and then doubled again between 1973 and 1982–83. Taiwan trains 50 percent more engineers in proportion to its population than the United States.

Although there has been no shortage of profitable investment outlets for Taiwan firms to exploit, the opposite has been true of savings. Over the years, however, as a proportion of gross national product (GNP), savings have risen phenomenally. This has spared Taiwan the mutilation of overextended international indebtedness, as discussed earlier. Savings as a percentage of national income were less than 5 percent in 1952, 6.5 percent in 1962, 26.8 percent in 1972, and almost one-third a decade later. The composition of savings has also altered. The share of foreign savings has nose-dived, from around 40 percent from 1952 to 1960, the heyday of U.S. aid, to a negative percentage in the period since 1972, whereas the shares of both public and private domestic savings have risen. . . .

A few remarks on the relationship between the Nationalist government and Taiwan firms are in order, lest it be thought that the interests of capital have been served by the state unstintingly. Taiwan's ability, by comparison with, say, a Latin American country, to situate its economy in the lap of the international market has rested in part on the clout that the state has used against private producers. Because the governance of private producers is nowhere clearly defined, capital everywhere imagines incursions into its domain by the state, but it is understandable why such complaints are so vocal in Taiwan.

We have already noted how "the arm of the state reaches down to virtually every farmer." Similarly, "the government is deeply involved in all aspects of industry." Even after most import and foreign exchange controls were lifted, the government exercised its will through the myriad licenses necessary for a firm to operate; the requirement of prior approval for foreign loans and technology agreements; public ownership of the banking system, which held interest rates much higher than in most Third World countries; vagueness in tax laws such that politically uncooperative firms could be threatened with audits; and so on. All businesspersons agree that they could be put out of business at the caprice of the state in a matter of months. . . .

Rentiers and capitalists alike in Taiwan have, in the past, experienced the dismembering or disabling effects of state power: the former were expropriated by a land reform, and the latter succumbed to the liberalization reforms that ushered in export-led growth. When a government charts a new economic course, entrenched interests are threatened. In the case of a turn to export-led growth, class conflict is stirred up by devaluation and deflation. A liberalization of imports hurts import-substituting firms and the banks that are financing them. When these are foreign, they can bring extraeconomic power to bear against new policy directives. These consequences of the turn to export-led growth were relatively mild in Taiwan. For one thing, the economy was both far less industrialized and far less inflationary than, say, some of the Latin American economies, so that fewer entrenched interests were upset. The state also controlled many sectors that would otherwise have been hurt, and foreign firms and foreign banks were absent. Nevertheless, private domestic firms that were not satisfied with the sweeteners of export subsidies and protection for second-generation import substitutes were swept away. In short, Taiwan was better able to turn to the international market than other poor countries because the balance of power between the state and both labor and capital was weighted far more to the state's advantage.

To a certain degree Taiwan enjoyed an edge over other developing countries in its export effort because of historical and geopolitical specificities: Taiwan's careful study of its erstwhile colonizer enabled it to absorb the Japanese economic experience and to appreciate that export-led growth was a viable strategy. In addition, the way was paved for the acceptance of Taiwan products in the U.S. market, first by Japanese exports and then by those of U.S. multinationals, which had chosen Taiwan as an export platform after U.S. aid had secured it for democracy. Clearly, however, these explanations of Taiwan's ability to exploit the international market—whereas most developing countries appear instead to have been exploited by it—are dwarfed by those explanations that focus on the forceful manipulation of Taiwan's political economy by the state.

Economic Growth and the Changing Nature of the State

The initial puzzle of the role of the Taiwan state was not just a question of magnitude. In terms of scope, Taiwan is simply a particularly striking example of the positive association between state intervention and the acceleration of economic growth. . . . What made Taiwan particularly interesting was that the state was so effective despite the clear priority the military placed on defense over development and the clear dominance of the military within the state apparatus. The discussion so far has not resolved this puzzle. On the contrary, the turn to export-led growth seems to make the relation between apparent military dominance of the state and successful economic policy even more perplexing.

The important role of public enterprises, like the early economic self-sufficiency promoted by the state, is quite consistent with what can be presumed to be the interests of the military. Import-substitution industrialization, low reliance on foreign investors, and a focus on greater output of basic foodstuffs would all square with the military's presumed preference for autarky. Export-led growth, on the other hand, appears to contradict the policies the military could be expected to favor. Why should a regime fanatically committed to national security tolerate a policy change that made the

Taiwan economy highly vulnerable to foreign supply and demand as well as more dependent on foreign-owned firms?

The answer to this question is complex. First, it must be emphasized that the increased reliance on international markets and capital that characterized the civilian economy did not extend to defense production. The military ran its own production facilities, supplied with basic inputs by state enterprises. In addition to state enterprises, there are many special-status companies that obtain favors and/or incentives from the state. Among these are the enterprises owned or invested in by the Guomindang or by the Vocational Assistance Committee for Retired Soldiers, a complex of more than forty firms reputed to be the largest single enterprise on the island. By the 1960s, military arsenals produced much of the equipment and less sophisticated weaponry and ammunition needed by the armed forces. . . . This mushrooming military economy may have made the generals less concerned with the diminishing autarky of the civilian sector.

Export-led growth, then, was consistent with the maintenance, and even expansion, of previous levels of autarky in the sectors that were most critical for warfare. Nevertheless, there is abundant evidence, beginning at the time of Taiwan's turn to export-led growth, that the influence of the military over economic affairs began to wane. For instance, the government began to support family planning, whereas it was once deterred by the insistence of party elders that such a policy would reduce the number of soldiers available for retaking the Mainland. Taiwan ceased being self-sufficient in basic foodstuffs because it was more profitable to specialize in cash crops for export. Defense spending as a percentage of GNP and of government expenditures also fell. . . . In 1960, when export-led growth was just getting underway, military expenditure as a percentage of GNP was roughly 13 percent and, as a percentage of government expenditure, 65 percent. By 1978, these figures had fallen to 8 percent and 34 percent, respectively.

Part of the answer to the apparent contradiction between the turn to export-led growth and the military's interests is that these interests were no longer reflected in state policy as monolithically as they had been in the period immediately following the takeover of Taiwan. And even if the military had held complete sway, it would have had little option other than to turn to export-led growth. Given the exhaustion of import-substitution industrialization and foreign reserves, the continued pursuit of increased autarky would have been economically suicidal, although reliance should not be placed on the functionalist argument that because a decision was economically necessary the military would endorse it even at the expense of its own geopolitical ends.

More understanding is gained, however, by a closer examination of the changing relationship over time of economic and geopolitical factors. On the one hand, the dream of retaking the Mainland grew dimmer as the communist regime there proved its durability. The repossession of China "had begun as a fierce resolve; it became an aspiration, then a myth, then a liturgy." At the same time, it became less clear that Taiwan could rely simply on its anticommunist credentials to ensure support from its major ally, the United States.

From this perspective, increased reliance on foreign investment, which went along with export-led growth, might be seen to be as valuable in securing powerful political allies as in reaping economic benefits.

The key to the changing logic of Taiwan's international position, however, was bread and butter. Taiwan, as well as communist China, was proving itself to be a viable economic entity, as evidenced by its control over inflation and its fast growth. The economic viability of Taiwan meant that the population of Mainlanders as a social collectivity no longer needed to retake China to enrich itself. This was all the more true when it became clearer in the 1960s that economic gains in Taiwan were being realized not on the ephemeral basis of plunder, as they had been between 1945 and 1949, or of buying cheap and selling dear, as they had been to some extent during the earliest years of import-substitution industrialization, but rather on the sustained basis of capital accumulation. I think that this, more than anything else, is what underlay the military's acceptance of export-led growth and its exit from the center of the stage of Taiwan's political economy.

In the last analysis, despite the continued power of the military within the state, Taiwan provides an interesting commentary on Engels's classic dictum that when "the internal public force of a country stands in opposition to its economic development. . . . [i]nexorably and without exception, the economic evolution has forced its way through." Engels's concern was with the open contest between an economically reactionary elite's attempt to maintain its rule by political means and the transformative power of economic change. Taiwan does not exactly fit this description, but one can observe in Taiwan the powerful effect of economic change on the orientation of political force. The military was not overcome by the emergence of successful capitalist development, but it does seem that it found the expanding opportunities such development offered to be more attractive than the shrinking ones that were promised by a continued fixation on geopolitical struggle.

Taiwan, then, is more than a case in which the essential contribution of state intervention to economic development can be observed. It is a case that demonstrates the reciprocal interaction between the structure of the state apparatus and the process of economic growth. The Taiwan state, which appeared on its arrival from the Mainland to be an unlikely instrument for the promotion of development, proved to be a most effective one. At the same time, changes in the nature of the state itself appear to have been an important by-product of economic development. The state, in short, can be said both to have transformed Taiwan's economic structure and to have been transformed by it.

7

Rational Choice Analysis

Rational choice IPE extends the logic and analytic techniques of neoclassical economics to the study of political questions. It is, therefore, rooted in the liberal tradition. Although much rational choice analysis is consistent with its liberal heritage, in recent years it has been employed to bolster some neomercantilist and Marxist arguments. This crossover is but one example of the eclecticism common to contemporary IPE theory. The two excerpts offered here fall within the purview of liberalism, but they provide a good overview of the rudiments of rational choice analysis and the prospects it offers for broader theoretical synthesis.

Mancur Olson and Richard Zeckhauser's classic, "An Economic Theory of Alliances," analyzes issues of international organization, especially the North Atlantic Treaty Organization (NATO). Drawing on Olson's earlier book, *The Logic of Collective Action,* they develop a model that explains why some NATO members bear a disproportionate share of the costs of maintaining the alliance and why NATO goals are not fulfilled optimally. At the heart of their argument is the concept of a "public good," a special situation in which all members of a group benefit irrespective of an individual's contribution to the provision of the good. Security, NATO's primary objective, is a public good because the absence of war benefits all countries of a particular region regardless of the defense burden of individual states. Olson and Zeckhauser contend that the collective action necessary for securing a public good is beset by a paradox because group members seek to maximize their individual benefits and minimize their individual costs. Since each knows that it will enjoy the good even if it does not pay an equal share of the requisite cost, then all will tend to evade their collective duties and, as a consequence, the public good may not be provided. Thus, international organizations are inherently inefficient; the perverse logic of collective action works against the fulfillment of common interests.

Why, then, has NATO not disintegrated? Quite simply, some members place a higher value on the alliance and, therefore, provide a disproportionate share of its public good. For a variety of reasons, the absolute value that the United States places on defense is greater than Belgium's. If they were not drawn together in an alliance, the United States would naturally spend more on defense, even in per capita terms, than Belgium. When the United States and Belgium join together, the military power of the United States is so great that it provides, in and of itself, much of Belgium's defense requirements. This creates a disincentive for Belgium to bear its "fair" share of alliance costs. Olson and Zeckhauser demonstrate with indifference maps how "larger" countries—those that place a higher value on a particular public good—may thus be exploited by smaller countries. In sum, disproportionality is due to neither the "moral superiority" of some states nor the irresponsibility of others; rather, it is the logical outcome of individual states rationally pursuing their own best interests.

Olson and Zeckhauser's argument resonates, to a certain extent, with international relations realism, a precursor of neomercantilist IPE. The efficacy of international organizations, according to realism, is a function of the particular national interests of member states. Insofar as this conclusion is consistent with the logic of collective action outlined above, rational choice analysis and realism are compatible. On the other hand, rational choice analysis does not rest upon the historical specificity embraced by many realist theorists. Instead, it deduces individual behavior from a few core assumptions.

Bruno Frey explicates the postulates of rational choice analysis. The perspective envisions a world of "economic men." Individuals are held to be rational utility maximizers with constant and transitively ordered preferences. The approach focuses on how such individuals strategically interact to secure their interests. It thus assumes that a single logic of formal rationality (as opposed to questions of substantive rationality) motivates a very wide range of human activity, from peasant revolution in Vietnam to nuclear deterrence. Rational choice analysis can be very simple, considering the interactions of only two individuals, or it may be highly complex, examining the strategies of many. Its assumption of rational individuality can be applied across levels of analysis, from individual states in an international system to individual consumers within one country. Frey illustrates how rational choice arguments move well beyond the special case of public goods as evidenced by "politicometric modelling" and game theory. He also notes that the methodology of rational choice is positivist; its abstract logic must be challenged by rigorous empirical scrutiny.

Frey provides examples of rational choice analysis in two areas: tariffs and international organization. On tariffs, rational choice is able to explain why Adam Smith's ideal of free trade is not realized. The benefits of a tariff reduction are a public good; all consumers gain regardless of their effort in bringing it about. Individuals, therefore, have no incentive to incur the "costs" of time and energy required to secure lower tariffs. Conversely, import-competing interests that are threatened by lower tariffs are more willing to assume the organizational costs of lobbying and political action. If the political system is open to specific social pressure, tariffs will not be reduced, because those who stand to gain from lower tariffs are diffuse and unconcerned while potential losers are focused and active. Moreover, Frey argues, the "supply" of tariffs may serve the interests of certain public officials, a situation that further undermines the chances for lower tariffs. The political market tends to favor protection. Regarding international organizations, Frey discusses rational choice analyses that confirm and refine Olson and Zeckhauser's conclusions. In addition, he shows how "constitutional agreements," in the form of various voting rules, might be employed to overcome some of the problems of collective action.

Although he states that rational choice analysis is a variant of economic reasoning, Frey suggests that it opens the way for new syntheses in IPE theory. Some findings of rational choice studies may complement "political science-based" IPE arguments. However, more extensive use of rational choice analysis within theoretical systems not based in liberalism raises an important epistemological question: is the central tenet of individual rationality consistent with the assumptions and argumentation of nonliberal theories? This issue has sparked heated debate among Marxists and is likely to be an ongoing controversy of rational choice analysis.

An Economic Theory of Alliances

MANCUR OLSON, JR. AND RICHARD ZECKHAUSER

I. Introduction

This article outlines a model that attempts to explain the workings of international organizations, and tests this model against the experience of some existing international institutions. Though the model is relevant to any international organization that independent nations establish to further their common interests, this article emphasizes the North Atlantic Treaty Organization, since it involves larger amounts of resources than any other international organization, yet illustrates the model most simply. . . .

There are some important respects in which many observers in the United States and in some other countries are disappointed in NATO and other ventures in international cooperation. For one thing, it is often argued that the United States and some of the other larger members are bearing a disproportionate share of the burden of the common defense of the NATO countries, and it is at least true that the smaller members of NATO devote smaller percentages of their incomes to defense than do larger members. There is also some concern about the fact that the NATO alliance has systematically failed to provide the number of divisions that the NATO nations themselves have proclaimed (rightly or wrongly) are necessary or optimal. . . .

Some suppose that the apparent disproportion in the support for international undertakings is due largely to an alleged American moral superiority, and that the poverty of international organizations is due to a want of responsi-

This article originally appeared in *Review of Economics and Statistics,* Vol. XLVIII, No. 3, August 1966. Reprinted with permission of Review of Economics and Statistics. (c) President and Fellows of Harvard College, 1966.

Table 1. NATO Statistics: An Empirical Test

Country	Gross National Product 1964 (billions of dollars)	Rank	Defense Budget as Percentage of GNP	Rank	GNP Per Capita	Rank
United States	569.03	1	9.0	1	$2,933	1
Germany	88.87	2	5.5	6	1,579	5
United Kingdom	79.46	3	7.0	3	1,471	8
France	73.40	4	6.7	4	1,506	6
Italy	43.63	5	4.1	10	855	11
Canada	38.14	6	4.4	8	1,981	2
Netherlands	15.00	7	4.9	7	1,235	10
Belgium	13.43	8	3.7	12	1,429	9
Denmark	7.73	9	3.3	13	$1,636	3
Turkey	6.69	10	5.8	5	216	14
Norway	5.64	11	3.9	11	1,484	7
Greece	4.31	12	4.2	9	507	12
Portugal	2.88	13	7.7	2	316	13
Luxembourg	.53	14	1.7	14	1,636	4

Ranks:

GNP	1	2	3	4	5	6	7	8	9	10	11	12	13	14
Defense Budget as % of GNP	1	6	3	4	10	8	7	12	13	5	11	9	2	14
GNP Per Capita	1	5	8	6	11	2	10	9	3	14	7	12	13	4

Source: All data are taken from the Institute for Strategic Studies, *The Military Balance 1965–1966* (London, November 1965).

bility on the part of some other nations. But before resorting to any such explanations, it would seem necessary to ask whether the different sized contributions of different countries could be explained in terms of their national interests. Why would it be in the interest of some countries to contribute a larger proportion of their total resources to group undertakings than other countries? The European members of NATO are much nearer the front line than the United States, and they are less able to defend themselves alone. Thus, it might be supposed that they would have an interest in devoting larger proportions of their resources to NATO than does the United States, rather than the smaller proportions that they actually contribute. And why do the NATO nations fail to provide the level of forces that they have themselves described as appropriate, i.e., in their common interest? These questions cannot be answered without developing a logical explanation of how much a nation acting in its national interest will contribute to an international organization.

Any attempt to develop a theory of international organizations must begin with the purposes or functions of these organizations. One purpose that all such organizations must have is that of serving the *common* interests of member states. In the case of NATO, the proclaimed purpose of the alliance is to protect the member nations from aggression by a common enemy. Deterring aggression against any one of the members is supposed to be in the interest of all. The analogy with a nation-state is obvious. Those goods and services, such as defense, that the government provides in the *common* interest of the citizenry, are usually called "public goods." An organization of states allied for defense similarly produces a public good, only in this case the "public"—the members of the organization—are states rather than individuals.

Indeed, almost all kinds of organizations provide public or collective goods. Individual interests normally can best be served by individual action, but when a group of individuals has some common objective or collective goal, then an organization can be useful. Such a common objective is a collective good, since it has one or both of the following properties: (1) if the common goal is achieved, everyone who shares this goal automatically benefits, or, in other words, nonpurchasers cannot feasibly be kept from consuming the good, and (2) if the good is available to any one person in a group it is or can be made available to the other members of the group at little or no marginal cost. Collective goods are thus the characteristic outputs not only of governments but of organizations in general.

Since the benefits of any action an individual takes to provide a public or organizational good also go to others, individuals acting independently do not have an incentive to provide optimal amounts of such goods. Indeed, when the group interested in a public good is very large, and the share of the total benefit that goes to any single individual is very small, usually no individual has an incentive voluntarily to purchase any of the good, which is why states exact taxes and labor unions demand compulsory membership. When—as in any organization representing a limited number of nation-states—the membership of an organization is relatively small, the individual members may have an incentive to make significant sacrifices to obtain the collective good, but they will tend to provide only suboptimal amounts of this good. There will also be a tendency for the "larger" members—those that place a higher absolute value on the public good—to bear a disproportionate share of the burden, as the model of alliances developed below will show.

II. The Model

When a nation decides how large a military force to provide in an alliance, it must consider the value it places upon collective defense and the other, nondefense, goods that must be sacrificed to obtain additional military forces. The value each nation in an alliance places upon the alliance collective good vis-à-vis other goods can be shown on a simple indifference map, such as is shown in Figure 1. This is an ordinary indifference map cut off at the present income line and turned upside down. Defense capability is measured along the horizontal axis and valued positively. Defense spending is measured along the vertical axis and valued negatively. The cost curves are assumed to be linear for the sake of simplicity. If the nation depicted in Figure 1 were not a part of any alliance, the amount of defense it would obtain (OB) could be found by drawing a cost curve coming out of the origin and finding the point (point A)

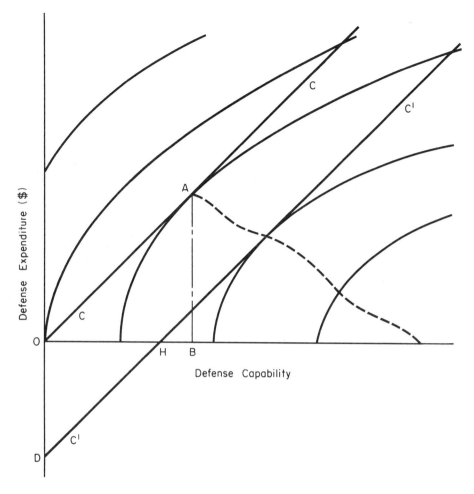

Figure 1. Indifference Map

where this cost curve is tangent to the "highest" (most south-easterly) indifference curve.

In an alliance, the amount a nation spends on defense will be affected by the amount its allies provide. By moving the cost curve down along the vertical axis beneath the origin we can represent the defense expenditure of allied nations as the distance between the origin and the juncture of the cost curve and the vertical axis. If a nation's allies spend OD on defense, and their cost functions are the same as its own, then it receives OH of defense without cost. This is directly equivalent to an increase in income of OD. The more defense this nation's allies provide, the further the cost constraint moves to the southeast, and the less it spends on defense. By recording all the points of tangency of the total cost curve with the indifference curves, we can obtain this nation's reaction function. The reaction function indicates how much defense this nation will produce for all possible levels of defense expenditure

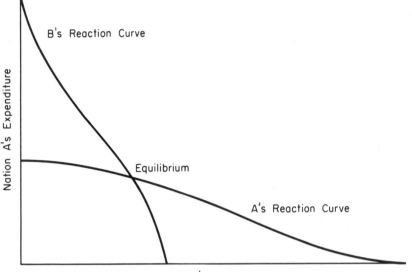

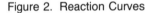

Figure 2. Reaction Curves

by its allies. The amount of defense that this nation provides will in turn influence the defense output of its allies, whose reaction curves can be determined in the same way.

Figure 2 shows the reaction curves for a two-country model (which can easily be generalized to cover N countries). The intersection point of the two reaction curves indicates how much of the alliance good each ally will supply in equilibrium. The two reaction curves need not always intersect. If one nation has a very much larger demand for the alliance good than the other, its reaction curve may lie at every point outside that of the other, in which case it will provide all of the defense. . . .

In equilibrium, the defense expenditures of the two nations are such that the "larger" nation—the one that places the higher absolute value on the alliance good—will bear a *disproportionately* large share of the common burden. It will pay a share of the costs that is larger than its share of the benefits, and thus the distribution of costs will be quite different from that which a system of benefit taxation would bring about. This becomes obvious when income effects—i.e., the influence that the amount of non-defense goods a nation has already forgone has on its desire to provide additional units of defense—are neglected. This is shown in Figure 3 below, which depicts the evaluation curves of two nations for alliance forces. The larger nation, called Big Atlantis, has the higher, steeper valuation curve, V_B, because it places a higher absolute value on defense than Little Atlantis, which has evaluation curve V_L. The CC curve shows the costs of providing defense capability to each nation, since both, by assumption, have the same costs. In isolation, Big

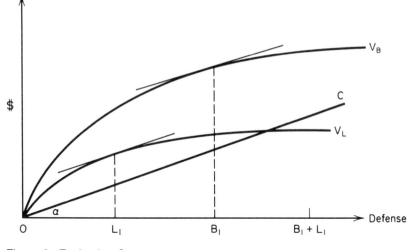

Figure 3. Evaluation Curves

Atlantis would buy B_1 units of defense and Little Atlantis L_1, for at these points their respective valuation curves are parallel to their cost functions. If the two nations continued to provide these outputs in alliance each would enjoy B_1 plus L_1 units of defense. But then each nation values a marginal unit at less than its marginal cost. Big Atlantis will stop reducing its output of deterrence when the sum applied by the two nations together is B_1. When this amount (or any amount greater than L_1) is available, it is not in Little Atlantis' interest to supply any defense whatever. The two nations are therefore simultaneously in equilibrium *only* when Big Atlantis provides B_1 of defense and Little Atlantis provides no defense whatever.

The disproportionality in the sharing of burdens is less extreme when income effects are taken into account, but it is still important. This can be seen most easily by supposing that Big Atlantis and Little Atlantis are identical in every respect save that Big Atlantis is twice the size of Little Atlantis. Per capita incomes and individual tastes are the same in both countries, but the population and GNP of Big Atlantis are twice that of Little Atlantis. Now imagine also that Big Atlantis is providing twice as much alliance defense as Little Atlantis, as proportionality would require. In equilibrium, the marginal rate of substitution of money for the alliance good (MRS) must equal marginal cost for each of these countries, i.e., $MRS_{Big} = MRS_{Little} =$ marginal cost. But (since each country enjoys the same amount of the collective good) the MRS of Big Atlantis is double that of Little Atlantis, and (since the cost of an additional unit of defense is the same for each country) either Big Atlantis will want more defense or Little Atlantis will want less (or both will be true), and the common burden will come to be shared in a disproportionate way.

There is one important special case in which there will be no tendency toward disproportionality. That is when the indifference maps of the member nations are such that any perpendicular from the ordinate would intersect all indifference curves at points of equal slope. In this case, when the nation's cost constraint moves to the right as it gets more free defense, it would not reduce its own expenditure on defense. In other words, none of the increase in income that the nation receives in the form of defense is spent on goods other than defense. Defense in this situation is, strictly speaking, a "superior good," a good such that all of any increase in income is used to buy the good.

This special case may sometimes be very important. During periods of all-out war or exceptional insecurity, it is likely that defense is (or is nearly) a superior good, and in such circumstances alliances will not have any tendency toward disproportionate burden sharing. The amount of allied military capability that Great Britain enjoyed in World War II increased from 1941 to 1944 as the United States mobilized, adding more and more strength to the allied side. But the British war effort was maintained, if not increased, during this period.

Although there is then one exception to the rule that alliance burdens are shared disproportionately, there is no equivalent exception to the rule that alliances provide suboptimal amounts of the collective good. The alliance output will always be suboptimal so long as the members of the alliance place a positive value on additional units of defense. This is because each of the alliance members contributes to the point where its MRS for the good equals the marginal cost of the good. In other words, the result of independent national maximization in an alliance, when the cost function is linear and the same for all members, is that $MRS_1 = MRS_2 = \ldots MRS_N = MC$. There could be an optimal quantity of the collective good only if the total value which all of the alliance members together placed on an additional unit of the good equalled marginal cost, i.e., only if $MRS_1 + MRS_2 + \ldots MRS_N = MC$. The individual nations in an alliance would have an incentive to keep providing additional alliance forces until the Pareto-optimal level is reached only if there were an arrangement such that the alliance members shared marginal costs in the same proportions in which they shared additional benefits (that is, in the same ratio as their marginal rates of substitution of money for the good). When there is such a marginal cost sharing scheme, there need be no tendency toward disproportionality in the sharing of burdens.

III. Qualifications and Elaborations

One simplification assumed in the foregoing model was that the costs of defense were constant to scale and the same for all alliance members. Although military forces are composed of diverse types of equipment and manpower, and thus probably vary less both in cost from one country to another and with scale of output than many single products, it is still unlikely that costs are constant and uniform. For some special types of weapon systems there are undoubtedly striking economies of large scale production, and for conventional ground forces there are probably rising costs as larger proportions of a nation's population are called to arms. Because of this latter tendency, a small country can perhaps get a considerable amount of conventional capability with the first few percentiles of its national income. This tends to keep the military expenditures of small nations in an alliance above the very low level implied by our constant cost assumption. In any event, cross-country variations in marginal costs should not normally alter the basic conclusions deduced from the model. The differences in the amounts which member nations would be willing to pay for marginal units of an alliance good are typically so great that the cost differentials could hardly negate their effect. Even if there were very large differences in marginal costs among nations, there is no reason to assume that national cost functions would vary systematically with the valuation a country places on alliance forces.

A nation's valuation of alliance forces obviously depends not only on its national income, but also on other factors. A nation on the enemy's border may value defense more than one some distance away. A nation that has a large area and long frontiers in relation to its resources may want a larger army than a compact country. On the other hand, if bomb and missile attacks are the main danger, a crowded country may wish to invest more in defense against attack by air. Similarly, a nation's attitudes or ideologies may partly determine its evaluation of defense. Many observers think that the uniformity and intensity of anti-communism is greater among the NATO countries with the highest per capita incomes, and these also happen to be the largest countries in the alliance. It also seems that many people in small and weak countries, both inside and outside of NATO, tend to be attracted to neutralist or pacifist ideologies. This pattern of attitudes may perhaps be partly explained by our model for it suggests that small nations, which find that even large sacrifices on their part have little effect on the global balance, would often be attracted to neutral or passive foreign policies, and that large nations which know that their efforts can decisively influence world events in their own interest will continually need to emphasize the urgency of the struggle in which they are engaged. The popularity of pacific ideologies, the frequent adoption of neutralist policies in small and weak countries, and the activist attitudes and policies of the United States and the Soviet Union are at least consistent with our model.

Whatever the reasons for the different evaluations different nations have for military capabilities in an alliance, the model here still applies. If two countries in an alliance had equal national incomes, but one was more concerned about the common enemy for geographic, ideological, historical, or other reasons, the more concerned nation would not only put a higher valuation on the alliance's military capacity, but would bear a share of the total alliance costs that was even greater than its share of the total benefits. The model deals with the general case of differences in the absolute valuation that nations put upon additional units of an alliance good, whether these differences are due to differences in national income or to other reasons.

Another assumption in the model developed in the foregoing section was that the military forces in an alliance provide only the collective benefit of alliance security, when in fact they also provide purely national, non-collective benefits to the nations that maintain them. When Portugal mobilizes additional forces to suppress the independence movement in Angola, a national goal unrelated to the purposes of NATO, she may at the same time be increasing the total strength of the alliance. Similarly, allied nations may be suspicious of one another, even as they cooperate in the achievement of common purposes, and may enlarge their military forces because of conceivable future conflicts with each other. In any situations in which the military forces of alliance members provide important non-collective benefits as well as alliance benefits, the degree of suboptimality and the importance of the disproportionality will decrease because the non-collective benefits give the member nations an incentive to maintain larger forces.

This fact leads to the paradoxical conclusion that a *decline in the amity, unity, and community of interests among allies need* not *necessarily reduce the effectiveness of an alliance,* because the decline in these alliances "virtues" produces a greater ratio of private to collective benefits. This suggests that alliances troubled by suspicions and disagreements may continue to work reasonably well. To be sure, the degree of coordination among the allies will decline, and this will reduce the efficiency of the alliance forces (in a sense leaving them on a poorer production function), but the alliance forces will be larger.

However important the non-collective benefits of alliances may be, there can be little doubt that above all alliances produce public goods. It is not easy to think of alliances that provide only private goods, though such alliances are perhaps conceivable. If nations simply trade sites for military bases, no common interests or public goods would necessarily be involved. An alliance might also be set up simply to provide insurance in the sense that two nations without any common purpose or common enemy would agree to defend each other in case of attack, but in which neither knew in advance which would suffer aggression. On the other hand, if these two nations thought (as they presumably would) that the fact of their alliance would make it less profitable for other nations to attack either of them, the alliance would provide a public good—a degree of deterrence that could deter an attack on either or both of these nations about as well as it could deter an attack on one alone. There is, moreover, no reason to describe a mere transaction in private goods as an alliance, and the word does not normally appear to be used in that way. A transaction in private goods would be quite as useful between enemies as between "allies," and would normally be completed by a single pair of actions or a single agreement which would not require the continuing consultation, cooperation, and organization characteristic of alliances.

Normally, an additional member can be added to an alliance without substantially subtracting from the amount of defense available to those already in the alliance, and any good that satisfies this criterion is by definition a public good. Suppose two nations of the same size face a common enemy with an army larger than either of them provides by itself. They then form an alliance and maintain a level of military forces larger than either of them had before, but smaller than the sum of their two pre-alliance armies. After alliance both nations enjoy (1) more military security, and (2) lower defense costs, than they had before. This result comes about, not only because a military force can often deter attack by a common enemy against an additional nation without a substantial increase in cost, but also because an alliance may make a greater level of security economically feasible and desirable, and the gains from obtaining this extra security can leave both nations better off.

Another defining characteristic that is sufficient (but not necessary) to distinguish a collective good is that the exclusion of those who do not share the cost of the good is impractical or impossible. Typically, once an alliance treaty has been signed, a member nation is legally bound to remain a member for the duration of the treaty. The decisions about how the common burden is to be shared are not, however, usually specified in the alliance treaty. This procedure works to the disadvantage of the larger countries. Often the smaller and weaker nations gain relatively more from the existence of an alliance than do the larger and stronger powers, and once an alliance treaty has been signed the larger powers are immediately deprived of their strongest bargaining weapon—the threat that they will not help to defend the recalcitrant smaller powers—in any negotiations about the sharing of the common burden. Even at the time an alliance treaty is negotiated exclusion may very well not be feasible, since most alliances are implicit in an already existing danger or goal common to some group of states. That common danger or goal gives the nations that share it an incentive tacitly to treat each other as allies, whether or not they have all signed a formal agreement. A nation can only lose from having another nation with whom it shares a common interest succumb to an enemy, for that will strengthen the enemy's side at the expense of the first nation. It may well be that most alliances are never embodied in any formal agreement. Sometimes a nation may have a geo-political position (e.g., behind an alliance member serving as a buffer state) such that it would be unusually difficult, if not impossible, to deny it the benefits of alliance protection. Then, if it regards alliance membership as a special burden, it may have an incentive to stay out of, or when legally possible to withdraw from, the alliance's formal organization.

This paper also made the simplifying assumption that no alliance member will take into account the reactions other members may have to the size of its alliance contribution. The mutual recognition of oligopolistic interdependence can be profoundly important in small groups of firms, but in the NATO alliance at least, it seems to have been somewhat less important (except with respect to the infrastructure which will be considered later). There are at least two important reasons why strategic bargaining interaction is often less important in alliances than in oligopolistic industries. First, alliances are often involved in situations that contain a strong element of irreversibility. Suppose that the United States were to threaten to cut its defense spending to nothing to get its allies to bear larger shares of the NATO burden. The Soviet Union, if it has the characteristics that American policy assumes, would then deprive the United States of its independence, in which case future defense savings would have little relevance. The United States threat would have only a limited credibility in view of the irreversibility of this process. The second factor which limits strategic bargaining interaction among alliance members stems from an important difference between market and non-market groups. In an oligopolistic group of firms, any firm knows that its competitors would be better off if it were made bankrupt or otherwise driven out of the industry. Large firms thus sometimes engage in price wars or cutthroat competition to drive out the smaller members of an oligopolistic group. By contrast, non-market groups and organizations, such as alliances, usually strive instead for a larger membership, since they provide collective goods the supply of which should increase as the membership increases. Since an ally would typically lose from driving another member out of an alliance, a bargaining threat to that effect may not be credible. This will be especially true if the excluded nation would then fall to the common enemy and (as we argued before) thereby strengthen the enemy at the expense of the alliance.

Even when strategic interaction is important in alliances, the advantage paradoxically still rests in most cases with the smaller nations. There are two reasons for this. First, the large country loses more from withholding an alliance contribution than a small country does, since it values a given amount of alliance force more highly. In other words, it may be deterred by the very importance to itself of its own alliance contribution from carrying out any threat to end that contribution. Second, the large country has relatively less to gain than its small ally from driving a hard bargain. Even if the large nation were successful in the bargaining it would expect only a relatively small addition to the alliance force from the small nation, but when the small nation succeeds in the bargaining it can expect a large addition to the alliance force from the large nation. There is, accordingly, no reason to expect that there is any disparity of bargaining in favor of the larger ally that would negate the tendency toward disproportionality revealed by our model.

IV. Empirical Evidence

When other things are equal, the larger a nation is, the higher its valuation of the output of an alliance. Thus, if our model is correct, the larger members of an alliance should, on the average, devote larger percentages of their national incomes to defense than do the smaller nations. This prediction is tested against the recent data on the NATO nations in Table 1. The following specific hypotheses are used to test the model's predictions:

H_1— In an alliance, there will be a significant positive correlation between the size of the member's national income and the percentage of its national income spent on defense. This hypothesis will be tested against:

H_0— There will not be a significant positive correlation between the variables specified in H_1.

. . . . The Spearman rank correlation coefficient for Gross National Product and *defense budget as a percentage of* GNP is .490. On a one-tailed test this value is significant at the .05 level. We therefore reject the null hypothesis and accept H_1. There is a significant positive correlation indicating that the large nations in NATO bear a disproportionate share of the burden of the common defense. Moreover, this result holds even when the level of per capita income is held constant. [Hypotheses on U.N. funding and foreign aid are also tested and supported.]

Our model indicated that when the members of an organization share the costs of marginal units of an alliance good, just as they share in the benefits of additional units of that good, there is no tendency toward disproportionality or suboptimality. In other words, if each ally pays an appropriate percentage of the cost of any additional units of the alliance good, the results are quite different from when each ally pays the full cost of any amount of the alliance good that he provides. The costs of the NATO infrastructure (common supply depots, pipelines, etc.), unlike the costs of providing the main alliance forces, are shared according to percentages worked out in a negotiated agreement. Since each ally pays some percentage of the cost of any addition to the NATO infrastructure, we have here a marginal cost sharing arrangement.

Thus our model suggests that the burdens of the NATO infrastructure should be borne quite differently from the rest of the NATO burdens. There are other reasons for expecting that the infrastructure burden would be shared in a different way from the main NATO burdens. For one thing, the infrastructure facilities of NATO are all in continental European countries, and ultimately become the property of the host nation. Their construction also brings foreign exchange earnings to these countries, which for the most part are the smaller alliance members. In addition, infrastructure costs are very small in relation to the total burden of common defense, so a small nation may get prestige at a relatively low cost by offering to bear a larger percentage of the infrastructure cost. There are, in short, many private benefits for the smaller alliance members resulting from the infrastructure expenditures. Because of these private benefits, and more important because of the percentage sharing of marginal (and total) costs of the infrastructure, we would predict that the larger members of the alliance would bear a smaller share of the infrastructure burden than of the main alliance burdens.

This prediction suggests that the following hypotheses be tested:

H_4— In an alliance in which the marginal costs of certain activities are *not* shared (but fall instead upon those members who have an incentive to provide additional units of the alliance good by themselves), and in which the marginal costs of other activities are shared (so that each member pays a specified percentage of any costs of these activities), the *ratio* of a member's share of the costs of the activities of the former type to his share of the costs of activities of the latter type will have a significant positive correlation with national income.

H_0— There will be no significant positive correlation between the variables in H_4.

Table 2. NATO Infrastructure

Country	National Income 1960[a] (billions of dollars) (1)	Infrastructure % Reconsidered in 1960[b] (2)	R = (2)/(1) (3)	Military Budget 1960 (billions of dollars) (4)	T = (4)/(2) (5)
United States	411.367	36.98	.0899	41.000	1.1087
Germany	51.268	13.77	.2686	2.072	.1504
United Kingdom	57.361	9.88	.1722	4.466	.4520
France	43.468	11.87	.2731	3.311	.2789
Italy	24.950	5.61	.2248	1.076	.1922
Canada	28.178	6.15	.2183	1,680	.2732
Netherlands	9.246	3.51	.3800	.450	.1282
Belgium	8.946	4.39	.4907	.395	.0900
Turkey	4.929	1.75	.3550	.244	.1394
Denmark	4.762	2.63	.5569	.153	.0582
Norway	3.455	2.19	.6338	.168	.0767
Greece	2.684	.87	.3242	.173	.1989
Portugal	2.083	.28	.1344	.093	.3321
Luxembourg	.386	.17	.4404	.007	.0412

Ranks:

(1)	1	3	2	4	6	5	7	8	9	10	11	12	13	14
(3)	14	9	12	8	10	11	5	3	6	2	1	7	13	4
(5)	1	8	2	4	7	5	10	11	9	13	12	6	3	14

[a]United Nations, *Yearbook of National Accounts Statistics,* (New York, 1964); and *Balance of Payments Yearbook,* Vol. 15 (Washington, D.C.: International Monetary Fund, 1964).

[b]Charles Croot, "Coordination in the Sixties," reprinted from *NATO Letter* (August 1960).

To test these hypotheses we calculated the correlation coefficient between *national income* and *variable T* in Table 2. The Spearman rank correlation coefficient between these variables is .582, which is significant at the .05 level. We therefore reject the null hypothesis and conclude that the larger members bear a larger proportion of the costs of the main NATO forces than they do of those NATO activities for which the costs of each unit are shared. The difference between the distribution of infrastructure costs and the distribution of alliance burdens generally is quite striking, as the tests of the following hypotheses indicate:

H_5— In the NATO alliance there is a significant negative correlation between national income and the percentage of national income devoted to infrastructure expenses.

H_0— There is no significant negative correlation between the variables in H_5.

The Spearman rank correlation coefficient between *national income* and *variable R* in table 2 is −.538, which is significant at the .05 level. Thus, not only is it the case that the larger nations pay a smaller share of the infrastructure costs than of other alliance costs; it is also true that there is a significant negative correlation between national income and the percentage of national income devoted to the NATO infrastructure, which is in vivid contrast to the positive correlation that prevails for other NATO burdens. This confirms the prediction that when there are marginal cost sharing arrangements, there need no longer be any tendency for the larger nations to bear disproportionately large shares of the costs of international organizations. If it happens at the same time that the smaller nations get greater than average private benefits from their contributions, they may even contribute greater percentages of their national incomes than the larger members.

V. Conclusions and Recommendations

All of the empirical evidence tended to confirm the model. . . . In NATO there is . . . a statistically significant positive correlation between the size of a member's national income and the percentage of its national income devoted to the common defense.

As our model indicated, this is in part because each ally gets only a fraction of the benefits of any collective good that is provided, but each pays the full cost of any additional amounts of the collective good. This means that individual members of an alliance or international organization have an incentive to stop providing the collective good long before the Pareto-optimal output for the group has been provided. This is particularly true of the smaller members, who get smaller shares of the total benefits accruing from the good, and who find that they have little or no incentive to provide additional amounts of the collective good once the larger members have provided the amounts they want for themselves, with the result that the burdens are shared in a disproportionate way. The model indicated two special types of situations in which there need be no such tendency toward disproportionality. First, in cases of all-out war or extreme insecurity defense may be what was strictly defined as a "superior good," in which case a nation's output of a collective good will not be reduced when it receives more of this good from an ally. Second, institutional arrangements such that the members of an organization share marginal costs, just as they share the benefits of each unit of the good, tend to work against disproportionality in burden sharing, and it is a necessary condition of an efficient, Pareto-optimal output that the marginal costs be shared in the same proportions as the benefits of additional units. The NATO nations determine through negotiation what percentages of any infrastructure expenditure each member will pay, and this sharing of marginal costs has led the smaller members to bear a very much larger share of the infrastructure burden than they do of the other NATO burdens. The fact that the model predicts not only the distribution of the principal NATO burdens, but also the greatly different distribution of infrastructure costs, suggests that the results are in fact due to the processes described in the model, rather than to some other cause.

The model's implication that large nations tend to bear disproportionate shares of the burdens of international organization, and the empirical evidence tending to confirm the model, does *not* entail the conclusion that the small nations should be told they "ought" to bear a larger share of the common burdens. No moral conclusions can follow solely from any purely logical model of the kind developed here. Indeed, our analysis suggests that moral suasion is inappropriate, since the different levels of contribution are not due to different moral attitudes, and ineffective, since the less than proportionate contributions of the smaller nations are securely grounded in their national interests (just as the disproportionately large contributions of the larger countries are solidly grounded in their national interests). Thus, American attempts to persuade other nations to bear "fair" shares of the burdens of common ventures are likely to be divisive and harmful even to American interests in the long run.

The model developed here suggests that the problems of disproportionality and suboptimality in international organizations should be met instead through institutional changes that alter the pattern of incentives. Since suboptimal provision is typical of international organizations, it is possible to design policy changes that would leave everyone better off, and which accordingly may have some chance of adoption. Appropriate marginal cost sharing schemes, such as are now used to finance the NATO infrastructure, could solve the problem of suboptimality in international organizations, and might also reduce the degree of disproportionality. Substituting a union for an alliance or international organization would also tend to bring about optimality, for then the unified system as a whole has an incentive to behave in an optimal fashion, and the various parts of the union can be required to contribute the amounts their common interest requires. Even a union of smaller members of NATO, for example, could be helpful, and be in the interest of the United States. Such a union would give the people involved an incentive to contribute more toward the goals they shared with their then more nearly equal partners. Whatever the disadvantages on other grounds of these policy possibilities, they at least have the merit that they help to make the national interests of individual nations more nearly compatible with the efficient attainment of the goals which groups of nations hold in common.

A final implication of our model is that alliances and international organizations, as presently organized, will not work efficiently, or according to any common conception of fairness, however complete the agreement and community of interest among the members. Though there is obviously a point beyond which dissension and divergent purposes will ruin any organization, it is also true that some differences of purpose may improve the working of an alliance, because they increase the private, non-collective benefits from the national contributions to the alliance, and this alleviates the suboptimality and disproportionality. How much smaller would the military forces of the small members of NATO be if they did not have their private fears and quarrels? . . . The United States, at least, should perhaps not hope for too much unity in common ventures with other nations. It might prove extremely expensive.

The Public Choice View
of International Political Economy

BRUNO S. FREY

There can be no question that the study of international political economy has received insufficient attention in both economics and political science. As Joan Spero puts it,

> in the twentieth century the study of international political economy has been neglected. Politics and economics have been divorced from each other and isolated in analysis and theory. . . . Consequently, international political economy has been fragmented into international politics and international economics.[1]

Though this gap still exists today, it has been narrowed considerably by the emergence of a new field from international relations theory, a field commonly known as "international political economy." . . .

Political science-based scholars quite outspokenly claim international political economy as their proper and exclusive domain. R.J. Barry Jones, for example, argues that "the foundations of a realistic study of the international political economy are not dissimilar to those of conventional political analysis."[2] Accordingly, "power" and "authority" are taken to be the central concepts with which to study problems. In addition, the analysis has to be "dynamic" and has to take historical processes into account. It is not surprising that, as a consequence, there is a marked tendency to reject any approaches based on economic theory. . . .

This rejection of economic theory does not, however, seem to be based on an extensive knowledge of the literature. In particular, the economic approach to politics, usually called "public choice," seems to be almost totally

Reprinted from *International Organization,* Vol. XXXVIII, 1984, Bruno Frey, "The Public Choice View of International Political Economy" by permission of The MIT Press, Cambridge, MA.

disregarded. The "classic" writers in the public choice tradition, such as Arrow, Downs, Buchanan, Tullock, and Niskanen, are hardly, if ever, mentioned. It is due to this oversight that Roger Tooze, writing as recently as 1981, can maintain that "neo-classical theory . . . treats political and social processes perfunctorily, as extraneous, and, at best, exogenous factors."[3] Yet what public choice has done is exactly to treat political processes as *endogenous* factors.

In this article, I endeavor to show that, first, public choice has been applied specifically to international political economy, and that there is a large and rapidly growing literature on the subject. Second, public choice offers an interesting and worthwhile approach to the area, an approach that complements the political science-based views of international political economy in a useful way. Consequently, the claim for exclusivity made by some writers based in political science should be replaced by the realization of the need for mutual cross-fertilization of the two (partly competing) approaches. Section 1 provides a short survey of those parts of the public choice approach most relevant for international political economy.

1. The Public Choice Approach

General Characteristics

Public choice, sometimes called the "economic theory of politics" or "(new) political economy," seeks to analyze political processes and the interaction between the economy and the polity by using the tools of modern (neoclassical) analysis. It provides, on the one hand, an explicit positive approach to the workings of political institutions and to the behavior of governments, parties, voters, interest groups, and (public) bureaucracies; and it seeks, on the other, normatively to establish the most desirable and effective political institutions. Public choice is part of a movement that endeavors to apply the "rational behavior" approach to areas beyond traditional economics. In recent years, an increasing number of political scientists, sociologists, and social psychologists have taken up this approach. It thus constitutes one of the rare successful examples of interdisciplinary research.

Both the rational behavior approach to social problems and public choice theory are characterized by three major features. First, the individual is the basic unit of analysis. The individual is assumed to be "rational" in the sense of responding in a systematic and hence predictable way to incentives: courses of action are chosen that yield the highest net benefits according to the individual's own utility function. Contrary to what nonspecialists often believe, it is not assumed that individuals are fully informed. Rather, the amount of information sought is the result of an (often implicit) cost-benefit calculus. Indeed, in the political arena it often does not pay the individual to be well-informed—this is known as "rational ignorance."

Second, the individual's behavior is explained by concentrating on the changes in the constraints to which he or she is exposed; that is, the preferences are assumed to be constant. Individuals are assumed to be capable of comparing alternatives, of seeing substitution possibilities, and of making marginal adjustments.

The third characteristic is that the analysis stresses rigor (and is sometimes formal). The results must yield a proposition that (at least in principle) can be subjected to econometric or politicometric testing.

There is no need to go into general public choice theory here; only its applications to problems of international political economy are relevant to this discussion.

The Concepts Applied in International Political Economy

In the international field, some theoretical concepts developed in public choice are used particularly often. Public goods theory and politico-economic modeling will be briefly mentioned here in order to illuminate the public choice approach to international political economy.

Public good theory. Public goods is the concept most frequently used within economic-based international political economy. Its usefulness is well illustrated in a contribution by Charles Kindleberger, in which he looks at various aspects of the international economy from the point of view of public goods, and at the tendency for free riding, in which a public good is available to all irrespective of whether they have contributed to its supply.[4] Thus, law and order can be considered a public good forming an important complement to foreign trade. Its absence can lead to serious disruption in international exchange. The institution of the state may also be regarded as a public good. The high costs arising when it does not exist are illustrated by the example of Germany in 1790. At that time there were 1,700 tariff boundaries with three hundred rulers levying tolls as they pleased. Under such circumstances it was no wonder that the advantages of trade exchange could not be exploited to any great degree. The existence of national monetary institutions may also be looked upon as a public good.

There are a great many other applications of the public goods concept and the concomitant free-rider problem, such as trade liberalization, nationalism, alliances, and burden sharing. A further application is the preservation of nature beyond natural frontiers, such as the campaign against whaling or the protection of the atmosphere.

The public goods concept is extremely useful and intuitively plausible. The ease of application may, however, sometimes hide underlying problems. The exact conditions under which free riding occurs are still unknown; often it is simply assumed that actors do not contribute to the common cause. Laboratory experiments on public goods situations suggest that free riding does not occur as often as pure economic theory would have us think. Moreover, institutional conditions are often such that free riding is discouraged.

Even when national actors fully perceive that it is advantageous for them to cooperate in the provision of a public good, it is difficult and sometimes even impossible to coordinate joint action. In view of the general impossibility of forcing independent national actors to cooperate, the free-rider problem can be overcome by finding *rules* or *constitutional agreements* that lay down the conditions for cooperation.

In order to find a set of rules that the participants are willing to accept in a state of (partial) uncertainty about the future (i.e., beyond the veil of ignorance), the actors must believe that obeying the rules will be advantageous to them. The agreement must lead to a beneficial change according to the expectations of all actors (Pareto-superiority), because only under these conditions will there be voluntary cooperation—that is, unanimity among the participants. These conditions are not easily set up and maintained in the international system. Once a set of rules or a constitution has been agreed upon, the problem is to ensure that the rules are observed and that individual nations have no incentive to back out of or attempt to alter the agreement. The "constitutional" approach has been applied to various problems in international political economy, among them environmental and fisheries pacts, international public health accords, cooperation about forecasting (and in the future possible influencing) the weather, the use of outer space, and the international judicial system.

The establishment and enforcement of rules has occupied a central position in two areas. First, *international monetary arrangements* may be considered to be, if well designed, advantageous to all, but the incentives for deviation are also marked. It is therefore necessary to consider not only the Pareto-superiority of an international monetary scheme but also the benefits and costs to the individual participating nations. This aspect has been overlooked in the many proposals made in this area; they usually assume (implicitly) that there is a "benevolent international dictator" who will put them into effect.

An important related question is why certain rules have not influenced behavior as much as one might have expected. One example is provided by the Bretton Woods system, in which changes in exchange rates have been made too infrequently, and generally too late. The reason is that forces militate against both devaluation and revaluation. Voters, it is believed, interpret devaluation as an admission of financial failure, with negative consequences for the government in power. Revaluation is good for the voters (as consumers) but very bad for well-organized groups of exporters and import competitors; so the government may again run into trouble. In view of this unwillingness to adjust exchange rates, an agreement allowing freely flexible exchange rates may be preferable because the issue is then taken out of government (and central bank) politics.

The second international area in which rules play an important role is that of *international common property resources*. The need for international conventions and rules is obvious in view of the pollution of the atmosphere and the overfishing and overexploitation of the oceans. The difficulty in reaching agreement on what these rules should be is equally well known. It is hard to obtain consensus because no country can be forced to accept rules. The only acceptable rules are those that produce such high aggregate net benefits that they can be distributed among the participating countries in such a way that everyone finds it advantageous to agree and to stick to the rules. Such rules do not usually exist; it is quite possible that agreement on some of the current proposals concerning common international property resources would be worse for participating countries than no agreement at all.

Politico-economic modeling. Politico-economic models or, as they are often called, political business-cycle models, study the interdependence between the economy and the polity by explicitly analyzing the behavior of actors. They test the resulting propositions using econometric, or rather politico-metric, techniques. The simplest such model analyzes a circular system: the state of the economy influences the voters' evaluation of the government's performance, which is reflected by a vote or government popularity function. If the government considers its chances of re-election to be poor, it uses economic policy instruments to influence the state of the economy and thus the voters' decisions. (The government's actions may depend on its ideology if it considers its re-election chances to be good.) The model is, of course, a great simplification of reality, but it has already been shown that the framework can be extended to incorporate additional actors and relationships.

A politico-economic model for a closed country can be extended in two ways to include international politico-economic relationships. The first approach concentrates on the *internal* connections between the economy and the polity but also introduces international influences. In this case the politico-economic model outlined above is amended by factors emerging from the international sphere. . . .

International political events may also affect votes and government popularity. Empirical studies of the United States show that, when the country is subjected to an international political crisis, the population tends to "rally round the flag." Another influence that may be introduced into politico-economic models is the foreign intervention in a country's internal polity that may occur if a foreign nation considers the results of a particular election undesirable. Government politicians may also have specific international political preferences and influence the internal economy accordingly, provided that their re-election chances are not thereby seriously diminished.

. . . . [T]he use of economic policy instruments is influenced by international economic conditions. The possibility of creating a political business cycle aimed at improving re-election chances depends on institutional conditions with the international economy. An expansionary economic policy yields more favorable short-run inflation-unemployment (or real income) trade-offs within a system of adjustable pegs than with a depreciating exchange rate. A system of adjustable pegs may thus be expected to increase the government's incentive to attempt to gain votes by introducing an expansionary policy before elections and devaluing thereafter.

The second approach goes one step further, by considering the *mutual interdependence* of domestic and foreign economies and polities. This research strategy is particularly well-developed with regard to arms race models. Such models have traditionally analyzed the mutual responses of two nations to each other's defense outlays in a rather mechanistic way. . . . In the last few years, however, the decision-making structure has been greatly improved by the introduction of elements of public choice. In particular, it has been recognized that a nation's response to another nation's armament depends on the government's utility, and is subject to the constraints imposed by the desire to be re-elected as well as by economic resources. The models have been econometrically estimated and their behavior has been analyzed with the help of extensive simulations.

Both of the aforementioned approaches are useful; the second is, of course, much more far-reaching and may therefore be difficult to apply to politico-economic interaction as a whole. It may therefore be advisable to restrict it to one particular issue at a time.

The next two sections illustrate the substantive contributions that public choice has made to the theoretical and empirical analysis of international political economy. No complete survey of all the applications of public choice is intended. I omit, for example, public choice's applications to the interdependence between foreign trade flows and political conditions, and the determinants of foreign direct investment and of international aid. Rather, I concentrate on two particular areas, the formation of tariffs and trade restrictions (section 2) and international organizations (section 3).

2. Tariffs and Trade Restrictions

Most economists approach the analysis of tariffs and other restrictions on trade from the same standpoint. They start from the basic proposition of international trade theory: that free trade leads to higher real income and is desirable not only for the world as a whole but also for individual countries. The problem for political economists of the neoclassical public choice orientation, therefore, is to explain why tariffs nonetheless exist, and why governments so rarely seem to take the welfare-increasing (Pareto-optimal) step of abolishing tariffs. A government might be expected to win votes by abolishing tariffs, either because a majority of the electorate would directly benefit or because the government could redistribute the gains so that a majority of the electorate would be better off than in a situation with tariffs. If citizens were to determine tariffs by a single direct majority vote in an assembly, the *median voter* would vote in favor of free trade.

The simplistic assumptions of the median-voter model must, however, be modified in a number of important respects if it is to represent reality. This provides an explanation for the continuing existence and possibly even growth of tariffs. At least five modifications must be considered.

The first is that the losers in any tariff reduction, the people engaged in the domestic production of the goods concerned, are not compensated. If they form a majority, they will obstruct the reduction or the elimination of tariffs.

The second necessary modification is to consider the fact that prospective gainers have less incentive than prospective voters to participate in the vote, to inform themselves, and to organize and support a pressure group. Tariff reductions are a public good whose benefits are received by everybody, including those not taking the trouble and incurring the cost to bring about the reduction. The prospective cost of tariff reduction to the losers is, however, much more direct and concentrated, so that it is worth their while to engage in a political fight against tariff reduction. In addition, the well-defined short-term losses to be experienced by the losers are much more visible, and therefore better perceived, than uncertain gains to be made in the distant future by the winners. The fight over trade restrictions benefits those sectors protected from competition but otherwise serves no socially useful purpose, because it wastes scarce resources. This aspect is the subject of the *theory of rent seeking*. It is useful to differentiate between two activities, both of which, from society's point of view, waste resources. "Rent seeking" is the activity by which trade restrictions (tariffs, quotas) generate rents to one's advantage; "revenue seeking" is the fight over the distribution of revenues, and is thus a general distributional phenomenon.

A third modification of the simple median-voter model considers the possibility that the prospective losers in a free-trade regime may be better represented in parliament and in the government than the prospective winners, depending on the system of voting.

A fourth modification reflects the fact that logrolling or vote trading can make it possible for two measures, each of which would increase the country's welfare, both to be defeated by a majority. Vote trading may happen if groups of voters have unequal preference intensities for two issues. This is very likely to be the case where tariffs are concerned. Consider a group I of voters engaged in domestic import-competing activities. The group's main preference is against the reduction of tariffs for its *own* products; it weakly favors the reduction of tariffs for some other products. Assume a group II of voters whose main interest lies in maintaining the tariff for the latter products, and who have a weak preference for a tariff reduction for the former products. If neither of the two groups commands a majority, and the other voters perceive the benefits of free trade, the tariff reduction would pass and free trade would be established. If, however, groups I and II combined have a majority, they can agree to trade votes: group I votes against the tariff reduction that group II strongly opposes provided group II votes against the tariff reduction that group I strongly opposes. This leads to a majority vote against tariff reductions, reducing overall welfare. Vote trading, however, does not always decrease social welfare. The fact that a market is established in which mutually advantageous trades can take place may increase social welfare, provided all the actors affected by the relevant activity take part in the vote-trading process.

The final modification of the median-voter model recognizes that tariffs provide revenue for governments, which in their absence would find it even more difficult to finance public expenditure. This is especially true in developing countries where, due to the inefficiency of the tax system, there is little tax revenue. A government will therefore wish to secure this income source and hence will oppose free trade.

These five modifications of the simple median-voter model combine to explain why free trade, which is optimal from the point of view of the country as a whole, is not found in reality. The discussion suggests that there is, on the contrary, a *political market for protection*. Protection is demanded by particular groups of voters, firms, and associated interest groups and parties, and supplied by politicians and public bureaucrats. Thus, the public choice approach to international political economy stresses the importance of interest groups. . . .

Another actor plays an important role in tariff formation: the *public administration*. This body has considerable influence on the "supply side" of tariff setting because it prepares, formulates, and implements trade bills once government and parliament have made a decision.

The activity of public bureaucrats with respect to tariffs may be analyzed with the help of the "rational" model of behavior, for example, by maximizing utility subject to constraints. The main elements in the bureaucrats' utility function may be assumed to be the prestige, power, and influence that they enjoy relative to the group of people they are officially designed to "serve," their clientele. In most cases this clientele will be located in a specific economic sector; in the case of public officials in the ministry of agriculture, for example, the clientele would be those groups with agricultural interests. They are, moreover, proud of being able to show that they are competent to perform their job ("performance excellence"). Public bureaucrats will therefore tend to fight for the interests of "their" economic sector, and will work for tariffs and other import restrictions in order to protect it from outside competition. They will prefer to use instruments under their own control rather than to follow general rules imposed by formal laws. They will thus prefer various kinds of nontariff protection and support (subsidies) to general tariffs.

The public bureaucracy faces constraints imposed by parliament and government. However, both of these actors have little incentive to control public administration more tightly, because they depend on it to attain their own goals. In addition, political actors have much less information available to them than the public bureaucracy does, in particular with respect to the sometimes very complex issues of protection. The limited incentive of politicians to control the public administration gives bureaucrats considerable discretionary power, which they use to their own advantage.

Public choice theory has also been used to try to explain differences in international protection, that is, the intersectoral *structure of tariffs*. It is hypothesized that the more concentrated industries find it easier to organize and to muster political pressure because a smaller number of enterprises is more willing to bear the transaction, organization, and lobbying costs involved in getting tariff protection. . . .

This discussion of the various factors that may be used to explain tariffs and other trade restrictions shows that the study of international political economy based on public choice is well under way, and that useful theoretical and empirical results have been achieved using an approach that differs strongly from political scientists' international political economy. Research is, however, only at an early stage, and various aspects of the analysis must be improved. First, the behavior of the actors (government, interest groups, and public bureaucracy) must be modeled more carefully, taking their characteristic preferences and constraints into account. Second, the equations used for econometric estimation need to be more closely and consistently linked with the theoretical models. Third, the framework of the analysis should be extended, so that all the relevant causal relationships can be included in the analysis. Politico-economic conditions do not only affect tariffs; tariffs also affect the state of the economy and polity. Thus, both directions of the interdependence between tariffs and the political economy should be considered.

3. International Organizations

Interesting contributions have been made within public choice to the study of the benefits and costs of joining international organizations, their decision rules, and their internal bureaucracy, as well as to the study of bargaining in an international setting.

Benefits and Costs of Joining International Organizations

An international organization may perform various services: it may provide public goods and services, coordinate the activities of actors in the international system, and form an institutional setting for alliances. International organizations may also be used to further private (i.e., national) aims; it would therefore be a mistake to assume that they maximize the collective economic welfare either of the individuals of a particular country or of the world as a whole.

Much of the output of international organizations has the character of a public good, thus providing an incentive for countries to behave as free riders. Under these circumstances the organization will only be able to operate effectively if it involves a small group of countries, permitting direct interaction and imposing high costs on free riders; if private goods are offered selectively to the members of the organization, providing an incentive for individual countries to join and participate in the financing of the organization; or if participation is achieved by coercion.

It has been empirically shown that small, regional or international organizations are indeed more successful than large ones. The second option, creating selective incentives for members, is very common in international organizations. The existence of such private goods is a very important bargaining tool used by governments in persuading parliaments to agree to join. Considerable effort is therefore devoted to transforming public goods into private goods owned by the organization. Finally, coercion is difficult and often impossible in an international context, because the member countries are unwilling to give up their independence. However, as long as the international system is composed of sovereign states, the assumption that coercion is possible solves the problem of international organization by definition.

An organization may also be formed if the potential participants' perception of the advantages of membership and the social pressure to belong to it can be increased by education and propaganda. As in the case of coercion, this approach has very little chance of success in the international system. The solution of international politico-economic problems is therefore not to be found in one or several supranational authorities.

The Bureaucracy of International Organizations

It has been suggested that the characteristics of bureaucracies are more pronounced in the international than in the national setting. The main reason is that they have greater room for discretionary action, because there is neither the opportunity nor the incentive to control them. Control is difficult because the "output" of an international organization is undefined and usually cannot be measured. There are no political institutions that would gain by tightly controlling an international organization: national governments would only run into trouble with other national governments if they tried to interfere with the workings of such institutions. They therefore prefer to let things go and only intervene if they feel that their own nationals employed in the organization are being unfairly treated or that their national interests are being threatened by the organization's activity. The lack of incentives is another example of the free-riding problem.

Due to the lack of effective control in an international organization, none of the layers in the hierarchy has any real incentive to work toward the "official product," because their utility depends hardly at all on their contribution. The national quotas for positions that are a feature of many international organizations drive a further wedge between the individual's utility and the organization's official function. This particular incentive structure leads to a growth of international bureaucracies quite independent of the tasks to be performed, because all bureaucrats benefit from larger budgets and a greater number of employees. International bureaucracies are also characterized by a low degree of efficiency and a profusion of red tape, because the formalized internal workings of the organization become dominant. A considerable share of the budget will be used for internal purposes, and to provide side benefits for the bureaucrats themselves.

This theory of international bureaucracy still has to undergo empirical testing.

International Bargaining

Modeling international bargaining is a formidable task, because the process has little structure and involves many variables. There have therefore been few public choice studies of international bargaining. Those that do exist have each concentrated on a particular aspect of the problem.

In international negotiations, linkages between various issues are quite a common feature. R.D. Tillison and T.D. Willett have shown that linkages are more important when the distribution of benefits from agreements is highly biased toward a small number of countries. The linkage of issues whose distributional consequences offset one another can help promote agreements that would otherwise fail because of distributional effects. On the other hand, linkages play a small role when the benefits from an agreement are considered to be "fairly" distributed across countries. In this case a consensus can be reached without introducing an additional dimension in the form of linked issues. Such hypotheses are plausible but, again, have not yet been empirically tested.

4. Concluding Remarks

The aim of this survey has been to show that public choice has made considerable and valuable contributions to international political economy. The approach has shed some new light on the field and should be of interest to all social scientists concerned with bridging the gap between international economics and international (political) relations. Due to limitations of space, I have only been able to provide some characteristic examples, and some selected fields of application, of the public choice approach to international political economy.

The public choice approach to international political economy has both strengths and weaknesses, a proposition, of course, true for any approach, including that adopted by political scientists. Five points merit amplification.

First, the public choice view provides *fresh insights* into the area, in the same way that the economics-based approach illuminated general politics. This is not to claim that the approach is superior to any other; rather, that it is able to illuminate particular aspects of international political economy (while being unable to contribute much in other areas). As will become clear from these concluding remarks, the specific strengths of the public choice view are also responsible for its specific weaknesses. This is true whenever one considers the advantages of applying a new method to an already established field, such as international political economy. There is a tendency to use theoretical and empirical methods without paying sufficient attention to the particular historical and institutional conditions existing in the field of study. A quick application is tempting, because it is seemingly easy to undertake, and the shortcomings of the analysis may not be obvious. It is necessary, however, to investigate thoroughly whether particular theoretical concepts such as public goods and free riding really capture the essential features of reality.

Second, an advantage of the public choice approach to international political economy is that the analysis is based on an explicit and unified *theory of human behavior,* and on a *technical apparatus* capable of producing theoretical solutions and empirically testable propositions. This technical elegance leads, however, to a tendency to sacrifice relevance for rigor. There are already some areas of this type of international political economy where the heavily formalistic apparatus used is out of all proportion to the resulting advances in knowledge.

Third, the public choice approach concentrates on specific aspects of international political economy, making it possible to isolate and analyze relatively simple relationships. The *high degree of abstraction* allows public choice scholars to gain major insights into complex problem areas. But it also involves the danger of leaving out relevant aspects or of keeping constant (by the "ceteris paribus" assumption) variables that are so closely and importantly connected with the problem being studied that they should be considered an endogenous part of the model. While this survey has concentrated on microanalytical and partial analyses, there are approaches within public choice that attempt to provide view (in particular the politico-economic models).

Fourth, the emphasis on deriving propositions that are at least in principle amenable to *empirical testing* is healthy, because it forces reality on the researcher. Econometric, or rather politicometric, analyses also provide factual knowledge about the relationships among the variables being studied. The disadvantage of this empirical orientation is that aspects difficult or impossible to measure quantitatively are easily excluded. Thus, the relationships for which data are easily available are those that tend to be studied. A common shortcoming of empirical economic research is that the operationalization of individual theories is often done in a rather cavalier way. In that respect economists could certainly learn from quantitative political scientists, as well as from other social scientists.

Empirical research has so far been predominantly concerned with the United States. This makes it more difficult to evaluate the contribution of public choice to international political economy, because it is difficult to know what part of the results is due to the public choice view, what part to the particular conditions obtaining in the United States. It is therefore important that empirical tests of the theories should be undertaken for other nations.

Fifth and finally, the public choice view is *interdisciplinary,* in a specific sense of the word: it combines the economic and political aspects of international political economy but uses a single theoretical approach. (Usually, interdisciplinary is understood to mean that theoretical approaches have to be combined.) This has the advantage that the two areas can be fused together, but it carries the already mentioned danger that only selected aspects of their interrelationship will be treated. There can be little doubt, however, that economists engaged in research on international political economy can gain from the work done by political scientists, especially from their experience of the institutions and political processes encountered in the international sphere. Up to now, there has been relatively little contact between public choice researchers and other scholars in the field. This survey will have achieved its goal if it has convinced the reader that the opposite proposition is also true: political scientists would benefit from considering and studying the public choice approach to international political economy.

Notes

1. J.E. Spero, *The Politics of International Economic Relations* (London: Allen & Unwin, 1977), pp. 1–2.

2. R.J. Barry Jones, "International Political Economy: Problems and Issues," Part II, *Review of International Studies* 8 (1982), p. 50.

3. R. Tooze, "Economics, International Political Economy and Change in the International System," in B. Buzan and R.J.B. Jones, eds., *Change and the Study of International Relations: The Evaded Dimension* (London: Pinter, 1981), p. 130.

4. C.P. Kindleberger, *Government and International Trade,* Princeton Essays in International Finance no. 129 (Princeton, N.J., July 1978).

8

Hegemonic Power and Stability

All three major schools of IPE thought discuss hegemonic power and its consequences. Unlike rational choice analysis, however, the idea of hegemony is not grounded in a particular paradigm; consideration of hegemony does not necessarily entail acceptance of a particular set of theoretical assumptions. It is, rather, an empirical question that is examined from different perspectives. Studies of hegemonic power do, nonetheless, open a new avenue for theoretical contention. Although each theory qualifies its understanding in specific ways, the shared engagement of hegemony has drawn the disparate approaches together in a complemetary, albeit eclectic, manner.

Immanuel Wallerstein develops a world-systems interpretation of hegemony, derived largely from his reading of the Marxist IPE canon. For Wallerstein, hegemony is a temporary characteristic of the world-system as a whole. It exists when a single country dominates simultaneously global processes of capital accumulation and international balances of military power. This general definition is basically consistent with neomercantilist and liberal notions of hegemony. Wallerstein differs from these contending theories, however, by emphasizing a particular economic logic of hegemonic power. Although he recognizes the political aspect of the world-system, he focuses on secular trends of economic growth ("A phases") and recession ("B phases") as the driving force of hegemonic rise and decline. These "long cycles," or "Kondratieff cycles" (named for a pioneering Soviet economist), reflect the dynamism of capitalism as a world-economy. Comparative advantages change as the locus of accumulation shifts around the globe. Wallerstein suggests a historical sequence of a country first acquiring dominance in agro-industrial production, then international commerce, and finally world finance. Only when one state enjoys predominance in all three of these areas does the system possess a hegemonic concentration of power.

Hegemony, as such, is very rare. Wallerstein contends that only three countries have attained the status of global hegemon since the seventeenth century: the United Provinces of the Netherlands in the mid-seventeenth century; the United Kingdom in the mid-nineteenth; and the United States in the mid-twentieth. Hegemony is, in addition, very unstable. The systemic forces that create it also work against its durability.

Wallerstein also considers the politics of hegemony. Interstate military balances, he suggests, parallel economic transformations. As hegemonic powers achieve economic dominance, they also gain a clear edge in naval and air power. Wallerstein does not posit a crudely economistic explanation of international military power; rather, he believes that global economics and politics are interactive and that the "logistics" which explain this interaction have yet to be fully analyzed. Moreover, international politics can, at times, be relatively autonomous from world-economic conditions. Hegemony is not empire; even though economic power can be highly concentrated, political power is distributed in a bipolar or multipolar fashion. The major wars engendered by political decentralization serve to restructure the world-system and usher in periods of hegemony. On the other hand, Wallerstein argues that global economic preeminence clearly shapes the definition of the hegemon's national interest. Simply put, hegemons tend to identify their interests with liberal international trade, investment, and finance.

Ironically, liberalism, which serves the interests of a hegemon at the height of its power, contributes to hegemonic decline. The coincidence of comparative advantages that defines hegemony is undermined by international openness and technological diffusion. As a consequence, the agreements and alliances forged by the hegemonic power come unstuck, and by this argument, global political and economic instability are likely to increase.

The question of hegemonic decline, especially whether or not the United States has fallen from global preeminence, has sparked a great deal of debate in recent years. Susan Strange outlines the major points of the "school of decline," those who argue the United States no longer holds a hegemonic position, and takes the opposite position, that the "American empire," though now somewhat different from thirty years ago, remains intact. Although she is not addressing his interpretation directly, at several points Strange differs with Wallerstein.

On the question of global power, Strange holds that the dispersion of production out of the United States is not a good indicator of failing hegemony. The control, rather than the location, of production and, more importantly, finance, is a primary determinant of global predominance. U.S. banks and corporate headquarters (wherever production facilities may be) still, she believes, manage the greatest share of the world's economic activity. When added to the other facets of "structural power," military force and cultural influence, these elements create an American "nonterritorial empire" that is unequalled globally.

Strange takes exception to the reading of history that many theorists of hegemony, Wallerstein included, employ to bolster their arguments. A more inclusive survey of world empires, she holds, reveals a wider range of experience than that of the Netherlands, Great Britain, and the United States. Most notably, the Roman Empire proved to be more durable than these others. The ebb and flow of global preeminence may not follow the regular wavelike pattern that Wallerstein and others suggest. Empires, Strange states, "are like trees. Some grow fast and fall suddenly without warning. Others grow slowly and decay very gradually, even making astonishing recoveries from shock or injury."

Strange's interpretation of hegemonic power is also less deterministic than that of most analysts in the "school of decline." Power may be structural in her analysis, but specific choices and actions still make a difference. She recognizes that a certain disorder has seized international financial markets, and that the United States appears weaker today than thirty years ago, but this does not lead her to the conclusion that the United States is experiencing hegemonic decline. Rather, "a series of American managerial decisions of dubious wisdom" are responsible for whatever confusion exists in global markets. Bad policy choices caused international economic disorder, she believes, and better choices can overcome it.

The Three Instances
of Hegemony in the History
of the Capitalist World-Economy

IMMANUEL WALLERSTEIN

When one is dealing with a complex, continuously evolving, large-scale historical system, concepts that are used as shorthand descriptions for structural patterns are useful only to the degree that one clearly lays out their purpose, circumscribes their applicability, and specifies the theoretical framework they presuppose and advance.

Let me therefore state some premises which I shall not argue at this point. If you are not willing to regard these premises as plausible, you will not find the way I elaborate and use the concept of hegemony very useful. I assume that there exists a concrete singular historical system which I shall call the "capitalist world-economy," whose temporal boundaries go from the long sixteenth century to the present. Its special boundaries originally included Europe (or most of it) plus Iberian America but they subsequently expanded to cover the entire globe. I assume this totality is a *system,* that is, that it has been relatively autonomous of external forces; or, to put it another way, that its patterns are explicable largely in terms of its internal dynamics. I assume that it is an *historical* system, that is, that it was born, has developed, and will one day cease to exist (through disintegration or fundamental transformation). I assume lastly that it is the dynamics of the system itself that explain its historically changing characteristics. Hence, insofar as it is a system, it has structures and these structures manifest themselves in cyclical rhythms, that is, mechanisms which reflect and ensure repetitious patterns. But insofar as this system is historical, no rhythmic movement ever returns the system to an

Reprinted from *International Journal of Comparative Sociology,* 24, 1–2 (1983), Immanuel Wallerstein, "Three Instances of Hegemony in the History of the Capitalist World Economy" by permission of E.J. Brill (USA), Inc.

equilibrium point but instead moves the system along various continua which may be called the secular trends of this system. These trends eventually must culminate in the impossibility of containing further reparations of the structured dislocations by restorative mechanisms. Hence the system undergoes what some call "bifurcating turbulence" and others the "transformation of quantity into quality."

To these methodological or metaphysical premises, I must add a few substantive ones about the operations of the capitalist world-economy. Its mode of production is capitalist; that is, it is predicated on the endless accumulation of capital. Its structure is that of an axial social division of labor exhibiting a core/periphery tension based on unequal exchange. The political superstructure of this system is that of a set of so-called sovereign states defined by and constrained by their membership in an interstate network or system. The operational guidelines of this interstate system include the so-called balance of power, a mechanism designed to ensure that no single state ever has the capacity to transform this interstate system into a single world-empire whose boundaries would match that of the axial division of labor. There have of course been repeated attempts throughout history of capitalist world-economy to transform it in the direction of a world-empire, but these attempts have all been frustrated. However, there have also been repeated and quite different attempts by given states to achieve hegemony in the interstate system, and these attempts have in fact succeeded on three occasions, if only for relatively brief periods.

The thrust of hegemony is quite different from the thrust to world-empire; indeed it is in many ways almost its opposite. I will therefore (1) spell out what I mean by hegemony, (2) describe the analogies in the three purported instances, (3) seek to decipher the roots of the thrust to hegemony and suggest why the thrust to hegemony has succeeded three times but never lasted too long, and (4) draw inferences about what we may expect in the proximate future. The point of doing all this is not to erect a Procrustean category into which to fit complex historical reality but to illuminate what I believe to be one of the central processes of the modern world-system.

1

Hegemony in the interstate system refers to that situation in which the ongoing rivalry between the so-called "great powers" is so unbalanced that one power is truly *primus inter pares;* that is, one power can largely impose its rules and its wishes (at the very least by effective veto power) in the economic, political, military, diplomatic, and even cultural arenas. The material base of such power lies in the ability of enterprises domiciled in that power to operate more efficiently in all three major economic areas—agro-industrial production, commerce, and finance. The edge in efficiency of which we are speaking is one so great that these enterprises can not only outbid enterprises domiciled in other great powers in the world market in general, but quite specifically in very many instances within the home markets of the rival powers themselves.

I mean this to be a relatively restrictive definition. It is not enough for one power's enterprises simply to have a larger share of the world market than any other or simply to have the most powerful military forces or the largest political role. I mean hegemony only to refer to situations in which the edge is so significant that allied major powers are *de facto* client states and opposed major powers feel relatively frustrated and highly defensive vis-à-vis the hegemonic power. And yet while I want to restrict my definition to instances where the margin or power differential is really great, I do not mean to suggest that there is ever any moment when a hegemonic power is omnipotent and capable of doing anything it wants. Omnipotence does not exist within the interstate system.

Hegemony therefore is not a state of being but rather one end of a fluid continuum which describes the rivalry relations of great powers to each other. At one end of this continuum is an almost even balance, a situation in which many powers exist, all somewhat equal in strength, and with no clear or continuous groupings. This is rare and unstable. In the great middle of this continuum, many powers exist, grouped more or less into two camps, but with several neutral or swing elements, and with neither side (nor *a fortiori* any single state) being able to impose its will on others. This is the statistically normal situation of rivalry within the interstate system. And at the other end lies the situation of hegemony, also rare and unstable.

At this point, you may see what it is I am describing but may wonder why I am bothering to give it a name and thereby focus attention upon it. It is because I suspect hegemony is not the result of a random reshuffling of the cards but is a phenomenon that emerges in specifiable circumstances and plays a significant role in the historical development of the capitalist world-economy.

2

Using this restrictive definition, the only three instances of hegemony would be the United Provinces in the mid-seventeenth century, the United Kingdom in the mid-nineteenth, and the United States in the mid-twentieth. If one insists on dates, I would tentatively suggest as maximal bounding points 1620–72, 1815–73, 1945–67. But of course, it would be a mistake to try to be too precise when our measuring instruments are both so complex and so crude.

I will suggest four areas in which it seems to me what happened in the three instances was analogous. To be sure, analogies are limited. And to be sure, since the capitalist world-economy is in my usage a single continuously evolving entity, it follows by definition that the overall structure was different at each of the three points in time. The differences were real, the outcome of the secular trends of the world-system. But the structural analogies were real as well, the reflection of the cyclical rhythms of this same system.

The first analogy has to do with the sequencing of achievement and loss of relative efficiencies in each of the three economic domains. What I believe occurred was that in each instance enterprises domiciled in the given power in

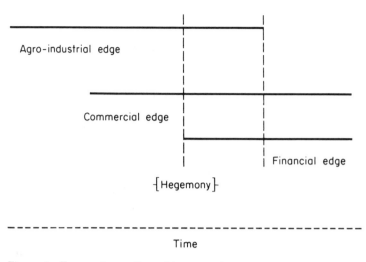

Figure 1. Economic position of hegemonic power

question achieved their edge first in agro-industrial production, then in commerce, and then in finance. I believe they lost their edge in this sequence as well (this process having begun but not yet having been completed in the third instance). Hegemony thus refers to that short interval in which there is *simultaneous* advantage in all three economic domains.

The second analogy has to do with the ideology and policy of the hegemonic power. Hegemonic powers during the period of their hegemony tended to be advocates of global "liberalism." They came forward as defenders of the principle of the free flow of the factors of production (goods, capital, and labor) throughout the world-economy. They were hostile in general to mercantilist restrictions on trade, including the existence of overseas colonies for the stronger countries. They extended this liberalism to a generalized endorsement of liberal parliamentary institutions (and a concurrent distaste for political change by violent means), political restraints on the arbitrariness of bureaucratic power, and civil liberties (and a concurrent open door to political exiles). They tended to provide a high standard of living for their national working classes, high by world standards of the time.

None of this should be exaggerated. Hegemonic powers regularly made exceptions to their anti-mercantilism, when it was in their interest to do so. Hegemonic powers regularly were willing to interfere with political processes in other states to ensure their own advantage. Hegemonic powers could be very repressive at home, if need be, to guarantee the national "consensus." The high working-class standard was steeply graded by internal ethnicity. Nevertheless, it is quite striking that liberalism as an ideology did flourish in these countries at precisely the moments of their hegemony, and to a significant extent only then and there.

The third analogy is in the pattern of global military power. Hegemonic powers were primarily sea (now sea/air) powers. In the long ascent to hegemony, they seemed very reluctant to develop their armies, discussing openly the potentially weakening drain on state revenues and manpower of becoming tied down in land wars. Yet each found finally that it had to develop a strong land army as well to face up to a major land-based rival which seemed to be trying to transform the world-economy into a world-empire.

In each case, the hegemony was secured by a thirty-year-long world war. By a world war, I shall mean (again somewhat restrictively) a land-based war that involves (not necessarily continuously) almost all the major military powers of the epoch in warfare that is very destructive of land and population. To each hegemony is attached one of these wars. World War Alpha was the Thirty Years' War from 1618 to 1648, where Dutch interests triumphed over Hapsburg in the world-economy. World War Beta was the Napoleonic Wars from 1792 to 1815, where British interests triumphed over French. World War Gamma was the long Euroasian wars from 1914 to 1945, where US interests triumphed over German.

While limited wars have been a constant of the operations of the interstate system of the capitalist world-economy (there having been scarcely any year when there was not some war somewhere within the system), world wars have been by contrast a rarity. In fact their rarity and the fact that the number and timing seems to have correlated with the achievement of hegemonic status by one power brings us to the fourth analogy.

If we look to those very long cycles that Rondo Cameron has dubbed "logistics," we can see that world wars and hegemony have been in fact related to them. There has been very little scholarly work done on these logistics. They have been most frequently discussed in the comparisons between the A–B sequences of 1100–1450 and 1450–1750. There are only a few discussions of the logistics that may exist after the latter point in time. But if we take the prime observation which has been used to define these logistics— secular inflation and deflation—the patterns seems in fact to have continued.

It therefore might be plausible to argue the existence of such (price) logistics up to today using the following dates: 1450–1730, with 1600–50 as a flat peak; 1730–1897, with 1810–17 as a peak; and 1897–?, with an as yet uncertain peak. If there are such logistics, it turns out that the world war and the (subsequent) hegemonic era are located somewhere around (just before and after) the peak of the logistic. That is to say, these processes seem to be the product of the long competitive expansion which seemed to have resulted in a particular concentration of economic and political power.

The outcome of each world war included a major restructuring of the interstate system (Westphalia; the Concert of Europe; the UN and Bretton Woods) in a form consonant with the need for relative stability of the now hegemonic power. Furthermore, once the hegemonic position was eroded economically (the loss of the efficiency edge in agro-industrial production), and therefore hegemonic decline set in, one consequence seemed to be the erosion of the alliance network which the hegemonic power had created patiently, and ultimately a serious reshuffling of alliances.

In the long period following the era of hegemony, two powers seemed eventually to emerge as the "contenders for the succession"—England and France after Dutch hegemony; the US and Germany after British; and now Japan and Western Europe after US. Furthermore, the eventual winner of the contending pair seemed to use as a conscious part of its strategy the gentle turning of the old hegemonic power into its "junior partner"—the English vis-à-vis the Dutch, the US vis-à-vis Great Britain . . . and now?

3

Thus far I have been primarily descriptive. I realize that this description is vulnerable to technical criticism. My coding of the data may not agree with everyone else's. I think nonetheless that as an initial effort this coding is defensible and that I have therefore outlined a broad repetitive pattern in the functioning of the interstate question. The question now is how to interpret it. What is there in the functioning of a capitalist world-economy that gives rise to such a cyclical pattern in the interstate system?

I believe this pattern of the rise, temporary ascendancy, and fall of hegemonic powers in the interstate system is merely one aspect of the central role of the political machinery in the functioning of capitalism as a mode of production.

There are two myths about capitalism put forward by its central ideologues (and strangely largely accepted by its nineteenth-century critics). One is that it is defined by the free flow of the factors of production. The second is that it is defined by the non-interference of the political machinery in the "market." In fact, capitalism is defined by the *partially* free flow of the factors of production and by the *selective* interference of the political machinery in the "market." Hegemony is an instance of the latter.

What defines capitalism most fundamentally is the drive for the endless accumulation of capital. The interferences that are "selected" are those which advance this process of accumulation. There are however two problems about "interference." It has a cost, and therefore the benefit of any interference is only a benefit to the extent it exceeds this cost. Where the benefits are available without any "interference," this is obviously desirable, as it minimizes the "deduction." And secondly, interference is always in favor of one set of accumulators as against another set, and the latter will always seek to counter the former. These two considerations circumscribe the politics of hegemony in the interstate system.

The costs to a given entrepreneur of state "interference" are felt in two main ways. First, in financial terms, the state may levy direct taxes which affect the rate of profit by requiring the firm to make payments to the state, or indirect taxes, which may alter the rate of profit by affecting the competitivity of a product. Secondly, the state may enact rules which govern flows of capital, labor, or goods, or may set minimum and/or maximum prices. While direct taxes always represent a cost to the entrepreneur, calculations concerning indirect taxes and state regulations are more complex, since they represent costs both to the entrepreneur and to (some of) his competitors. The chief concern in terms of individual accumulation is not the absolute cost of these measures but the comparative cost. Costs, even if high, may be positively desirable from the standpoint of a given entrepreneur, if the state's actions involve still higher costs to some competitor. Absolute costs are of concern only if the loss to the entrepreneur is greater than the medium-run gain which is possible through greater competitivity brought about by such state actions. It follows that absolute cost is of greatest concern to those entrepreneurs who would do best in open-market competition in the absence of state interference.

In general, therefore, entrepreneurs are regularly seeking state interference in the market in multiple forms—subsidies, restraints of trade, tariffs (which are penalties for competitors of different nationality), guarantees, maxima for input prices and minima for output prices, etc. The intimidating effect of internal and external repression is also of direct economic benefit to entrepreneurs. To the extent that the ongoing process of competition and state interference leads to oligopolistic conditions within state boundaries, more and more attention is naturally paid to securing the same kind of oligopolistic conditions in the most important market, the world market.

The combination of the competitive thrust and constant state interference results in a continuing pressure towards the concentration of capital. The benefits of state interference inside and outside the state boundaries is cumulative. In political terms, this is reflected as expanding world power. The edge a rising power's economic enterprises have vis-à-vis those of a competitive rising power may be thin and therefore insecure. This is where the world wars come in. The thirty-year struggle may be very dramatic militarily and politically. But the profoundest effect may be economic. The winner's economic edge is expanded by the very process of the war itself, and the postwar interstate settlement is designed to encrust that greater edge and protect it against erosion.

A given state thus assumes its world "responsibilities" which are reflected in its diplomatic, military, political, ideological, and cultural stances. Everything conspires to reinforce the cooperative relationship of the entrepreneurial strata, the bureaucratic strata, and with some lag the working-class strata of the hegemonic power. This power may then be exercised in a "liberal" form—given the real diminution of political conflict within the state itself compared to earlier and later periods, and to the importance in the interstate arena of delegitimizing the efforts of other state machineries to act against the economic superiorities of the hegemonic power.

The problem is that global liberalism, which is rational and cost-effective, breeds its own demise. It makes it more difficult to retard the spread of technological expertise. Hence over time it is virtually inevitable that entrepreneurs coming along later will be able to enter the most profitable markets with the most advanced technologies and younger "plant," thus eating into the material base of the productivity edge of the hegemonic power.

Secondly, the internal political price of liberalism, needed to maintain uninterrupted production at a time of maximal global accumulation, is the creeping rise of real income of both the working strata and the cadres located in the hegemonic power. Over time, this must reduce the competitivity of the enterprises located in this state.

Once the clear productivity edge is lost, the structure cracks. As long as there is a hegemonic power, it can coordinate more or less the political responses of all states with core-like economic activities to all peripheral states, maximizing thereby the differentials of unequal exchange. But when hegemony is eroded, and especially when the world-economy is in a Kondratieff downturn, a scramble arises among the leading powers for the smaller pie, which undermines their collective ability to extract surplus via unequal exchange. The rate of unequal exchange thereby diminishes (but never to zero) and creates further incentive to a reshuffling of alliance systems.

In the period leading to the peak of a logistic, which leads towards the creation of the momentary era of hegemony, the governing parable is that of the tortoise and the hare. It is not the state that leaps ahead politically and especially militarily that wins the race, but the one that plods along improving inch by inch its long-term competitivity. This requires a firm but discrete and intelligent organization of the entrepreneurial effort by the state-machinery. Wars may be left to others, until the climactic world war when the hegemonic power must at last invest its resources to clinch its victory. Thereupon comes "world responsibility" with its benefits but also its (growing) costs. Thus the hegemony is sweet but brief.

4

The inferences for today are obvious. We are in the immediate post-hegemonic phase of this third logistic of the capitalist world-economy. The US has lost its productive edge but not yet its commercial and financial superiorities; its military and political power edge is no longer so overwhelming. Its abilities to dictate to its allies (Western Europe and Japan), intimidate its foes, and overwhelm the weak (compare the Dominican Republic in 1965 with El Salvador today) are vastly impaired. We are in the beginnings of a major reshuffling of alliances. Yet, of course, we are only at the beginning of all this. Great Britain began to decline in 1873, but it was only in 1982 that it could be openly challenged by Argentina.

The major question is whether this third logistic will act itself out along the lines of the previous ones. The great difference is the degree to which the fact that the capitalist world-economy has entered into a structural crisis as an historical system will obliterate these cyclical processes. I do not believe it will obliterate them but rather that it will work itself out in part through them.

We should not invest more in the concept of hegemony than is there. It is a way of organizing our perception of process, not an "essence" whose traits are to be described and whose eternal recurrences are to be demonstrated and then anticipated. A processual concept alerts us to the forces at play in the system and the likely nodes of conflict. It does not do more. But it also does not do less. The capitalist world-economy is not comprehensible unless we analyze clearly what are the political forms which it has engendered and how these forms relate to other realities. The interstate system is not some exogenous, God-given variable which mysteriously restrains and interacts with the capitalist drive for the endless accumulation of capital. It is its expression at the level of the political arena.

The Future of the American Empire

SUSAN STRANGE

Make no mistake. Questions about American decline—true or untrue, avoidable or inevitable—which have been much in the public eye this last couple of years, are not just the subject of an academic debate, a kind of intellectual jousting match of absorbing interest to the protagonists but of only passing interest to the spectators. In my opinion, it is much more than that. This is one of the comparatively rare occasions on which the perceived outcome of an academic debate actually has some significance and impact outside the classroom and beyond the pages of professional journals. At the end of the day the apparent victor in the argument, and the broad conclusions that the spectators draw, will crucially affect decisions in the real world. It cannot help but affect the policy choices made in the future by people in business, banking, and government, in the United States and in other countries around the world.

Personal, corporate, and party policy-making decisions will vary according to the perceived outcome—whether the conviction becomes general that the United States is a superpower already in decline and destined to decline still further; or whether the view gains ground that the decline has been exaggerated and misunderstood and can be halted or reversed; or whether yet another interpretation takes hold, that there has not really been a decline at all, only a change in the basis of American power, as when a person shifts weight from one foot to another. Because perceptions of the debate will affect strategic choices by decision makers, and because those decisions will in turn affect the lives of ordinary people who have never even heard of any of the professors engaged in the debate, it seems to me a matter of such importance that it justifies return to a subject on which I have already written.

At the time of writing, it looks as though the "school of decline," as it has been called, has thus far got the best of the intellectual joust. Although a few voices of dissent have been heard in America, and though opinion outside the United States is still far from convinced that American power is declining, the challenges that have been made to the major propositions of this school have not registered much of a dent. But the tournament is far from over and the verdict of the present and coming generation of students in the social sciences, and especially in international relations, has still to be given.

To that end, it may help first to disentangle the three major propositions of the school of decline. These are:

- American power, once predominant, is now less than it was, and that it is (or soon will be) matched or exceeded by that of others.
- Such declines of great powers are normal and explicable and are to be anticipated, especially when such states are committed to heavy military spending.
- When such states do decline in power, one likely consequence is political instability and economic disorder in the international system.

Though distinctly separate, all three propositions are interrelated and thus often conflated in one argument. When that is done, the implications are strongly deterministic. For if indeed it is true that American power has declined, and if it is also true that such a decline is normal, even unavoidable, then the resulting disorder in the international system is also, in large degree, preordained. This suggests that there is little that can be done about it. We have therefore to plan on uncertainty, anarchy, conflict, and misrule and to behave accordingly. This is a counsel of despair not to be taken too lightly.

For readers to clarify their own thinking, therefore, the three propositions must first be considered separately, together with the refuting counter-propositions, for it is not logically necessary to accept or reject all three. For example, the theme of Robert Keohane's *After Hegemony,* and of much current literature by international economists, is that although American power has declined and although this has led to the erosion of international regimes, there is still a substitute for American hegemony to be found in international cooperation and the coordination of monetary and fiscal policies. Thus, accepting the first proposition does not necessarily mean accepting the third.

By laying out the main grounds on which I think each of the three propositions can be legitimately questioned, a different conclusion becomes possible. It is based on the analysis of structural power in international political economy which I have developed at greater length elsewhere. It leads to the conclusion that although there are current weaknesses in the American Empire, they are not irreparable and they are much less important than its continuing structural power. However, a necessary condition for the needed reforms is the development of a political will to change. And that will not come until it is more widely recognized that the school of decline has grossly overdone its Cassandra act.

To be fair, however, it has to be said that it is the simplifications and vulgarizations by the media and the politicians of what the gloomy academics have actually said that have been grossly overdone. Paul Kennedy, for example, in his epilogue quotes Bismarck to abjure determinism and to insist that the governments of states "travelling on the stream of Time" may still "steer with more or less experience." And although in public appearances he has sometimes weakened and pontificated confidently about international affairs, in his book he carefully plays the role of the nonpartisan historian, merely presenting his large body of data to the political scientists "concerned with the larger patterns of war and change in the international order" for them to analyze. Time and again, when the reader looks more closely at the small print, there is found to be more common ground between the school of decline and its opponents (like myself) than would at first appear. . . .

Where I think we are all in agreement is on the critical nature of the present end-of-century decade. We share a common perception that mankind—and more particularly the governments it acknowledges as possessing the authority to make decisions—is standing at a fork in the road, at the end of a long stretch of comparative order and stability, and facing momentous choices in the way ahead. That is why there is shared concern to understand where we are now and how we got there and to seek in the lessons of history some guidance for future action. In the last resort, it may well be that this common concern is more significant than the differences of interpretation to which I now turn.

American Power

Paul Kennedy, in common with the rest of the decline school, starts from the age-old premise that "to be a great power demands a flourishing economic base." Following Adam Smith the liberal, and Friedrich List the mercantilist, this is then interpreted to mean an economic base of manufacturing industry located within the territorial boundaries of the state. It is this interpretation of "a flourishing economic base" that is obsolete and therefore open to doubt. Smith and List are both long dead. More recent changes, noted by Peter Drucker, among others, in the character of the world-economy throw doubt on whether it is manufacturing that is now most important in developing the sinews of war; and, whether it is location within the boundaries of the territory that matters most.

My contention (which should surely be sustained by the champions of American service industries) is that it is the information-rich occupations, whether associated with manufacturing or not, that confer power, much more now than the physical capacity to roll goods off an assembly line. Second, I contend that the location of productive capacity is far less important than the location of the people who make the key decisions on what is to be produced, where and how, and who design, direct, and manage to sell successfully on a world market. Is it more desirable that Americans should wear blue collars and mind the machines or that they should wear white collars and design, direct, and finance the whole operation?

That is why all the figures so commonly trotted out about the U.S. share of world manufacturing capacity, or the declining U.S. share of world exports of manufactures are so misleading—because they are territorially based. Worse, they are irrelevant. What matters is the share of world output—of primary products, minerals, and food and manufactured goods and services—that is under the direction of the executives of U.S. companies. That share can be U.S.-directed even if the enterprise directly responsible is only half owned by an American parent, and even, in some cases of technological dependence, where it is not owned at all but where the license to produce is granted or refused by people in the United States. The largest stock of foreign direct investments is still held by U.S. corporations—even though the figures are neither precise, complete, nor comprehensive. The fact that the current out-flow from Japan is greater than that from the United States merely means that the gap is narrowing. But the Japanese still have a long way to go to rival the extent of U.S. corporate operations in Europe, Latin America, Australasia, the Middle East, and Africa, the assets of which are often valued at their historical prices, not at their current values.

U.S.-controlled enterprise outside the territorial United States is still grow-ing very fast in new fields of technology like software services, biotechnology, medical products, data retrieval, environmental management, or new basic materials. IBM is still unrivaled in its field and has stayed so by strategic agility in overcoming its rivals and imitators. Genentech is still the world's biggest biotechnology corporation and Cray Research is the largest producer of supercomputers. What these leading American companies have in common is that more of their output is produced outside the territorial United States than is produced inside it. For example, an estimate of middle-sized U.S. companies associated within the American Business Conference found that 80 percent of their revenues in 1986 came from production overseas; only 20 percent came from exporting from the United States. Two conclusions were drawn from their success. One was that Jean-Jacques Servan Schreiber had been quite wrong in seeing the "American Challenge" to the rest of the world as coming from the giant corporations like ITT or General Electric. Today, the challenge is more likely to come from relatively new and smaller American enterprises. The other conclusion was that trade figures are not the best measure of competitiveness and that it would be better to judge by corporate world market shares. In these terms, Japanese companies just now beginning to shift production to America, Europe, and mainland Asia are only following the American lead—and the trade figures, eagerly (and wrongly) watched for indications of competitiveness, will soon begin to show it.

At this point some people will object that when production moves away from the territory of the United States, the authority of the U.S. government is diminished. At the same time, the same people sometimes complain against the "invasion" of the United States by Japanese companies, as if "selling off the farm" is diminishing the authority of the United States government. Clearly, both cannot be right. Rather, both perceptions seem to me to be wrong. What is happening is that the American Empire is spilling out beyond the frontier and that the very insubstantial nature of frontiers where produc- tion is concerned just shows the consolidation of an entirely new kind of nonterritorial empire.

It is that nonterritorial empire that is really the "flourishing economic base" of U.S. power, not the goods and services produced within the United States. One obvious indication of this fact is that foreign central banks last year [1987] spent roughly $140 billion supporting the exchange value of the dollar. Another is that Japanese and other foreign investors financed the lion's share of the U.S. government's budget deficit by buying U.S. government securities and investing in the United States. An empire that can command such resources hardly seems to be losing power. The fact that the United States is still the largest and richest (and mostly open) market for goods and services under one political authority means that all successful foreign compa- nies will want to produce and sell there and will deem it prudent also to produce there, not simply to avoid protectionist barriers but in order to be close to the customers. And the worldwide reach of U.S.-controlled enter- prises also means that the capacity of the United States to exercise extraterrito- rial influence and authority is also greater than that of any other government. If only for security reasons, the ability of Washington to tell U.S. companies in Japan what to do or not to do is immeasurably greater than the ability of Tokyo to tell Japanese companies in the United States what to do.

This points to another major fallacy in the decline school's logic—its inattention to matters of security. The U.S. lead in the ability to make and deliver the means of nuclear destruction is the complement to its lead in influencing, through past investments overseas, the nature, modes, and pur- poses of modern industrial production. Here, too, the gap may be narrowing as South Africa, Israel, India, and others claim nuclear capability. Yet there is still no comparison between the military power of the United States to confer, deny, or threaten the security of others with that of minor noncommunist states. That military power is now based far less on the capacity to manufac- ture nuclear weapons than on the capacity to recruit scientists, American or foreign, to keep ahead in design and invention, both offensive and defensive.

Historical Parallels

The decline school so far has succeeded in promoting the idea that history teaches that it is "normal" for great states and empires to decline, especially when they become militarily overextended; or else when they become socially and politically sclerotic, risk-averse, and resistant to changes or when they overindulge in foreign investment; and for any or all of these reasons when they lose preeminence in agricultural and industrial production, or in trade and military capability. In almost all the American literature on the rise and fall of empires, great attention and weight is characteristically (and for rea- sons of language and culture, perhaps understandably) given to the British experience. But the trouble with history, as the first great realist writer on international relations, E.H. Carr, rightly observed, is that it is necessarily selective—and that the historian selects facts as a fish shop selects fish, choosing some and discarding or overlooking others. In this debate, the historical analogy between Britain and America is particularly weak; and the other examples selected for consideration show a strong tendency to concentrate on the empires whose decline after the peaking of their power was more or less steady and never reversed.

First, it is not too difficult to show that what Britain and America have had in common—such as a tendency to invest heavily overseas—is much less important than all the differences that mark their experience. Britain's economic decline, beginning around the 1880s, was the result of a neglect of the then advanced technologies—notably in chemicals and engineering. This neglect reflected the weakness and low status of manufacturing industry in British politics and society—a social disdain such as American industry has never had to contend with. Even more important was the effect of two long, debilitating wars on the British economy, by comparison with which the American experience of Vietnam was a flea bite. It is arguable that the British economy, dependent as it was on financial power, would not have suffered so great a setback if the whole international financial system on which it lived and prospered had not been twice destroyed—first in the Great War and then in the Second World War. The interwar period was too short—and policies were also ill-chosen—to allow a reversal of this British decline.

Finally, there is the great difference between a small offshore island running a large territorial empire and a great continental power managing (or sometimes mismanaging) a large nonterritorial empire. The island state made the fatal mistake after the Second World War of relying on sheltered colonial and sterling area markets—with disastrous effects on the competitiveness of its export industries and even some of its old, established multinationals. The continental power's confidence in its ability to dominate an open world-economy, plus the strong commitment to antitrust policies at home, has created no such weakening crutches for its major transnational corporations.

Second, any historical study of empires of the past fails to reveal any standard or uniform pattern of rise and fall. They are like trees. Some grow fast and fall suddenly without warning. Others grow slowly and decay very gradually, even making astonishing recoveries from shock or injury. One author, Michael Doyle, who has shared less in the media attention perhaps because his work lends itself less readily to deterministic interpretations, drew an important conclusion from an analytical survey of empires that included those of the ancient world as well as the later European ones. It is worth quoting:

> The historical alternatives had divided between persistence, which necessitated imperial development in both the metropole and the periphery, and decline and fall. Persistence in an extensive empire required that the metropole cross the Augustan threshold to imperial bureaucracy, and perhaps became in effect an equal political partner with the metropole.

In plainer language, what I interpret this to mean is that the empires that lasted longest were those that managed to build a political system suited to the administration of the empire out of one suited to managing the core. In addition, those empires that survived managed to blur the distinction between the ruling groups of the core and the participating allies and associates of the periphery. This is a notion closely related to Gramscian concepts of hegemony and explanations of the persistent strength of capitalist political economies.

Michael Doyle's attention to the Roman Empire, which was much longer-lived than any of the nineteenth-century European empires, is important for the debate. This is so partly because there have been so many conflicting interpretations of its decline, from Edward Gibbon and Thomas Macaulay to Joseph Schumpeter and Max Weber, and partly because most historians seem to agree that it passed through periods of regeneration and reform before it finally broke up in disorder. Michael Mann, for instance, recently identified one such period of reform and regeneration in the twenty years after the accession of Septimus Severus in A.D. 193:

> Severus began withdrawing crack legions from the frontiers to mobile reserve positions, replacing them at the frontier with a settler militia. This was a more defensive, less confident posture. It also cost more, and so he attempted financial reform, abolishing tax farming and the tax exemption of Rome and Italy.

This comment by a sociologist is interesting because it focuses on two important elements of power in imperial states: relations with key groups in the periphery, and the fiscal system by which unavoidable imperial expenditures are financed. When we consider the future of the American Empire, we find that these two issues are once again crucial to the outcome between Doyle's two alternatives—persistence or decline. Mann describes the Roman Empire as a "legionary empire," indicating that the role and character of the legions were important in explaining Roman power.

I would argue that America's "legions," in the integrated financial and production economy of today's world, are not military but economic. They are the corporate enterprises on which the military depends—as President Dwight Eisenhower foresaw in talking about the military-industrial complex. The American Empire in sociological terms therefore could be described as a "corporation empire" in which the culture and interests of the corporations are sustained by an imperial bureaucracy. But this bureaucracy, largely set up after the Second World War, was not simply a national American one based in Washington, D.C. A large and important part of it was and is multinational and works through the major international economic organizations such as the International Monetary Fund (IMF), the World Bank, the Organization for Economic Cooperation and Development (OECD) in Paris, and the General Agreement on Tariffs and Trade in Geneva.

The other feature of the Roman Empire that I believe is relevant to the current debate is that citizenship was not a matter of domicile and that there were gradations of civil and political rights and responsibilities, ranging from slaves to senators, which did not depend on what we, today, understand by "nationality," indicated by possession or nonpossession of a passport. If we can once escape the corsetlike intellectual constraints of the conventional study of international relations and liberate our minds to ask new questions, we begin to see new things about America's nonterritorial empire. Here, too, citizenship is becoming much more complex and graded than it used to be. The managers of U.S. corporations, in Brazil, for example, may hold Brazilian and not U.S. passports. But they are free to come and go with indefinite visas into the United States and they often exercise considerable delegated power in the running of U.S.-directed enterprises vital to the Brazilian economy. Participation in the cultural empire depends not on passports but on competence in the American language and in many cases participation in U.S.-based professional organizations. . . . Similarly, participation in America's financial empire depends on the possession and use of U.S. dollars and dollar-denominated assets and the ability to compete with U.S. banks and in U.S. financial markets.

Rather like a chrysalis in the metamorphosis from caterpillar to butterfly, the American Empire today combines features of a national-exclusive past with features of a transnational-extensive future. In military matters, it is still narrowly exclusive—though where advanced technology is concerned, even that is changing. Certainly, in financial and cultural matters, the distinction between first-class, passport-holding citizens and second-class, non-passport-holding participants is increasingly blurred. The peripheral allies have been unconsciously recruited into the American Empire.

This is why it is important for the current debate not to think that the mine of imperial histories has been finally and totally exhausted by Paul Kennedy, Mancur Olson, and company. The variety of forms in which empires of the past have handled the personal identity question (citizenship), the territorial limit-of-authority question, and the ideological conformity question calls for a lot more careful scholarly work. For instance, not so much has been done on the Austro-Hungarian Empire of the nineteenth century, which lasted surprisingly long considering its backward economy. A comparison of the Napoleonic Empire, which was militarily based and heavily hegemonic, with the Venetian Empire so beloved of John Ruskin might be instructive. For while the one was ideological and comparatively short-lived, the *Serenissima,* being commercially based, was, from the first, strikingly nonideological and permissive in its dealing with Islamic infidels—and like the late Hapsburg Empire, surprisingly long-lived. One obvious feature of the American Empire, like that of Venice, has been that despite the political rhetoric on the subject of liberty, democracy, and free trade, its governments have been remarkably unfussy on all three counts in their choice of allies and associates.

Power and Systemic Disorder

The third proposition of the decline school has been the one under longest discussion among scholars in international relations. Over most of the past decade, the lead in these discussions has been taken by specialists in the study of international organizations (for example, Joseph Nye, Robert Keohane, John Ruggie, and Ernst Haas). It seems to me that they share a wishful reluctance to admit that international organizations, when they are not simply adaptive mechanisms through which states respond to technical change, are either the strategic instruments of national policies and interests, or else merely symbolic gestures toward a desired but unattainable world government. This reluctance to admit the inherent limitations of international organizations leads them subconsciously to the conclusion that it must be hegemonic decline that is the cause of economic instability and disorder and the coincident erosion of earlier international regimes.

This is a proposition that does not stand up well to either the record of recent international economic history or the structural analysis of power in the international political economy. I do not want to repeat myself, but *Casino Capitalism* was an attempt to show two things (among others): there were more ways than one of interpreting recent developments in the international monetary and financial system; and these developments of the last fifteen years or so could be traced to a series of crucial (and mostly permissive) decisions by governments. Hence, the precarious and unstable state of the global financial structure—which has already been dramatically demonstrated once and probably will be so again—was no fortuitous accident of fate or history.

Since that book was written, I find confirmation that it was not a decline of American power but rather a series of American managerial decisions of dubious wisdom that accounts quite adequately for financial and monetary disorder, without any need to adduce the decline of American hegemonic power. Not only is this the theme of David Calleo's *The Imperious Economy,* but it is also to be found buried in the text of Robert Gilpin's chapters on international money and finance:

> Beginning with the Vietnam war and continuing into the Reagan Administration, the United States had become more of a "predatory hegemon." . . . less willing to subordinate its own interests to those of its allies; instead it tended more and more to exploit its hegemonic status for its own narrowly defined purposes.

Gilpin repeats the point twenty pages later, adding: "Most of the troubles of the world economy in the 1980s have been caused by this shift in American policy."

It will not escape careful students of this important text that Gilpin's historical analysis, and the use of the word "mismanagement" with reference to American domestic and foreign financial policy, fundamentally contradicts his concluding thesis that a stable and prosperous world-economy in the future calls for an American–Japanese condominium because of lost American hegemony.

Similarly, *States and Markets* extends the definition of international political economy beyond the conventional politics of international economic relations to ask more basic who-gets-what questions. In that volume I find that a structural analysis of the basic issues in any political economy, when applied to the world system, strongly suggests that on balance American structural power may actually have increased in recent decades. It has done so through four interlocking structures. These structures concern the power conferred by the ability to offer, withhold, or threaten security (the security structure); the ability to offer, withhold, or demand credit (the financial structure); the ability to determine the locus, mode, and content of wealth-creating activity (the production structure); and, not least, the ability to influence ideas and beliefs and therefore the kind of knowledge socially prized and sought after, and to control (and, through language, to influence) access to and communication of that knowledge (the knowledge structure).

Such a structural analysis suggests the existence under predominant American power and influence of an empire the likes of which the world has never seen before, a nonterritorial empire, whose only borders are the frontiers of the socialist great powers and their allies. It is not, in fact, such an eccentric idea. Two former U.S. secretaries of state recently wrote:

> Far into the future, the United States will have the world's largest and most innovative economy, and will remain a nuclear superpower, a cultural and intellectual leader, a model democracy and a society that provides exceptionally well for its citizens.

What, Then, Must Be Done?

The power Henry Kissinger and Cyrus Vance describe is structural power. The objectives they advocate for the guidance of the next president lie not only in the field of foreign policy but in the political changes they judge necessary for the better management of the world-economy and, consequently, for the creation of a more secure base for long-term U.S. national interests. Specifically, they mention a more efficient, trustful, and well-defined relationship between the Congress and the White House, and a clearer definition, and limitation, of the role of the media in shaping U.S. policies at home and abroad. Such recommendations may suggest to the historian a transition to an Augustan system relying more on a career bureaucracy and less on the vagaries of party politics. . . .

Curiously, perhaps, rather similar conclusions are to be found in the recent study by a Japanese journalist/scholar, Yoichi Funabashi, of international efforts at exchange rate management and policy coordination between the United States, Japan, and the European Community. He suggests a greater and more responsible role in policy-making for the major committees in both houses of Congress—in other words, a more structured and formalized process of bipartisan decision making on crucial issues of trade and finance.

It seems that those individuals whose past professional experience in government or as informed observers best qualify them to judge do not share the enthusiasm for "international policy coordination" that has recently overwhelmed so many professional economists and some publicists. Summit meetings without long and careful preparation by officials, and Group of Seven market interventions without visible changes in economic management are not the answer. At this critical juncture in world affairs, the United States as hegemonic power has, as usual, to take the lead.

In the past two years or so, the Japanese have been conducting among themselves a lively and sometimes quite heated debate on their "identity," that is, their role in the international political economy. According to Chalmers Johnson and others, despite some discussion of the possibilities of "Pax Nipponica" replacing Pax Americana (just as that in turn replaced Pax Britannica), such an outcome is not seen by most Japanese as lying within the realm of practical politics, if only because of the exclusivity of Japanese culture and the difficulties others have with the Japanese language. Nor, because of the disordered and unstable state of world trade and finance, is muddling through on the basis of the status quo a very practical or desirable alternative. A third option, "Pax Consortis" (the Japanese term for international policy coordination), has turned out to be more difficult to achieve than it sounds; "many meetings but little Pax," in Johnson's words. Interest is, therefore, growing in the possibilities and nature of a joint U.S.–Japan hegemony. It does not mean splitting the world-economy into three economic blocs, as in the 1930s. The economies of North America, Japan, and Europe are far too closely intertwined today to allow that. Nor, in the considered opinion of several influential elder statesmen in Japan, does it mean an equal balance of power between the United States and Japan. Naohiro Amaya, a former vice minister at the Ministry of International Trade and Industry, for instance, calls it a "Pax Ameripponica," but adds that "if it were a company the United States would be president and Japan vice president." He does not think the opposite is possible.

What this implies, it seems to me, is that reforms should be set in motion that would create between the United States and Japan—now the world's major creditor and banker—the same sort of symbiotic relationship between senior and junior partner that the Americans developed with the British before, during, and after World War II. Leadership—a term Charles Kindleberger, who started the whole hegemonic stability debate, has always used in preference to hegemony—rests with America. But there has to be something more in it than there is now for Japan. And Americans have to make more strenuous efforts than they have made so far to tackle the dilemma of their two deficits—the budget deficit and the trade deficit. Unless they look as if they mean to do so, the sustaining flow of capital out of Japan into the United States is going to look precarious, inducing uncertainty and continuing volatility in exchange rates and interest rates. The markets will react accordingly. Consequently, not only must fat be cut out of the U.S. defense budget—at home as well as in Europe and the Middle East—but something must also be done to encourage savings in place of the unremitting consumerism characteristic of the United States and some parts of its nonterritorial empire. Long-term assets underwritten in a basket of currencies and tax concessions for small savers are the sorts of policy instruments that need examination.

"New Deals" are needed internationally and not just nationally as in the 1930s. A New Deal with Japan would give better long-term assurance of financial support for the expenses of empire in return for more generous power-sharing in organizations like the IMF, the World Bank, the OECD, and the regional development banks in Asia and Latin America. A New Deal with Europe would exchange increased financial responsibility for the costs of NATO for Europeanization (Calleo's term) of its command structure. . . . A New Deal for Latin America—in some ways the most solid part of the American Empire—would take up the Japanese proposal, brushed too contemptuously aside at the Toronto summit, for a long-term solution of its chronic debt problems, in return perhaps for some commitments to liberalize trade and secure investments.

New Deals, however, do not drop like manna from heaven. They do not come about without political vision and inspiration, or without hard intellectual effort to find the sustaining optimal bargain. Optimal bargains are those that last because they go some way to satisfy the needs and aspirations of the governed as well as those of the governors. Only then can the power of those in charge of empires (as of states, local party machines, or labor unions) be sustained over the long run. The next four years will show not only Americans but the rest of us who live and work in the American Empire whether the defeatist gloom of the school of decline can be dissipated. They will show whether the necessary vision can still be found in the White House for a series of global New Deals and whether the necessary intellectual effort to design and negotiate them will be generated not only in the bureaucracies, national and international, but in the universities and research institutes of all our countries.

9

Regimes and Epistemic Communities

The study of "international regimes," like the rational choice approach, emerged from liberal theory. It, too, has been integrated into other theoretical systems, especially neomercantilism, and has developed into a distinct subfield of IPE. Unlike rational choice, which is basically a methodological technique, regime analysis centers on relationships and governing principles among global actors in particular issue-areas. Theoretical synthesis centered on regime analysis does not involve the same kind of epistemological problems as rational choice; neomercantilists employ the concept without compromising their statist assumptions. In recent years, however, the study of regimes, and the allied concept "epistemic communities," has pushed away from neomercantilist theory, suggesting greater theoretical compatibility with its parent, liberalism.

The regime analysis of Donald J. Puchala and Raymond F. Hopkins is consistent with the liberal tradition. They take up the time-honored liberal issue of the role of principles in international affairs. Their definition of regimes—"a set of principles, norms, rules and procedures around which actors' expectations converge"—is conventional, but their application of the concept is broader than other regime analysts'. Puchala and Hopkins see normative forces at work in virtually every issue-area of international relations. This suggests that regime-based principles and norms have greater efficacy than realist theory would allow. Puchala and Hopkins argue that regime analysis, as such, is an improvement over cruder power politics variants of realism. They do not lapse into unwarranted idealism, but clearly resuscitate long-standing liberal positions.

The question for Puchala and Hopkins is, therefore, to explain why some regimes are more effective in constraining state behavior than others. They consider the extent to which certain internal characteristics influence regime effectiveness. Regimes may be specific to one issue or more diffuse, involving numerous related issues; they may be formal or informal; subject to evolutionary or revolutionary change; and distinguished by certain distributive biases. Puchala and Hopkins examine two regimes with very different configurations: colonialism (diffuse, informal, subject to revolutionary change, and very biased) and food (specific, formal, open to evolutionary change, and less biased) in an effort to clarify the significance of these variables.

Their conclusions are reminiscent of interdependence theory. Although internal characteristics are helpful in understanding the dynamics of specific regimes, on a more general level regime effectiveness is influenced by the broader international context. Regimes are likely to constrain state behavior when they mediate relations among countries of relatively equal power. Additionally, regimes are important in situations where power is diffused, as in international organizations, and at moments of power transitions. In short, the global distribution of power and the definition of national interests are not negated by the existence of regimes. Thus, Puchala and Hopkins, in a manner similar to Keohane and Nye's notion of complex interdependence, do not completely reject realist analysis; they qualify it. They argue that regimes: "tend to have inertia or functional autonomy and continue to influence behavior even though their norms have ceased either to reflect the preferences of powers or to be buttressed by their capabilities." This implies that, under certain circumstances, state action may be significantly influenced by relatively autonomous international regimes, a point that undermines state-centric realist arguments.

Peter M. Haas's discussion of epistemic communities further emphasizes the transformative power of regimes. Unlike Puchala and Hopkins, Haas focuses more on the internal workings of regimes, especially the coherence and power of groups of like-minded experts—"epistemic communities"—and less on the global context. In the case of Mediterranean pollution control, an epistemic community of United Nations officials and government officials in various countries, linked together by a common ecological outlook and access to certain international organizations, played an important part in strengthening the marine environmental regime in the region.

Epistemic communities can strengthen regimes through a process of learning, which, in turn, hinges on political influence. Haas finds that state leaders can learn to accept regime principles and norms, thus changing the definition of national interests, if constituents of the epistemic community have sufficient bureaucratic standing within the state apparatus and adequate support from relevant international bodies. He shows that environmental policy in Algeria and Egypt changed in accord with regime principles as the power and resources of the ecological epistemic community expanded in those countries. Where environmentalists had less power within the bureaucracy, as in France, state policy was somewhat less congruent with regime principles.

In focusing on the domestic political dynamics of particular countries, Haas reminds us that IPE inquiry requires a comparative as well as global perspective. Different political systems do not react to global issues in the same manner and attention must be paid to local particularities.

International Regimes:
Lessons from Inductive Analysis

DONALD J. PUCHALA AND RAYMOND F. HOPKINS

Rising interest in the concept "international regime" in the 1970s is much like that accorded to "international system" in the 1950s. It has become intellectually fashionable to speak and write about regimes. Current faddishness notwithstanding, the purpose of this article is to show that the notion of regime is analytically useful, and that the concept is therefore likely to become a lasting element in the theory of international relations. As realist and other paradigms prove too limited for explaining an increasingly complex, interdependent, and dangerous world, scholars are searching for new ways to organize intellectually and understand international activity. Using the term regime allows us to point to and comprehend sets of activities that might otherwise be organized or understood differently. Thinking in terms of regimes also alerts us to the subjective aspects of international behavior that might be overlooked altogether in more conventional inquiries.

A regime . . . is a set of principles, norms, rules, and procedures around which actors' expectations converge. These serve to channel political action within a system and give it meaning. For every political system, be it the United Nations, the United States, New York City, or the American Political Science Association, there is a corresponding regime. Regimes constrain and regularize the behavior of participants, affect which issues among protagonists move on and off agendas, determine which activities are legitimized or condemned, and influence whether, when, and how conflicts are resolved.

Several particular features of the phenomenon of regimes, as we conceive

Reprinted from *International Organization*, Vol. XXXVI, No. 2, Donald J. Puchala and Raymond F. Hopkins, "International Regimes: Lessons from Inductive Analysis," by permission of The MIT Press, Cambridge, MA.

of it, are worth noting, since other authors do not stress or, in the case of some, accept these points. We stress five major features.

First, a regime is an attitudinal phenomenon. Behavior follows from adherence to principles, norms, and rules, which legal codes sometimes reflect. But *regimes themselves are subjective:* they exist primarily as participants' understandings, expectations or convictions about legitimate, appropriate or moral behavior.

Second, an international regime includes tenets concerning appropriate procedures for making decisions. This feature, we suggest, compels us to identify a regime not only by a major substantive norm (as is done in characterizing exchange rate regimes as fixed or floating rate regimes) but also by the broad norms that establish procedures by which rules or policies—the detailed extensions of principles—are reached. Questions about the norms of a regime, then, include who participates, what interests dominate or are given priority, and what rules serve to protect and preserve the dominance in decision making.

Third, a description of a regime must include a characterization of the major principles it upholds (e.g., the sanctity of private property or the benefits of free markets) as well as the norms that prescribe orthodox and proscribe deviant behavior. It is especially useful to estimate the hierarchies among principles and the prospects for norm enforcement. These bear upon the potential for change.

Fourth, each regime has a set of elites who are the practical actors within it. Governments of nation-states are the prime official members of most international regimes, although international, transnational, and sometimes subnational organizations may practically and legitimately participate. More concretely, however, regime participants are most often bureaucratic units or individuals who operate as parts of the "government" of an international subsystem by creating, enforcing or otherwise acting in compliance with norms. Individuals and bureaucratic roles are linked in international networks of activities and communication. These individuals and rules govern issue-areas by creating and maintaining regimes.

Finally, a regime exists in every substantive issue-area in international relations where there is discernibly patterned behavior. Wherever there is regularity in behavior some kinds of principles, norms or rules must exist to account for it.

Regime Distinctions Important for Comparative Study

. . . . Our examination of several international regimes suggests four characteristics of theoretical importance.

1. Specific vs. Diffuse Regimes

. . . . Regimes can be differentiated according to function along a continuum ranging from specific, single-issue to diffuse, multi-issue. They may also be categorized by participants according to whether a few or a great many actors subscribe to their principles or at least adhere to their norms. No international regimes command universal adherence, though many approach it. More specific regimes often tend to be embedded in broader, more diffuse ones—the principles and norms of the more diffuse regimes are taken as given in the more specific regimes. In this sense we may speak of normative *superstructures,* which are reflected in functionally or geographically specific normative substructures or regimes. For example, in the nineteenth century, principles concerning the rectitude of the balance of power among major actors (the normative superstructure) were reflected in norms legitimizing and regulating colonial expansion (a substructure), and in those regulating major-power warfare (another substructure). . . .

2. Formal vs. Informal Regimes

Some regimes are legislated by international organizations, maintained by councils, congresses or other bodies, and monitored by international bureaucracies. We characterize these as "formal" regimes. The European Monetary System is one example. By contrast, other, more "informal" regimes are created and maintained by convergence or consensus in objectives among participants, enforced by mutual self-interest and "gentlemen's agreements," and monitored by mutual surveillance. For example, Soviet–American detente between 1970 and 1979 could be said to have been governed by a regime that constrained competitiveness and controlled conflict in the perceived mutual interests of the superpowers. Yet few rules of the relationship were ever formalized and few institutions other than the Hot Line and the Helsinki accords were created to monitor and enforce them.

3. Evolutionary vs. Revolutionary Change

Regimes change substantively in at least two different ways: one preserves norms while changing principles; the other overturns norms in order to change principles. Regimes may change qualitatively because those who participate in them change their minds about interests and aims, usually because of changes in information available to elites or new knowledge otherwise attained. We call this *evolutionary change,* because it occurs within the procedural norms of the regime, usually without major changes in the distribution of power among participants. Such change, undisturbing to the power structure and within the regime's "rules of the game," is rather exceptional and characteristic mainly of functionally specific regimes.

By contrast, *revolutionary* change is more common. Most regimes function to the advantage of some participants and the disadvantage of others. The disadvantaged accept regime principles and norms (and diminished rewards or outright penalties) because the costs of noncompliance are understood to be higher than the costs of compliance. But disadvantaged participants tend to formulate and propagate counterregime norms, which either circulate in the realm of rhetoric or lie dormant as long as those who dominate the existing regime preserve their power and their consequent ability to reward compliance and punish deviance. However, if and when the power structure alters, the normative contents of a prevailing regime fall into jeopardy. Power transition ushers in regime transformation; previously disadvantaged but newly powerful participants ascend to dominance and impose new norms favoring their own interests. In extreme cases the advantaged and disadvantaged reverse status, and a new cycle begins with regime change contingent upon power change. Such revolutionary change is more characteristic of diffuse regimes, highly politicized functional regimes, or those where distributive bias is high.

4. Distributive Bias

All regimes are biased. They establish hierarchies of values, emphasizing some and discounting others. They also distribute rewards to the advantage of some and the disadvantage of others, and in so doing they buttress, legitimize, and sometimes institutionalize international patterns of dominance, subordination, accumulation, and exploitation. In general, regimes favor the interests of the strong and, to the extent that they result in international governance, it is always appropriate to ask how such governance affects participants' interests. The degree of bias may make a considerable difference in a regime's durability, effectiveness, and mode of transformation. "Fairer" regimes are likely to last longer, as are those that call for side payments to disadvantaged participants. . . .

In the next two sections, we use the regime framework to discuss international relations in two contrasting issue-areas, 19th century colonialism and mid-twentieth century food affairs. Readers will recognize that these two regimes differ significantly along each of the four analytical dimensions we have elaborated. The colonial regime was diffuse, largely informal, subject to revolutionary transformation, and distinctly biased in distributing rewards. By contrast, the food regime is more specific, more formalized, probably in the process of evolutionary transformation, and more generally rewarding to most participants. Our primary intention is to highlight and clarify our theoretical definitions and the variables we have identified as useful for comparative analysis. Conclusions will push toward generalizations concerning regime outcomes and patterns of stability and change.

Colonialism, 1870–1914

Historians identify the years 1870 to 1914 as the heyday of European colonial expansion. Our analysis reveals that during this period the international relations of the imperial powers were regulated by a regime that prescribed certain modes of behavior for metropolitan countries vis-à-vis each other and toward their respective colonial subjects. Save for the United States, which entered the

colonial game rather late (and Japan, which entered later and never participated in the normative consensus until after it had come under challenge), all of
the colonial powers were European. The "regime managers" by 1870 were the
governments of major states, where ministries and ministers made the rules of
the colonial game and diplomats, soldiers, businessmen, and settlers played
accordingly. In addition, a variety of subnational actors, including nebulous
"publics" such as church societies, militarist lobbies, trade unions, and bankers, held opinions on issues of foreign policy and in some countries exercised
substantial influence over the formulation of colonial policy.

The international relations of colonialism were evident in distinctive patterns of political and economic transactions and interactions. Flows of trade
and money were typically "imperial" in the sense implied by Hobson or
Lenin: extracted raw materials flowed from colonies to metropolis, light manufactures flowed back, investment capital flowed outward from European centers, and profits and returns flowed back.

But much more important than the characteristic transaction flows of colonialism were the interaction patterns in relations among imperial powers and
between them and their respective colonies. There was a pronounced competitiveness among metropoles as each country sought to establish, protect, and
expand its colonial domains against rivals. Yet there was also a sense of limitation or constraint in major-power relations, a notion of imperial equity, evidenced in periodic diplomatic conferences summoned to sort out colonial issues
by restraining the expansiveness of some and compensating others for their
losses. Constraint and equity were also reflected in doctrines like "spheres of
influence" and "open doors," which endorsed the notion that sharing and
subdivision were in order. . . . In inter-imperial relations, then, there were
distinct elements of international management over selected parts of the non-
European world. This management rested upon implicit codes for managing
colonies, rationales like "civilizing mission," which were given credence, and
growing willingness to agree on imperial borders by diplomatic conferences.

With regard to relations between the metropolitan powers and subject
peoples, little equity prevailed. Commands, directives, and demands flowed
from colonial ministries to colonial officers and then either to compliant local
functionaries or directly to subjects. Deference and compliance flowed back.
Defiance usually brought coercive sanctions, with success largely guaranteed
by the technological superiority of European arms. . . .

Norms of the Colonial Regime

The legitimacy in colonization was founded upon consensus in a number of
norms that the governments of the major powers recognized and accepted.
These subjective foundations of the international regime may be treated under six headings.

a. The Bifurcation of Civilization. Looking from the metropolitan capitals
outward, the world was perceived as divided into two classes of states and

peoples, civilized and uncivilized. Europe and northern North America occupied the civilized category, and all other areas were beyond the pale, save perhaps other "white-settled" dominions. . . . From this, it followed politically that inequality was an appropriate principle of international organization and that standards and modes of behavior displayed toward other international actors depended upon which category those others fell into. . . .

b. *The Acceptability of Alien Rule.* The zenith of European imperialism occurred before the principle of national self-determination became a tenet of world politics, and indeed before Europe itself had largely settled into the pattern of "one nation, one state". . . . Thus, the imposition of foreign rule and the superimposition of white elites on indigenous elites were approved as right and proper, especially when such behavior was also perceived as "civilizing" or "Christianizing."

c. *The Propriety of Accumulating Domain.* During the period 1870 to 1914 states' positions in the international status hierarchy were determined in considerable measure by expanses of territory (or numbers of inhabitants) under respective national jurisdictions. Domain was the key to prestige, prestige was an important ingredient in power, and power was the wherewithal to pursue a promising national destiny. The expansion of domain was therefore accepted by the European powers as a legitimate goal of imperial foreign policy and, indeed, reluctance to pursue such policies was considered unorthodox; it raised questions about the according of status. . . .

d. *The Importance of Balancing Power.* Intra-European relations in the late 19th century were stabilized by principles of a multipolar balance of power (even though the bipolarization that would harden by the eve of World War I was already in evidence). There was a widespread recognition of the efficacy of the balance of power and a general consensus among foreign offices that it should be preserved and perfected. This principle also justified colonial expansion and it further supported the norm of compensation. As a matter of right all colonial governments expected compensation for adjustments in the boundaries of colonial empires. . . .

e. *Legitimacy in Neomercantilism.* Economic exclusivity was a norm of colonialism since, as we have noted, colonies were considered to be zones of economic exploitation. Hence metropolitan powers endorsed their rights to regulate the internal development and external commerce of their colonies for the benefit of the home country, and, when appropriate or necessary, to close their colonial regions to extra-empire transactions. . . .

f. *Noninterference in Others' Colonial Administration.* As colonial domains were considered to lie under the sovereign jurisdiction of metropolitan governments, external interference in "domestic" affairs was not countenanced. The colonial powers could, and did, chip away at each others' domains via strategic diplomacy and occasional military skirmishes. But seldom did any one power question the internal administration of another's colonies. . . .

It is easy to see how these various tenets of the colonial regime affected international behavior. They abetted behavior directed toward establishing relationships of dominance and subordination, rationalized conquest and whatever brutalities it might involve, justified subjugation and exploitation, impelled a continuing major-power diplomacy concerning colonial matters, and necessitated periodic conferences and continuing bureaucratic-level communication. Such communication was aimed at limiting overexpansiveness, providing compensation, and maintaining the balance of power, and it had the effect of insulating empires from extra-imperial scrutiny and intervention. In this normative setting, colonization was deemed right and legitimate. It flourished.

The fundamental principles of the colonial regime were all challenged, even in their heyday, and eventually undermined during the years after 1920. By the 1970s dominance-subordination was considered an illegitimate mode of international relations, alien rule had become anathema, economic exploitation was condemned and attacked, territorial compensation was considered diplomatically ludicrous, and the internal affairs of empire (of which only small remnants remained) became matters of continuing international public disclosure and debate in the United Nations and elsewhere. . . .

Why did the regime change? First, and obviously, the power structure of the international system changed; western European power was drained in two world wars; the United States and the Soviet Union rose to fill the power vacuum; new elites had come to power in both the United States and Russia after World War I and their preferences were distinctly anticolonial (though for ideologically different reasons). After World War II, new power emerged to buttress new principles and to support new institutions like the United Nations, where anticolonialism, promoted by the Soviet Union and acquiesced in by the United States, was taken up by smaller countries and proclaimed by excolonial states, whose ranks swelled yearly. A new global consensus was formed in the General Assembly under pressure from the Committee of Twenty-Four, and this held the tenets of the new anticolonial regime that prevails at present.

Some Analytic Characteristics of the Colonial Regime

The international regime that governed turn-of-the-century European colonialism was obviously diffuse, both geographically and functionally. Its tenets pertained to relations among metropolitan countries, and to relations between them and their subjects. Whatever the substance of relations among metropoles, principles of exclusivity, compensation, and power balancing applied. In metropolitan-colonial relations of whatever substance principles prescribing dominance-subordination and abetting exploitation applied. To the extent that there was also geographically or functionally specific sub-regimes operative during the imperial era, such as American hegemonism in the Caribbean, the antislavery system, or intracolonial trade, they tended to embody as given the main tenets of the colonial regime. Interestingly, the colonial regime itself embodied some of the more general principles of 19th century international relations, as for example the central and explicit importance of power balancing, and the linkage between international stature and control over "domain." This suggests the hierarchical interrelationship of *superstructural* and *substructural* regimes discussed earlier.

Managing the colonial regime was a pluralistic exercise conducted largely by mutual monitoring and self-regulation practiced in national capitals. The regime was therefore, by and large, informal; there were few codified rules and no permanent organizations. . . . Formalization would have amounted to a spelling out of the rules, as for example those necessitating compensation, and would have jeopardized major-power relations by calling attention to constraints that rival governments could not admit to in public. The less said formally, the better, and the more durable the regime.

While our description of the colonial regime only hints at its transformation in the middle of the 20th century, the change was obviously of the revolutionary variety. There was little changing of minds or goals on the part of the colonial powers (save perhaps for the United States, whose government began to seek decolonialization almost as soon as the Pacific territories were annexed). Instead, counterregime norms took form in the European colonies in the 1920s and 1930s as nationalist elites emerged and movements were organized. The Russian Revolution created a formally anti-imperialistic state, thus breaking the European consensus that supported the principles of colonialism and modestly transferring power from the forces of imperialism to its challengers. Two world wars in the first half of the 20th century eclipsed European power and with it the capacity to retain great empires. After World War II the United States became aggressively anti-imperialistic for a time, thus shifting more power away from the supporters of the colonial regime. With the onset of the Cold War the United States subdued its anticolonialism in the interest of western unity (but Washington never admitted the legitimacy of empires). Meanwhile, counterregime norms prescribing decolonization had been legitimized and institutionalized by the United Nations General Assembly and its subsidiary bodies in the early 1960s. As the power to preserve the old regime waned, the power to replace it expanded. Personalities changed, norms changed, and power changed. As a result an international regime was discredited, eliminated, and replaced. The transformation was nothing less than a comprehensive change in the principles by which governments conducted their international relations.

Food, 1949–1980

Food constitutes a functionally rather specific regime, at least in comparison with diffuse regimes such as colonialism. Nonetheless, it conditions diverse policies and activity. Food trade, food aid, and international financing for rural development and agricultural research, for example, are all affected by the principles and norms of the international food regime. In contrast to the colonial regime, the food regime is more formal. Several organizations shape and spread regime norms and rules, and many rules are explicit and codified. . . .

Many of the regime's principles and norms are codified in treaties, agreements, and conventions such as the FAO [Food and Agricultural Organization] Charter, the International Grains Agreement, and the Food Aid Convention. The norms of the food regime are biased to favor developed and grain-trading countries, which have long enjoyed special weight in the IWC and FAO forums. Still, in contrast to the colonial regime, most participants in the food regime benefit to some extent from their compliance with norms. The regime is now in transition though, again in contrast to the colonial regime, change is taking place in evolutionary fashion.

For illustrative purposes we will focus on wheat as a key commodity in the international food regime, mainly because the international economics and politics of wheat have been thoroughly researched and we can therefore discuss regime influences with some confidence.

The national actors dominating the international wheat market since World War II have been the United States and Canada. In 1934–38 these North American countries supplied 20 percent of the wheat, coarse grain, and rice traded, while in 1979 they supplied 70 percent. These countries also held very large surpluses until 1972 (a byproduct of their domestic agricultural politics). Their common interests led them to operate as an informal duopoly. Together they controlled and stabilized international prices for two decades, though at the cost of allowing the price of internationally traded wheat to decline in constant terms by nearly one-half between 1950 and 1963–69. Other important actors in the food regime, as reflected by their participation in the wheat sector, include 1) major producers and consumers such as members of the European Communities (EEC), eastern European countries, and the Soviet Union; 2) other principal exporters such as Australia and Argentina; 3) poor importers such as China, Bangladesh, and Egypt; and 4) various international bodies such as the World Food Council, the Committee on Surplus Disposal of the FAO, and the major grain-trading firms. Of course, in more concrete terms the participants in the food regime are not really states and organizations but individuals, an international managerial elite of government officials who are responsible for food and agricultural policy within countries, and for bargaining about food affairs in international forums. Their network usually includes executives from the trading firms, some scientific experts, and occasionally representatives from public-interest organizations. But its core is a cluster of agricultural and trade officers. . . .

Norms of the food regime

In regulating food affairs over the last several decades, regime managers have been able to find consensus on a number of norms. Some of these reflect the overarching principles or superstructure of the state system; others are more specifically aimed at regulating food transfers. Eight norms in particular tend either to be embodied in the charters of food institutions, or to be recognized as "standard operating procedures" by food managers.

Respect for a Free International Market. Most major participants in the food trade of the post-World War II era adhered to the belief that a properly functioning free market would be the most efficient allocator of globally traded foodstuffs (and agricultural inputs). . . . Communist countries did not accept this norm for Soviet bloc trade, but abided by it nonetheless in East–West food trade. Actual practice often deviated rather markedly from free-trade ideals, as the history of attempts at demand and supply controls testifies, but in deference to the regime norm these were either rationalized as means towards a free market or criticized for their unorthodox tenets.

National Absorption of Adjustments Imposed by International Markets. This derives from norms worked out in the more diffuse trade and state-system regimes. The relative price stability that prevailed in international grain markets during much of the postwar era can be accounted for in large measure by American and Canadian willingness to accumulate reserves in times of market surplus and to release them, commercially and concessionally, in times of tightness. Of course, these practices occurred largely for domestic reasons. Yet there was still the almost universal expectation that North Americans could and would hold reserves for the world and would manipulate them in the interest of market stability. Hence this major norm—that each group dependent on the market should bear, through its own policies, burdens created by large price swings—was made easier to maintain as long as North American reserves acted to prevent large price variations.

Qualified Acceptance of Extramarket Channels of Food Distribution. Food aid on a continuing basis and as an instrument of both national policy and international program became an accepted part of the postwar food regime. By 1954 it was institutionalized by national legislation in the United States and by international codes evolving through the FAO's Committee on Surplus Disposal. Yet in a system oriented toward free trade, participants' acquiescence in extramarket distribution could be obtained only on the stipulation that market distribution was to take precedence over extramarket distribution. Therefore, food aid was acceptable to American and foreign producers and exporters as long as aid did not dramatically reduce income from trade or distort market shares. Rules to this effect were explicitly codified in national and international law. . . .

Avoidance of Starvation. The accepted international obligation to prevent starvation is not peculiar to the postwar period; it derives from more remote times. There has been and remains a consensus that famines are extraordinary situations and that they should be met by extraordinary and charitable means.

The Free Flow of Scientific and Crop Information. Whereas most of the other norms of the international food regime (and, more specifically, the wheat regime) emerged during the postwar era largely because of American advocacy and practice, "free information" emerged in spite of U.S. misgivings. Freedom of information about the results of agricultural research was a notion nurtured by the FAO and welcomed by those seeking technology for development. With American acquiescence, especially after 1970, it became a norm of the food regime and has become nearly universal.

Low Priority for National Self-Reliance. Partly because the global food system of the past thirty years was perceived by most participants as one of relative abundance and partly because of international divisions of labor implicit in free-trade philosophies, national self-reliance in food was not a norm of the international food regime. Indeed, food dependence was encouraged and becoming dependent upon external suppliers was accepted as legitimate and responsible international behavior. . . . Measures that reduce dependence in rich importers, such as the Common Agricultural Policy of the EEC and the subsidization of domestic rice production in Japan, . . . conflict with this norm implictly. Such policies, however, reflect domestic political pressures rather than explicit goals of food self-reliance; hence they do not directly conflict with the emphasis on food trade *per se.*

National Sovereignty and the Illegitimacy of External Penetration. The international food system of the last thirty years existed within the confines of the international political system, so that principles governing the latter necessarily conditioned norms of the food regime. Among them, the general acceptance of the principle of national sovereignty largely proscribed external interference or penetration into matters defined as "domestic" affairs. In practice this meant that food production, distribution, and consumption within countries, and the official policies that regulated them, remained beyond the legitimate reach of the international community; a "look the other way" ethic prevailed even in the face of officially perpetrated inhumanities in a number of countries. . . .

Low Concern About Chronic Hunger. That international transactions in food should be addressed to alleviating hunger and malnutrition, or that these concerns should take priority over other goals such as profit maximization, market stability or political gains, were notions somewhat alien to the international food regime of the postwar era. It was simply not a rule of international food diplomacy that hunger questions should be given high priority, or, in some instances, it was not considered appropriate that they should even be raised when there was a danger of embarrassing or insulting a friendly country by exposing malnutrition among its citizens. . . .

Regime Consequences

Some effects of the prevailing food regime upon the international food system during the postwar era are easily discernible. In setting and enforcing regime norms for commercial transactions, the United States worked out trading rules in conjunction with key importers and other exporters. . . . Communist countries remained peripheral participants in these arrangements. They worked out their own rules within COMECON, although they occasionally interacted with "western" food traders, playing by western rules when they did. World trade in foodstuffs attained unprecedented absolute levels, and North America became grain merchants to the world to an unprecedented degree. Through concessional transactions the major problems of oversupply and instability in the commercial markets were resolved. Surpluses were disposed of in ways that enhanced the prospects for subsequent growth of commercial trade by the major food suppliers. Especially with respect to grain trading, adherence to regime norms enhanced the wealth and power (i.e., market share and control) of major exporters, most notably farmers and trading firms in the United States. The nutritional well-being and general standard of living of fairly broad cross-sections of populations were also enhanced within major grain-importing countries. Adhering to regime norms, however, also encouraged interdependence among exporters and importers, an interdependence that, over time, limited the international autonomy and flexibility of both. With regard to concessional food flows, regime norms facilitated global humanitarianism and enhanced survival during shortfalls and famines. . . . On the other hand, regime norms also contributed to huge gaps in living standards between richer and poorer countries; they helped to perpetuate large gaps between rich and poor within countries; and they failed to correct chronic nutritional inadequacies of poor people worldwide. By promoting transfers of certain types of production technology as well as foodstuffs, the food regime also contributed to the spread of more capital-intensive farming and specialized rather than self-reliant crop choices. Overall, the food regime reflected and probably reinforced the global political–economic status quo that prevailed from the late 1940s to the early 1970s. It was buttressed by, and in turn buttressed, the global power structure of American hegemony.

The period 1970–78 was one of substantial instability in markets and concern for food distribution, food insecurity, and malnutrition. . . . Production actually declined worldwide and the traded tonnage expanded dramatically, and wheat prices tripled in the two years between the summer of 1972 and 1974. Sufficient concern was aroused both in and beyond the circle of elite regime managers that a World Food Conference was held in November 1974, to institute a series of reforms in the regime. Three substantive major defects in the world food system, as well as many minor ones, were identified at the Conference. The first was inadequate food reserves to assure reasonable stability in markets and security for consumers; second, the use of food aid in ways that reflected low priority for the food problems of less developed countries; and third, inadequate and inappropriate investment flows with respect to food production capacity in food-deficit areas.

These defects arose because behavior according to regime norms, which previously had not led to a conflict between domestic and international interests, now did so. The stockpiles that had guaranteed international price stability (though not the food security of those unable to buy food) had not been created or maintained with the purpose of providing international stability. No norm had been institutionalized that prescribed reserves for international purposes. Reserves, held mainly by the United States and Canada, had been largely a function of political and economic responses to income demands of the politically significant farm populations in exporting countries. The norm held that adjustment to market conditions was a national responsibility. When reserves were no longer required for adjustment purposes in North America they were gladly, not cautiously, depleted. . . . Food aid was a mechanism to reduce such stocks and to promote new markets. In addition, the largest donor, the United States, allocated the bulk of its food aid on the basis of political rather than nutritional criteria and in direct proportion to the size of American stocks. . . . Dietary adequacy in poorer countries was not prescribed by the regime. Thus, Egypt, South Korea, Taiwan, Israel, and even Chile got aid, while near-famine occurred in Bangladesh. Finally, investment in food production, especially in poor countries, was low because it was not seen as attractive by the dominant philosophy of economic development—import-substituting industrialization. Nor was it relevant to the largest motivation that shaped private capital flows, namely, the search for cheap sources of supply. As noted, agricultural development was not prescribed by the regime. These considerations abetted the transfer of existing rather than new technologies, and leaned against investment in rural areas and in food crops for local consumption (as opposed to fibers or tropical products such as coffee, tea, and pineapples). . . .

In the seven years since the World Food Conference, has the regime changed? The answer is "marginally," and by evolution. First, there has come to be a greater emphasis on rural development. . . . New norms emphasizing food in development planning have been codified by a special conference on rural development held in Rome in 1979 and by continuing World Food Council resolutions. . . . A second change is that greater security for food-aid recipients has been assured. This results from a new Food Aid Convention, agreed to in March 1980, which raised the minimum aid donor pledges from four-and-a-half to eight million tons, and from the four-million-ton emergency international wheat reserve of the United States signed into law in January 1981. . . . A violation of older, nonintervention norms is reflected in the way this aid intervenes in the domestic food policy of aid recipients. Another norm change is reflected in increased programming of food aid according to nutritional rather than political criteria, which has occurred in the food aid programs of the WFP, Australia, Canada, and Europe.

These changes constitute the evolution of new norms that challenge the priority of market principles and give higher priority to chronic hunger, food security, and food self-reliance. . . .

In other respects the tenets of the old regime prevail, and priorities remain as they were in the early 1970s. National policies dominate international policies and "free market" mechanisms are still held to be ideal for the bulk of food allocations flowing in international channels. With respect to reserves to increase stability and security, progress has been limited. . . .

Food security remains tenuous. The internationally coordinated system of reserves for food security called for at the World Food Conference has not been created. . . .

All current trends suggest that food deficits will grow in a number of regions of the world, particularly in Asia and Africa. Furthermore, the rising cost of production, ecological deterioration, and the decline of subsistence agriculture all point to increasing vulnerability in the relationship between food supplies and needy customers. Regime changes since 1974 to cope with this problem of maldistribution are almost certainly inadequate.

We expect that the higher degree of formalization of the food regime and its large number of voluntary participants will lead to continuing and accelerated efforts to change substantially the norms of the food regime. These efforts will occur within the frameworks of public and private organizations—United Nations agencies, special forums and secretariats, centers, councils, committees, conferences, and companies. Setting the rules of the game will remain the prerogative of powerful national governments, especially those whose foodstuffs dominate in trade and aid flows, and in particular the United States. To the extent that there has been incremental change in the global food regime, pressures from formal international institutions have been helpful. . . .

Otherwise, the food regime does not look very different or function very differently from other regimes. Its principles have legitimized unequal distributions of food and unequal distributions of benefits from buying and selling food. Its norms have given authority to the powerful, both informally and in formal international bodies. Interestingly, though, there has been little formulation or articulation of revolutionary norms.

Conclusions

Six General Conclusions

Our two cases, colonialism and food, suggest some conclusions. They are hardly definitive or universal, but they might be subject to broader generalization and further refinement.

Without intending to be trivial let us first underline that *regimes exist.* In international relations there are revered principles, explicit and implicit norms, and written and unwritten rules, that are recognized by actors and that govern their behavior. Adherence to regimes may impose a modicum of order on international interactions and transactions. Our two case studies demonstrate that actors are guided by norms in diverse issue-areas. We would suggest that regimes exist in all areas of international relations, even those, such as major-power rivalry, that are traditionally looked upon as clear-cut examples of anarchy.

Second, taking regimes into account contributes to explaining international behavior by alerting students of international affairs to subjective and moral factors that they might otherwise overlook. Once this subjective dimension of international relations is included, explanations of international behavior can be pushed beyond factors such as goals, interests, and power. Our case study reveals that regimes mediate between goals, interests, and power on the one hand, and behavior on the other. Such normative mediation is most effective, and hence most theoretically significant, between two limiting sets of conditions. At one extreme, a regime may be an empty facade that rationalizes the rule of the powerful by elevating their preferences to the status of norms. Under such conditions a regime exists because subordinate actors recognize the rules and abide by them, but knowing this would not significantly improve upon our ability to explain behavior as all we would need to know are the identities of the powerful and their interests and goals. Under the colonial regime, for example, knowledge of norms contributed little to explaining the dominance of metropolis over colonies. Similarly, under the food regime, the knowledge that there were norms revering free markets does not contribute greatly to explaining major trends in the trading behavior of the major exporters. These actors pressed for free trade because it was in their interest. . . .

At the other extreme are conditions where regimes are determinative, where codified international law or morality is the primary guide to behavior, and where the separate goals, interests or capabilities of actors are inconsequential. Such conditions are extraordinarily rare in international relations. Where they prevail (in narrow, highly technical issue-areas like smallpox control or international posts and telegrams) consequent international behavior is analytically uninteresting. . . .

Between the limits of major-power hegemony and legal or moral order is a rather broad range of international relations where regimes mediate behavior largely by constraining unilateral adventurousness or obduracy. The case studies suggest conditions under which such normative mediation takes place. For example, it occurs in relations among powers of comparable capability, where the exertion of force cannot serve interests. Here, norms and rules tend to order oligarchies, establishing the terms of a stable and peaceful relationship, mediating and moderating conflict, and preserving collective status and prerogatives against outsiders. Relations among the colonial powers, for example, were obviously mediated by norms, and knowing this adds to our ability to explain behavior that had large consequences for colonial regions. Under the food regime, exporters' direct and indirect relations with each other were mediated by norms such as those proscribing concessional dealings until commercial markets were cleared. . . .

Regimes also mediate under conditions of diffused power, or under conditions where asymmetries in power are neutralized, as in one-state-one-vote international forums. Here, consensus about appropriate decision-making procedures and their legitimacy keeps pluralism from deteriorating into anarchy, and consensus about legitimate objectives makes policy possible.

Finally, regimes mediate during transitions of power. They tend to have inertia or functional autonomy and continue to influence behavior even though their norms have ceased either to reflect the preferences of powers or to be buttressed by their capabilities. This is one of the most fascinating and useful aspects of regime analysis, where compliance with norms explains why patterns of behavior continue long after reasoning in terms of power and interest suggests that they should have disappeared. . . .

Our third conclusion is that functionally specific and functionally diffuse regimes differ importantly with regard to the locus of management and the nature of managers. Functionally specific regimes such as the food regime are directed by technical specialists and middle-echelon administrators in participating governments. Such officials are recruited for their expertise and skills, traits that are well dispersed internationally. As a result, specific regimes tend to follow rather democratic procedures, at least as concerns policies pursued by managers. By contrast, functionally diffuse regimes such as the colonial regime are more often managed by diplomatic generalists and higher-level political officers. Not only does this suggest that diffuse regimes are likely to be much more highly politicized than specific ones, but also that conflicts which arise in the contexts of various regimes will be different. Resistance to issue linkage, for example, will be more common in specific regimes, where managers will variously seek to insulate (or, alternatively, expand) their jurisdictional domains. On the other hand, difficulties in enforcing norms, and greater deviance and regime challenges, are likely in diffuse regimes.

Fourth, international regimes are formalized in varying degrees. Our analysis suggests that degrees of formality tend to have relatively little to do with the effectiveness of regimes measured in terms of the probabilities of participants' compliance. With the two regimes we considered, one formal and one informal, both predictably and consistently constrained most participants' behavior over considerable periods of time. The colonial case suggests that some of the most effective regimes are those that are quite informal. This would seem to be true especially for regimes that regulate the general political behavior of major powers. . . .

While there may be few differences in the effectiveness of formal and informal regimes, our analyses suggest that "formalization" itself may be a dynamic factor. Regimes tend to become more formal over time, as with the colonial regime, where multilateral diplomatic conferences became increasingly important in the latter years of the imperial system; or with the food regime, where organizations, institutions, and rules seem now to be proliferating to fill a void in management created by American reluctance to provide informal leadership. We believe that regimes formalize over time because maintenance often comes in one way or another to require explicitness. As those rewarded by a regime's functioning become either accustomed to or dependent upon such benefits, they tend to formalize interaction patterns in order to perpetuate them. . . .

Fifth, effectiveness in terms of compliance with rules and procedures of any given regime depends largely upon the consensus or acquiescence of participants. Formal enforcement is extraordinary and coercive enforcement is rare despite its prevalence in relations between metropolis and colonies during the colonial era. Usually it is self-interest, broadly perceived, that motivates compliance.

Most participants in international regimes, whether they are advantaged or disadvantaged under the regime's normative biases, usually comply because compliance is calculated to be more rewarding or less costly than deviance. Saying this is perhaps pushing the obvious. But what is intriguing is how regime participants calculate their benefits and costs, and especially how they assign weights to perceived "moral" benefits of acting in accord with norms, or perceived "moral" costs of acting against them. . . .

Sixth and finally, our comparative case studies of regimes suggest that regime change is closely linked to two classical political concepts—power and interest. Most regime change results from changes in the structure of international power. For diffuse regimes, the relevant power structure is the global political-strategic balance, as was the case with the colonial regime, which began to change when major powers such as Russia (the Soviet Union) and the United States defected from the normative consensus. On the other hand, for more functionally specific regimes, relevant power also must include command over specific resources within particular issue-areas, as with the oil companies during the 1930s and the oil states in the 1970s, and the food-supplying states in the food regime. Of course, principles such as sovereignty may extend from the diffuse state system to affect or be part of the features of these specific regimes as well.

Revolutionary change is the more frequent pattern of regime change, and such change most often comes after changes in the structure of power. On the other hand, regime change via cognitive learning and the recasting of goals among dominant elites also occurs. This evolutionary change seems less frequent than revolutionary change, perhaps because major wars, from the Thirty Years War to World War II, have preceded and been instrumental in regime change.

Regime change without significant changes in power structure occurs when leading elites seek to preserve their status and their control of the regime by eliminating "dysfunctional" behavior, either in the substantive performance or in the decision procedures of a regime. This results when learning and technology foster new or changed goals. Changes in interests and goals have arisen from expanding knowledge of the world and its environmental exigencies. New understanding and capability with respect to disease, food technology, and air travel are important instances of regime change and even regime creation. The norm that no one should be hungry is not accepted by the current food regime, but it has sparked major efforts at regime change, including the creation of international reserves and external aid to increase food production in areas of the world that are most chronically malnourished. Unfortunately, it is only rarely the case that controlling elites—especially the fragmented and oligarchic elites of the international system—learn enough in sufficient time to change from within.

Do Regimes Matter? Epistemic Communities and Mediterranean Pollution Control

PETER M. HAAS

An important and persistent question facing analysts of international regimes is: Do regimes matter? Much attention has been paid to regime creation and regime maintenance, but few authors have studied the substantive nature of regimes or their direct effects on national behavior. Regimes are not simply static summaries of rules and norms; they may also serve as important vehicles for international learning that produce convergent state policies. This role for regimes has been seriously underestimated in the theoretical and empirical literature, which has tended to focus on two correlates of regimes—political order and economic growth—rather than on the transformative processes that regimes may initiate or foster. The literature has also paid little attention to the fact that some regimes stem from communities of shared knowledge and not simply from domestic or transnational interest groups.

Through the examination of the Mediterranean Action Plan (Med Plan), a regime for marine pollution control in the Mediterranean Sea, I seek to demonstrate that this regime played a key role in altering the balance of power within Mediterranean governments by empowering a group of experts, who then contributed to the development of convergent state policies in compliance with the regime. In turn, countries in which these new actors acquired channels to decision making became the strongest proponents of the regime.

The Med Plan is widely hailed as a success. Commentators from a variety of viewpoints cite it as the crowning achievement of the United Nations Environment Programme's (UNEP's) Regional Seas Programme and an exemplary case of interstate cooperation. Its success is distinctive because of the number of compelling factors militating against it. The extensive pollution of the Mediterranean is the result of intense coastal population pressures, combined with largely unregulated industrial, municipal, and agricultural emission practices. . . . Thus, effective protection required the coordinated efforts of all the coastal states. Common pollution control standards had to be adopted for pollutants from tankers, offshore dumping, and a variety of land-based sources. Contending uses of the sea also had to be balanced: for instance, fishermen and tourists require much cleaner waters than do tanker and industrial interests.

Pollution of the Mediterranean Sea was widely regarded as a collective goods problem, since one country's pollutants could wash up on its neighbor's beaches. The Riviera, for example, is polluted by discharges from Spain, France, Italy, and Monaco. If France were the only country to build sewage treatment plants and to require coastal industries to reduce their emissions, the quality of the coast would only be partially improved, and French industry would be hampered by additional production costs that would not be met by Spanish and Italian competitors and would thus reduce the comparative advantage of French industries. Other Mediterranean basins, such as the Adriatic and Aegean Seas and the eastern basin, posed similar problems. Pollutants were not exchanged throughout the entire Mediterranean, but the entire Mediterranean region faced a number of smaller collective goods problems that impeded coordinated national action to control pollution. The political antipathies and economic disparities in the region militated against effective and equitable cooperation, and the global recessions of 1973–75 and 1980–84 made the expensive compliance with the regime even more problematic. . . .

Even though the Med Plan was successfully negotiated, its maintenance poses an anomaly in terms of conventional understanding of how regimes operate. The most intriguing puzzle regarding the Med Plan's effectiveness is why states comply, given the fact that so many were initially opposed to it. As Oran Young and Robert Keohane have noted, the most compelling argument for a regime's importance in promoting international order is the fact that compliance is achieved even when the regime's norms and principles run counter to the short-term interests of the participants (or the hegemon). The highly technical dimension of the Med Plan makes it a "most expected case" for an explanation that emphasizes consensual scientific knowledge. However, the diversity of political interests in the region and the widespread political antipathy to international environmental protection initially inhibited the easy influence of scientists on their governments.

The Med Plan's successful creation was promoted by a community of ecologists and marine scientists. They served in UNEP's secretariat and were often granted formal decision-making authority in national administrations. In addition to their involvement in the policy-making process, they were given responsibility for enforcing and supervising pollution control measures. The members of this group became partisans for adopting the regime, complying with it, and strengthening it to deal with more pollutants from more sources. Following the involvement of these new actors, state interests came to increasingly reflect their environmental view, as seen in diplomats' statements and government policies, and state behavior came to reflect their interests as well, as was evident from state investment patterns and diplomatic actions. Compliance, as measured by the adoption of new policies which are consonant with the regime's norms and which ease its enforcement, has been strongest in countries in which the experts were able to consolidate their power most firmly.

As the case of the Med Plan shows, regimes may be transformative, leading to the empowerment of new groups of actors who can change state interests and practices. According to the explanation suggested here, if a group with a common perspective is able to acquire and sustain control over a substantive policy domain, the associated regime will become stronger and countries will comply with it. Such groups are most likely to be consulted after a crisis, especially when decision makers are uninformed about the technical dimensions of the problem at hand or are uncertain about the costs and benefits of international cooperation. New national policies, often in compliance with the regime, would then reflect the interests of the group consulted and empowered, and the duration of the new policies would depend upon the group's ability to consolidate and retain its bureaucratic power. The substantive nature of the regime would reflect the group's cause-and-effect beliefs. Because of the usual institutional rigidities and the overall administrative inertia at reviewing past decisions, such power would be likely to persist until a subsequent crisis incited other decision makers to consult with a new group or until the current group was weakened by internal disagreements or as a result of bureaucratic infighting with another group. It would follow logically, then, that the loss of consensus within the group or the loss of the group's access to high-level decision making would lead to a breakdown in compliance.

In the following sections, I describe the regime, analyze in greater detail the role of the new actors and the process by which national compliance occurred, and contrast this analysis with more conventional analyses of regimes and policy change.

The Mediterranean Action Plan

The Med Plan is a collectively negotiated, ongoing set of arrangements for the progressive control of Mediterranean marine pollution. It was developed under the auspices of UNEP, which provided $18.5 million and administrative support during the program's first eight years and continues to oversee it. With Albania's attendance at the 1985 meeting of the Contracting Parties, all eighteen littoral states now participate. . . .

In Stephen Krasner's by now familiar definition, the Med Plan is a regime, consisting of

> . . . sets of implicit or explicit principles, norms, rules, and decision-making procedures around which actors' expectations converge in a given area of international relations. Principles are beliefs of fact, causation, and rectitude. Norms are standards of behavior defined in terms of rights and obligations. Rules are specific prescriptions or proscriptions for action. Decision-making procedures are prevailing practices for making and implementing collective choice.

The principles are that Mediterranean currents and wind patterns transmit pollutants across national borders and that these pollutants interfere with other uses of the sea (such as recreation, tourism, fishing, and navigation), thereby necessitating coordinated national pollution control policies. . . .

The rules and decision-making procedures consist of annual intergovern-mental meetings at which the secretariat's administration of the joint monitor-ing projects is reviewed and the Contracting Parties' attempts to develop and enforce national legislation for pollution control are held up to nominal public scrutiny. A weak provision for arbitration exists but has never been invoked.

Until 1976, there was a very loose framework for evaluation. After 1976, the rule became stronger as the parties adopted protocols covering a more comprehensive range of sources and types of pollutants. The rules have grown in scope from banning marine dumping to controlling a wide variety of land-based sources of pollution, including agricultural sprays and industrial and municipal wastes. They also govern pollutants transmitted to the Mediterra-nean through rivers and the atmosphere. In addition to its early focus on dumping and oil spills, the Med Plan now "eliminates" the emissions of nine groups of toxic substances, "limits" the emissions of thirteen groups of less hazardous substances, and requires states to develop specific guidelines for control of these substances. . . .

Following the evolution of a stronger regime, the quality of the Mediterra-nean has improved. Beaches have been protected from organic wastes, such as municipal garbage. Environmental quality data on inorganic pollutants, such as industrial wastes, remain anecdotal at best. In 1976, about 33 percent of Mediterranean beaches were unsafe for swimming. Ten years later, only 20 percent were deemed unsafe by World Health Organization (WHO) and UNEP standards. This improvement is largely due to the construction of sewage treatment plants inspired by the Med Plan. . . .

The Ecological Epistemic Community and the Med Plan

The success of the Med Plan is attributable to the involvement of ecological and marine scientists who set the international agenda and directed their own states toward support of international efforts and toward the introduction of strong pollution control measures at home.

In the Mediterranean in the early 1970s, government leaders became in-creasingly concerned about the extent of pollution of the Mediterranean Sea. Jacques Cousteau alerted the world to the potential "death" of the sea, but government officials did not know whether such predictions were valid (they turned out not to be), nor did they know the extent of the problem, the sources and types of pollutants, or the means of preventing or controlling pollution. Therefore, they turned to the region's marine scientists for informa-tion and to UNEP for the development of environmental policies and the drafting of a treaty to protect the Mediterranean Sea.

UNEP officials, some secretariat members from other specialized agencies (notably WHO and the Food and Agriculture Organization [FAO]), and like-minded governmental officials in the region composed an "epistemic community." Together, they acted as an informally coordinated lobbying group. They also shared a common ecological outlook. In this ecological epistemic community, the members had similar beliefs about the need to preserve the quality of the physical environment and similar views on the origins and severity of pollutants, the policies necessary to control pollution, and the research needed to determine the physical linkages between sources of pollution and the health of the sea by evaluating all economic activities and possible uses of the sea within a broader ecosystemic framework. This epistemic community consisted of high-ranking UNEP officials and midlevel government officials from various countries (including France, Israel, Greece, Egypt, and Yugoslavia) and from a variety of disciplines and backgrounds (such as engineering, physics, oceanography, microbiology, urban planning, and diplomacy). Their political values entailed a belief that all governments should actively cooperate and intervene domestically to protect the environment, including the universal adoption of more comprehensive, rational forms of economic planning to internalize environmental considerations into virtually all forms of policy-making.

UNEP officials also forged transnational alliances with regional marine scientists, who shared an interest in controlling specific pollutants but lacked the overall holistic, causal framework that ecologists accepted. Effectively acting in harmony with UNEP, these scientists had the combined impact of persuading their governments to support the UNEP measures to control as many sources and types of pollution as possible, to move for stronger measures for their control, and to comply with Med Plan policies. Later, as environmental ministries were established in the Mediterranean countries, these scientists were invited to join their staffs, as were people who were firmly in the epistemic community.

Ecological principles were embraced by members of the epistemic community as their core set of beliefs about cause-and-effect relationships. . . .

As such, it [ecology] facilitated the formation of coalitions among scientists, because most contending views about what are important research questions and the appropriate levels and methods of analysis may be integrated within such a broad framework.

By promoting the adoption of a very broad definition of "pollution" which emanated from an ecological perspective, UNEP and members of the ecological epistemic community were able to encompass more parochial interests under its umbrella. . . .

Such a broad formulation of concerns blurred the distinctions between otherwise incompatible views, and this enabled UNEP and other members of its epistemic community to tie in with the broadest possible constituency by incorporating the concerns of many groups within those of UNEP. . . .

UNEP cemented the alliances by funding scientific research that was not supported by domestic sources, providing sophisticated monitoring equipment and training in its use, and publicizing the research findings. UNEP's discretionary control over the Med Plan budget allowed it to continue to distribute funds among the various members of the alliance during budgetary squeezes from 1979 to 1982. The provision of sophisticated equipment allowed scientists to conduct new studies and generate data revealing the widespread presence of organic and inorganic pollutants. The scientists were invited to attend biannual conferences convened by UNEP for the purpose of exchanging information, discussing techniques, and forming professional bonds with their colleagues throughout the Mediterranean. UNEP stressed the ambiguity of individual scientists' roles and loyalties by inviting them in their individual capacity as scientists rather than as formal representatives of their governments. Methodologies and findings were also exchanged in English-language journals such as *Ambio* and *Marine Pollution Bulletin* and in over thirty-six manuals released by UNEP and FAO in French, English, and Spanish.

The external support from UNEP enhanced the scientists' domestic prestige and strengthened their domestic political base. Although their work was only loosely coordinated by UNEP, the knowledge gained through collaborative efforts established or reinforced their authority in the issue-area of marine pollution control. When consulted by their governments, the scientists provided congruent policy advice about domestic pollution control measures and encouraged them to support the norms and principles outlined in the Med Plan. Through shaping their own governments' policies in convergent manners, they reinforced the regime's support internationally. They also led their governments to take more constructive approaches at international meetings on the Med Plan. Ultimately, a stronger regime resulted than was initially anticipated, since the states adopted and ratified new protocols controlling an even wider range of pollutants (new rules) and acted in compliance with the regime's injunctions.

Politics were also important in the negotiation of the Med Plan protocols. A number of compromises satisfied the demands of different groups. The protocols included pollutants of concern to both developed and developing countries, and the less developed countries (LDCs) received monitoring equipment from UNEP. Arab–Israeli conflicts were downplayed as a result of the deliberately low–profile stance adopted by Israeli delegates and the decision of UNEP not to invite the Palestine Liberation Organization to attend. The definition of the Mediterranean's geographic scope consciously excluded the Soviet bloc by setting the eastern limit at the southern end of the Dardanelles rather than at the northern end, which would open up Bulgarian participation. Scientific laboratories for the monitoring component of the Med Plan were chosen by UNEP on a geographic basis in order to reward countries for their participation at negotiating meetings.

The Epistemic Community's Influence on the Med Plan

In 1972, there had been very few measures for pollution control in the Mediterranean states. After the regime's successful negotiation, however, member countries began to introduce measures to accomplish the Med Plan objectives. From an early antipathy to dealing with environmental problems, many LDCs became much more constructive at international meetings. Accepting the need to control a growing number of hazardous substances, they ratified the international protocols within two years.

The actual form of policies varies among countries. Different countries specify different emission standards, ban different substances, and point to different indicators for cleanliness. Many LDCs simply apply thresholds suggested in the WHO's *Technical Reports Series*. Yet the movement in all cases is in the same direction, in conformity with the Med Plan's enunciated norms and principles.

The countries that have been the most supportive of the Med Plan are those in which the epistemic community has been strongest. Phrased slightly differently, the variance in compliance with the Med Plan is largely explained by the amount of involvement of the epistemic community in domestic policy-making. With increasing involvement of the epistemic community, countries became more supportive of the Med Plan, became more constructive participants at international meetings, and introduced more comprehensive pollution control policies at home, often supported by increased domestic funding for pollution control. The epistemic community influenced both foreign and domestic environmental policies.

In the early 1970s, most of the countries established coordinative environmental ministries, in keeping with the holistic environmental ethos galvanized by preparations for the 1972 United Nations Conference on the Human Environment. These ministries were staffed by members of the ecological epistemic community and by the marine scientists who were allied with UNEP, since they were the only ones with a strong reputation for expertise in pollution control. These groups had little affinity with other ministries in their own governments and felt more closely tied to their functional counterparts around the region. As members of UNEP's transnational alliance, they were all involved in the Med Plan negotiations, and they encouraged their own governments to support these negotiations and to comply with Med Plan arrangements.

With only small staffs, slim budgets, and little statutory authority, the coordinative environmental ministries were seldom able to compel other ministries to control pollution within their functional domains. However, once they were transformed into regulatory ministries, as occurred in seven countries . . . they usually had sufficient bureaucratic clout to usurp control over the environmental domain and convert their interests into national policies. Thus, through the capture of various regulatory environmental ministries, the epistemic community consolidated its control over environmental policy and became successful in encouraging governments toward convergent actions such as controlling a broader range of pollutants, increasing their support for the Med Plan, elevating environmental concerns on their national agendas, and pushing for increased investment in pollution control. Countries in which the epistemic community did not consolidate its hold through regulatory environmental ministries have been less supportive of the Med Plan and have undertaken fewer and weaker measures for pollution control.

The ecological epistemic community has been able to use the administrative base provided by environmental ministries to effectively promote its own preferred vision of pollution control, which is broader in scope and more clearly delineated than the vague, formal missions assigned to the ministries in various countries. In this respect, it has been a story of putting the foxes in charge of the chicken coop. For instance, in Israel and Greece, the foreign ministries ceded responsibility for Med Plan negotiations to the Israeli environmental protection service and to the Greek national council for physical planning and the environment (NCPPE), respectively, which were both staffed by members of the epistemic community. The NCPPE was instructed by its foreign affairs ministry to be "pro-environment," in essence making the Greek delegation an active environmental lobbyist and giving the scientific constituency within the government a free hand to formulate and pursue policy. With the NCPPE as a springboard, the staff introduced new domestic environmental legislation to Parliament and continually served as an "honest broker" to mediate conflicts at intergovernmental meetings. . . .

The importance of scientific access to government decision making is underscored by the Italian experience. With a large and experienced scientific community, replete with individuals who deeply believed in UNEP's message, but without an active environmental ministry for them to channel their concerns, domestic policy did not change for several years. Although the position of minister of ecology without portfolio was created in 1983, a full ministry of the environment was only established in 1986, at which time a budget of $6.7 million was allocated and sixty staff members were appointed. This staff now has the capacity to enforce the 1977 Merli Law, whose deadline for compliance had been frequently extended owing to the government's inability to enforce it and to the industries' reluctance to incur the high costs necessary for modifying production processes to reduce or eliminate emission of the hazardous substances covered under the law. . . .

In most cases, the environmental ministries' authority over pollution control in Mediterranean countries was not challenged by industrial groups or by commerce ministries. Multinational corporations potentially affected by the Med Plan arrangements were slow to recognize its implications and only weakly entered the process after most of the agreements had been concluded. In 1981, the Centre Europeen des Silicones, representing the European silicon industry, asked UNEP to remove organosilicons from the list of substances for which permits must be obtained from national authorities before they can be emitted into the Mediterranean, but their request was denied. The persistent uncertainty about the actual extent of regional pollution deferred challenges to the authority of the environmental ministries. There was prevailing sentiment that something had to be done, and the ministries were the only groups with anything to offer. . . .

A more detailed analysis of the process by which Algeria and Egypt came to support the Med Plan indicates the key role played by the epistemic community. At first, both of these countries were strongly opposed to introducing measures that would inhibit industrial growth and were highly suspicious of French motivations. However, following the involvement of the epistemic community, these positions were reversed. This is particularly striking given the fact that, as small countries, both would have been able to free-ride on arrangements once they were supported by France.

Algerian leaders had always been intransigent in asserting the primacy of industrial development over environmental protection. In the early 1970s, they opposed any pollution control measures that might impede or retard economic development, and they did not send a delegation to the 1976 Barcelona Conference. Following the inclusion of marine scientists in the Algerian administration after 1975, government preferences began to change, elevating pollution control to a more equal footing with economic development. Algeria acceded to the Barcelona Convention in 1981, ratified the protocol for control of pollution from land-based sources in 1983, and also adopted national environmental legislation in 1983. Algeria's law no. 83-3 of 1983 provides a broad framework for the development of a domestic environmental policy, although it fails to specify water quality standards. The fact that the 1983 legislation includes the control of industrial wastes is an indication of the change in Algerian position from refusing to accept constraints on economic development to imposing them.

These Algerian policy changes in the early 1980s followed the entrenchment of marine scientists in the government and their provision of domestically produced analyses of marine pollution. The Algerian scientific community originally obtained access to the government through its national committee for the environment, established in 1974, and its subsequent institutionalization within the hydrologic ministry, which became the secretary of state for forests and development. In 1983, a national agency for environmental protection was formed.

Policy advice also came from scientists in the Centre de Recherches Oceanographiques et des Peches in Algiers. CROP began monitoring pollution in 1975, in response to fears of a decrease in fishery production due to pollution. UNEP gave CROP scientists a gas chromatograph and an atomic absorption spectrophotometer to monitor industrial and agricultural wastes and also provided them with training in their use. With this new equipment, the Algerian assessment of levels of oil and other industrial wastes was consonant with that of other countries around the Mediterranean Basin. CROP's first reports, published in 1979 and 1980, described the industrial and public health dimensions of coastal pollution and generated concern within the government and among elites. The evidence of increasing marine pollution was finally accepted by the early 1980s, and policies began to change. . . .

The gradual involvement of the epistemic community also transformed Egyptian policy. Scientists were initially isolated from the government, having access only to the Egyptian academy of scientific research and technology. During early Med Plan negotiations, delegates from the foreign ministry focused on encouraging the transfer of technology on concessionary terms, but they did nothing substantive with regard to specific sources or types of pollutants to control. The delegates' attitude toward pollution control was one of ambivalence or even indifference.

However, scientists were consulted in the early 1980s, as the government convened commissions to decide whether Egypt should adopt the protocol for control of land-based sources of pollution and to determine what the domestic effects of ratification would be. Administrative reforms from 1980 to 1982 created a new environmental affairs agency and committees in the academy for scientific research and technology, which were charged with developing environmental policy and determining whether Egypt should ratify the various Med Plan treaties. Chaired and lobbied by individuals who were closely tied to UNEP, the committees, not surprisingly, advocated immediate compliance with the Med Plan norms, which the foreign ministry accepted. Egypt ratified the protocols to control pollution from land-based sources and to establish specially protected areas.

Already sensitive to the variety of pollution problems facing Egypt, marine scientists who were now invited into the policy arena began to encourage legislation to control the whole gamut of pollutants and sources of pollution. In 1982, the government introduced Egypt's law no. 48 to protect the Nile, followed by a number of ministerial directives aimed at controlling a variety of forms of pollution. In January 1983, President Mubarak announced that water quality control and sewage treatment were primary national concerns and called for an investment of $4.6 billion to develop water resources and control water pollution. The environmental affairs agency has advocated the widespread use of environmental impact assessments, expanded investment in sewerage and sewage treatment, and development of specific emission and ambient standards for coastal waters used for different purposes (recreation, navigation, and so forth). . . . In the early 1980s, the ministry of industry spent $24.6 million on controlling industrial wastes as part of a $153 million industrial production project supported by the USAID.

France provides the limiting case for the extent of an epistemic community's influence. Although the epistemic community consolidated its power in the French environmental ministry and was able to redirect domestic planning policy, it was relatively weak in influencing foreign environmental policy because the Quai d'Orsay would not cede authority to it. . . .

The environmental ministry was less powerful than the foreign affairs ministry, however, and was unable to prevail with regard to French Med Plan positions. Internationally, the foreign affairs ministry had broader geopolitical ambitions in the Mediterranean to which the Med Plan was subordinated, and it therefore kept the scientists on a tight rein. The Quai d'Orsay supported overall compliance with international environmental law and was willing to defer to the environmental ministry's abiding interest in integrated environmental planning, in which it had no interest; but French delegates from the foreign affairs ministry were reluctant to accept the provisions in the protocol for control of land-based sources of pollution which covered river-borne and airborne transmission of pollutants and which banned the emission of radioactive substances, even though the environmental ministry supported them. . . .

Domestically, the epistemic community had a much stronger impact in France, since it was able to utilize its bureaucratic leverage. Because French scientists already had extensive domestic resources and ongoing research activities, they had much less direct interest in the Med Plan than did colleagues from other Mediterranean countries, who could obtain new equipment and prestige by participating. Thus, UNEP's deliberate strategy of transnational alliance building would not work well in France, and U.N. officials did not try hard to mobilize French scientists, in part because they did not want to appear to the LDCs to be closely linked to the regionally dominant French. However, although less involved than their Mediterranean colleagues in the direct policy-making associated with the Med Plan, the marine scientists in the French environmental ministry did share the beliefs of their Mediterranean colleagues about the causes of marine pollution and the need to control them, so they advocated policies similar to those advocated elsewhere by marine scientists. . . .

Countries in which the epistemic community was unable to consolidate its power have been much less active in controlling pollution. In some states, such as Libya, Syria, and Morocco, there simply was not a domestic scientific establishment. In others, no strong domestic institution was put into place to provide the epistemic community with a channel to influence national policy. For example, Libya, Morocco, and Tunisia have only titular offices for the environment.

Epistemic Communities and Governmental Learning

In response to new information about Mediterranean pollution, the states in which the epistemic community was most active have not only developed more sophisticated environmental policies to control more pollutants but have also sought to develop economic plans that anticipate possible environmental degradation through the preparation of environmental impact assessments. To the extent that governmental planning agencies actually follow such procedures, one may say that double-loop learning about the relative role of the environment in overall economic development occurred. In the absence of these procedures, single-loop learning is evident in efforts to incrementally manage more types and sources of pollutants.

Learning occurred in two domains, through a different process in each. In the domain of foreign policy, governments committed themselves to a new environmental regime for the Mediterranean. Learning seems to have occurred by persuasion, as marine scientists and members of the ecological epistemic community informed foreign ministry officials of the need to control specific pollutants. Consensual knowledge proved compelling to the uninitiated. In 1977, all of the countries chose to control land-based sources of pollution as a consequence of a report of the sources of the region's pollution.

Tunisian and Moroccan delegates were convinced of the need to extend coverage to organophosphate pesticides, despite their heavy economic reliance on phosphate exports; and as a result of thorough documentation submitted by the secretariat, most of the LDCs were convinced of the need to control more industrial heavy metals than were covered under existing international law. The case of France, however, demonstrates limits of persuasion. With its regional foreign policy prestige at stake, the Quai d'Orsay was only willing to accept policy advice from the French environmental ministry in areas to which the Quai was indifferent.

In the domain of domestic policy, by which the states complied with the Med Plan, learning occurred through bureaucratic preemption of policy-making by the environmental ministries. The epistemic community usurped decision-making authority and promoted pollution control policies consistent with its own perspective. As observed earlier, no learning occurred in countries in which the epistemic community was unable to appropriate control. . . .

Learning did not result solely from the persuasive force of shared understanding. Persuasion did account for a small amount of the regime's broadened scope to include more sources and forms of pollution, but national compliance came from the power acquired by a new group of actors. Consensual knowledge is the common bond within this group, but it did not serve as a process of regime change. Instead, it served largely as a power resource for members of the epistemic community. With no basis for challenging their authority, they were able to use consensual knowledge to bolster their policy-making advice. The regime not only provided new evidence but, more important, it also empowered a group that was able to articulate what the evidence portended for Mediterranean governments and to suggest policies to alleviate anticipated problems.

In response to the advice provided by the epistemic community and its allied domestic marine scientists, as well as through their consolidation of domestic bureaucratic power, state interests were transformed. Algeria moved from a position of staunchly opposing the control of industrial pollutants to one of compliance with the Med Plan, as did Egypt. The governments learned to accept the fact that ecosystemic transfer of pollution imposed limitations on the undifferentiated pursuit of their short-term objectives, which required more comprehensive management in order to minimize possible trade-offs between them. Long-term objectives, such as economic development and enhancement of autonomy, remained unchanged. The governments thus became willing to accept the need to control new sources of pollution, even at reasonably high short-term costs.

Alternative Explanations

The process of regime compliance described above contradicts three common explanations for the development of convergent state policies: foreign pressure (coercion), public opinion, and the rational anticipation of future benefits by a unitary government. Thus, the analysis offered in this case varies from the conventional (often tacit) analyses suggested by hegemonic stability theorists, the comparative analyses of domestic politics, and the more recent functional-institutionalist approaches of Robert Keohane and Robert Axelrod.

Neither the regime nor compliance was "imposed." The persistence of the regime does not lie with hegemonic support through bargaining, tolerance of defections, or staunch enforcement of the regime's rules. France was the hegemonic power in the region, with 42 percent of the Mediterranean gross national product in 1978, with 20 percent of the region's marine research centers (second to Italy's 22 percent, but far in excess of the LDCs' capacities), and with a high proportion of regional trade. Yet Algerian support for the Med Plan came when France's principal tool of leverage over Algeria was at its lowest: Algerian dependence upon trade with France had dropped from 27.6 percent in 1973 to 17.3 percent in 1980. Contrary to conventional hegemonic stability arguments, Algerian compliance was actually strongest when French hegemony was weakest.

Compliance did not stem from popular mass politics in the Mediterranean countries, either. Domestically, issues of marine quality were not highly politicized, and they remained within the purview of a small group of elites and technocrats in the environmental ministries. Citizen response was generally too weak and too delayed to influence the decision to control marine pollution. Although public acceptance and support of "environmental values," at least in Western Europe, were on the rise, such support did not extend to marine issues. . . .

Nor did compliance stem from the rational anticipation of future benefits or from guarantees that other partners would not ride freely. The Med Plan does provide many of the functional goods that Keohane and Axelrod identify as being absent in international society (such as information about the environment and other actors' choices, a stable forum for interactions that reduce transaction costs, and a set of iterated sequences in which actors may hope to receive reciprocated concessions in the future), but their provision is insufficient to explain the full force of compliance with the regime. For example, the Algerian leaders' initial antipathy to cooperation was so severe that it does not seem credible that they were only grandstanding in order to obtain subsequent concessions. Algeria could have ridden freely in 1980 after observing France's decision to unilaterally enforce pollution control regulations; instead, within two years, Algeria chose to follow the French example. Viewed through "rational choice" lenses, a crude cost-benefit analysis might suggest that defection would have been more profitable than cooperation for Algeria. By avoiding the expenditures related to pollution control, Algerian industry would have gained a comparative advantage that benefited Algeria as a whole, and the state would also have forgone investment expenditures in coastal factories . . . and municipal sewage treatment facilities. For Algeria and Egypt as well, the costs of controlling pollution may have outweighed the economic benefits of improved coastal water quality (for instance, benefits of increased fishery yields, decreased medical costs, and increased income from tourism) and the marginal benefits of technology transfer and training provided by UNEP. UNEP would most likely have continued to provide this support, and support in the functional areas identified by Keohane and Axelrod, even in the absence of constructive Algerian and Egyptian diplomacy and domestic policy changes. Nonetheless, these two countries chose to comply fully with the Med Plan in the sphere of developing more comprehensive national policies.

Conclusion

The most notable aspect of the Med Plan is the domestic compliance with it. In the literature on international relations, few studies have focused on the reasons for which states actually comply with regimes. As argued above, coercion, public opinion, and anticipation of benefits do not fully explain the extent of compliance. The Med Plan's success was due to the regime's introduction of new actors who influenced national behavior and contributed to the development of coordinated and convergent policy-making in the Mediterranean states. In the face of uncertainty, a publicly recognized group with an unchallenged claim to understanding the technical nature of the regime's substantive issue-area was able to interpret for traditional decision makers facts or events in new ways and thereby lead to new forms of behavior.

Common principles and norms gave rise to a common set of rules for pollution control. The principles also empowered new domestic groups of marine scientists, who led their governments to comply more strongly with the regime and to negotiate more constructively internationally. In turn, the regime's scope was broadened and stronger rules were negotiated—rules with which most states have complied.

As this analysis of the process of compliance with the Med Plan shows, regimes can play a transformative role in international affairs. Within the analytic framework explicitly or tacitly accepted by most proponents of international regime theory, regimes are valued as stable forms to order international behavior and mitigate conflict in an anarchic world. But the conventional approach does not go far enough. Regimes may also contribute to the empowerment of new groups. By relating shared norms and principles to the codified social conventions of a specific group, light is shed on the origins of a regime's substantive nature, often overlooked in most regime analyses. With the presence and durability of new groups, regimes may not be static arrangements. They may be evolving arrangements that contribute to greater understanding, recognition of common interests, and convergence on a new set of policies.

Epistemic communities may introduce new policy alternatives to their governments, and depending on the extent to which these communities are successful in obtaining and retaining bureaucratic power domestically, they can often lead their governments to pursue them. In the case of the Mediterranean, where the new policies were more integrative and reflected more acceptance of the interplay between a number of different environmental forces, the pursuit of these policies constituted governmental learning. Governments learned about the complexity of the pollution problem and accepted the need for more comprehensive and coordinated policies to accomplish state and regional goals. Thus, both power and knowledge can be viewed as explanatory variables for state behavior.

10

Postmodernisms

Postmodern, a term fraught with ambiguity, can refer to a historical moment as well as a theoretical perspective. Its time is the present, beginning, perhaps in the 1960s, with the transformation of economic organization away from the highly centralized, hyperstandardized mass production regime of Fordist capitalism—and its cultural correlates of linear progress, absolute truths, and rational planning—toward new forms of globally dispersed, decentralized, flexible accumulation and new frontiers of commodification, which bring in their wake cultural fragmentation, incoherence, chaos. To accept this historical process as "postmodern," however, is not necessarily to assume a postmodern theoretical position, a stance that explores, and often celebrates, the uncertainties of the age and the impossibilities of universal explanation.

David Harvey is a master chronicler of the postmodern historical turn, but is less enamored of the theoretical play of postmodernism. In his book, *The Condition of Postmodernity,* he outlines the cultural contours of postmodernism (excerpted below), describes contemporary transformations of global capitalism, and links the two through a discussion of how economic practices shape understandings of space and time and, by extension, culture.

Harvey begins by pointing out that postmodernism is embedded in modernism, that the loss of certainty is a theme articulated by writers and artists for centuries. What distinguishes the postmodern is its abandonment of the possibility of rediscovering a transcendent Truth. Existence is not orderly and simple. It is, as argued by Michel Foucault, heterotopian, an unkempt collection of "a large number of fragmentary possible worlds." This view suggests that meta-narratives, grand theories or themes that proffer comprehensive (or at the very least comprehensible) understanding, are merely pleasant fictions, unable to capture the complexities of multiple realities.

Questions of identity, individual and collective, thus loom large in postmodernism. The self is not assumed to be singular and settled. Rather, if the world is in flux, then identity is contingent upon shifting contexts, circumstances that defy neat summation into a unified whole but jostle uneasily in riotous montage. Subjectivity is not an immutable, essential quality but is a social construct; it is continually renegotiated and remade in the flow of human interaction. As Harvey notes, schizophrenia is a favorite postmodern image.

Cultural dissolution and identity crisis do not, in Harvey's words, occur in a political–economic vacuum; postmodernism's "rootedness in daily life is one of its most patently transparent features." Further on in his book, Harvey builds upon Fredric Jameson's argument that postmodernism is the cultural logic of late capitalism. Harvey argues that "Post-Fordist" capitalism, which rests upon flexible production processes that can respond to rapidly changing niche markets, compresses both space and time. Spatially, technological transformation of communications and transportation not only enables a corporation to scatter its facilities worldwide in search of maximum profits, but also broadcasts consumer fads far and wide. Distance is hardly an obstacle for production managers and marketing agencies. Temporally, electronic links allow capital to speed around the globe in the blink of a cursor, rendering markets ever more volatile. The closer space and quicker pace of contemporary capitalism provide a material context for postmodern culture.

Harvey rues the political consequences of postmodernism. He worries that efforts to create alternatives will be frustrated by its focus on "schizophrenic circumstances induced by fragmentation and all those instabilities (including those of language) that prevent us from even picturing coherently, let alone devising strategies to produce, some radically different future." In other words, shattered political subjects are not effective revolutionaries. Other writers, however, see in the postmodern condition new chances for freedom and liberation.

Michael Shapiro is one such author. In the article excerpted below, "Sovereignty and Exchange in the Orders of Modernity," he assumes a postmodern theoretical perspective, one that sees in the classic state/market dichotomy struggles for political identity.

On the one hand, he outlines the sovereignty impulse, as seen in the thought of Thomas Hobbes, which attempts to secure an autonomous sense of national self free from the influences of others. Margaret Thatcher's imagined Britain is sovereign, in charge of its own affairs, able to protect its citizens' prosperity and the value of the Pound sterling. On the other hand, Shapiro extrapolates from Adam Smith to illustrate the necessity of exchange, not simply economic but also social and linguistic. It is impossible to construct a political identity in isolation from others; "Britain" has no meaning independent of "Europe" or "United States" or whatever. Markets, the avenue of exchange, are thus the conduits not only of commodities but of powerful symbolic currencies as well. States, whose claims to sovereignty are enlivened by appeals to national identities, cannot do without exchange.

Shapiro offers no resolution to the tensions of sovereignty and exchange. To press the sovereignty impulse too far, as Margaret Thatcher did (one thinks here of an audacious Popeye character intoning "I am what I am") is untenable insofar as the defense of national symbols will ultimately collide with economic practices, in this case the fact that the value of British currency is well beyond the control of the British government. But exchange, while it may confound sovereignty, never finally trumps it. The state can respond to flows of symbols and commodities with new renderings of national identity that reassert its central place in politics (though not invoked by Shapiro, China's post-Mao experience is a good example of this dynamic). For Shapiro, exchange continually destabilizes sovereignty and sovereignty redefines itself in the face of exchange.

New interpretations of key IPE concepts are Shapiro's contribution. For example, to the usual critique of protectionism as economically inefficient and therefore politically unsustainable, he adds that it may spark a crisis of national identity, a crisis from which there is no easy escape. His postmodern aversion to closure does not lead him to Harvey's pessimism, however. Quite to the contrary, postmodern theory ". . . can enable the continuous assertion of human rights, human hopes, and human affinities to dimensions of the planet and its inhabitants unrecognized in state-level conceits."

The Condition of Postmodernity

DAVID HARVEY

"Modernity," wrote Baudelaire in his seminal essay "The Painter of Modern Life" (published in 1863), "is the transient, the fleeting, the contingent; it is the one half of art, the other being the eternal and the immutable."

I begin with what appears to be the most startling fact about postmodernism: its total acceptance of the ephemerality, fragmentation, discontinuity, and the chaotic that formed the one half of Baudelaire's conception of modernity. But postmodernism responds to the fact of that in a very particular way. It does not try to transcend it, counteract it, or even to define the "eternal and immutable" elements that might lie within it. Postmodernism swims, even wallows, in the fragmentary and the chaotic currents of change as if that is all there is. Foucault . . . instructs us, for example, to "develop action, thought, and desires by proliferation, juxtaposition, and disjunction," and "to prefer what is positive and multiple, difference over uniformity, flows over unities, mobile arrangements over systems. Believe that what is productive is not sedentary but nomadic." To the degree that it does try to legitimate itself by reference to the past, therefore, postmodernism typically harks back to that wing of thought, Nietzsche in particular, that emphasizes the deep chaos of modern life and its intractability before rational thought. This does not imply, however, that postmodernism is simply a version of modernism; real revolutions in sensibility can occur when latent and dominated ideas in one period become explicit and dominant in another. Nevertheless, the continuity of the condition of fragmentation, ephemerality, discontinuity, and chaotic change in both modernist and postmodernist thought is important. I shall make much of it in what follows.

Embracing the fragmentation and ephemerality in an affirmative fashion implies a whole host of consequences. . . . To begin with, we find writers like Foucault and Lyotard explicitly attacking any notion that there might be a meta-language, meta-narrative, or meta-theory through which all things can be connected or represented. Universal and eternal truths, if they exist at all, cannot be specified. Condemning meta-narratives (broad interpretative schemas like those deployed by Marx or Freud) as "totalizing," they insist upon the plurality of "power-discourse" formations (Foucault), or of "language games" (Lyotard). Lyotard in fact defines the postmodern simply as "incredulity towards meta-narratives."

Foucault's ideas—particularly as developed in his early works—deserve attention since they have been a fecund source for postmodernist argument. The relation between power and knowledge is there a central theme. But Foucault . . . breaks with the notion that power is ultimately located within the state, and abjures us to "conduct an ascending analysis of power, starting, that is, from its infinitesimal mechanisms, which each have their own history, their own trajectory, their own techniques and tactics, and then see how these mechanisms of power have been—and continue to be—invested, colonized, utilized, involuted, transformed, displaced, extended, etc. by ever more general mechanisms and by forms of global domination." Close scrutiny of the micropolitics of power relations in different localities, contexts, and social situations leads him to conclude that there is an intimate relation between the systems of knowledge ("discourses") which codify techniques and practices for the exercise of social control and domination within particular localized contexts. The prison, the asylum, the hospital, the university, the school, the psychiatrist's office, are all examples of sites where a dispersed and piecemeal organization of power is built up independently of any systematic strategy of class domination. What happens at each site cannot be understood by appeal to some overarching general theory. Indeed the only irreducible in Foucault's scheme of things is the human body, for that is the "site" at which all forms of repression are ultimately registered. So while there are, in Foucault's celebrated dictum, "no relations of power without resistances," he equally insists that no utopian scheme can ever hope to escape the power–knowledge relation in nonrepressive ways. He here echoes Max Weber's pessimism as to our ability to avoid the "iron cage" of repressive bureaucratic–technical rationality. More particularly, he interprets Soviet repression as the inevitable outcome of a utopian revolutionary theory (Marxism) which appealed to the same techniques and knowledge systems as those embedded in the capitalist system it sought to replace. The only way open to "eliminate the fascism in our heads" is to explore and build upon the open qualities of human discourse, and thereby intervene in the way knowledge is produced and constituted at the particular sites where a localized power-discourse prevails. Foucault's work with homosexuals and prisoners was not aimed at producing reforms in state practices, but dedicated to the cultivation and enhancement of localized resistance to the institutions, techniques, and discourses of organized repression.

Foucault evidently believed that it was only through such a multifaceted and pluralistic attack upon localized practices of repression that any global challenge to capitalism might be mounted without replicating all the multiple repressions of capitalism in a new form. His ideas appeal to the various social movements that sprang into existence during the 1960s (feminists, gays, ethnic and religious groupings, regional autonomists, etc.) as well as to those disillusioned with the practices of communism and the politics of communist parties. Yet it leaves open, particularly so in the deliberate rejection of any holistic theory of capitalism, the question of the path whereby such localized struggles might add up to a progressive, rather than regressive, attack upon the central forms of capitalist exploitation and repression. Localized struggles of the sort that Foucault appears to encourage have not generally had the effect of challenging capitalism, though Foucault might reasonably respond that only struggles fought in such a way as to challenge all forms of power-discourse might have such a result. . . .

Such "local determinisms" have been understood by others . . . as "interpretive communities," made up of both producers and consumers of particular kinds of knowledge, of texts, often operating within a particular institutional context (such as the university, the legal system, religious groupings), within particular divisions of cultural labor (such as architecture, painting, theater, dance), or within particular places (neighborhoods, nations, etc.). Individuals and groups are held to control mutually within these domains what they consider to be valid knowledge.

To the degree that multiple sources of oppression in society and multiple foci of resistance to domination can be identified, this kind of thinking has been taken up in radical politics, even imported into the heart of Marxism itself. We thus find Aronowitz arguing in *The Crisis of Historical Materialism* that "the multiple, local, autonomous struggles for liberation occurring throughout the post-modern world make all incarnations of master discourses absolutely illegitimate." . . . Aronowitz is here seduced, I suspect, by the most liberative and therefore most appealing aspect of postmodern thought— its concern with "otherness." Huyssens . . . particularly castigates the imperialism of an enlightened modernity that presumed to speak for others (colonized peoples, blacks and minorities, religious groups, women, the working class) with a unified voice. The very title of Carol Gilligan's *In a Different Voice*—a feminist work which challenges the male bias in setting out fixed stages in the moral development of personality—illustrates a process of counterattack upon such universalizing presumptions. The idea that all groups have a right to speak for themselves, in their own voice, and have that voice accepted as authentic and legitimate is essential to the pluralistic stance of postmodernism. Foucault's work with marginal and interstitial groups has influenced a whole host of researchers, in fields as diverse as criminology and anthropology, into new ways to reconstruct and represent the voices and experiences of their subjects. Huyssens, for his part, emphasizes the opening given in postmodernism to understanding difference and otherness, as well as the liberatory potential it offers for a whole host of new social movements (women, gays, blacks, ecologists, regional autonomists, etc.). Curiously, most movements of this sort, though they have definitely helped change "the structure of feeling," pay scant attention to postmodernist arguments, and some feminists (e.g., Hartsock . . .) are hostile. . . .

Interestingly, we can detect this same preoccupation with "otherness" and "other worlds" in postmodernist fiction. McHale, in emphasizing the pluralism of worlds that coexist within postmodernist fiction, finds Foucault's concept of a heterotopia a perfectly appropriate image to capture what that fiction is striving to depict. By heterotopia, Foucault means the coexistence in "an impossible space" of a "large number of fragmentary possible worlds" or, more simply, incommensurable spaces that are juxtaposed or superimposed upon each other. Characters no longer contemplate how they can unravel or unmask a central mystery, but are forced to ask instead, "Which world is this? What is to be done in it? Which of myselves is to do it?" The same shift can be detected in the cinema. In a modernist classic like *Citizen Kane* a reporter seeks to unravel the mystery of Kane's life and character by collecting multiple reminiscences and perspectives from those who had known him. In the more postmodernist format of the contemporary cinema we find, in a film like *Blue Velvet,* the central character revolving between two quite incongruous worlds—that of a conventional 1950s small-town America with its high school, drugstore culture, and a bizarre, violent, sex-crazed underworld of drugs, dementia, and sexual perversion. It seems impossible that these two worlds should exist in the same space, and the central character moves between them, unsure which is the true reality, until the two worlds collide in a terrible denouement. A postmodernist painter like David Salle likewise tends to "collage together incompatible source materials as an alternative to choosing between them." . . . But to accept the fragmentation, the pluralism, and the authenticity of other voices and other worlds poses the acute problem of communication and the means of exercising power through command thereof. Most postmodernist thinkers are fascinated by the new possibilities for information and knowledge production, analysis, and transfer. Lyotard . . . , for example, firmly locates his arguments in the context of new technologies of communication and, drawing upon Bell's and Touraine's theses of the passage to a "postindustrial" information-based society, situates the rise of postmodern thought in the heart of what he sees as a dramatic social and political transition in the languages of communication in advanced capitalist societies. He looks closely at the new technologies for the production, dissemination and use of that knowledge as a "principal force of production." The problem, however, is that knowledge can now be coded in all kinds of ways, some of which are more accessible than others. There is more than a hint in Lyotard's work, therefore, that modernism has changed because the technical and social conditions of communication have changed.

Postmodernists tend to accept, also, a rather different theory as to what language and communication are all about. Whereas modernists had presupposed that there was a tight and identifiable relation between what was being said (the signified or "message") and how it was being said (the signifier or "medium"), poststructuralist thinking sees these as "continually breaking apart and re-attaching in new combinations." "Deconstructionism" (a movement initiated by Derrida's reading of Martin Heidegger in the late 1960s) here enters the picture as a powerful stimulus to postmodernist ways of thought. Deconstructionism is less a philosophical position than a way of thinking about and "reading" texts. Writers who create texts or use words do so on the basis of all the other texts and words they have encountered, while readers deal with them in the same way. Cultural life is then viewed as a series of texts intersecting with other texts, producing more texts (including that of the literary critic, who aims to produce another piece of literature in which texts under consideration are intersecting freely with other texts that happen to have affected his or her thinking). This intertextual weaving has a life of its own. Whatever we write conveys meanings we do not or could not possibly intend, and our words cannot say what we mean. It is vain to try and master a text because the perpetual interweaving of texts and meanings is beyond our control. Language works through us. Recognizing that, the deconstructionist impulse is to look inside one text for another, dissolve one text into another, or build one text into another.

Derrida considers, therefore, collage/montage as the primary form of postmodern discourse. The inherent heterogeneity of that (be it in painting, writing, architecture) stimulates us, the receivers of the text or image, "to produce a signification which could be neither univocal nor stable." Both producers and consumers of "texts" (cultural artifacts) participate in the production of significations and meanings (hence Hassan's emphasis upon "process," "performance," "happening," and "participation" in the postmodernist style). Minimizing the authority of the cultural producer creates the opportunity for popular participation and democratic determinations of cultural values, but at the price of a certain incoherence or, more problematic, vulnerability to mass-market manipulation. However this may be, the cultural producer merely creates raw materials (fragments and elements), leaving it open to consumers to recombine those elements in any way they wish. The effect is to break (deconstruct) the power of the author to impose meanings or offer a continuous narrative. Each cited element, says Derrida, "breaks the continuity or the linearity of the discourse and leads necessarily to a double reading: that of the fragment perceived in relation to its text of origin; that of the fragment as incorporated into a new whole, a different totality." Continuity is given only in "the trace" of the fragment as it moves from production to consumption. The effect is to call into question all the illusions of fixed systems of representation. . . .

There is more than a hint of this sort of thinking within the modernist tradition (directly from surrealism, for example) and there is a danger here of thinking of the meta-narratives in the Enlightenment tradition as more fixed and stable than they truly were. Marx, as Ollman . . . observes, deployed his concepts relationally, so that terms like value, labor, capital, are "continually breaking apart and re-attaching in new combinations" in an open-ended struggle to come to terms with the totalizing processes of capitalism. Benjamin, a complex thinker in the Marxist tradition, worked the idea of collage/montage to perfection, in order to try and capture the many-layered and fragmented relations between economy, politics, and culture without ever abandoning the standpoint of a totality of practices that constitute capitalism. Taylor . . . likewise concludes, after reviewing the historical evidence of its use (particularly by Picasso), that collage is a far from adequate indicator of difference between modernist and postmodernist painting. . . .

The portrait of postmodernism I have so far sketched in seems to depend for its validity upon a particular way of experiencing, interpreting, and being in the world. This brings us to what is, perhaps, the most problematic facet of postmodernism, its psychological presuppositions with respect to personality, motivation, and behavior. Preoccupation with the fragmentation and instability of language and discourses carries over directly, for example, into a certain conception of personality. Encapsulated, this conception focuses on schizophrenia (not, it should be emphasized, in its narrow clinical sense), rather than on alienation and paranoia. . . . Jameson . . . explores this theme to very telling effect. He uses Lacan's description of schizophrenia as a linguistic disorder, as a breakdown in the signifying chain of meaning that creates a simple sentence. When the signifying chain snaps, then "we have schizophrenia in the form of a rubble of distinct and unrelated signifiers." If personal identity is forged through "a certain temporal unification of the past and future with the present before me," and if sentences move through the same trajectory, then an inability to unify past, present, and future in the sentence betokens a similar inability to "unify the past, present, and future of our own biographical experience or psychic life." This fits, of course, with postmodernism's preoccupation with the signifier rather than the signified, with participation, performance, and happening rather than with an authoritative and finished art object, with surface appearances rather than roots. . . . The effect of such a breakdown in the signifying chain is to reduce experience to "a series of pure and unrelated presents in time." Offering no counterweight, Derrida's conception of language colludes in the production of a certain schizophrenic effect, thus, perhaps, explaining Eagleton's and Hassan's characterization of the typical postmodernist artifact as schizoid. Deleuze and Guattari . . . , in their supposedly playful exposition *Anti-Oedipus,* hypothesize a relationship between schizophrenia and capitalism that prevails "at the deepest level of one and the same economy, one and the same production process," concluding that "our society produces schizos the same way it produces Prell shampoo or Ford cars, the only difference being that the schizos are not saleable."

A number of consequences follow from the domination of this motif in postmodernist thought. We can no longer conceive of the individual as alienated in the classical Marxist sense, because to be alienated presupposes a coherent rather than a fragmented sense of self from which to be alienated. It is only in terms of such a centered sense of personal identity that individuals can pursue projects over time, or think cogently about the production of a future significantly better than time present and time past. Modernism was very much about the pursuit of better futures, even if perpetual frustrations of that aim were conducive to paranoia. But postmodernism typically strips away that possibility by concentrating upon the schizophrenic circumstances induced by fragmentation and all those instabilities (including those of language) that prevent us even picturing coherently, let alone devising strategies to produce, some radically different future. Modernism, of course, was not without its schizoid moments—particularly when it sought to combine myth with heroic modernity—and there has been a sufficient history of the "deformation of reason" and of "reactionary modernisms" to suggest that the schizophrenic circumstance, though for the most part dominated, was always latent within the modernist movement. Nevertheless, there is good reason to believe that "alienation of the subject is displaced by fragmentation of the subject" in postmodern aesthetics. . . . If, as Marx insisted, it takes the alienated individual to pursue the Enlightenment project with a tenacity and coherence sufficient to bring us to some better future, then loss of the alienated subject would seem to preclude the conscious construction of alternative social futures. . . .

The invocation of Jameson brings us, finally, to his daring thesis that postmodernism is nothing more than the cultural logic of late capitalism. Following Mandel . . . , he argues that we have moved into a new era since the early 1960s in which the production of culture "has become integrated into commodity production generally: the frantic urgency of producing fresh waves of ever more novel seeming goods (from clothes to airplanes), at ever greater rates of turnover, now assigns an increasingly essential structural function to aesthetic innovation and experimentation." The struggles that were once exclusively waged in the arena of production have, as a consequence, now spilled outwards to make of cultural production an arena of fierce social conflict. Such a shift entails a definite change in consumer habits and attitudes as well as a new role for aesthetic definitions and interventions. While some would argue that the countercultural movements of the 1960s created an environment of unfulfilled needs and repressed desires that postmodernist popular cultural production has merely set out to satisfy as best it can in commodity form, others would suggest that capitalism, in order to sustain its markets, has been forced to produce desire and so titillate individual sensibilities as to create a new aesthetic over and against traditional forms of high culture. In either case, I think it important to accept the proposition that the cultural evolution which has taken place since the early 1960s, and which asserted itself as hegemonic in the early 1970s, has not occurred in a social, economic, or political vacuum. The deployment of advertising as "the official art of capitalism" brings advertising strategies into art, and art into advertising strategies. . . . It is interesting, therefore, to ruminate upon the stylistic shift that Hassan sets up in relation to the forces that emanate from mass-consumer culture: the mobilization of fashion, pop art, television, and other forms of media image, and the variety of urban life-styles that have become part and parcel of daily life under capitalism. Whatever else we do with the concept, we should not read postmodernism as some autonomous artistic current. Its rootedness in daily life is one of its most patently transparent features.

Sovereignty and Exchange in the Orders of Modernity

MICHAEL J. SHAPIRO

Introduction

According to one of her staunch defenders, "Margaret Thatcher has taught us that you have to own your money before you can spend it." Here in one sentence is contained the Thatcherian proposition that the interests of sovereignty must take priority over those related to exchange. It is supplemented by the corollary claim, emphasized in so many of Thatcher's statements, that the dynamics of exchange threaten the achievements of sovereignty.

The tenacity of this commitment was at least partly responsible for Thatcher's fall from office, for it informed her resistance to a process of European economic integration endorsed by influential members of her party. What was at issue, at the point at which her support crumbled, was the mode of British entry into the European Monetary Union (EMU). As Sir Geoffrey Howe stated in summarizing his reasons for resigning as Thatcher's deputy prime minister, "The Prime Minister has appeared to rule out from the start any compromise at any stage on any of the basic components which all the eleven other countries believe to be part of EMU—a single currency or permanently fixed exchange rates a central bank or common monetary policy."

Like many national leaders in Europe, Howe did not see a strict trade-off between sovereignty and exchange, as perceived by Thatcher. Whereas Thatcher declared that she "would never witness the end of British sovereignty, nor countenance the demise of sterling," Howe argued against seeing the issue "as some kind of zero sum game." According to Howe, the forthcoming merger of economies is not to be understood as a loss of sovereignty but as a way to strengthen it, and, in support of this view, he quoted Winston

Churchill's claim that such economic union is a step in "the gradual assumption by all nations concerned of that larger sovereignty, which can alone protect their diverse and distinctive customs and characteristics, and their national traditions."

This exemplary contention between the impulses of sovereignty and exchange has been repeated in other European nations, even those with reputations for zealously guarding their sovereignty. For example, Sweden's qualms about relinquishing neutrality have turned out to be far less significant than the fear of damage to industrial development if Sweden remains outside of the EMU. Like Howe, such nations see preserving sovereignty and joining the European Union as compatible, and what is feared "is a future outside the EC which sees industrial investment drain away and strips isolated national governments of any true influence over their economic fortunes."

In sum, what is at issue in the disparate positions taken by Thatcher and Howe is the degree of compatibility possible between maintaining sovereignty and facilitating an expanded level of exchange. The fundamental tension between them has especially crucial implications for claims to political identity. The sovereignty impulse tends toward drawing firm boundaries around the self, unambiguously specifying individual and collective identities, privileging and rationalizing aspects of a homogeneous subjectivity that is eligible for memberships and recognition, and constituting forms of nonidentical and ineligible otherness; and specifying and bounding both the spaces in which subjects achieve eligibility and those in which the collective as a whole has dominion.

In contrast, the exchange impulse encourages flows and thus (often) the relaxation of specifications of eligible subjectivities and territorial boundaries. The opposition between flows of exchange and the inhibitions of sovereignty is oriented around issues of selfhood and location and consequently involves an emphasis either on ownership and the maintenance of authority and control or on reciprocity, substitutability, and the relaxation of control in order to produce expanded domains in which things can circulate.

Despite this simple and familiar rendering of the opposing impulses of sovereignty and exchange, the interrelationships between them are exceedingly complex. In various cultural configurations, in different epochs in the histories of states and economies, and with respect to different aspects of association, sovereignty and exchange can be opposing, mutually facilitating, or relatively independent. . . .   .

Hobbes and Smith on the Self and the Other

Thomas Hobbes's *Leviathan,* written just after a fractious civil war, is an exemplar of a sovereignty-oriented treatise, for it is preoccupied with justifying a unifying, unambiguous, and absolutely dominant national proprietor: Hobbes's sovereign embodies the will and desire for protection of all subjects, who give up their individually sponsored coercive acts in order to achieve the paramount founding civic value, civil peace. *Leviathan* combines this valorizing and privileging of civil peace with the ideas Hobbes adopted from his fascination with mathematics and Galilean physics to produce a logical, rigorous, and inescapable justification for an absolute model of sovereignty.

Hobbes's sovereignty orientation is notable not only for an absolutist (preferably monarchical) view of sovereign displacement, but also for his conceptual building blocks, his proto-sovereign positions, of which the most important is his version of the civically relevant dimensions of human subjectivity. Like so many thinkers in the history of the political theory canon, Hobbes offered a mythic narrative in which drives toward consensuality, which are immanent in (or natural to) subjectivity, become a basis for the existing system of sovereign authority. Hobbes's individual subjects are constructed as being, in their initial condition, wholly "sovereign"; that is, as being the sole authors of their actions or proprietors of their deeds, except in cases in which they are duly constituted as representatives, authorized to act on behalf of another (owner) of the deeds to be carried out. Hobbes's persons are sovereign either as authors or actors. As an author, the person is a natural person— "he whose words or actions are considered either his own, or as representing the words or actions of another man." As an actor, the person is an artificial person: there are "persons artificiall" in that they "have their words and actions *Owned* by those whom they represent." In such a case, the representative is the "actor," and the "owner" is the "author." In short, persons, insofar as they are persons, hold a copyright to their words and deeds, and interactions among persons which affect proprietorship are matters of freely-entered-into covenants.

Just as persons hire actors by covenants that stipulate substitutions of actors for authors, they also hire an absolute sovereign. This choice, which is the covenant of the civic whole, tends to persist, for although persons exhibit a restless desire for power over others, they also have an innate aversion to death and a desire for "commodious living." To avoid the one and achieve the other, persons calculate that it is best to enter into the primary covenant by which they trade obedience for protection and accept the absolute power of the sovereign. This is the mythic tale that links proto-sovereignty with sovereignty, and subjectivity with the sovereign order.

The entry of the Hobbesian self into the relationship with the sovereign, by now an old story, amounts to a rational/consensual willingness to give up an aspect of proprietorship, of control over one's own protection. The sovereign state is constructed out of a series of covenants that, when viewed individually, are aimed at protection for each, and, when summed up, produce civil peace for the whole. The state as an entity thus amounts to a vast set of yielded proprietorships.

Hobbes recognized that there are rebellious aspects of human subjectivity, but rather than envisioning a less rigorous or normalizing form of civic order that would allow them space for legitimate articulation, he relegated them to the domain of the irrational. For example, he evoked the idea of madness, which manifests itself either as emotional extravagance (too much rage or laughter) or as discursive aberration, an "abuse of words." Concerned with maintaining a willed or consensual legitimation for absolute sovereignty, Hobbes marginalized all aspects of subjectivity that affront the order or appear to dilute consensuality.

It should be evident that this model of sovereignty contains a form of exchange, which can be conveniently represented through Marx's discussion of the extended and general value form in Volume I of *Capital*. When speaking of how value forms are extended, Marx stated, "the value of any commodity, such as linen, is expressed in terms of numberless other elements of the world of commodities." This extended form of value is analogous to the difference Hobbes noted between authors and actors, where another person—the "artificiall" person—is substituted. Such extensions or substitutions were, for Marx, merely an intermediate stage in the movement of the capitalist system toward what he called the general form of value represented by gold or money. The general form provides a means not only for substituting for various individual commodities but also, owing to its general representative character, for unifying exchange value. Hobbes's notion of the sovereign or monarch, whose will substitutes for those of all subjects, is analogous to Marx's notion of the sovereignty of gold, which monopolizes value just as the sovereign monopolizes normativity as a general representative. Gold, as a form of commodity, becomes sovereign; it achieves an "objective fixity and general social validity."

The Hobbesian sovereign state therefore contains an atrophied economy. The exchange dimension of Hobbesian sovereignty is overcome by a preoccupation with civil peace and unification. In effect, Hobbes offers a static economy of subjectivity exchange wherein the sovereignty impulse represses the exchange impulse. His economy is inaugurated with a primordial exchange and is followed by an inhibition of substitutions. Once the substitutions are willingly made (if only mythically), the process is to cease, for although he allowed for a right of rebellion against abusive sovereigns, Hobbes wanted to give to the sovereign (the monarch or sovereign assemby) total control over selecting a successor.

Another dimension must be added to the sovereignty-exchange relationship to determine what is at stake in Hobbes's repression of the economies within his version of sovereignty. The question of value has to be raised. Jacques Lacan made a relevant contribution here by noting the necessary complementarity between sovereignty and exchange in the process of discourse. In stating that "the signifier requires another locus—the locus of the Other," Lacan suggested that value emerges precisely in the trade-off involved. To participate in intelligible exchanges, the subject must recognize the subordination of its identity to a hegemonic model of otherness. The entry into discourse therefore concedes this form of otherness, and the value that emerges is a compensation. In exchange for the loss of control over meaning, subjects acquire the ability to enter into the social order referenced in the signification process.

A recognition of the inherent compromises of the sovereignty of subjectivity in the exchange dimension of language—that is, of the domination of the sociosymbolic dimension over that of the individual with respect to meaning and value—provides the opportunity of interrogating Hobbesian thought at two levels. At the level of civic sovereignty, Hobbes institutes a strict form of inhibition, which stifles the exchange dimension of sovereignty with an obsessive concern with peace and safety. Because of this, the value emerging from the collective sovereign relationship is compromised in that it is not re-experienced through continuous, participatory reactivation. Hobbesian sovereignty subverts exchange by being based on a single, mythic exchange, which constitutes an end to all exchange. On the other level, that of individual subjectivity, Hobbes represses the dimension of exchange by repressing the otherness of the social, which is always already there in the subject's ability to engage in self-recognition. Precisely because of his emphasis on the originary sovereignty of the subject, its ownership or authorship of its acts (as though conduct has meaning without a prior system of social inscription), Hobbes neglects that aspect of otherness—the symbolic exchanges between self and other through which selves are constituted—that produces a socially available form of subjectivity.

A telling contrast with the Hobbesian privileging of both an absolutist, unifying sovereignty and a wholly self-contained model of proto-sovereign subjectivity is found in the writings of Adam Smith, who, like Hobbes, wrote in response to a sovereignty crisis. In Smith's case, the crisis was related not to the issue of maintaining civil peace but of fitting a model of home rule to the need for access to markets. Hobbes was certainly writing at a time when a bourgeois market society had already begun to emerge, but his gaze on this aspect of the order was inconsistent: "now he saw it, now he didn't," as Macpherson put it. In sharp contrast, Adam Smith's gaze was well and consistently focused on this aspect of the order. Writing a century later, he was responding in part to the turmoil produced in connection with the Scottish-English Union, which had been effected in 1707 after a tumultuous national debate in Scotland. The debate had been primarily concerned with the degree of compensation to be gained through an increased trading advantage obtained by giving up a large measure of Scottish sovereignty. Ultimately, the Treaty of Union required Scotland to give up some venerable institutions in order to gain some economic advantages.

Despite his preference for a robust and broad economy an anemic degree of centralized control, Smith was not without a sovereignty orientation. He addressed himself assiduously (albeit with highly selective historical evidence) to the proprieties of legislation as well as to surrounding judicial and executive powers. Treating these issues in his lectures on Jurisprudence, Smith did much of his reasoning on the basis of long historical fantasies (one of his primary methods in his *Wealth of Nations*). imagined, not unwisely, for example, that hunting and shepherding societies had little use for robust legislative functions. He also resorted occasionally the writings of the ancients on the Greek city-state and, putting these together with his historical fables and anthropological fantasies, came up model of the natural progression of the art of government, which is a more or less material-ist version of the evolution of governmental forms.

At the level of specific preference, Smith wanted to locate primary sover-eignty in a legislative body—a preference that followed from his narrative, in which he saw his society at the appropriate evolutionary stage because of its emphasis on manufacture and trade. According to Smith, this situation was well beyond the management capabilities of a chieftain, and he claimed to demonstrate that only parliamentary sovereignty could provide the manage-ment necessary for Britain's mode of economy (although, as is well known, Smith wanted a minimalist form of management that would allow the natural social mechanisms, especially those related to the division of labor and market impulses, to provide the necessary regulation).

However nonabsolutist may be Smith's version of sovereignty, what pri-marily distinguishes him from Hobbes is not only his preference for a sover-eignty shared between a legislature and social mechanisms rather than located in a monarch but also his well-elaborated version of society. Whereas in Hobbes, the sovereignty relationship emphasizes owner/author subjects and representing rulers to whom the subjects defer to obtain social peace, in Smith it is a social body made up of social beings involved in economic exchange and the exchange of sentiments that provides the basis of the sovereign relation-ship. The political relation for Smith is oriented toward this robust version of the social, for politics is conceived in the classical liberal sense of subordinat-ing the political relation to the natural mechanisms operating at the level of social relations.

What is especially notable also by way of the Hobbes–Smith contrast is the attenuated sovereignty implicit in Smith's proto-sovereign notions. The Smithian individual is not the sovereign, self-contained owner or author of actions but, rather, a dynamic, reflective, immanently social system of sym-bolic exchanges. Hobbes figured the person-thing relationship within a scien-tific heuristic, based on a Galilean concept of motion. Objects set up forces of attraction, and the appetite of the subject produces initiating energy forces as well. Subject-object or subject-subject relations, which result in attitudes or sentiments, are to be understood as the result of a co-motion—a meeting of the motions produced by the subject and the object. This leaves little space for immanent sociality.

In contrast, Smith figured the social domain within a visual and reflective rhetoric. For him, a person's understandings and sentiments form a complex set of points of observation. Smith's person is not a self-contained, sovereign actor but a forced or double self, containing both an actor and an imag-ined observer through whom action predicates are mediated. The appetite is therefore subordinated to two points of view, one belonging to the subject, and the other to an imagined disinterested observer, whose viewpoint is con-structed as too were involved in the external appraisal or judgment. Through the reflexivity of the individual's gaze, the imagined observer there-fore functions a social representative within. Smith's nonabsolutist version of state sovereignty is thus reinforced by a compatible proto-sovereignty—a construction of an individual who is prepared for an attenuated sovereignty by his or her own acts of self-attenuation.

With his immanently socialized subject in place, Smith mounted a resistance to a strong sovereignty model at the level of the collectivity. His contributions to notions of governance are clearly influenced more by the forces impelling circulation and exchange than those militating in the direction of the imposed unities and cohesions, which require firm and unchallenged models of sovereign control. Although this position represents a significant shift from the preoccupations of Hobbes, it is not a radical departure from the changes in emphasis in political treatises from the seventeenth to the eighteenth centuries. With his focus on managing an economy to secure the well-being of the population as a whole, Adam Smith addressed themes that had been blocked throughout the seventeenth century because of "the preeminence of the problem of the exercise of sovereignty." Certainly there were concerns addressed in connection with the problem of wealth prior to Smith's *Wealth of Nations,* but under the system of mercantilism, political treatises—preoccupied as they were with the power of the sovereign—treated wealth from the point of view of its functioning as a resource for the sovereign to protect the realm, not its potential increase. In this context, Smith's view of wealth participated in a more general departure from the legalistic obligation of the citizen to the sovereign and moved toward an interest in an aggregate effect, the problem of producing and maintaining conditions for the well-being—health, wealth, longevity—of the "population." Rather than neglecting sovereignty, Smith helped to shift the problematic from the originary flow of loyalty to the top, that is, from sovereignty as a series of displacements to a concern with a different flow, with the management activity of the sovereign with respect to the flows of exchanges within the social domain. The problem of sovereignty for Smith was therefore based on facilitation rather than control—on the selection of the appropriate model to maintain the flow of goods and services necessary to improve the population's condition.

With Smith, the "social" had become the primary alibi for the political. The very meaning of politics had shifted from the Hobbesian notion of a contract between previously wholly sovereign individuals and their general representative equivalent, the monarch, to a notion of the political arising from the social. The political had developed "a social referent," and once this happened, the problem of sovereignty became one of managing the social configuration.

With Smith, therefore, the world becomes unstuck. In place of a static, legalistic, and protection-oriented model of sovereignty, Smith articulated one congenial to the movement of things within an "art of government" concerned with the management of the relationship of persons to things. In this context, Smith's labor theory of value, based on the cost of maintaining labor power, plays the role of producing a system of calculation for that management. Moreover, the space of governance is reconstituted. It is no longer simply concerned with the maintenance of the realm as a whole, but the encouragement of private ownership of the means of production. Smith's sovereignty thus takes up its primary locus in the society, especially in its productive venues, and the center of authority is viewed more as a steering mechanism (through the appropriate legislation) than a repository of authority.

Summarizing this change from a focus on sovereignty as the maintenance of a legalistic unity to sovereignty as the maintenance of well-being through the management of flows, Michel Foucault referred to the development of a "governmental state," understood less as a territorial extension and more in terms of the various energies and flows produced by its population. Smith, among others, helped to produce this understanding.

Given that it was circulation and mobility rather than sovereignty and stasis that organized Smith's approach to governance, and that his gaze was on the social configuration rather than the ruler-ruled relationship, he was able to notice that the exchange impulse arising out of the social domain was surging well beyond the inhibitions constituted by the absolutist form of sovereignty that had been theorized by Hobbes and had remained intrinsic to the mercantilist management of wealth. Accordingly, Smith stressed a form of governance compatible with his notion that a general well-being would emerge from a facilitation of the productive capacities of the "individual." This emphasis is, of course, predicated on some ideational shifts that had already come to pass especially on various desacralizing modes of thought (to which Hobbes had contributed). In short, by Smith's time there was such a thing as an individual, whose activities could be facilitated.

There is a strong narrative commitment guiding and supporting Smith's orientation toward governance as management of flows rather than as the maintenance of a static sovereignty—a narrative incorporating the materialist version of the history of governance noted above. In contrast with Hobbes's "mythic plot," with its discrete history of the origin of state authority, Smith offered a more continuous model in which forms of governance evolve. They arise, he argued, naturally, meaning that they shift to provide the appropriate context for the particular mode of production in effect. Smith thought that little governance of any kind was needed and did not arise until property relations became complex, as in the case in which people changed their vocations from hunting to herding. He surmised, further, that with the growth of manufacture and trade, forces were unleashed that weakened the monarchy and strengthened the House of Commons.

This materialist narrative had the effect of naturalizing Smith's preference for a form of governance oriented around facilitating trade. Even his treatment of the issue of the security function was influenced by his interest in exchange, for by "security" he meant not merely the maintenance of civil peace but also the protection of property relations and the production of a general well-being.

Although Smith's interest in commerce controlled his interest in governance, his desire to avoid inhibiting the "market" must be understood in the premodern sense. His conception of a market was not what is meant when one now refers to the global systems of exchange characteristic of contemporary capitalism. Smith's market concept was more akin to the idea of limits to the desire for goods. Indeed, given his concern with morals as a social interaction, he would have been distressed with the extent to which the global vectors along which economic exchanges now occur have loosened the bonds of mutuality.

However, although Smith did not conceive of the market as anything but the arbitrary boundaries of exchange, he recognized the significance of money in creating the conditions of possibility for uninhibited exchange. While, of course, Marx was to later indict the money form's role in alienating value from its source in human productive activity, Smith was fixated on the encouragement of trade and primarily concerned with extracting the idea of money from old notions of hoarding and accumulating so that it could circulate in an uninhibited way, into and out of British ports. Arguing vigorously for the advantages of free trade, he stated:

> Britain should by all means be made a free port, that there should be no interruptions of any kind made to foreign trade, that if it were possible to defray the expenses of government by any other method, all duties, customs and excises should be abolished, and that free commerce and liberty of exchange should be allowed with all nations and for all things.

Smith was clearly and unmistakably resistant to the idea that there could be any inhibition to the circulation of money. For him, money was not bound up even at a symbolic level with sovereignty. It was not a mark of wealth or national integrity, but solely an instrument to facilitate exchange. Despite the distance of Smith's position from that recently adopted by Margaret Thatcher, he was not without some Thatcher-like qualms. At the level of governance, he tended to think that the evolving forms, which had encouraged commerce, would also provide liberty and security for each individual. However, "security" here meant the protection of property and livelihood. When it came to such a thing as national security, Smith did not share Thatcher's worries, because trade and military technology were not, in his time, dissolving old boundaries. But he did express a deep concern about the diminution of the "martial spirit" among citizens who are totally oriented toward commerce. Among the bad effects of commerce, he noted, was that it "sinks the courage of mankind." As his lament continued, he expressed the opinion that when the defense of the country is left to specialists, others with "their minds constantly employed on the arts of luxury" grow "effeminate and dastardly."

Money, Sovereignty, and Modernity

If by "effeminate" and "dastardly" Adam Smith meant a reluctance to bear arms and a generalized fear of bellicosity, Margaret Thatcher's sovereignty orientation has been neither. Her resistance to European union has been based both on her opposition to relinquishing unilateral control of defense and warmaking (as her Falklands/Maldives war attests) and her unwillingness to subsume the British economy within a wider system of sovereign control (one, she complained, in which bankers instead of parliaments make decisions).

Thatcher's anachronistic view of money, which emerged most recently in her resistance to the European Monetary Union, is especially noteworthy for purposes of theorizing the sovereignty-exchange relation. For better (Smith et al.) or worse (Marx et al.), when one is dealing with an exchangeable currency, it is already not controlled by an independent mode of sovereignty. Contemporary control over national currencies is widely dispersed. A currency's value is based on a system of interrelationships that extend well beyond the identity/sovereign dimensions involved in the initiation of exchanges. Indeed, modernity can be understood as, among other things, a condition in which relations of capital have displaced relations between persons and collectivities. It is a situation of "an unprecedented rift between intersubjective relations and what function henceforth as economic relations." At all levels of identity—person, family, tribal group, or nation—the meanings attached to subjectivity have paled as exchanges have become "rather abstract relations between *positions*."

The significance of this rift becomes especially evident when modern capital exchange relations are contrasted with the symbolic ties between subjects that control barter relations among tribal societies. For example, among the Narringeri peoples studied by Geza Roheim, exchange relations were connected so closely with intersubjectivities that there were actual exchanges of body substances accompanying the exchange of goods. There was, for example, the custom of a father ceremoniously preserving a child's umbilical cord to be later passed on to a man from another tribe. With this bodily exchange, a future intersubjectivity was established. The child and children of the recipient would become "certified traders of various products exchanged between the two tribes," once they reached adulthood. United by the umbilical cord, the traders do not have their reciprocity deferred through money, which, as a much more abstract symbolizing instrument, depersonalizes exchange, suppressing its sovereignty dimensions by connecting abstract persons whose reciproclty is too mediated to allow for mutual recognition.

To extend the comparison, we can consider an intermediate level represented by the money forms used by the Trobriand Islanders and the North American Iroquois. The Trobriand armshells and necklaces and Iroquois wampum were media of exchange, but they were also "pledges, linked to the persons who use them and who in turn are bound by them." By contrast, in modern capitalist societies, money or species payments are instruments through which both subjectivities and places are dissolved rather than reinforced or formed. This dissolving of subjectivity and locationality is precisely a challenge to sovereignty, for what "sovereignty" implies in its most general sense is the authoritative control over domains and subjects.

When exchange becomes wholly abstract—a matter of goods destined for abstract persons in abstract positions—the rudiments of sovereignty (subjects and places) are no longer easily identifiable. It is not the case that intersubjectivity has vanished. Rather, it is the case that the forms that it takes are disinstantiated from the concrete subjects affected by the exchanges. The identities of the exchangers exist within sovereign domains, and the exchanges, which link subjects across domains, do not apply to specific subjects and are often part of a pattern that affects the very identity spaces within which subjects operate.

In the face of this modern tendency, nationalist inhibitions, such as those expressed in Thatcher's attempt to maintain "British money," are increasingly inefficacious because no one sovereignty domain controls either the exchanges or the subjectivities around which they are organized. Money, now shorn of its reference to specific subjectivities, has been largely deprived of its sovereign vestiges, and given the recent tendency to effect transactions electronically, money is becoming not only more abstract but wholly dematerialized. This is well captured in Don DeLillo's novel *Players,* in which one of the characters becomes aware of this qualitative change in money's existence:

> He'd seen the encoding rooms, the microfilming of checks, money moving, shrinking as it moved, beginning to elude visualization, to pass from paper existence to electronic sequences, its meaning increasingly complex, harder to name. It was condensation, the whole process, a paring away of money's accidental properties, of money's touch. . . .

Toward a New Formulation of Sovereignty

This charged intimacy between sovereignty and exchange, the paradoxical combination of antagonism and symbiosis, can be found in more aggregate institutional contexts, notably at the level of the state. In order to discern the effects at this level, it is necessary to seek a formulation of sovereignty and exchange that transcends the static limitations of traditional political discourses which fail to capture the dynamics and complexities in the simple equating of sovereignty with the authority.

The first step is toward a more general rendering of the idea of sovereignty. . . . Sovereignty is a stabilized system of authoritative control. But what stabilizes it? One aspect is the firmness and continuity of its domain— the space of its authority. For example, one reason why sovereignty has been understood in such a state-centric way is because of the power, authority, and persistence of the discourse within which state sovereignty is inscribed. The apparent domain of this discourse (the geostrategic map of the world constructed in typical policy discourses), which arose as a particular answer to the question of political community, is maintained in part by the discourse's implicit claim to timelessness and universal validity as it both suppresses its specific origins and turns a blind eye toward various processes of globalization that threaten it.

The geopolitical map of the world, produced by a state-centric view of sovereignty, has had significant competitors of late, all provoked by various processes of globalization in various domains, as with transnational regroupings such as the European Union. And, increasingly, the state-as-coherent-actor or unitary entity has been destabilized as various "subnational" or tribal and ethnic groups have asserted desires to reoccupy old sovereignties that preexist the current geopolitical map.

Closely related to the growing instability in what has been understood as international space is an instability in the other dimension of what stabilizes claims to sovereignty: the dimension of subjectivity. When, for example, the person-as-citizen who depends on "rights" flowing from a state affiliation is accompanied by the person as trader-consumer within an authority frame of a supranational economic union, the domain of subjectivity, over which states have claimed control, has become ambiguous, and this has obvious implications for the stability of state sovereignty.

In addition to such pressures on sovereignty as spaces and subjectivities becoming reordered, there are accompanying textual changes that these dynamics encourage. As old sovereignty models break down, the ideational structures supporting them begin to dissolve or experience disturbances and reversals. Of these, one of the most significant is the traditional narrative, lodged in the history of political theory, through which the state has achieved much of its legitimacy. In arguing that "statecraft is mancraft," Richard Ashley contributed to one such reversal. He claimed that contrary to the traditional narrative, in which the state arises as the appropriate political form to house the preexisting forms of human nature, character, concerns, or modes of production, is the narrative implied in statecraft as mancraft, in which the state produces a model of human subjectivity as a legitimating device. At a textual level, modern statecraft is "an art of domesticating the meaning of man by constructing his problems, his dangers, his fears."

What Ashley called a "paradigm of sovereignty" is what I have called above a commitment to a form of proto-sovereignty—a version of human subjectivity upon which sovereignty is predicated. The proto-sovereign model dominating modern state discourse is "a specific, historically fabricated, widely circulated, and practically effective intepretation of man as a sovereign being." More specifically, it is a model of "reasoning man" employed to promote the illusion (central to Hobbes's sovereignty version) that the legal and coercive structures of the state are those that "reasoning man knows to be the necessary conditions of his free use of reason."

In addition, part of the locational strategy used to construct modern subjectivity is temporal. "The effect of acceleration obtains in the sense that dangers produced through practices of statecraft, far from being indefinitely postponable into some ambiguous future, are immediately and unambiguously encountered here and now in the time of man." This imbrication of space and time has also had a marked effect on the strategies that the sovereignty impulse has had to effect, for in addition to basing its sovereignty claim on the dangers to reasoning man is a spatiotemporal mapping of the world in which it locates the dangers—from various locations, coming with little or no degree of warning, and so on. The state thus produces its sovereignty justification by producing both subjectivity and space within a world that is experiencing increasing disturbances to both.

An adequate formulation of the roles of sovereignty and exchange in the modern period thus requires a language within which such dynamisms can be captured, the flows that increasingly threaten sovereignty-oriented inhibitions, and the reinscriptions that occur as reactions when sovereignty-oriented reactions try to contain the flows. Flows and inscriptions are, in fact, the primary concepts with which Gilles Deleuze and Feliz Guattari have attempted to capture the dynamics and complexities of the sovereignty-exchange interaction. . . .

To illuminate the interpretive impositions involved in the state's inhibitions of the exchange dynamic, Deleuze and Guattari employed the terms *codes* and *flows* in their model of force and counterforce. Inasmuch as the sovereignty impulse involves a heavy investment in the interpretive containment or marking of subjectivities and domains, the counterforce dimension of the sovereignty dynamic is driven by a dread of "decoded flows." Because the state, as a domain for sovereignty, operates through fixing residence, its additional activities, which go beyond its initial territorializing, must involve attempts to code all flows, and some flows are especially troublesome in that they exceed territorial boundaries either in fact or interpretation. The most dangerous of these are, of course, those that threaten to dissolve the state's territoriality in the process of exceeding the boundaries (at least with respect to some functions, as with the European Monetary Union). To understand territory not as a thing, but as a dynamic, to understand "territorializing" and "deterritorializing" forces at work, one can recall, for example, the historical period in which the medieval church began to lose the ability to authoritatively territorialize the world, and to code domains in relation to divine sanction. The process by which civil authorities took over this coding, often on behalf of commercial interests, amounted to a deterritorializing as the church's codes lost their grip. This was followed by a reterritorializing as state-oriented coding became institutionalized. In the face of deterritorializing dynamics, forms of sovereignty assert themselves. For example, lands that lost their meaning within a theological discourse, which identifies their functioning as a locus for divine bounty, were ultimately recoded as domains controlled by earthly "proprietors" that yield "products" as the fruits of labor.

This recoding has, of course, been markedly successful, and although contemporary prayers still refer to some goods as "God's bounty"—as gifts entailing spiritual obligations—it is the market and distribution of proprietorship rather than the person–God covenant that largely determines their value. However, the state's triumph over the church has not produced an end to all coding. Flows across territorial boundaries of the state continue to threaten existing codes and to attenuate the state system of sovereignty as a whole. As money, labor forces, weapons, and scientific technology become subject to exchange dynamics that are increasingly global, the inhibitory responses by those who, like Margaret Thatcher, are defenders of old sovereignty systems become more frantic.

Moreover, the forces producing the flows, which exceed and endanger old sovereignties (and thus old coding strategies), operate within a modernity whose general characteristic has been the dissolution of geographic space. As noted above, modern exchanges privilege temporality or speed rather than site, making space what Virilio has called "chronospace." In this space, activities around the globe involve a speed of transmission of messages, weapons, money, and so on. In a world based more on time than on territory, distance, in the old sense, is displaced by speed and acceleration. As a result, the inhibition of flows must involve modifying pace and trajectory rather than simply containing things. Sovereignty maintenance tactics must therefore change. For example, as commercial enterprises begin drawing labor from around the globe by moving either people or production facilities, the state begins to lose the ability to regulate work. As labor supplies respond to demands by becoming mobile or displaced, sovereign entities inhibit the labor exchanges not only through legal prohibitions but also through a slowing of credentialing processes. A slowing of the paper flow has been one of sovereignty's tactics for slowing and thus managing the labor flow as well as other flows.

Another telling case of a flow threatening the state sovereignty system is the flow of scientific exchanges in the domain of space exploration. Since 1972, Soviet and U.S. scientists have engaged in exchanges of information and data related to space technology. Whereas the interests of scientists produce impulses toward more rapid and comprehensive exchanges, state authorities, governed by the geostrategic, security dimension of the sovereignty impulse, engage in inhibitions of these exchanges. Thus a five-year exchange of data treaty established in 1977 was allowed to lapse in 1982 by the U.S. government, which wanted to use this as a mechanism to sanction Soviet policy toward Poland. And the U.S. National Aeronautics and Space Administration (NASA) has been continually wary of uninhibited flows of Soviet–U.S. scientific exchange related to space technology. To inhibit such exchanges, NASA has limited the size and frequency of symposia.

Contemporary Disturbances

Having established the frame for conceiving the sovereignty-exchange tension, what remains is to point briefly toward aspects of present global structures and processes within which the two impulses contend. In recent years, the process of "inscription," wherein the prevailing state sovereignty structure attempts to maintain its control, has had especially to contend with two types of dynamics. The first is related to the flow of capital. If, as has been noted above, the system of exchange requires a sovereignty dimension to function, so that exchanges must always be tied to a set of identities that articulates with the flows to determine value, any qualitative change in the system of circulation will necessarily produce "transformations of the identity structure." For example, in recent decades the flow from central, industrial powers has tended to be more in the form of export capital than manufactured goods. This "deindustrialization of the center" affects accumulations and activities at the periphery, which, in turn, impact not only on the economies there but also on the cultural frames or identity structures with which economic activities are associated.

Second, to appreciate the impact on sovereignty structures of these changes, it is necessary to recognize an ongoing dynamic that is not clearly referenced within the more static renderings of the sovereignty problematic. However stable may be the names of existing national states, the processes of official transfers of power, and the recognition of their authority structure by other states and supranational agencies, every state harbors varying degrees of centrifugal force, of resistance to officially inscribed, state-oriented subjectivities.

Therefore, states always find themselves involved to some degree in attempts to maintain central control by overcoming the old affiliations that have never been fully integrated into centralized, state-controlled structures. This assertion of centralizing control takes the form not only of direct coercion but also of interpretive activity. The state engages in what Deleuze and Guattari called "overcoding"—an inscription process that attempts to reinterpret old activities based on old affiliations within the state-oriented code. But such inhibition strategies become strained when changes in the structure of exchanges provoke subsumed but not wholly incorporated cultural groupings to react with new, identity-affirming activities, and attempt to "reestablish a culturally unified way of life," that does not accord with the sovereignty direction of the state as a whole.

More specifically, in varying degrees, states contain a "fourth world" that has participated in the capitalist sector of the economy but has retained a resistant group identity and solidarity ready to reassert itself and threaten existing sovereignty structures when it is disturbed by demands to adjust to shifting identity spaces. This dynamic is very much involved in the current tensions between the Soviet regime in Moscow and some of the Soviet republics. In effect, polities whose sovereign surfaces appear smooth and untroubled contain dormant resistances below the surface, which can be awakened when various unleashed forces disturb the inscription process that is responsible for smoothing the surface. Deleuze and Guattari liken the state to a great wall. In appropriating and subsuming old forces and affiliations, the state's overcoding—its territorial inscriptions through which it contains subjects within a demarcated space—"allows the old territorial inscriptions [the spatial practices of existing subsumed groupings] to subsist as bricks on the new surface." However, as flows increase, the overcoding cannot always keep pace, and reassertions of dissident identity and spatial practices occur. It becomes evident that the state's debts have not all been redeemed, and that the sovereignty wall has bricked in old grievances.

Similarly, at an international level, the sovereignty system of separate states represses structures of grievance. For example, during the recent Gulf War, President George Bush of the United States treated the conflict as if it were a disturbance in an otherwise stable and untroubled system of Middle Eastern sovereignties, and he explicitly envisioned the postwar period as a return to quiescence. But if one heeds the constitutive debts of the various state sovereignties in the region, what is apparent is that they rest on an economy of grievances. This repressed economy within the sovereignty system of the region is not apparent when one simply speaks, as did Bush, of the territorial integrity of each state. The grievances are built into the various territorialities. It is less the case that there are territories with grievances than it is that the existing pattern of state sovereignties constitutes territorial grievances. There is thus no quiescence or tranquillity to which they can return after the war, for this "peace" exists only within the alibi of a wholly sovereignty-oriented discourse that fails to acknowledge the deep system of exchanges it represses. Just as disturbances in systems of exchange awaken grievances within sovereignty structures by disturbing subsumed identity structures, disturbances in the sovereignty system awaken grievances by summoning repressed dimensions of exchange.

Conclusion

The orders of modernity both within and among the state entities on the globe now confront new instabilities as the sovereignty-exchange nexus is tested by new flows and ever more intense efforts at reinscription. To summarize, a politics of sovereignty is a politics of control over subjectivities and domains. Because stable patterns of subjectivity and space are a function of both the regulation of things and people and the interpretative impositions that give them meaning, sovereignty cannot be supported simply by exhibits of raw matter, of land or flesh and blood. The process of asserting or making sovereignty models, as well as that of challenging them, involves active, interpretive struggles. But struggles against what? Sovereignty maintenance involves first and foremost the activity of creating and maintaining inhibitions, of controlling and directing flows of exchange that continually threaten extant boundaries and subjectivities. Some threats are constant. They are continually activated forces, propelled by self-conceptions at odds with those within the authorized discourses of the state, and they exert a more or less constant pressure against sovereignty-maintaining constraints. These come often from aspects of culture and society that are never wholly subsumed or domesticated within the sovereignty system. Some are episodic.

The episodic disturbances to sovereignty arrrangements are various. . . . In the domain of "international relations," there have been changes in weapons technology, such as the development of all-terrain vehicles that "dissolve the earth," and the development of floating and flying arsenals that also dissolve the geographic defenses of the sovereign integrity of nations.

Some episodic disturbances are ideational. It is these that more clearly evoke interpretive struggles, for they occur in the domain of the sovereign control over texts. . . . At the level of state systems, adjustments in the perceived space of divinity as various civic versions of neo-Copernican cosmology developed, helping to precipitate the historical shift from religious to civic forms of sovereign authority. Extensions of the Copernican thought system also led to the ultimate triumph of civic authority over the theological version of sovereignty by encouraging a different construction of the space of personhood. Commercial societies achieved their sovereignty justifications through the proto-sovereign construction of the individual proprietor on the Earth, a successor to the brief sojourner occupying a symbolic place with a temporary, divinely sanctioned permit.

At a minimum, once we recognize that the present global condition of sovereignty is a relatively recent and contentious set of practices rather than a naturally evolving form of wisdom, we are in a position to resist theoretical frames that reify existing political arrangements. But more than the stultification of academic theorizing is at stake. Theoretical practices affect the conditions of possibility for political practices. Insofar as one can think in a way that disenables old sovereignty-oriented inhibitions, a space for new forms of self-assertion is created, and new modes of reasoning are allowed to contend with rigidly institutionalized reasons of state. More specifically, theory can enable the continuous assertion of human rights, human hopes, and human affinities to dimensions of the planet and its inhabitants unrecognized in state-level conceits. This will allow for the emergence of discursive challenges to the more austere reasons of state, helping to liberate flows of ideas and sentiments that will never allow existing systems of authority to secure an unchallenged place to hide.

Index